REGULATING GOVE

This book examines government ethics rules and their enforcement in China (as well as in three other jurisdictions for comparative insights). Empirical research methods (involving primarily semi-structured interviews) were employed to explore the dynamics of actual enforcement policies and practices in China. This book formed an analytical framework through reviewing existing theories on government ethics regulation and general regulation literature and analysing government ethics rules in the US, the UK, and Hong Kong. Using this framework, it seeks to explore the patterns and features of government ethics rules and their enforcement in China. It shows that the inadequacy of government ethics rules per se and the deterrence-oriented criminal enforcement style of government ethics regulation are important but ignored elements of the problem of rampant corruption in China. Such analysis has generated important and practical policy implications for China's government ethics rules and their enforcement.

CHONGHAO WU received his PhD in Law from the University of Hong Kong in 2014.

REGULATING GOVERNMENT ETHICS

An Underused Weapon in China's Anti-Corruption Campaign

CHONGHAO WU

CAMBRIDGE
UNIVERSITY PRESS

CAMBRIDGE
UNIVERSITY PRESS

University Printing House, Cambridge CB2 8BS, United Kingdom

One Liberty Plaza, 20th Floor, New York, NY 10006, USA

477 Williamstown Road, Port Melbourne, VIC 3207, Australia

314-321, 3rd Floor, Plot 3, Splendor Forum, Jasola District Centre, New Delhi - 110025, India

79 Anson Road, #06-04/06, Singapore 079906

Cambridge University Press is part of the University of Cambridge.

It furthers the University's mission by disseminating knowledge in the pursuit of
education, learning and research at the highest international levels of excellence.

www.cambridge.org
Information on this title: www.cambridge.org/9781108735223

© Cambridge University Press 2016

First published 2016
First paperback edition 2018

A catalogue record for this publication is available from the British Library

Library of Congress Cataloging in Publication data
Names: Wu, Chonghao, author.
Title: Regulating government ethics : an underused weapon in China's
anti-corruption campaign / Chonghao Wu.
Description: Cambridge, United Kingdom : Cambridge University Press, 2016. | Based on
author's thesis (doctoral - University of Hong Kong, 2014) issued under title: Regulating
government ethics in China | Includes bibliographical references and index.
Identifiers: LCCN 2015051001 | ISBN 9781107123519 (Hardback)
Subjects: LCSH: Political corruption–Law and legislation–China. | Political ethics–Law
and legislation–China. | Corruption–Prevention–China.
Classification: LCC KNQ4516 .W7 2016 | DDC 345.51/02323–dc23 LC record
available at http://lccn.loc.gov/2015051001

ISBN 978-1-107-12351-9 Hardback
ISBN 978-1-108-73522-3 Paperback

CONTENTS

FIGURES

TABLES

FOREWORD

Regulating government ethics is the missing but essential component in China's struggle against corruption. This is the central thesis in Dr Chonghao Wu's book. It is a thesis that needs to be taken seriously. President Xi Jinping's crackdown on corruption has made international headlines, but it is only another example in a long series of such campaigns in China's history. Though unprecedented in its breadth and intensity, it will not be China's last. While the current campaign stretches to all corners of the earth in search of fugitives and stolen assets, it remains a backwards-looking journey. What is missing is the forward-looking campaign that inculcates a culture of compliance with integrity rules and leads to a sustainable system of prevention. This is where Dr Wu's study makes an important contribution. With reference to the experiences of three jurisdictions that rank within Transparency International's top twenty least corrupt countries, Dr Wu makes the case for establishing in China a two-tier system of regulating ethics and prosecuting corruption crimes. He finds that China lacks a comprehensive set of public sector integrity rules and a suitable agency to enforce such rules and promote compliance. He provides an incisive critique of the discipline inspection committees and explains why a separate government ethics agency is urgently needed. This book is essential reading for anyone interested in the reform and sustainability of China's anticorruption system.

Dr Wu is to be congratulated on his in-depth study of a serious problem that continues to hold China back from reaching its full potential. As his supervisor, I could not have wished for a more diligent and talented student. As my first student to graduate, Dr Wu sets a high standard for all those to follow.

Simon N. M. Young
The University of Hong Kong

ACKNOWLEDGEMENTS

First and foremost, I would like to express my sincere gratitude to Professor Simon N. M. Young, who supervised my PhD thesis on which this book is based, for his encouragement, dedication, patience, and support. He guided me in the right direction with the breadth and depth of his knowledge of public law in general and anti-corruption law in specific. He always provided timely and valuable advice and comments on my research throughout the time of my PhD study. He also provided me with the opportunities to attend several ICAC conferences in which I met some helpful experts in the area of anti-corruption law. He continued to give support and advice as I revised the thesis into a book. I could not have completed this book without his support and guidance. In addition to his academic training and guidance, he is also genuinely interested in my personal well-being and career development. Professor Young is a great supervisor and I consider myself extremely lucky to be his first PhD student.

I would like to thank Professor David Donald, Professor Fu Hualing, Mr Benny Tai, and three anonymous reviewers who provided encouraging and constructive comments on an early draft of the book.

I also owe my appreciation to a number of people who have helped my research. First, I would like to thank all the interviewees and survey participants for their participation in the research. Second, I would like to thank the staff at the Faculty of Law, law library, and main library at the University of Hong Kong for their professional support.

I would like to express my gratitude to Jennifer Eagleton for her help on proofreading.

I would also like to thank Joe Ng, Finola O'Sullivan, and Claire Wood at Cambridge University Press for their help and encouragement during various stages of preparing this book for publication.

Finally, I am most thankful for the support and encouragement from my parents. I would like to dedicate this book to my parents.

ABBREVIATIONS

CCDI	Central Commission for Discipline Inspection
CCP	Chinese Communist Party
CSB	Civil Service Bureau
DAEO	Designated Agency Ethics Official
DICs	Discipline Inspection Committees
ICAC	Independent Commission against Corruption
IPSA	Independent Parliament Standards Authority
MP	Member of Parliament
NIS	National Integrity System
OGE	Office of Government Ethics
POBO	Prevention of Bribery Ordinance

1

Introduction

1.1 Corruption and anti-corruption

Although corruption in the public sector in countries and regions such as Sweden, New Zealand, Singapore, and Hong Kong is not a major social concern, it is still not unusual to read of corruption scandals in those countries. In China, corruption is still a major social concern. On 23 October 2014, China's president, Xi Jinping pointed out at the Second Meeting of the Third Plenary Session of the 18th Central Committee of the CCP, that the work of fighting corruption still faces a complicated and difficult situation: corruption in some areas is still prevalent; in some cases, corruption hits a whole entity or a whole region; and some officials are even committing more aggravated offences.[1] In 2014 alone, according to the statistics of the Supreme People's Procuratorate, more than 55,101 officials, 7.4 per cent higher than 2013, were prosecuted for corruption. Of them, there are 4,040 county/department level officials, 589 bureau level officials and 28 officials at or above ministry/province level.[2]

The consequences of corruption are great. Research has shown that corruption can distort the market,[3] undermine the government's ability to deliver security and order,[4] and negatively influence investment and economic growth.[5] Corruption in some specific sectors, such as in the

---

[1] 'Xi Jinping's Speech at the Second Meeting of the Third Plenary Session of the 18th Central Committee of the CCP: the work of fighting corruption still faces a complicated and difficult situation', available at www.ccdi.gov.cn/special/xilun/zyls/201501/t20150111_49941.html (last visited on 19 May 2015).

[2] 'Annual Work Report of the Supreme People's Procuratorate 2014', available at www.spp.gov.cn/gzbg/201503/t20150324_93812.shtml (last visited on 1 June 2015).

[3] Alexandra Addison Wrage, *Bribery and Extortion: Undermining Business, Governments, and Security* (Westport, CT and London: Praeger Security International, 2007), p. 27.

[4] Ibid.

[5] Paolo Mauro, 'Why worry about corruption?' *IMF Economic Issues*, 6, 24 (February 1997), available at www.imf.org/external/pubs/ft/issues6/index.htm (last visited on 23 September 2009).

judiciary,[6] could be more detrimental than others, since judicial corruption may be the cause of other sorts of corruption.[7] Recent corruption scandals in China vividly demonstrate the detrimental consequences of corruption. One case to illustrate this is of Zheng Xiaoyu. Zheng was the former head of the National Bureau of Food and Drug Administration of China. He received bribes worth RMB 6.5 million and in return approved six fake drugs.[8] It is difficult to imagine how many people were actually victims of these fake drugs, but the number would not be small.

In 2008, Norad (Norwegian Agency for Development Cooperation) conducted a literature review of studies on the prevention of corruption which surveyed about 150 studies covering both academic sources and publicly available documents by organizations such as the World Bank and United Nations agencies.[9] It identified anti-corruption efforts as belonging to six groups: political structure reform; rule of law (control and prosecution of corruption); public administration and system reforms; addressing specific sector corruption (some sector corruption should be understood best as a function of the sector itself); measures focusing on the civil society; and capacity building of anti-corruption agencies.

These approaches focus mainly on the corruption itself; this is largely 'rooting out the bad apples' thinking. Another philosophy of fighting corruption is focused on the opposite side of corruption: the integrity of the government officials. One of the most well-known integrity-building theories is the National Integrity System (NIS), first put forward by Jeremy Pope, which is a framework composed of twelve key institutional pillars: an elected legislature, the role of the executive, an independent judicial system, the auditor general, the ombudsman, independent anti-corruption agencies, public services to serve the public, local government, an independent and free media, civil society, the private corporate sector,

[6] Ting Gong, 'Dependent judiciary and unaccountable judges: judicial corruption in contemporary China', *China Review*, 4, 2 (Fall 2004), pp. 33–54.
[7] Zou Keyuan asserted 'the negative impact of judicial corruption on society is more damaging than corruption in other government agencies due to the nature and functions of the judiciary'. Keyuan Zou, 'Judicial reform versus judicial corruption: recent developments in China', *Criminal Law Forum*, 11, 3 (2000), p. 323.
[8] 'China executes former food and drug safety chief', *New Scientist* (10 July 2007), available at www.newscientist.com/article/dn12230-china-executes-former-food-and-drug-safety-chief.html (last visited on 21 September 2009).
[9] Norad, 'Anti-corruption approaches: a literature review' (2008), available at www.norad.no/en/Tools+and+publications/Publications/Publication+Page?key=119213 (last visited on 12 April 2010).

and international actors and mechanisms.[10] However, the result is not satisfactory if only a single pillar of the system is addressed in isolation to other pillars.[11]

1.2 Regulating government ethics

Recent research on government integrity tends to centre on regulations/rules governing integrity, especially their development. For example, Ian Scott 's article 'Promoting integrity in a changing environment: Hong Kong's public sector after 1997', explores the development of regulations and rules against the environment change mainly due to Hong Kong's transition to Chinese sovereignty.[12] Ting Gong examined the emergence of rules on asset declaration in three cities in China in her article 'An "institutional turn" toward rule-based integrity management in China'.[13] Christopher Hood et al.'s book *Regulation Inside Government* systematically examined regulation activities inside governments.[14] Regulation in this book referred not to norms and rules but to the various activities that governments do to regulate themselves in order to make the government behave better.

Regulation, as used in its common context, generally refers to the state regulating the private sector such as the business and financial sectors. However, there is no generic word to describe the sum of activities inside the government in the same way as regulation is used for the private sector. Hence, Hood et al. extends the scope of regulation into situations where government shapes its own behaviour.[15] The central idea of regulation inside government is that the ethics of the government should be guided, monitored, and administrated. Broadly speaking, a regulatory

[10] Jeremy Pope, *Confronting Corruption: The Elements of A National Integrity System* (Berlin: Transparency International, 2000), available at http://info.worldbank.org/etools/docs/library/18416/00.pdf (last visited on 17 October 2012).

[11] Ibid.

[12] Ian Scott, 'Promoting integrity in a changing environment: Hong Kong's public sector after 1997', Collaborative Governance and Integrity Management Conference, Centre of Anti-corruption Studies of the ICAC, Hong Kong, 2010.

[13] Ting Gong, 'An "institutional turn" toward rule-based integrity management in China', Collaborative Governance and Integrity Management Conference, Centre of Anti-corruption Studies of the ICAC, Hong Kong, 2010.

[14] Christopher Hood, Colin Scott, Oliver James, George Jones, and Tony Travers, *Regulation Inside Government: Waste-Watchers, Quality Police, and Sleaze-Busters* (New York: Oxford University Press, 1999).

[15] Ibid., especially p. 8.

enforcement system against public corruption mainly regulates public ethics (or public integrity). Public corruption is mainly generated in situations where organizational dysfunction exists, and where public bureaucracies can intervene in the transfer of a large amount of capital.[16]

Criminal law and administrative law mainly focus on traditional corruption such as embezzlement, bribery, and fraud. Although serious acts of corruption in the form of abuses of public power for private gain have been criminalized, many undesired ethical behaviours actually arise from maladministration and/or misconduct and/or poor internal regulations. As Australia's Public Sector Standards Commissioner stated, 'integrity refers to the application of good values, principles, and standards by public officials in the daily operations of public sector organizations'.[17] Integrity means to act honestly and transparently, using power responsibly and behaving in a way which earns and sustains public trust.[18] Maladministration, misconduct and corruption are the opposite of integrity. Thus, integrity regulation can, to a large extent, address the problem of public corruption. Rules governing public ethics, regulators and the regulatory enforcement process are the main aspects of the regulatory system of public ethics. Earlier research mainly covered rules and some isolated best practices of regulatory enforcement and regulators. Since the 1960s, rules governing public ethics and regulatory bodies experienced rapid development in countries and regions such as the United States, the United Kingdom and Hong Kong.

After a short review of literature on public ethics regulation in the United States, the United Kingdom, and Hong Kong, some observations can be identified. First, the war on corruption has been extended from traditional corruption offences to broad public ethics regulation. Second, the regulation of public ethics is reflected mainly in two aspects: making and revising public ethics rules and regulations, and setting up regulatory bodies. Third, the scope of regulated behaviour is broad, but it mainly lies in four aspects: conflicts of interest, appearance of corruption, financial disclosure and outside employment regulation/activities. These four aspects are not mutually exclusive but overlap to some degree.

---

[16] Endrius Eliseo Cocciolo, 'Checking the integrity of government', Droit Administratif Compare, europeen et global seminar paper, Paris, 2008.

[17] Public Sector Standards Commissioner (Victoria, Australia), 'Review of Victoria's integrity and anti-corruption system' (2010), available at www.vic.ipaa.org.au/sb_cache/profes sionaldevelopment/id/193/f/PSSC_Integrity_Review.pdf (last visited on 17 April 2010).

[18] Ibid.

Unlike the United Kingdom and the United States, where government ethics regulation was developed earlier in the twentieth century and became more systematic from the 1970s, in China, the regulation of public ethics has, at best, only just begun to emerge. Even defined by traditional criminal corruption, China still has a long way to go. The authorities have to first deal with serious criminal corruption and leave government ethics (considered minor in nature compared with criminal corruption) unchecked, or at least under-checked.

Some scholars argue that China has begun to follow a more rule-guided integrity management style over the past decade.[19] It is true that the Communist Party and the government have made a large body of rules relevant to government ethics. However, that does not mean a government ethics regulatory system has been established in China. First, many public ethics regulations are made in a very abstract way so their enforceability is very weak. As observed by Li Chengyan, in China, the overall plan of civil servants' honesty management at the national level has not been made, and the basic regulations governing civil servant honesty is missing.[20] The existing regulations are abstract, scattered and unenforceable.[21]

Second, many regulations on conflicts of interest and the appearance of corruption regulations are almost nonexistent. For example, assisting a third party by an official in this third party's dealing with the government is not prohibited by law. Further, the need to avoid an appearance of corruption is almost a foreign notion in China's fight against corruption.

Third, many existing rules regulating government ethics is actually not the counterpart of public ethics regulation in the United Kingdom, the United States, or Hong Kong. Many behaviours governed by government ethics rules in China are considered serious acts of criminal corruption in the United Kingdom, the United States, and Hong Kong. For example, taking a bribe of less than RMB 5,000 in China usually does not amount to criminal corruption.[22] However, a small bribe (say several hundred) will be subject to criminal punishment in the United States, the United

---

[19] Gong, 'An "institutional turn"'; Ting Gong and Stephen K. Ma (eds.), *Preventing Corruption in Asia: Institutional Design and Policy Capacity* (London: Routledge, 2009).

[20] Chengyan Li, 'Government honesty building up and civil servant honesty management', ICAC Integrity Management Conference paper, Hong Kong, 2010.

[21] Ibid.

[22] Article 386 of the Criminal Law of the People's Republic of China (1997) states that '[w]hoever commits the crime of accepting bribes is to be punished on the basis of Article 383 of this law according to the amount of bribes and the circumstances. A heavier

Kingdom, and Hong Kong. In the three selected jurisdictions, the government ethics rule system mainly regulates conflicts of interest, appearance of corruption, financial disclosure, and outside employment; these rules are inherently more preventative than criminal corruption laws as the former focus mainly on various corruption risks and potential.

Finally, in practice, much maladministration and misconduct is not subject to any formal regulatory control in China even if the relevant rules are there. For example, using government cars for private business is prohibited by government and party rules. However, in reality officials violating this rule are seldom monitored; occasionally some officials may be punished as 'showcases' mainly because they are exposed by the media or Internet and have led to strong public resentment. Generally speaking, unethical conduct by civil servants in China is less likely to be challenged compared with those in the United States, the United Kingdom and Hong Kong.

The expression 'ethics' is frequently used throughout the book. In its philosophical meaning, ethics can refer to Aristotle's virtues determining human behaviour in a way that benefits both the person possessing the virtues and that person's society.[23] This is different from the meaning used in the context of 'government ethics' in this book. For the purpose of this book, government ethics refers to clean and honest conduct of government officials and employees.

1.3   Argument of the book

Researchers working on corruption and/or government ethics in China generally agree that the problem in fighting corruption mainly lies in the enforcement of existing anti-corruption legislation and not the weakness or absence of such laws. Lin Zhe, a law professor at Party

---

punishment shall be given to whoever demands a bribe.' Article 383 (4) of the Criminal Law of the People's Republic of China states that '[i]ndividuals who have engaged in graft with an amount of less than 5,000 yuan, with the situation being serious, are to be sentenced to less than two years of fixed-term imprisonment or criminal detention. In lighter cases, they will be given administrative action to be decided by the unit to which they belong or the higher administrative organ. Toward those who have committed repeated crimes of graft, all amounts of graft of unhandled cases are to be added in meting out punishment.'

[23] Oxford Dictionaries (online), available at www.oxforddictionaries.com/definition/english/ethics; see also Aristotle, *Nicomachean Ethics* (Chicago, IL: University of Chicago Press, 2011).

College of the Central Committee of China Communist Party (CCP) said to a journalist that:

> Though our country has made many rules on anti-corruption and integrity, these rules are mainly in the form of party rules and administrative rules. Now what we need to do is to integrate these rules into an Anti-corruption Law. It can be said that the promulgation of an Anti-Corruption Law is an important landmark for the establishment of an anti-corruption system. In this modern age, anti-corruption varies greatly from one country to another; however, no matter what anti-corruption method a country adopts, an *Anti-Corruption Law* is absolutely necessary.[24]

The logic behind Lin's proposal is that a national anti-corruption law will be better enforced than party rules and administrative rules. This is actually calling for transferring rules into more formal and perhaps stricter national laws rather than challenging the coverage of existing rules on unethical behaviour. Indeed, even if some countries have special anti-corruption statutes (such as the Prevention of Bribery Ordinance in Hong Kong and the Bribery Act in the United Kingdom) officials' conduct in these countries is not mainly addressed by these statutes. Codes of conduct and other regulations and guidelines set forth detailed requirements for government officials. An article in the *Beijing Times* commenting on Xi Jinping's speech about 'confining power into a cage of regulation' stated that China 'does not lack anti-corruption laws and regulations as well as institutions; what China lacks is the ability to enforce these anti-corruption laws and regulations'.[25] It is plausible at its first sight to argue that China does not lack anti-corruption rules. This illusion is mainly derived from the observation that China has large number of rules and regulations regulating the conduct of officials. However, having a large number of rules does not necessarily mean most undesired ethical behaviours have been regulated. For example, China has issued many circulars and documents regulating issues such as accepting club memberships, gifts, cash, securities, travel and special products. However, these specific prohibition rules omit many types of transfers of economic value from private

[24] Yonggang Li, 'Lin Zhe, Professor at Central Party Committee College, proposed that anti-corruption institutions shall be upgraded to anti-corruption statutes', *Huashang Daily*, available at http://sx.sina.com.cn/news/kuai/2012-03-14/18729.html (last visited on 25 May 2013).

[25] Qiao Wu, 'Legal measures against corruption: confining public power into the cage of regulation', *Beijing Times* (17 December 2012), p. A02.

sources to a government official as new forms of advantage that have not been prohibited can always be created.

Thus, the first research question is: to what extent are China's government ethics rules adequate (or inadequate) or comprehensive (or incomprehensive)? This question is important because different answers will suggest different anti-corruption responses. If it is found that China lacks rules on government ethics, a systematic rule-making response is required. In order to address this question, many other related questions must also be answered. These questions can be put into two groups. The first group includes questions about the general framework used to analyze government ethics rules: What are the key categories of government ethics rules? What are the major activities regulated? Why should these activities be regulated (in other words, how can these rules be justified)? Answers to these questions will provide a systematic skeleton to examine rules concerning government ethics. Further, rules on government ethics can cover a very broad range of activities as this concept is in itself vague; clear answers to these questions will help define the scope of this research.

The other group of questions concerns government ethics rules in three selected jurisdictions, the United States, the United Kingdom and Hong Kong: What are the patterns of government ethics rules in the three countries (jurisdictions)? To what extent do these patterns conform to the analytic frameworks developed for the questions in group one? Research on these questions can test whether the analytic frameworks are appropriate in analyzing real government ethics rules. Further, the patterns of rules in the three jurisdictions, together with the categories and key principles in general addressed in group one questions, will provide both a practical and a theoretical baseline for the research of government ethics in China.

The second group of key research questions are as follows: What is the state of government ethics enforcement in China and how do we evaluate the effectiveness of enforcement? To address these questions, many related sub-questions, which can be put into three groups, need to be answered. The first group is about analytic framework for government ethics enforcement: What are the key elements of government ethics enforcement? Can law enforcement knowledge in general be extended to government ethics enforcement? The second group is about government ethics enforcement in the three selected jurisdictions: Who are the government ethics enforcers in the three jurisdictions? What is the enforcement style adopted by these agencies? What powers and responsibilities have been given to these agencies? What are the tools and techniques available to these agencies and how do they use these tools? In general, what are the patterns of government ethics enforcement in the three jurisdictions? The third group is about the enforcement in China: What are the enforcement patterns/features in China with respect to the agencies, enforcement styles, enforcement powers and responsibilities, enforcement tools and enforcement resources? What types of actions are regulated in everyday life?

The third key group of research questions are: What implications regarding government ethics rule reform and enforcement policies can be generated? Are these proposed changes practical in the sense of being feasible given the existence of the one-party political environment in China? In other words, to what extent may these proposed reforms be adopted by the top authority of China?

This book addresses these questions through both doctrinal and empirical approaches. These questions mainly involve two aspects, government ethics rules and their enforcement. Discussion of the rules was addressed by desktop research – specifically speaking, by rule searching and rule analysis methods. First, literature on government ethics principles and categories in general was examined to figure out the appropriate frameworks to analyze government ethics rules and their enforcement. Second, government ethics rules in three selected jurisdictions (the United States, the United Kingdom, and Hong Kong) were systematically examined (the reasons for choosing these three jurisdictions will be discussed at the end of this section). The features and patterns of the government ethics rules in the three countries provide a standard to examine China's rules. Finally, government ethics rules in China were searched and then analyzed. As enforcement is about how to maintain adherence to the rules in reality, it is not enough to examine this based solely on academic literature, especially for China where existing research on this area is limited. Thus, fieldwork (specifically, interviews, internal documents review [archive study] and questionnaires) was carried out on government ethics enforcement in China (see Appendix A for a more detailed description of the research methods).

This book argues that government ethics rules in China are problematic in four ways. First, existing rules have not yet regulated much of the unethical behaviour of government officials (such as representing a third party in dealing with government, and the appearance of using official influence for private purposes). Second, some unethical behaviour in China is subject to narrower regulation compared with that in the three selected jurisdictions. For example, the scope of the items for financial disclosure is narrower than that in the United States, the United Kingdom, and Hong Kong. For another example, regarding transfer of economic value from a private source to a government official, China mainly restricts transfers connected to the official's official duties and leaves the transfer made in the official's private capacity unregulated, whereas the three jurisdictions prohibit both. Third, the rules are technically poorly made. China has more than seventy government ethics rules, but they are scattered, repeated, and ambiguous. Finally, certain rules cannot be justified because these rules play only a marginal role (or even no role) in achieving the expected results and at the same time impose a more than necessary burden on the regulated officials. Take rules prohibiting the spouse and children of covered officials from running a business as an example. These rules cannot effectively prevent officials from abusing power for private gains as they can still benefit private businesses controlled by their other relatives or close friends. On the other hand, officials' spouses and children are burdened more than is necessary as it is not wrong for them to run a business as long as they do not profit from official power. Thus, it is argued that these rules shall be repealed and the problem of abusing power for private gain should be addressed by criminal corruption law and government ethics rules (especially conflicts of interest rules and appearance of corruption rules).

Further, the book argues that China's government ethics enforcement suffers from the lack of separation of criminal corruption enforcement and government ethics enforcement. Both criminal corruption and government ethics are enforced by Discipline Inspection Committees (DICs). DICs' attention focuses on criminal enforcement. They seldom regularly enforce many existing government ethics rules (such as using government cars for private use). Their enforcement style and tools are shaped by their criminal enforcement. The DICs do not distinguish government ethics enforcement from criminal corruption enforcement. Nor do they realize the systematic difference between the two systems. They enforce government ethics rules in the same manner as they enforce criminal corruption: their style is deterrence oriented in contrast to being compliance oriented. For example, the DICs' power mainly involve investigation and punishment, and they seldom conduct department audits, review financial disclosure forms or require register of conflicts of interest, which are typical compliance enforcement methods. However, government ethics regulation requires a completely different enforcement style: compliance oriented enforcement style. Thus, it is argued that China should first establish a separate government ethics enforcement agency. This will help to transfer the system from being a deterrence-oriented enforcement system to a compliance-oriented enforcement system in regulating government ethics.

This book also argues that a regulatory approach against corruption has special applicability to China. Government ethics enforcement is different from criminal enforcement in terms of their influence on the CCP's political legitimacy. The latter may damage public confidence in the party and government because a large number of prosecutions of party and government officials show the problems in the party system. On the other hand, the former may strengthen the public's confidence in the government because government ethics regulation mainly involves constantly monitoring compliance with government ethics standards to control the risk of corruption. This reflects an early intervention in the government officials' public conduct involving corruption risks rather than actual corruption. It will prevent a possible corruption risk from developing into full-blown criminal corruption if the risk is identified and properly corrected at an early stage. A stricter enforcement of government ethics may generate more confidence in the government as it can reduce or even eradicate corruption risks. Take the following analogy. Putting out fires is like criminal corruption enforcement and setting various standards (such as exit signs in public buildings, compulsory requirements for equipping fire extinguishers in public buildings, installation of a fire alarm system and regular fire drills) and monitoring the compliance with these standards is like government ethics enforcement. An increase in the number of fire calls will reduce the public's feeling of safety; on the other hand, stricter requirements for setting the various aforementioned standards will strengthen the public's confidence in the fire service departments. Thus, most of the proposed changes (such as making more systematic government ethics rules, especially rules governing conflicts of interest and appearance of corruption, and separating government ethics regulation from criminal corruption enforcement) will not face strong resistance from the top authorities, though some changes (such as rules governing conflicts between party interests and official government duties) are less likely to happen in the near future due to the political system in China.

There are several reasons for choosing these three jurisdictions: first, the three countries are ranked at (or near) the top in terms of government integrity, and thus lessons about rule reform may be learned from them; second, research on government ethics regulation in the United States and the United Kingdom is abundant; third, all three jurisdictions use English as their official language which makes thorough research of the rules in the three countries possible.

It might be thought that the comparative study between the three selected countries and China is problematic as the three countries are not comparable with China in several aspects. Politically, China is a communist one-party authoritarian state, whereas the United States and the United Kingdom are democracies and Hong Kong can be considered as a semi-democracy. Economically, all three selected jurisdictions are developed countries, whereas China is a developing country and its development is unbalanced. In terms of media monitoring, all three countries have a free media which are very eager to report government corruption scandals, whereas in China the media is still subject to strict censorship.

However, that does not necessarily mean comparison of government ethics regulation between the three selected jurisdictions and China is meaningless. Whether a comparative study makes sense or not, to some extent, depends on the comparative framework or standard and the study's purpose. The purpose of this research is not to transplant a specific law or code from a specifically selected country to China, but to concentrate on common government ethics issues and conceptions. China can address these key government issues but at the same time be flexible in adopting specific responses.

Indeed, though the three selected jurisdictions share many commonalities (e.g. they are all clean countries and all belong to the common law system) they are also considerably different in a variety of aspects. Politically, the United States is a presidential system whereas the United Kingdom is a parliamentary kingdom. Both the United States and the United Kingdom are highly democratic countries but Hong Kong is not a real democracy as both its Chief Executive and Legislative Council are not selected by universal suffrage currently. Further, politically Hong Kong is not an independent state though it enjoys executive, legislative, and independent judicial power. Political parties in Hong Kong are less developed than that in the United States and the United Kingdom. Culturally, in Hong Kong Confucian culture is still very influential, whereas the United Kingdom and the United States share similar Western cultures. In terms of geographic and population size, the United States is big in both, whereas Hong Kong is only a city with a population of around 7 million. However, comparison of government ethics regulation between the United States, the United Kingdom, and Hong Kong makes sense within the same analytical framework (see Chapter 3 and

Chapter 4 for the detailed comparison between the three selected juris-dictions). Thus, comparative study of government ethics between the three selected countries and China can shed light on China's situation even if the contexts are different. It would be problematic if the purpose was to introduce a specific government ethics code or tool into China from the United States, the United Kingdom, or Hong Kong without carefully considering the country's context. For example, rules governing conflicts of interests between the government and political parties from these countries are difficult, if not impossible, to be adopted in China; given the CCP's ruling status and operation, there is a blurring of government and party roles (e.g. CCP officials' salaries are covered by government revenue and they are considered civil servants).

1.4 Organization of the book

The remainder of the book is composed of four parts. Chapter 2 will first discuss the concept of 'government ethics regulation' so that the research scope can be clearly defined. Then, it will discuss the role of government ethics regulation as compared to the criminal approach against corruption both in general and in a Chinese context. The two approaches form the broad legal approach against corruption, but government ethics regulation is largely ignored in China. Next, it will discuss the connection between an important political factor, the CCP's legitimacy, and each of the two legal approaches against corruption. The chapter will argue that the role of government ethics regulation has not been realized and it has a special applicability to China's political environment.

Chapter 3 will examine government ethics rules in China. Specifically, it will explore four key categories of government ethics: conflicts of interest, appearance of corruption, financial disclosure and outside employment/activities. It will identify the weak areas and loopholes of existing rules and put forward policy implications for rule improvement.

Chapter 4 will focus on enforcement of government ethics rules in China. Enforcement agencies, enforcement powers and responsibilities, enforcement styles, enforcement tools and techniques, and enforcement resources will be examined respectively. It argues that China's government ethics rules are enforced in a deterrence-oriented criminal style which should be replaced by a compliance-oriented regulatory enforcement style.

Chapter 5 will conclude the book. It will first summarize key findings of the research. Then, it will discuss the contributions of the research. Finally, it will point out possible directions for further research.

2

The role of a regulatory enforcement system
against corruption in China

2.1 Introduction

This chapter will explore the role a regulatory approach against corruption would have in China. The central argument of this chapter is that a regulatory approach against corruption can play a more important role in China than it does now. This argument can be justified from three aspects. First, by its nature, a regulatory approach against corruption can prevent more serious corrupt offences from occurring and will not damage the CCP's political legitimacy.

Second, the effectiveness of a criminal approach against corruption in China is largely constrained due to considerations regarding the CCP's political legitimacy (strict criminal law enforcement will lead to an increasing number of prosecutions, which might increase people's resentment towards the CCP). However, this is not to say that criminal enforcement against corruption is not important in China or that the criminal and regulatory approaches are the only weapons against corruption. In addition to the criminal and regulatory approaches, other institutions such as a free media, social norms, and democratic politics, to name a few, all have a role to play. But it appears clear that a regulatory approach and criminal approach are two basic pillars in fighting corruption; if criminal enforcement already faces serious political constraints, the regulatory aspects must be strengthened. Otherwise, the level of integrity in China cannot be improved. Thus the central focus of this research is the regulatory approach.

Third, China's regulatory regime against corruption has largely lagged behind countries such as the United States, the United Kingdom, and Hong Kong – many forms of integrity deviance are not regulated in China (this point will be examined in Chapter 3); the enforcement of existing government ethics rules is not regulatory-oriented but deterrence-oriented in terms of enforcement style and enforcement tools (this will be discussed in Chapter 4).

To establish my argument, the features of the regulatory approach and the criminal approach will be compared both in a general context and in a China-specific context to demonstrate the potential room for an expanded regulatory approach against corruption in China. China's political state also supports the further development of a regulatory approach. Although in this chapter China-specific information (mainly its political features, criminal enforcement against corruption, and details on acts of corruptions) has been touched upon many times, it serves mainly as background information against which the potential effect of regulatory regimes can be better understood. Details of China's current regulatory regime against corruption will be discussed in Chapters 3 and 4. The remaining part of this chapter will be organized as below.

Section 2.2 will briefly introduce the idea of a regulatory regime against corruption. As the definition of the term 'regulation' varies from one study to another, it is important to make clear the scope of regulation against corruption for the purpose of this research.

Section 2.3 will discuss the relationship between the regulatory approach and the criminal approach against corruption. First, both approaches are necessary and each complements the other. Second, although anti-corruption criminal law reform is always needed, in terms of criminal enforcement, both punishment magnitude for corruption and punishment rate in China is difficult, if not impossible, to be strengthened due to not only the nature of criminal enforcement of corruption but also to political factors. Victims of corruption are often not so apparent compared with other crimes such as rape or robbery. Thus the detection rate for corruption is lower than that of other crimes such as street violence in which the victims themselves play an important role in helping to catch the offenders. Third, a regulatory approach still has much room for development in China in that much misconduct and maladministration has not been subject to any effective regulation so far. Finally, the regulatory approach plays a very important preventive role as minor deviance often paves the way for more serious criminal corruption.

Section 2.4 will explore how the ruling legitimacy of the CCP is influenced by the two anti-corruption approaches previously mentioned. It argues that criminal enforcement has the potential to ruin CCP's political legitimacy. The government may keep one eye closed regarding criminal enforcement against corruption since a continuous stream of corrupt officials being prosecuted will likely arouse public resentment towards the CCP and the government. The section further argues that a regulatory approach against corruption is likely to improve the public's confidence in the CCP. It implies that a regulatory approach against corruption is more likely to be supported by the top authorities if its role is recognized by these authorities. The last section, Section 2.5, will summarize the key arguments of Chapter 2 and briefly introduce the focus of the next chapter.

2.2   What is a regulatory regime against corruption?

Before regulation of government ethics is discussed, it is necessary to briefly discuss regulation in general. Although the definitions of regulation vary greatly from one study to another, they all touch three dimensions: 'who regulates', 'how to regulate' (regulatory methods), and 'whom to regulate'.

Regulation can be very broadly referred to as all mechanisms of social control or influence which can affect or shape behaviour.[1] In line with this argument, almost everything such as culture and social norms is within the boundary of regulation. However, as pointed out by Freiberg, 'if regulation is everywhere and everything, then the idea means nothing'.[2] Further, it is not possible to carry out in-depth and comprehensive research on regulation under this broad conception of regulation as the boundary cannot be set clearly.

Regulation is also frequently restricted to government activities. For example, the UK Better Regulation Task Force defines regulation as 'any government measure or intervention that seeks to change the behaviour of individuals or groups'.[3] The scope of this definition is considerably narrower than the one above. However, they are identical in that 'whom to regulate' refers to private individuals or groups even if this is not explicitly stated.

Hood et al. shifts the focus of 'whom to regulate' from regulating private business sectors by governments (the traditional scope of regulation research) to regulating the government itself. Hood et al. restricted regulatees to government organizations.[4] That means the government regulates itself.

---

[1] Robert Baldwin, Colin D. Scott, and Christopher Hood (eds.), *A Reader on Regulation* (Oxford: Oxford University Press, 1998).

[2] Arie Freiberg, *The Tools of Regulation* (Sydney: The Federation Press, 2010), p. 2.

[3] Better Regulation Task Force, 'Principles of good regulation' (2003), p. 1, available at www.cabinet-office.gov.uk/regulation/TaskForce/2000/PrinciplesLeaflet.pdf (last visited on 23 October 2012).

[4] Christopher Hood, Colin Scott, Oliver James, George Jones, and Tony Travers, *Regulation inside Government: Waste Watchers, Quality Police, and Sleaze-busters* (Oxford: Oxford University Press, 1999).

Although the three dimensions framework is very useful to understanding the scope of regulation, a further dimension can be added that further clarifies the particular scope of this research. Each regulator usually has a specific area to regulate. For example, a factory's licence is regulated by the business administration; but the same factory's sewage disposal system is regulated by the environment administration. Again, the same factory's fire alarm system is regulated by the fire service department. The fourth dimension is 'what to regulate'.

In terms of who regulates, this book will focus on public bodies (including government bodies) with *primary* official authority in regulating government ethics. However, judicial organs (such as prosecutors and courts) are excluded from the scope because these entities are more closely associated with the criminal system. Government bodies like auditors and ombudsmen will also be excluded from the scope of the research because though these entities have a role in government integrity they are not *primarily* in charge of government ethics.[5] For example, auditors are mainly responsible for monitoring whether government expenditure is spent in accordance with budgetary policy. Spending may be challenged if it violates budgetary policies. A typical regulator within the scope of this research is the US Office of Government Ethics.

Regarding 'whom to regulate', this book focuses on only government bodies and government officials (including CCP entities and party officials). That means the ethics of private parties will not be discussed. The reason is that government integrity mainly concerns the behaviours of government employees. Codes of conduct for government officials are the fundamental regulation tools for government integrity. Unlike national laws, these rules technically are not binding for individuals who are not government officials.

With respect to 'regulatory methods', this book mainly concentrates on binding legal methods that may take many forms, including laws, regulations, ordinances, orders, codes, standards, guidelines, circulars, and documents which have a binding or persuasive authority in government ethics.

---

[5] Office of the Ombudsman in the Philippines plays a very important role in anti-corruption. It has the power to 'determine the causes of inefficiency, red tape, mismanagement, fraud, and corruption in the Government and make recommendations for their elimination and the observance of high standards of ethics and efficiency'. See Office of the Ombudsman, 'Powers, Functions and Duties', available at www.ombudsman.gov.ph/index.php?home=1& navId=MQ==&subNavId=ODY (last visited on 11 September 2013).

For 'what to regulate', this research concerns government ethics. Before discussing government ethics, it will briefly discuss ethics in general; in so doing, the former concept will be better understood. According to Earl A. Molander, 'Ethics refers to the principles of right and wrong conduct which guide the members of a group, profession or society'.[6] These principles in most times are unwritten. For example, a person is expected to be honest and thus telling lies is in general considered unethical. This is not a written guide but this principle can be observed in daily life. The unwritten principles may be vague in certain contexts. For example, Linda recently learned that she was given the wrong baby when she gave birth to her son in the hospital twelve years ago. Now, Linda finds she is in a dilemma about whether to tell the truth to her twelve-year-old son or not. She knows her son will be hurt if she told the truth to him. However, she also knows that her son should have the right to know the truth, especially when he grows up. In this case the unwritten social norm cannot give Linda guidance on ethical choice as the principle is very general and vague.

Sometimes these principles are written down, mainly in the forms of ethical codes such as, to mention a few, ethical codes for nurses, ethical codes for psychologists, and ethical codes for doctors. Written codes have at least two apparent benefits compared with unwritten ethical principles. First, written codes can remind a person of the relevant ethics principles; this can reinforce the guidance function of the ethics principles as this reminds the person that this is a value shared by the community to which he or she is belonging. For example, a research ethics code which clearly defines what plagiarism is and expressly states that plagiarism is not allowed (especially when a signed pledge is required) will work better in reducing plagiarism than unwritten ethical principles, while most university students may already know roughly what constitutes plagiarism and know that it is unethical.

Second, though in most cases a person can figure out what is ethical and what is unethical by resorting to unwritten principles, violation of these principles will usually bring the violators no more than embarrassment, shame, or public blame. Written codes are not a mere search of the unwritten values in order to restate them. They can supplement the general principles with specific prohibitions, even with concrete examples. More importantly, it can make clear what disciplinary actions will be

[6] Earl A. Molander, 'A paradigm for design, promulgation and enforcement of ethical codes', *Journal of Business Ethics* 6, 8 (1987), p. 619.

made if the codes are violated, and this will result in reliable enforce-ment.[7] Take the above example again. A university student is more likely to violate the plagiarism rule if it is unwritten. Though the student knows this principle (plagiarism is unethical), he or she may risk this as he or she does not expect serious consequence for violating this rule. The same student is more likely being deterred from plagiarism if the written code states that a student who intentionally plagiarizes will be suspended or even expelled from the university. Thus, many organ-izations (such as companies and universities) and professions (such as teachers, nurses, doctors, and accountants) prefer putting in place written ethical codes.

Thus, in transforming ethical principles into written ethical codes, the above two aspects must be kept in mind. First, ethical codes should contain both general precepts and the prohibition of specific practices. Without specific prohibitions, the code may be too vague to guide the target members' behaviour. The code, then, becomes no more than window dressing. On the other hand, without general principles, its coverage will be very limited and may send the dangerous signal that 'anything not covered in the code is acceptable behaviour'.[8] This prob-lem can be found in China's government ethics rules (see Chapter 3 for detailed discussion). This dilemma will be greatly overcome by combin-ing general precepts and specific practices together into a code.[9] Second, each prohibition rule must clearly state what enforcement actions will be triggered if such rule is violated. Otherwise, these rules will not be treated seriously by the people.

Ethics codes are made and enforced by specific organizations, associ-ations, and professions, and thus the codes can only regulate their own members. Further, though ethics codes usually have disciplinary actions, these actions are limited to very mild sanctions. The most serious punishment is expelling the violator. Thus, compliance to ethics codes is still largely relying on enforcement mechanisms for unwritten ethics principles such as avoiding embarrassment and peer pressure; sanction based enforcement mechanisms are only occasionally used. Therefore, ethics codes mainly regulate minor offences; serious offences need tough reactions such as fines and imprisonment which ethics codes cannot offer. These serious offences such as fraud, robbery, rape, and murder are addressed by criminal law.

---

[7] Ibid.   [8] Ibid., p. 619.   [9] Ibid.

Unwritten ethical principles are one of the important sources of criminal law: the early form of criminal principles (raw criminal law) are themselves ethics principles (e.g. the old Chinese saying that life for life [杀人偿命; *sha ren chang ming*] is a well-known ethics principle). Criminal law can be viewed as a special form of written codes. It is written by a country and needs to be passed by legislators in modern countries. A common feature of unwritten ethical principles, ethical codes, and criminal law is that all of them are primarily interested in human actions and in their legality or illegality.[10] Thus, the regulation of human conduct can be thought of as a continuum from unwritten ethical values to law with the ethical code in the middle; one characteristic of the continuum is that, from ethical values to law, it becomes increasingly more reliable in enforcement and more formal.[11] This book will mainly focus on the middle ground of the continuum, the written ethical codes.

Government ethics mainly involves misconduct or malpractice not serious enough to constitute criminal corruption. The opposite of public integrity is various forms of behaviour conducted by public position holders which are not in conformity with impurity, efficiency, honesty, and integrity principles. These undesired behaviours in the public sector form a continuum from very minor wrongdoing such as delivering public services inefficiently to much more serious offences such as embezzlement and bribery. Although the level of seriousness and culpability of a behaviour varies from one to another it is possible and helpful to group these behaviours for analysis.

A useful framework is to categorize this undesired behaviour into three groups: traditional corruption (such as bribery, embezzlement, fraud, and extortion), misconduct (conscious rule breaking), and maladministration (inappropriately performed administrative tasks such as bad decision making; see Figure 2.1).[12] The three groups of undesired activities form a spectrum as shown below from least serious to most serious; the darker the colour, the more serious the behaviour.

Traditional acts of corruption, which are considered criminal offences, are mainly addressed by criminal enforcement, whereas less serious misconduct and maladministration are mainly addressed by regulation. Much of the existing scholarly debate in China centres on traditional

---

[10] Patrick J. Sheeran, *Ethics in Public Administration: A Philosophical Approach* (Westport, CT and London: Praeger, 1993), p. 52.

[11] Molander, 'A paradigm for design'.

[12] Public Sector Standards Commissioner (Victoria, Australia), 'Review of Victoria's integrity and anti-corruption system' (2010), available at www.vic.ipaa.org.au/sb_cache/profes sionaldevelopment/id/193/f/PSSC_Integrity_Review.pdf (last visited on 17 April 2010).

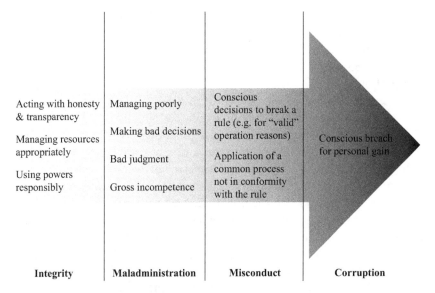

| Integrity | Maladministration | Misconduct | Corruption |

Figure 2.1   Integrity system spectrum of behaviour.

Source: Public Sector Standards Commissioner (Victoria, Australia), "Review of Victoria's Integrity and Anti-corruption System", 2010, p. 3, available at http://www.vic.ipaa.org.au/sb_cache/ professionaldevelopment/id/193/f/PSSC_Integrity_Review.pdf (last visited on 17 April, 2010). (Note: the figure was adapted from Treasury Board of Canada Secretariat, *The Financial Administration Act: Responding to Non-compliance*, 2005).

corruption. This research will shift the anti-corruption research focus from the fight against traditional corruption to the promotion of public integrity. Although the fourth dimension (what to regulate) is confined to government ethics, it seems the scope is still very broad. More specifically, the research concentrates mainly on four key categories of government ethics: conflicts of interest, the appearance of corruption, financial disclosure, and outside employment/activities (this will be discussed in detail in Chapters 3 and 4).

Though this research is not focused on criminal enforcement against corruption, it also discusses criminalized government ethics offences where necessary because these offences are not criminal in nature. A feature of modern criminal law is that it has incorporated many regulatory rules both in general and in the area of anti-corruption. This incorporation of regulation into criminal law is due to the difficulties of proving intent which resulted in the development of strict liability.[13]

[13] Hazel Croall, 'Combating financial crime: regulatory versus criminal control approaches', *Journal of Financial Crime*, 11, 1 (2003), pp. 45–55.

Many criminal corruption offences are actually not really criminal in nature (*mala inse*), but regulatory offences, also named technical offences (*mala prohibita*).[14] For example, unexplained sources of wealth and failure to disqualify oneself when faced with conflicts of interest are this kind of offence.

A regulatory system mainly relies on three types of mechanisms to secure compliance with certain standards: monitoring mechanisms, behaviour changing mechanisms, and sanction (disciplinary) mechanisms. The priority is on constant monitoring of compliance or noncompliance. For example, a food regulator's major work is setting specific standards for food producers and sellers and then constantly monitoring the state of compliance in the market. Even a very minor deviation from the standard, the regulator must intervene early to correct the misbehaviour. This is the behaviour changing mechanism. The food regulator, for example, can require a restaurant to prepare facilities to make sure cooked and raw food are stored and cut separately. The regulator can revoke the restaurant's licence if the restaurant failed to do so. Licence revocation is the sanction mechanism which is usually used as a backup to make sure the regulated is willing to change their misbehaviour. A regulatory regime against corruption is similar to the food regulator; a government ethics regulator usually also has the same kinds of mechanisms. It can monitor compliance with integrity code through devices such as financial reports review and government ethics auditing. If a minor deviation is found (e.g. an official is negotiating future employment with a possible future employer), it can require the official stop doing that. A government ethics regulator also has sanction tools such as warning, demerit, and even expulsion.

2.3 The relationship between regulation against corruption and criminal approach in anti-corruption

2.3.1 Both are necessary and complementary

Both criminal enforcement and regulation against corruption are necessary as each addresses different areas of the integrity system spectrum of behaviour shown in Figure 2.1. Actually, it is difficult to imagine a country where the public sector is clean and efficient at the same time

---

[14] Claire Andrews, *The Enforcement of Regulatory Offences* (London: Sweet & Maxwell, 1998).

that the criminal law and its enforcement against corruption is weak or underdeveloped. In Asia, the cleanest counties (or regions) are Singapore and Hong Kong; they ranked seventh and seventeenth respectively in Transparency International's 2014 Corruption Perceptions Index ranking.[15] Both Hong Kong and Singapore are well known for their anti-corruption laws and law enforcement. Special anti-corruption laws (the Prevention of Bribery Ordinance in Hong Kong and the Prevention of Corruption Act in Singapore) and law enforcement agencies (Independent Commission against Corruption [ICAC] in Hong Kong and Corrupt Practices Investigation Bureau in Singapore) were created and the laws are enforced very effectively in real life. Effective criminal enforcement against corruption in Hong Kong and Singapore is a crucial factor in their success in fighting corruption.

Of course, criminal enforcement alone cannot solve the problem of corruption. Since the ICAC successfully controlled the police corruption in the 1970s and 1980s, traditional corruption offences (mainly including bribery, embezzlement and fraud) have not been a major concern for the public sector in Hong Kong.[16] However, public ethics/integrity attracted and is attracting more attention. Conflicts of interest and potential conflicts of values in the public sector have become a concern for the government and the public.[17] Regulatory bodies such as Civil Service Bureau and the Select Committee of the Legislative Council play an important role in regulating public integrity in Hong Kong. Below are two cases which highlight the tough standards that the Hong Kong government has towards government integrity.

The Leung Chin-man case concerns conflicts of interest in post-Civil Service employment. Leung was a former director of housing who officially retired in 2007. In 2008, after a one year sanitization period, he joined a property development company to whom below-market price land projects were sold when he was still in office in 2004. His new position in the company was considered a benefit for the favours he granted to the company in 2004. In the face of public pressure, he resigned from the company. The public was not only concerned about Leung's conflicts of

---

[15] Transparency International, 'Corruption perceptions index 2014', available at http://cpi .transparency.org/cpi2014/results/ (last visited on 23 May 2015).

[16] Ian Scott, 'Promoting integrity in a changing Environment: Hong Kong's public sector after 1997', Integrity Management and Collaborative Governance Conference, ICAC, Hong Kong, 2010.

[17] Ibid.

interest but also the approval of Leung's application for his new job by the Secretary for Civil Service (SCS). The Chief Executive, Donald Tsang, asked the SCS to reevaluate the approval and submit a report to him. This case demonstrates that the Hong Kong government and society are sensitive to public ethics at the individual level as well as at the institutional level.

Another case in point is the Leung Ming-yin case which illustrates the government's strong attitude to maintain high ethical standards in the public sector. Leung Ming-yin was the Director of Immigration in 1996. The government claimed that Leung had violated the terms of the Housing Loan scheme and had not declared the full detail of his investments. Although he had been cleared by the ICAC after investigation, the government still asked him to retire for the reason that he had violated civil service regulations and the government had lost confidence in his integrity.[18]

Apparently, both the stringent regulation of public integrity and effective criminal enforcement are important legal responses towards corruption. Addressing only one aspect is less likely to achieve the desired result. Of course, anti-corruption efforts are not limited to the two approaches. It is not denying the roles of other factors such as the free media, democracy, and social norms, but these are not the focus of this research.

Each approach can strengthen the effect of the other. Put in other words, 'when performed effectively they can even have the added benefit of reinforcing' the other.[19] On the one hand, regulation has a preventive role: regulation focusing largely on misconduct and mal-administration can raise public officials' awareness of public integrity and hence help them avoid improper conduct which might result in criminal enforcement (such as investigation, prosecution, and sanctions) against them. On the other hand, effective prosecution and punishment against corruption may 'have the potential to encourage further compliance to the policies and systems that have been established to prevent misconduct'.[20]

---

[18] Ian Scott, *The Public Sector in Hong Kong* (Hong Kong: Hong Kong University Press, 2010), p. 115.

[19] Amy Comstock, 'Maintaining government integrity: the perspective of the United States Office of Government Ethics', in Cyrille Fijnaut and Leo Huberts (eds.), *Corruption, Integrity and Law Enforcement* (Kluwer Law International, 2002), p. 219.

[20] Ibid.

2.3.2   Limited room for improvement of criminal enforcement against corruption

The room for the criminal enforcement approach is relatively limited compared with the regulatory approach. The effect of the criminal approach against any crime lies on its deterrent effect derived mainly from punishment; there is no exception for corruption. Two main dimensions of punishment are punishment magnitude and the probability of punishment. In order to make punishment deter an act, the expected sanction must be equal to or above the benefits gained from committing an act. The expected sanction is approximately equal to the maximum sanction stipulated by the law or regulations multiplied by the sanction probability. Hence, examination of the room for criminal enforcement approach against corruption involves analysis of the benefits gained from committing corruption and the expected punishment (punishment magnitude multiplied by punishment probability).

Regarding the expected punishment for corruption, both punishment magnitude and punishment probability suffers from certain limits. Most serious criminal sanctions for corruption include economic sanctions, imprisonment, and the death penalty. There are constraints on the magnitude of both imprisonment and the death penalty. A basic sanction principle is that magnitude of punishment must be proportionate to the culpability of a crime. A person may perceive a punishment as disproportionate to the act performed.[21] For example, a sentence of death for corrupt officials would be considered too cruel and disproportionate.

In terms of sanction magnitude, a regulation regime can provide a wider range of sanctions for government ethics offences compared with a criminal regime against corruption. For the latter, punishment mainly includes economic penalties, imprisonment, disqualification orders, and in some places the death penalty; for the former, sanctions range from oral warning, formal warning, demerit, and demotion, to dismissal from post and expulsion. The reason is that under the regulation regime the range of consequences for breach is considerably wider than that in the criminal regime against corruption. For example, a violation may be very minor such as ignorance of potential conflicts of interest or failure to satisfy certain technical standards (e.g. financial report). The consequence could also be more serious such as accepting a gift. Responses

---

[21] Steven Shavell, 'The optimal structure of law enforcement', *Journal of Law and Economics*, 36, 1 (1993), pp. 255–287.

to these consequences under the regulation regime are more compliance-oriented because most of these consequences are focused on risk, potential, or reasonable suspicion of the public.

Furthermore, if punishment for corruption is fixed and severe (say, the death penalty or long-term imprisonment) regardless of the seriousness of the offence, the penalty will have no deterrent effect on those who have passed the corruption threshold.[22] Although serious punishment for even minor corruption will have a larger deterrent effect for those who had never carried out a corrupt act, those who have already committed minor corruption will be more likely to risk more serious corruption because their first offence has already constituted sound legal grounds for punishment by death. This situation can be illustrated by the act of smoking. If a smoker is told by a doctor that no matter whether they have smoked for one day or half a year and no matter whether they give up smoking or not, they will have the same possibility of dying of lung cancer, it is reasonable to expect that they will continue smoking or even smoke more heavily.

In addition to the above constraints, the death penalty and imprisonment also have their practical limits. Capital punishment is seen as a means whose advantages can be achieved by other alternative means of punishment and their disadvantages cannot be removed unless it is abolished.[23] One of the practical constraints on the death penalty is the pressure from the worldwide anti-capital punishment movement.[24] For imprisonment, the most serious practical problem is the burden on national budget. According to David J. Rothman, the cost of maintaining one inmate for one year in New York City is 58,000 USD, at least twice the tuition fee and living costs when attending a private university. On average, the cost for each of the 5 million or so men imprisoned is 54,000 USD per year.[25] In China, though in theory the death penalty can be applied to officials who embezzle 0.1 million RMB or above, in practice,

---

[22] Susan Rose-Ackerman, 'Corruption and the criminal law', *Forum on Crime and Society*, 2, 1 (2002), pp. 3–21.

[23] Andrew Von Hirsh, 'Penal theories', in Michael Tonry (ed.) *Handbook of Crime and Punishment* (New York and Oxford: Oxford University Press, 1998), p. 674.

[24] Terence D. Miethe and Hong Lu, *Punishment: A Comparative Historical Perspective* (Cambridge: Cambridge University Press, 2005), p. 21.

[25] Mirta B. Gordon, J. R. Iglesias, Viktoryia Semeshenko, and J. P. Nadal, 'Crime and punishment: the economic burden of impunity', *The European Physical Journal B*, 68 (2009), pp. 133–144, available at http://arxiv.org/PS_cache/arxiv/pdf/0710/0710.3751v1.pdf (last visited on 13 April 2010).

the death penalty is rarely imposed on corruption offenders. Some scholars have even suggested abolishing the death penalty altogether for corruption.[26]

For economic sanctions, the natural limit is the total wealth of a corruption offender. However, it is not easy to recover all the ill-gotten gains from corruption, let alone the offender's total wealth which includes both illegal gains and legal assets.

The constraints of punishment magnitude for corruption have been examined. Now, the limits of the other factor of criminal enforcement deterrence, punishment probability for corruption, will be discussed. Generally speaking, punishment probability for corruption is lower than for other crimes such as rape, burglary, and robbery. Reporting by victims is a major way of identifying an act that violates the law (in many cases, the offender is directly identified by the victims). However, for crimes of corruption, in many cases victims do not realize they have been harmed by the corrupt act. That makes for a lower reporting rate for corruption than for other offences. Further, corrupt officials are those who are in power; they can use their power to retaliate against whistle-blowers. This also contributes to the lower reporting rate for corruption crimes.

Moving specifically to the situation in China, in addition to the usual reasons for the low reporting rate for corruption, another factor also contributes to the low punishment probability for corruption in China. A large number of prosecutions of corrupt officials would mean systemic failure of the CCP government. That would damage the political legitimacy of the Party and its government. As Minxin Pei has pointed out, it is a misperception that penalties for corruption are harsh in China, though long-term imprisonment and the death penalty are applied to corruptors because the Party actually only punishes a very small proportion of Party and government officials involved in corruption.[27] His research showed that almost 80 per cent of the 130,000 to 190,000 CCP members disciplined and punished annually for their corruption received only a

---

[26] Dan Shao, 'Feasibility of abolishing the death penalty for corruption crimes: implementing UNCAC', *The Legal System and Society*, 22 (2006), pp. 9–10; and Renwen Liu, 'Can we create conditions for abolishing the death penalty for corruption?' *Democracy and Legal System*, 22 (2010), pp. 32–34.

[27] Minxin Pei, 'Corruption threatens China's future', *Policy Brief* 55 (Washington, DC: Carnegie Endowment for International Peace, October 2007), available at www.carnegieendowment.org/files/pb55_pei_china_corruption_final.pdf (last visited on 15 June 2013).

warning. Only 20 per cent were expelled from the Party and only no more than 6 per cent actually received criminal punishment. In recent years, he found that half of the convicted corruptors received a suspended sentence. That means, putting all these percentages together, Minxin Pei estimated, that only three out of one hundred detected corruptors actually went to jail. This punishment pattern for detected corruptors is also identified in Wedeman's research, though the percentage for different punishments is slightly different.[28] Given that the detection rate itself is very low, the possibility of being punished is very small.

The limits of the magnitude of criminal sanctions for corruption in China can be better understood if they are viewed against the background of the gains from committing corruption. The meaning of the deterrence through punishment magnitude and punishment probability must be evaluated against the gains from committing a crime. According to the fundamentals of deterrence theory, in any case, the costs of committing a crime (punishment) must not be less than what is sufficient to outweigh that of the profit of the offence.[29] A rational person will decide to commit an offence if profit of the offence outweighs the cost of committing the offence; he or she will abide by the law if the punishment value is greater than the profit of crime. The cost of committing an offence is equal to the value of punishment severity multiplied by certainty of punishment. An ideal case from Entorf serves as a good example to illustrate the idea.[30] Consider the choice between paying €3 for a short-term city parking space or not paying the amount and taking the risk of a fine of €20. Assuming 10 per cent of the unpaid parking is detected and fined, that means the probability of punishment is 10 per cent. The profit then from unpaid parking would be €3 as the person will save €3 if undetected. The cost of illegal parking is €2 (punishment magnitude €20 multiplies punishment probability by 10 per cent), which is smaller than the profit, €3. Hence a rational driver would decide not to put a coin into the parking meter.

---

[28] According to Andrew Wedeman, of detected corruptors, 25 per cent were expelled from the Party, 6 per cent of the cases were transferred to the judiciary for criminal investigation, and 69 per cent resulted in various forms of internal party sanctions. See Andrew Wedeman, 'The intensification of corruption in China', *The China Quarterly* 180 (2004), pp. 895–921, especially p. 908.

[29] Jeremy Bentham, *An Introduction to the Principles of Morals and Legislation* (Oxford: Clarendon Press; New York: Oxford University Press, 1996).

[30] Horst Entorf, 'Certainty and severity of sanctions in classical and behavioral models of deterrence: a survey', IZA Discussion Paper No. 6516, Goethe University, 2012.

For crimes of corruption, the situation is more complicated and it is not possible to compare the value of punishment with gains from committing a corrupt act in the way it is calculated in mathematics like the above example. However, the evaluation framework is definitely helpful.

Economic gains will be explored first and then noneconomic gains will be examined. Regarding the amount of the money in corruption cases in China, a survey of corruption cases published on the Supreme People's Procuratorate official website from January to April 2009 shows that more than 70 per cent of the cases involve money more than 1 million RMB. The details of the money involved are shown in Table 2.1.

Let us conservatively assume that the average amount of money involved in corruption cases in China is 2 million. In order to effectively deter an act of corruption, the expected punishment must be equal to or greater than the 2 million. The corruption detection rate in China is not publically available, but a reasonable estimation can be made. According to comparative research on the detection rate for nonviolent crimes, detection rate in European countries is mainly between 10 to 20 per cent.[31] As mentioned earlier, the detection rate for corruption is lower than for other crimes. It is safe to estimate that the possibility of being detected for corruption in China is not bigger than 10 per cent. However, according to Minxin Pei no more than 6 per cent of detected officials receive criminal punishment; most of caught corruptors only receive a warning.[32] Thus, that means the probability of being criminally punished is only 0.006, or 0.6 per cent (10 per cent multiplying 6 per cent). Other noncriminal punishments such as administrative or party disciplinary punishments will not impose any monetary fine on officials.[33] The expected punishment = monetary punishment imposed after conviction × 0.6 per cent (the possibility of being criminally punished). To have a

---

[31] Paul R. Smit, Ronald F. Meijer, and Peter-Paul J. Groen, 'Detection rates, an international comparison', *European Journal on Criminal Policy and Research*, 10, 2–3 (September 2004), pp. 225–253.

[32] Pei, 'Corruption threatens China's future'.

[33] See Article 6, Regulation on the Punishment of Civil Servants of Administrative Organs. Disciplinary actions against civil servants in administrative organs are limited to: (1) a warning; (2) a demerit; (3) a gross demerit; (4) demotion; (5) dismissal from office; and (6) expulsion; See also Article 10, Regulation of the Communist Party of China on Disciplinary Actions. Party disciplinary actions are very similar to administrative sanctions, which include: a warning, a serious warning, being removed from a party position, being placed on probation within the party, or being expelled from the party.

Table 2.1 *The amount of money in corruption cases from January to April 2009.*

Money involved in corruption cases (RMB)	Number of cases	Percentage	Notes
Less than 5,000	0	0	
5,000 to less than 50,000	1	1.96	
50,000 to less than 100,000	2	3.92	
100,000 to less than 500,000	8	15.69	
500,000 to less than 1 million	2	3.92	
1 million to less than 10 million	21	41.18	Two cases are still under investigation
10 million to less than 100 million	4	7.84	
More than 100 million	4	7.84	One case is still under investigation
Huge	6	11.76	All six cases are still under investigation. The specific amount of money is not stated, but articles use the word 'huge' to describe the amount
Money not mentioned in the case	3	5.88	
Total	**51**	**100**	

Source: The Supreme People's Procuratorate website at www.spp.gov.cn/site2006/region/00027,1.html (last visited on 29 April 2009).

deterrence effect, the expected punishment must be equal to (or greater than) 2 million RMB. That means punishment severity (monetary punishment imposed after conviction) must be at least more than 333 million RMB (2 million ÷ 0.006). Looking at Table 2.1, for more than 25 per cent of cases, the benefit from corruption is more than 10 million RMB. If that is the case, in order to ensure that the punishment has a deterrent effect, the monetary punishment imposed must be at least 1,667 million RMB (10 million ÷ 0.006).

The purpose of doing the above mathematical calculations is not to exactly figure out the accurate amount of monetary punishment for corruption, but to show that the severity must be very huge to generate a deterrence effect. Monetary sanctions have a natural limit, that is, the total wealth of the corruptors including their benefits and their own legal wealth. The above calculation showed us that in most cases corrupt officials do not have that much wealth to be fined or confiscated. In practice, money confiscated or fined from corrupt officials is generally less than the benefits they have gained from committing corruption because a large part of the gains have already been lavishly spent and their own legal wealth is marginal relative to the corrupt gains. For example, in 2008 Cheng Xitong, the former party chief of Shanghai, was convicted of bribery (2.39 million RMB), but confiscation of personal wealth was only 0.3 million RMB.[34] In June 2013, money confiscated for the bribery offence (3.16 million RMB) of Lei Zhengfu, the former party chief of Beipei District, Chongqing city, was only 0.3 million RMB.[35]

Of course, punishments are not limited to monetary sanctions. However, benefits from corruption can also be extended to nonmonetary gains. Many corrupt officials in China, especially core leadership officials in various local government departments or party organs, live like kings. They eat meals in five-star restaurants using the public's budget; they have several mistresses and provide lavish housing for them; they go to Macau or foreign countries to gamble with public funds; they decide who will be promoted; and they decide whether a new office building will be constructed. For some, living a life like a king for a decade or two and then a stay in prison their later years is better than keeping clean as officials for their whole life. Let alone only a small percentage of those officials will be detected and only a small part of the detected will be heavily punished. It is true that monetary punishment and imprisonment are not exclusive and thus could be imposed simultaneously. However, corrupt officials in China also get huge amounts of monetary and nonmonetary benefits from being corrupt.

---

[34] 'Cheng Liangyu was sentenced to eighteen years imprisonment for his two offences', *Xinhua-News*, available at http://news.xinhuanet.com/newscenter/2008-04/11/content_7959849.htm (last visited on 13 September 2013).

[35] 'Lei Zhengfu was sentenced to thirteen years imprisonment and confiscated of personal wealth of 0.3 million RMB', *XinhuaNews*, available at http://news.xinhuanet.com/legal/2013-06/28/c_116329205.htm (last visited on 13 September 2013).

In order to put in place deterrence, either regarding sanction magnitude, sanction probability, or both, must be increased. However, sanction magnitude has constraints; increased benefits make corruption more attractive and thus induce more violators. More violators make detection even more difficult. A vicious circle results: more benefits → more violators → more difficult to detect → more violators. Thus, the room for the criminal law enforcement approach is very limited given that the primary tools for it are investigation, prosecution, and sanctions. The criminal approach against corruption in China also faces political constraints as strict criminal enforcement against corruption will ruin the CCP's political legitimacy. Section 2.4 will discuss this point further.

2.3.3   The potential for regulation against corruption

There is still much room for the development of regulations against corruption, especially maladministration and misconduct. Unlike the criminal system which has been long established, regulatory regimes against corruption have mainly developed since the 1960s in many developed countries such as the United States, the United Kingdom, and Hong Kong. Although the origin of public ethics regulation can be traced to early in the twentieth century (e.g. as early as 1917, federal employees in the United States were no longer allowed to accept any payment from any nongovernment sources[36]), this research will focus on development of such regulations mainly since the 1960s. As shown by Hood et al., rapid development of regulation inside government and regulatory agencies begins from the 1960s onwards.[37] A brief development of public ethics regulation in the United States, the United Kingdom, and Hong Kong will be discussed below; they will also be discussed in greater detail in Chapter 3.

Issues that dominated public ethics in the United States in the early days largely stressed putting the appropriate people in public posts; emphasis was on the personal character of possible candidates. The Kennedy administration marked an important change in public ethics management as the country began to experience rule-driven ethics.[38] This shift can be seen as the first stage or the emergence of modern

---

[36] Endrius Eliseo Cocciolo, 'Checking the integrity of government', Droit Administratif Compare, Europeen et Global Seminar Paper, Paris, 2008.
[37] Hood et al., *Regulation inside Government*.
[38] Cocciolo, 'Checking the integrity of government'.

public ethics regulation. In 1961, President Kennedy sent a message titled 'Ethical Conduct in Government' to Congress. This message established rules governing financial conflict-of-interest situations which might raise the public's doubts about the impartiality of the government.[39] It also governed outside employment. Outside employment, though, could be seen as one aspect of potential conflicts of interest, together with other employment requirements, it later developed to a very important and systematic sub-area of public integrity.

In 1965, President Johnson took a further step in public ethics regulation through Executive Order 11222. The new rules required federal employees to report the *details* of their personal finances.[40] Even more importantly, a new element was introduced into public ethics regulation: federal employees were required to avoid the *appearance* of corruption.[41] This new element greatly broadened the scope of public ethics regulation and developed into another important sub-area of public ethics regulation.

Later, in the Richard Nixon Administration, the Watergate scandal triggered another important principle in public ethics regulation, *legitimate suspicion*, on which the Ethics in Government Act commissioned in 1978 is based.[42] The Watergate scandal also gave birth to a new mentality in public ethics regulation; a key element of the new mentality is that a new corps of regulators must be established and they must be specialized in ethics laws.[43] In the United States, the Office of Government Ethics (OGE) was established under the Ethics in Government Act of 1978. In the same year, under the Inspector General Act of 1978, Inspector Generals (IGs) were established in twelve cabinet-level agencies.[44] According to Phyllis Fong, chair of the Council of the Inspectors General on Integrity and Efficiency of the United States, IGs identify fraud, waste, and abuse and can report their findings with recommendations to address their findings to their agencies, Congress, and the public.[45]

---

[39] Robert N. Roberts and Marion T. Doss, Jr., *From Watergate to Whitewater: The Public Integrity War* (Westport, CT: Praeger, 1997), p. 48.

[40] G. C. Mackenzie, *Scandal Proof: Do Ethics Laws Make Government Ethical?* (Washington, DC: Brookings Institution Press, 2002), p. 25

[41] Cocciolo, 'Checking the integrity of government'.   [42] Ibid.

[43] Mackenzie, *Scandal Proof*, pp. 31–32.

[44] Phyllis K. Fong, 'Working together: corruption and integrity investigations in the United States', *Collaborative Governance and Integrity Management Conference*, ICAC, Hong Kong, 2010.

[45] Ibid.

The United Kingdom's approach to public ethics management historically has developed through a less rule-bound tradition than that in many other jurisdictions.[46] However, since the 1990s, it seems that this trend has been challenged. In 1996, the Civil Service Code came into effect and was revised in 2006 and 2010. This code contains various requirements on conflicts of interest ('you must not accept gifts or hospitality or receive other benefits from anyone which might reasonably be seen to compromise your judgment or integrity ... you must not be influenced by ... the prospect of personal gain') and appearance of corruption ('you must always act in a way ... that deserves and retains the confidence of all those with whom you have dealings').[47] It is true that in terms of codification of ethical standards, the United Kingdom has lagged behind many other jurisdictions such as the United States. However, that does not mean in reality unethical activities are less likely to be subject to regulation.

According to Paul Heywood, there are currently at least fifteen public ethics watchdogs in the United Kingdom at the national level.[48] Take one of the regulatory agencies, the Committee on Standards in Public Life, for example. It regulates a broad range of public ethics activities. Many regulatory activities concern financial interests such as the expenses of Members of Parliament (MPs) and outside employment issues. The committee does not focus only on 'things going wrong; the Committee is equally interested to see evidence that arrangements already in place are working to ensure the highest standards of propriety in public life'.[49]

Corruption had been a serious issue for Hong Kong before and during the early period of the establishment of the ICAC. However, since the

---

[46] Paul M. Heywood, 'Integrity management and the public services ethos in the UK: patchwork quilt or threadbare blanket?' Collaborative Governance and Integrity Management Conference, ICAC, Hong Kong, 2010.

[47] Paragraph 6, 7 and 9 The Civil Service Code (the UK), 2010.

[48] These fifteen regulatory bodies are: Comptroller and Auditor General, Parliamentary and Health Service Ombudsman, Information Commissioner, Electoral Commissioner, Committee on Standards in Public Life, Civil Service Commissioners, Public Appointments Commissioner, Business Appointments Committee, House of Lords Appointments Committee, Commission for Equality and Human rights, UK Statistics Authority, Judicial Appointments Commission, Independent Advisor on Ministerial Interests, Audit Commission, Standards for England, and Parliamentary Standards Commissioner. See Heywood, 'Integrity management'.

[49] Committee on Standards in Public Life (the UK), 'Annual review and report 2009–10', 2010, p. 3, available at www.public-standards.gov.uk/wp-content/uploads/2012/11/2010_ANNUAL_REPORT___Final.pdf (last visited on 17 December 2012).

ICAC successfully controlled the police corruption in the 1970s and 1980s, traditional corruption offences (mainly including bribery, embezzlement, and fraud) have not been a major concern for the public sector in Hong Kong.[50] However, public ethics/integrity attracted, and is attracting, more attention. Conflicts of interest and potential conflicts of values in the public sector have become a concern for the government and the public due to the structural changes in the government resulting from the transition to Chinese sovereignty.[51] Prior to and after the transition, more and more senior positions in the government were gradually taken up by Hong Kong locals; these positions were earlier dominated by the British. Senior local officials tend to retire early and then enter the private sector. As a response to the new trend and triggered by a number of post-service employment cases involving conflicts of interest or potential conflicts, rules governing postservice employment and the reform of the Advisory Committee on Postservice Employment of Civil Servants have been discussed by the government, legislators, and the media.

From this short discussion of public ethics regulation in the United States, the United Kingdom, and Hong Kong, three conclusions can be made. First, anti-corruption campaigns have been extended from traditional corruption offences to broad public ethics regulation. Second, the regulation of public ethics is reflected mainly in two aspects: making and revising public ethics rules/regulations; and setting up regulatory bodies. Third, regulated areas mainly lie in four aspects: conflicts of interest, appearance of corruption, financial disclosure, and outside employment/activities. These four aspects are not exclusive and overlap to some degree.

Unlike the United Kingdom and the United States, where public ethics regulation began to become systematic from the 1970s onwards, modern public ethics regulation at best has only begun to emerge in China. Some scholars have argued that China has evolved to rule-guided integrity management only in the past decade.[52] It is true that the Party and the government have made, and is making, a large body of rules relevant to integrity/public ethics. However, that does not mean a regulatory

---

[50] Scott, *The Public Sector in Hong* Kong.   [51] Ibid.

[52] Ting Gong, 'An institutional turn toward rule-based integrity management in China', Collaborative Governance and Integrity Management Conference, ICAC, Hong Kong, 2010; Ting Gong and Stephen K. Ma (eds.), *Preventing Corruption in Asia: Institutional Design and Policy Capacity* (London and New York: Routledge, 2009).

enforcement system against corruption has been established in China. This is reflected in several features of the current regulation of government ethics in China. First, many public ethics regulations/rules are made in an abstract way so that their enforceability is very weak. As observed by Li Chengyan, in China an overall plan for the management of the honesty of civil servants at the national level has not been made and basic regulations/rules governing civil servant honesty is also missing.[53] The existing regulations are abstract, scattered, and unenforceable.[54] Second, many subcategories of conflicts of interest (such as assisting a third party in dealings with government) and appearances of corruption regulations are almost nonexistent.

Third, many existing administrative regulations (or party rules) governing corruption in China cannot be considered counterparts of public ethics regulations in the United Kingdom, the United States, and Hong Kong. Much behaviour governed by administrative/party regulations in China is considered serious criminal corruption in the United Kingdom, the United States, and Hong Kong. For example, taking a bribe of under 5,000 RMB usually does not amount to criminal corruption in China.[55] Apparently, a small bribe (say several hundreds) will be subject to criminal punishment in the United States, the United Kingdom, and Hong Kong.

Finally, in practice, many maladministration and misconduct actions are not subject to any formal regulatory control in China. Generally speaking, nonethical conduct by civil servants in China is less likely being challenged compared with that in the United States, the United Kingdom, and Hong Kong. Further, enforcement of government ethics in China is largely the same as its criminal enforcement (deterrence-oriented),

---

[53] Chengyan Li, 'Government honesty building up and civil servant honesty management', Collaborative Governance and Integrity Management Conference, ICAC, Hong Kong, 2010.

[54] Ibid.

[55] Article 386 of the Criminal Law of the People's Republic of China states that '[w]hoever commits the crime of accepting bribes is to be punished on the basis of Article 383 of this law according to the amount of bribes and the circumstances. A heavier punishment shall be given to whoever demands a bribe'. Article 383 (4) of the criminal law of the People's Republic of China states that 'Individuals who have engaged in graft with an amount of less than 5,000 yuan, with the situation being serious, are to be sentenced to less than two years of fixed-term imprisonment or criminal detention. In lighter cases, they will be given administrative action to be decided by the unit to which they belong or the higher administrative organ. Toward those who have committed repeated crimes of graft, all amounts of graft of unhandled cases are to be added in meting out punishment.'

whereas in the three selected countries a compliance-oriented enforcement style is practiced in government ethics regulation. Chapters 3 and 4 will examine these features in detail.

2.3.4 Minor maladministration and misconduct paves the way for serious corruption in government

There is a pattern that corruption offenders usually get more corrupt gradually; they seldom start from serious corrupt behaviour without experiencing minor violations. If less serious gratuities are allowed to occur, the condition for more serious bribes exists.[56] On the other hand, if a robust regulatory regime against maladministration and misconduct is in place and functions well, minor corrupt behaviour will be less likely to develop and become serious corruption as they will be interdicted at an early stage.

It is common practice that officers in many government bodies deviate from public ethics values and standards. These acts may be very minor in nature – for example, accepting a gift from a businessman. In many government agencies, such minor deviance is so common that it has become an acceptable way of doing business and has been considered too minor to warrant a formal response.[57] However, once a minor illegal act is justified, it will become easier for an official to commit more serious corruption; this is known as the slippery slope of corruption.[58]

This process of becoming corrupt gradually was also observed by Lawrence Sherman who described the process as 'becoming bent'.[59] Sherman summarized six stages of becoming bent for police. The first stage is free coffee and meals offered by restaurants, usually in a policeman's first days on duty, which is termed as 'minor "perks"'. If the minor perks are accepted, he is more likely to accept a drink from a bar owner and in return allow the bar to stay open after closing hours; this step was labelled 'bar closing hours'. The third stage is the policeman may accept a regulative bribe; for example, a motorist hands in the policeman his

---

[56] Lawrence W. Sherman, 'Becoming bent: moral careers of corrupt policemen', in Frederick A. Elliston and Michael Feldberg (eds.), *Moral Issues in Police Work* (Totowa, NJ: Rowman & Allanheld Publishers, 1985), pp. 253–265.

[57] Thomas Barker and David L. Carter, *Police Deviance* (Cincinnati, OH: Anderson Publishing, 1986), pp. 2–3.

[58] John P. Crank and Michael A. Caldero, *Police Ethics: The Corruption of Noble Causes* (Cincinnati, OH: Anderson Publishing, 2000), p. 66.

[59] Sherman, 'Becoming bent', pp. 253–265.

driver's licence with a five dollar bill in it and the policeman accepts the bill and ignores the driver's reckless driving. The fourth step is regular payoffs offered by a local gambling business. Usually, a newly recruited policeman will only be involved in this kind of payoff by other policemen receiving payoffs after he has already passed the tests of the first three steps. The fifth step is accepting bribes from prostitution providers (streetwalkers, pimps, or brothel operators). The sixth stage is accepting narcotics bribes.

Putting it more clearly, in Sherman's words, the process of 'becoming bent' is:

1. Minor 'perks'
2. Bar closing hours
3. Regulative crimes
4. Gambling
5. Prostitution
6. Narcotics

It is not to say that every policeman will follow this process of becoming corrupt. Some may either accept or reject a bribe at a certain stage. For example, a policeman accepting minor perks and bar drinks may still reject a regulative bribe, but Sherman argues that acceptance is made easier if the policeman is used to taking meals from restaurants and drinks from bars.[60] On the other hand, it is not usual to find a case where a policeman starts to become corrupt from committing the more serious corruption from narcotics graft directly without any previous experience of corruption.[61]

Although Sherman's research on 'becoming bent' is based mainly on Western police deviance literature and his own personal experience, it seems the slippery slope of corruption can be extended to other public officials in China. Of course, as other public officials have totally different powers compared with that of police, their form of deviance will not follow the six-stage deviance pattern discussed above. However, the central focus of this section is not about the deviance forms but the gradual process of becoming corrupt from minor deviance to serious corruption.

The Li Zhen case will be used to show the process. The reason for choosing this case is not because of the senior ranking of the official nor

---

[60] Ibid.   [61] Ibid.

the huge amount of his corrupt gains. The reason is because the available materials on the Li Zhen case provide a good opportunity to examine the process of becoming corrupt gradually. From the time of his arrest to his execution, Li Zhen was interviewed several times in jails by Qiao Yunhua, a journalist from the Xinhua News Agency. One year after Li Zhen was executed, Qiao Yunhua's interviews with Li Zhen were published in a work titled *Before the Gates of Hell: Conversations with Li Zhen before His Execution.*[62]

Qiao's interviews with Li Zhen were conducted with clear 'research questions' in mind. At the beginning of the book, Qiao said to Li that:

> In our last two meetings, you have clearly told me all your crime facts. Actually, I have finished my interview work for the media report purpose. However, ... I find, like many others think, many 'mysteries' of you have not been disclosed. For example, ... From refusing a multipack of cigarettes at the beginning to asking for millions of money at the end, how did your mindset change?[63]

Li Zhen's corruption began when he was the personal assistant to a deputy governor of Hebei Province in 1990. However, at the very beginning he hoped he could perform the job well. The following conversation showed his cleanness:

> QIAO (THE INTERVIEWER): What is your ideal when you become assistant to the vice governor?
> LI: Be a good assistant.
> QIAO: You did not have the idea of bribery in mind?
> LI: Actually, at the very beginning when I became [the deputy governor's] the assistant, I felt incredible when I heard of officials around me involved in corruption. I felt that is far from me. It is not easy to have these political powers, why not do something for the people? Why accept bribes?[64]

This stage can be referred to as the 'clean stage' where the official has not yet been corrupted. However, this period was very short for Li Zhen; he soon slipped to the step of accepting free meals. Li Zhen said to the interviewer that 'since the second week of my becoming the deputy governor's assistant I began to receive invitations for meals and I refused the first several invitations. However, once I refused an

---

[62] Yunhua Qiao, *Before the Gates of Hell: Conversations with Li Zhen before His Execution* (Beijing: Xinhua Publishing House, 2004).
[63] Ibid., pp. 24–25.   [64] Ibid., pp. 149–150.

invitation but eventually accepted. It is so hard to say no because they kept pleading'.[65]

The next step is accepting small gifts. Li's first experience in accepting a gift immediately followed his first free meal. Li recalled that 'after the meal somebody offered a multipack of cigarettes (10 packs of cigarettes). I strongly refused the offer. But, that guy was jamming it into my pocket in a way like a madman. I realized it was hard to refuse him; I took only one pack [of cigarettes]'.[66] Li continued: 'it was that pack of cigarettes that made me upset for a week. I felt very nervous every time I thought of this'.[67]

Then, gradually, the gifts became more expensive. Sometime later he went to attend a conference. Each conference participant was given a sweater as a souvenir by the conference organizer. He accepted the sweater but felt restless and uneasy.[68]

Not soon after he accepted the sweater, an official in Cangzhou city in Hebei Province visited Li Zhen and offered him a multipack of Zhonghua cigarettes and an electric razor while the official was reporting the work to the provincial leaders. Li Zhen accepted the gifts. However, when he took the gifts to his home he found that he could not open the door of his home. He was opening the home door with his bicycle key due to nervousness and fear.[69]

The next 'gift' he was offered was a jade Chinese cabbage:

> I did not dare to accept this when somebody offered me it. I do not know how much this jade Chinese cabbage was worth. The 'gift'-giver said to me 'this is not worth much. I bought it while I was on a business trip to south China.' In fact, I know this is not cheap. But his words reassured me that I could take it. I also thought, at that time, even if this was disclosed I still had an excuse. I could argue that I really did not know it was worth much money. I refused it once or twice before I accepted it.[70]

So far, his bribes were limited to 'gifts'. Four conclusions can be made from the above gradual process. First, the value of the 'gifts' was growing exponentially. Second, all the 'gifts' were taken in a passive manner – all these offers were initiated by the gift-givers rather than by Li Zhen. Third, he experienced a process ranging from strong resistance, soft resistance to no resistance when he was given these 'gifts'.

---

[65] Ibid., p. 150.   [66] Ibid.   [67] Ibid.

[68] Ling Xiu, *The Rise and Fall of Li Zhen: The Li Zhen Case and Li Zhen's Personal Life* (Beijing: Guangming Daily Press, 2004).

[69] Ibid.   [70] Qiao, *Before the Gates of Hell*, p. 246.

Finally, such acceptance will always arouse uncomfortable psychological experiences such as fear and nervousness.

Li Zhen's first money acceptance scene was described in detail in Xiu Lin's book.

> Li Guoting comes to Li Zhen's room. Li Zhen opened the door and saw Li Guoting. Li Zhen said 'Manager Li, sit down please. Please do not mind the simpleness and crudeness of my residence.' Li Guoting said: 'it does not matter. Young men should put study and work before everything. The conference will end tomorrow. [I will go home to Zhangjiakou city after the conference.] Is there anything I can do for you in Zhangjiakou city? You have to deal with many social functions, banquets, and parties very frequently. It must take a lot of money to do this. I give you 5,000 yuan; please accept it.'

> Li Zhen was shocked by so much money. This is the first time he is offered with money. 5,000 yuan, at that time, is equal to two-and-a-half years of his salary. Li Zhen strongly refused many times, but Li Zhen failed to stop him. Manager Li left the money with Li Zhen and went away quickly. The next day, Li Zhen reported this to the deputy governor he serves under. The deputy governor told him: 'you must return the money to him. You cannot accept the money.' Li Zhen returned the money to Li Guoting through another person. Soon after, Li came to Shijiazhuang again for a conference. He was not happy when he met Li Zhen. He said to Li Zhen: 'you look down on me.'[71] I was afraid of making him angry and thus accepted the 5,000 yuan.[72]

Li Zhen had two conflicting thoughts after accepting the 5,000 RMB. On the one hand, he makes up his mind secretly – it is terrible, thinking 'I must avoid accepting money later'. On the other hand, he thought given that gift-giving was so pervasive in the society he must turn down those gifts which are for obvious economic benefits (e.g. granting a bar licence to the gift-giver) but should consider taking gifts given by those who are high on the social scale and who have a close relationship with him.[73]

After a series of passively accepting 'gifts' and money, Li Zhen stepped up to initiate bribes (to 'borrow' things and money in Li Zhen's own words):

> QIAO: You just mentioned you passively accept gifts and money. Can you say something about asking for gifts and money?
> LI: I did not begin with asking for millions of money at the beginning . . . I was too ashamed to say that.

---

[71] Xiu, *The Rise and Fall of Li Zhen*, p. 118.   [72] Qiao, *Before the Gates of Hell*, p. 247.
[73] Ibid.

QIAO: But, you did say that. How did you say that the first time?

LI: I began with 'borrowing' ... borrowing a car from Zhang Tiemeng at first.

QIAO: Say a bit more about that.

LI: Zhang Tiemeng was detained by a procuratorate. He was released through my efforts. He wanted to thank me. A car caught my eye. It was a Lexus 400 worth 0.62 million at that time. I told Zhang Tiemeng the bank account of the sales agent of the car. Around February 1994, Zhang directly transferred the money to the bank account of the car seller.

QIAO: What is your mindset after you had gotten the car?

LI: I was pleased. I still can remember that I showed off the car to Yu Qiurong (Li's mistress).[74]

After Li 'borrowed' this car, he began to 'borrow' a flat worth 1 million RMB in 1996:

QIAO: How did you 'borrow' the flat?

LI: At the beginning of 1996, I was appointed as vice head of the Hebei Provincial Office of State Administration of Taxation. In March and April 1996, I went to Beijing for a conference. A friend of mine in Beijing visited me in my hotel and recommended a company, which could produce cheaper devices for the electronic declaration of tax, to me. On my return to Shijiazhuang, I recommended that company to the head of our office and the head appointed me as the in-charge person for the device purchase. I called my friend in Beijing and he soon came. Half a year later, I, on behalf of Hebei Provincial Office of State Administration of Taxation, signed the cooperation contract with that company. The money invested in this project was 18 million RMB.

QIAO: Did you ask for commission for this?

LI: I did not ask for a commission for facilitating this transaction. But, that friend said to me: 'both you and I will have benefited from this deal.' In 1997, I wanted to borrow a flat in Beijing so that I can have a place to stay when I visited Beijing. I fancied a flat and told this to my Beijing friend who paid for the purchase of the flat directly to the flat seller.[75]

After the 'borrowing' stages, Li Zhen began to initiate or even extort bribes from real estate developers who competed for projects of the Hebei Provincial Office of State Administration of Taxation.

From the second half of 1996 until he was detained in 1999, Li Zhen took or extorted bribes six times, amounting to several million RMB from office building construction projects. At this stage, Li's physiological reaction to bribery was totally different from the very early stages:

[74] Ibid., p. 252. [75] Ibid., pp. 253–254.

LI: It seems to me that taking many bribes made me get used to it and that it now seemed natural to take it. At that time, once construction projects were mentioned I could not but help to think about bribery.

QIAO: In 1999, why did you dare to ask for bribes for building projects given that you know you have caught the eye of Central Commission for Discipline Inspection of the CCP?

LI: It is the desire to be in possession of money that drove me. I wanted to collect money from project developers every time there was a new project in the Provincial Office of State Administration of Taxation. Regardless of difficulty, the developers I recommended must be selected. If a local leader had a different view on the selection of developer, I would exert my influence; if there were different opinions within the Hebei Provincial Office, I would make them see it my way. In any case, I must get the money once I decided that I wanted it.

QIAO: How did you feel mentally?

LI: I was not nervous any more. I felt calm when I was carrying out my plan. I became excited when my aim was about to be fulfilled. If I successfully 'made' a big amount of money in a certain case, I became fully immersed in the joy of success.[76]

Table 2.2 summarizes how Li Zhen gradually became corrupt. The table clearly shows the gradual process of becoming corrupt for Li Zhen. The 'Forms of gift/bribe' column shows that the value of gifts/bribe gradually increased from just a meal to several million RMB. The value is roughly positively linked to the seriousness of the corrupt behaviour because if more money was invested by a bribe-giver more profit should be earned from this investment. Thus, public power would be abused to a more serious degree in order to create more profit for the bribe-giver. Column 2 (initiated by bribe-giver) and column 3 (initiated by bribe-taker) together demonstrates that both for small gifts and money Li Zhen always begins with passive acceptance. Columns 4, 5 and 7 together illustrate that the official experienced a process from successful refusing, failed refusing but with strong resistance to bribery, to accepting with no hesitation.

Column 6 (psychological state) shows the official's physiological experience moving from nervousness, fear, upset, restlessness and uneasiness to calm, pleasure, excitement, and feelings of success. All the mentioned negative feelings are caused mainly by two psychological factors: fear (afraid of being caught and punished) and sense of guilt (afraid of being called corrupt). When Li received a multipack of

[76] Ibid., pp. 266–267.

Table 2.2 Process of moving from minor deviance to serious corruption for Li Zhen.

Forms of Gift/Bribe	Initiated by bribe-giver	Initiated by bribe-taker	Accepted	Refused	Psychological state	Note
(1)	(2)	(3)	(4)	(5)	(6)	(7)
(1) Meals	✓			✓		
(2) Meal	✓		✓		Not available	'It is so hard to say no because they kept pleading.'
(3) A multipack of cigarettes (10 packs of cigarettes)	✓		one pack	✓	Nervous and upset	'But, that guy was jamming it into my pocket in a way like a madman. I realized it was hard to refuse him; I took only one pack.'
(4) A sweater	✓		✓		Felt restless and uneasy	
(5) A multipack of Zhonghua cigarettes (10 packs) and an electric razor	✓		✓		Nervous and fear	
(6) A jade Chinese cabbage	✓		✓		Not available	'I refused it once or twice before I accepted it.'

Item					
(7) 5000 RMB	✓			Nervous and decided not to accept money in the future.	Li Zhen strongly refused for many times, but Li failed to stop him.
(8) Many small- to medium-sized monetary gifts	✓			Not available	
(9) A car		✓	✓	pleased	Too ashamed to ask for money directly. So he began with 'borrowing' a car.
(10) A flat		✓	✓	Not available	
(11) Asking office building constructors for bribes six times		✓	✓	Not nervous any more, calm, excited, and immersed in the joy of success	Even if faced with obstacles, he decided to use his power and influence to bend others to his will. 'In any case, I must get the money once I decided that I wanted it.'

Zhonghua cigarettes and an eclectic razor, his negative psychological experience was mainly driven by fear of being found out. Thus, he went back home with the gifts, but he could not open his house door, and it was because of nervousness he used his bicycle key instead of his house key. After receiving money and gifts passively many times, his feelings of fear have largely been overcome. But he was still too ashamed to initiate a bribe. He said to the businessman that he would like to borrow a car. This kind of shame is aroused mainly from a sense of guilt.

Each time a corrupt act is successfully conducted both the feeling of fear and guilt will be somehow weakened. After repeated success, negative feelings will disappear. In their place, pleasant feelings of success will be formed.

Though only a single case (Li Zhen) with respect to the process of becoming corrupt in China was analysed, it is safe to say that in general the process of becoming corrupt is from minor deviances to serious corrupt offences. This pattern of getting corrupt gradually is also observed by others. For example, Ma Sanshan, after reviewing several recent corruption cases in China, found that most corrupt officials experienced a process 'from minor to serious, from occasional offence to regular offence . . . and finally sliding into the abyss of criminal corruption'.[77]

It is worth pointing out that both officials (bribe-takers) and business people (bribe-givers) have gradually mastered the tact of coping with the sense of guilt. For many, a strong sense of committing a corrupt act can have a deterrent effect to those considering such an act though there are some who can easily overcome this sense of guilt. Further, being perceived corrupt by the public can be a deterrent factor as the actors are more likely to face strong pressure and be reported. Thus, corrupt actors tend to use certain tactics to make their behaviour look less offensive and themselves feel less guilty. As Smart and Hsu correctly pointed out, '[S]kill is particularly necessary to avoid practices from being labelled as corrupt. Inept performance can result in a gift exchange becoming disdained as a bribe'.[78] A study of the techniques used by corrupt actors to make their actions seem less corrupt is helpful for us to better understand the consequences of corruption in China.

---

[77] Sanshan Ma, 'Resisting corruption from six aspects', *Study Times*, p. 11, 5 August 2013.

[78] Alan Smart and Carolyn L. Hsu, 'Corruption or social capital? Tact and the performance of guanxi in market socialist China', in Monique Nuijten and Gerhard Anders (eds.) *Corruption and the Secret of Law: A Legal Anthropological Perspective* (Aldershot: Ashgate, 2007), p. 168.

The most common tactic is to make the boundary between corruption and *guanxi* (关系) blurred. Guanxi refers to personal connections with appropriate persons or government officials.[79] It connotes warm human sentiments and usually involves gift-giving. Guanxi does not necessarily carry a negative meaning as corruption does from the Chinese's viewpoint: 'Chinese could talk about guanxi without shame, unlike corruption'.[80] Thus, most clever people will carry out a corrupt transaction by using the expressions and practices commonly associated with guanxi. This skill at least can facilitate corruption transactions in three ways. First of all, some corrupt practices well conducted in the form of guanxi will be perceived as less offensive and therefore more acceptable. Imagine this circumstance. A train station official is conducting a money-for-train-ticket exchange. A bed ticket in a train before Chinese New Year is provided to a 'close friend'. Of course, at the same time, the train station official will receive a 'gift' and some money in a red envelope for his young child from this 'close friend' as a Chinese New Year Greeting gift. Another way of doing this is to conduct a pure exchange. Apparently, in the Chinese context, the first way of exchange is more tolerable because it is dressed up in the form of guanxi.

Second, the corruptors will have a weak sense of corruption if the transaction is done in the name of guanxi so that their sense of guilt can be easily overcome. If an official thinks he is helping his friends out by granting a business licence to them, he will probably have little guilt in breaking the law. However, if he has a clear sense that he is conducting a corrupt transaction he will at least feel somewhat guilty, which can serve as a deterrent though that may not always be very effective. Rivkin-Fish conducted excellent empirical research on bribes in Russia's healthcare industry by studying it through an anthropological perspective.[81] In the study, he asked Valya (the interviewee) about her strategies to gain competent and reliable healthcare in St. Petersburg. Valya offered the doctor vodka (a distilled beverage) in addition to some money for good services. Though this case was set in Russia, it is still useful to understand the role of a guanxi practice in

---

[79] Irene Y. M. Yeung and Rosalie L. Tung, 'Achieving business success in Confucian societies: the importance of guanxi (connections)', *Organizational Dynamics*, 25, 2 (1996), pp. 54–65.

[80] Smart and Hsu, 'Corruption or social capital?'.

[81] Michele Rivkin-Fish, 'Bribes, gifts and unofficial payments: rethinking corruption in post-Soviet Russian health care,' in Dieter Haller and Cris Shore (eds.) *Corruption: Anthropological Perspectives* (London and Ann Arbor, MI: Pluto Press, 2005). pp. 50–51.

diminishing the sense that a practice is corrupt in a Chinese context. The following comes from Rivkin-Fish's study:

> When I asked Valya why she gave the physician vodka in addition to the money, she explained that it was a gift, conveying a sense of gratitude and, I would add, obligation. In other words, the gift offered a way of diminishing the sense created by the exchange of money that the services he provided were indistinguishable from any other commodity exchange: the care and expertise he provided as a doctor were different and special, and she wanted to thank him (the doctor), not only pay him from them.[82]

Third, it is still useful for actors involved in bribery to adopt the forms and expressions of guanxi, even if 'savvy participants may be well aware that the substance of the transaction is a sham'.[83] In this case, using the practice of guanxi will at least make the transaction process smoother and friendlier. It is difficult to negotiate a corrupt exchange in the same way as negotiating a purely business transaction. However, if guanxi forms are used, the process will be more pleasant, the transaction cost will be reduced, and the successful transaction rate will by higher. Apparently, adoption of guanxi when the corruptors have a clear awareness of the guilt of corruption plays a purely instrumental effect in facilitating corruption just like the way the Internet facilitates communication.

The relationship between minor deviance and serious corruption discussed above implies that there must be sufficient anti-corruption resources devoted to even minor deviance. It is true that fighting corruption demands many resources, and many countries, especially developing countries, suffer from a shortage of funds and staff. It is also plausible that if resources are limited they should be devoted to the most serious corruption. However, the result may be far from satisfactory if limited resources are largely, or even exclusively, devoted to serious corruption. First, minor corruption is more likely to develop into serious corruption if not checked. Second, if reporting of minor corruption acts is ignored, whistle-blowers will be more likely not to report even serious corruption when it occurs.[84] Both consequences will increase the burden of fighting against serious corruption. Compared with the United States, the United Kingdom, and Hong Kong, minor deviances are still largely unchecked in China. On the other hand, if a government ethics regulatory regime (which specifically focuses on minor deviance) can be established, the

---

[82] Ibid., pp. 47–64.   [83] Smart and Hsu, 'Corruption or social capital?', p. 172.
[84] Yassin El-Ayouty, Kevin J. Ford, and Mark Davies (eds.), *Government Ethics and Law Enforcement: Toward Global Guidelines* (Westport, CT: Praeger, 2000), pp. 150–151.

burden of fighting serious criminal corruption will also be alleviated as most problems have been solved at an early stage.

2.4   Anti-corruption approaches and ruling legitimacy of the CCP

This section will examine anti-corruption approaches in relation to the ruling legitimacy of the CCP. It argues that the criminal approach against corruption in China cannot play a role as important as that in the United States, the United Kingdom, and Hong Kong because some aspects of criminal enforcement against corruption can destroy the ruling legitimacy of the CCP. On the other hand, the regulatory approach might strengthen the CCP's legitimacy and thus can gain support from the top authority if they learned the importance of regulation against corruption. The discussion will be organized under three headings: the ruling legitimacy of the CCP, the CCP's dilemma in fighting against corruption, and regulatory enforcement and ruling legitimacy of the CCP.

2.4.1   Ruling legitimacy of the CCP

It is widely accepted that democratic regimes, compared with authoritarian ones, have inherently much more popular legitimacy. One major flaw of authoritarianism is its lack of legitimacy.[85] In the world's largest authoritarian country, the CCP is more susceptible to challenges to its legitimacy to rule. The CCP's ruling legitimacy can be examined from two aspects: factors the CCP adopted, or are adopting, to build up its legitimacy; and factors that are ruining its legitimacy.

The CCP gained its ruling status in 1949 after its victory against the Kuomingtang (The Nationalist Party) in the civil war. However, the CCP's victory in the civil war does not necessarily give it legitimacy to rule. Around 1 million people fled China to Hong Kong to avoid the authority of the CCP.[86] In the 1950s, armed insurrections still occurred frequently in many areas of China and the country could be said to be

---

[85] Heike Holbig and Bruce Gilley, 'In search of legitimacy in post-revolutionary China: bring ideology and governance back in', German Institute of Global and Area Studies (GIGA) Working Papers No. 127, 2010, available at www.giga-hamburg.de/dl/download .php?d=/content/publikationen/pdf/wp127_holbig-gilley.pdf (last visited on 19 June 2013).

[86] Heike Holbig and Bruce Gilley, 'Reclaiming legitimacy in China', *Politics & Policy*, 38, 3 (2010), pp. 395–422.

only nominally under communist authority.[87] The CCP gradually gained its 'legitimacy through revolutionary ideology and concrete performance' under Chairman Mao's leadership (1949–1976).[88] In Mao's era, the formal ideology of China was Marxism, which regarded the proletariat or working class as the most progressive force of society.[89] Performance of the CCP in Mao's era is mixed. The CCP successfully ended the civil war, controlled inflation,[90] and conducted agricultural and industrial reform in the early years of its rule.[91] However, the Great Leap Forward (*dayuejin*), a campaign aiming to boost agricultural and industrial output to catch up with the United Kingdom and the United States at any cost, in 1958 and 1959 resulted in great loss – the economy was destroyed and millions of rural peasants died of starvation.

Mao died in 1976 and he was succeeded as leader of the CCP by Deng Xiaoping in 1977. Deng never formally cast aside Marxism, but shifted the focus from mass campaigns to economic development.[92] In 1978 the Opening up and Reform (*Gaige Kaifang*) policy was implemented. The country opened its door again to the international world, developed private economy in cities, and abolished the collective production of agriculture in rural areas. These policies had an immediate and great effect. From 1978 to 1984, the country witnessed growth of 5 per cent per annum for grain output; by the end of 1983, in urban areas around 17 million people had moved to the private sector, and this sector was still booming after 1983.[93] In 1992, Deng once again explicitly supported the opening up and reform policy in his Southern

---

[87] Jeremy Brown and Paul G. Pickowicz, 'The early years of the People's Republic of China: an introduction', in Jeremy Brown and Paul G. Pickowicz (eds.) *Dilemmas of Victory: The Early Years of The People's Republic of China* (Cambridge, MA and London: Harvard University Press, 2007), pp. 1–18.

[88] Holbig and Gilley, 'Reclaiming legitimacy in China'.

[89] Robert Weatherley, *Politics in China Since 1949: Legitimizing Authoritarian Rule* (London and New York: Routledge, 2006), p. 10.

[90] Holbig and Gilley, 'Reclaiming legitimacy in China'.

[91] Weatherley, *Politics in China Since 1949*, p.12.

[92] Zengke He, 'Corruption and anti-corruption in reform China', *Communist and Post-Communist Studies*, 33 (2000), pp. 243–270; and Jing Men, 'The search of an official ideology and its impact on Chinese foreign policy', paper presented on Regional Governance: Great China in the 21st Century, Asia-Link Conference, University of Durham, 24–25 October 2003, available at https://www.dur.ac.uk/resources/china.studies/The%20Search%20of%20An%20Official%20Ideology%20and%20Its%20Impact%20on%20Chinese%20Foreign%20Policy.pdf (last visited on 13 June 2013).

[93] Weatherley, *Politics in China Since 1949*.

China tour (*nanxun*) against the background in which some senior CCP leaders complained that the country might become a capitalist nation. He pointed out,

> Speed up the pace of reform and opening, with the courage to try and to rush. We must be brave in reform and opening, and dare to experiment. With regard to the problem of whether this is called capitalist or socialist, we must judge according to whether or not it promotes the development of the productive forces of socialism, whether or not it contributes to the comprehensive strength of the nation, and whether or not it raises the living standard of the people.[94]

Putting it more specifically, Deng's focus on the development of the country and raising of the living standard of the Chinese people (rather than ideology) posed problems for the legitimacy of the CCP.

Jiang Zeming was selected to be the core of the new leadership in 1989 by Deng, and he retired in 2002. In Jiang's era and beyond, the role of party ideology continued to be de-emphasized.[95] Ideology is no longer used as policy-making guidelines, but it still plays a role in justifying the CCP's policies.[96] During the Jiang era the economy was further liberalized. But, the rich–poor gap widened. China's Gini coefficient, an internationally accepted measurement of the extent of inequality of wealth distribution in a country, grew to 0.40 in 1994 and 0.46 in 2000, from 0.33 in 1980.[97] In early 2000, before his retirement, Jiang proposed the theory of the Three Represents (*sange daibiao*) against the growing social tension in order to strengthen the legitimacy of the CCP. In 2002 the Three Represents was formally expressed by Jiang in the Sixteenth Party Congress: 'Unyielding efforts will be made to ensure that our Party ... always represents the development trend of China's advanced productive forces, the orientation of

---

[94] Xiaoping Deng, *Selected Works of Deng Xiaoping*, Vol. 3 (Beijing: People's Publishing House, 1993), p. 72.

[95] Gungwu Wang and Yongnian Zheng, 'Introduction: reform, legitimacy, and dilemmas', in Gungwu Wang and Yongnian Zheng (eds.) *Reform, Legitimacy and Dilemmas: China's Politics and Society* (Singapore: Singapore University Press and World Scientific Publishing, 2000), p. 10.

[96] Yongnian Zheng, 'The politics of power succession', in Gungwu Wang and Yongnian Zheng (eds.) *Reform, Legitimacy and Dilemmas: China's Politics and Society* (Singapore: Singapore University Press and World Scientific Publishing, 2000), p. 30.

[97] Baogang Guo, 'Political legitimacy in China's transition: toward a market economy', in Lowell Dittmer and Guoli Liu (eds.), *China's Deep Reform: Domestic Politics in Transition* (Lanham, MD: Rowman & Littlefield, 2006), pp. 147–175.

China's advanced culture and the fundamental interests of the over-whelming majority of the Chinese people'.[98]

In 2002, Hu Jingtao became Party chief and retired in early 2013. From 2002 onwards, the country has maintained high-speed economic development. However, the growth is achieved but at great cost: an increasingly large rural–urban gap and serious environmental pollution. Many economists, especially Western economists, criticized China's growth rate, which cannot be sustained indefinitely.[99] Against this background, the CCP under Hu's leadership introduced the Concept of Scientific Development (*kexue fazhanguan*) of 'comprehensive, coordinated, and sustainable development' in 2004 and this was adopted as the guideline for social and economic development by the National People's Congress in the same year.[100] In 2007 at the Seventeenth Party Congress, Hu summarized the concept of scientific development: 'The Scientific Outlook on Development takes development as its essence, putting people first as its core, comprehensive, balanced and sustainable development as its basic requirement, and overall consideration as its fundamental approach'.[101]

It is clear that official ideologies under different CCP leaders vary considerably, especially between Chairman Mao who focused on class struggle and the next three leaders who stressed economic development. However, even in Mao's era, development was also an important justification for ruling legitimacy. One example was the Great Leap Forward that aimed to catch up to the West in agricultural and industrial production to show the world and the Chinese people the superiority of socialism over capitalism. In the post-Mao era, economic development

[98] Zemin Jiang, 'Report at the 16th Party Congress', available at www.china.org.cn/english/features/49007.htm#10 (last visited on 16 December 2011).
[99] Andong Zhu and David M. Kotz, 'The Dependence of China's Economic Growth on Exports and Investment' (2010), available at http://people.umass.edu/dmkotz/China_Growth_Model_%2010_09.pdf (last visited on 18 June 2013); Dani Rodrik, 'Growth Strategies', NBER working paper series, Working Paper 10050, October 2003, available at http://users.nber.org/~rosenbla/econ302/lecture/rodrick.pdf (last visited on 28 July 2013); James Xiaohe Zhang, 'Is the Chinese economic growth sustainable? A macroeconomic approach', *Journal of Business and Policy Research*, 7, 2 (July 2012), pp. 25–40.
[100] Heike Holbig, 'Ideological reform and political legitimacy in China: Challenges in the post Jiang era', in Thomas Heberer and Gunter Schubert (eds.) *Regime Legitimacy in Contemporary China: Institutional Change and Stability* (London and New York: Routledge, 2009), p. 28.
[101] Jintao Hu, 'Hu Jintao's report at the 17th Party Congress', especially section III, available at www.china.org.cn/english/congress/229611.htm#3 (last visited on 16 December 2011).

has even become the most important justification for the CCP's legitimacy. The logic is that the CCP provides the governed with continually increasing living standards and thus the CCP is a good ruler. It is also clear that although the CCP's ideologies changed at different times with different leaders, all stressed that the party was for the people; paraphrasing Jiang's words, the Party always represents the fundamental interests of the overwhelming majority of the Chinese people.

In addition to these two aspects (economic development and a 'for the people' image), nationalism and personal charisma are also frequently mentioned as sources for the CCP's legitimacy.[102] However, post-Deng leaders including Jiang Zemin and Hu Jintao lack the charisma which Mao and Deng had.[103] Nationalism as a source of legitimacy was not actively adopted in the Mao era or even in the Deng era. Hence, these two sources of legitimacy will not be discussed here.

Since Deng's economic reform, China has witnessed rapid economic growth for three decades. Although economic development, on the one hand, justified the CCP's legitimacy, on the other, reform also led to new problems regarding legitimacy. The most cited factors which erode the CCP's legitimacy include high inflation, corruption, unemployment,[104] the widening income gap, 'the deterioration of social welfare programs and the return of many "social evils" such as ... rising rate of serious crimes', and the erosion of social stability.[105] Corruption is thought of as the key factor eroding CCP's political legitimacy. From 1999 to 2004, opinion surveys of senior- and middle-level Party/government officials studying at the CCP's Central Party School found that corruption was ranked as either the most serious or second most serious social problem.[106] Research undertaken in Hunan Province in 2001 also showed that corruption was cited as being second only to underdevelopment as a source of legitimation problems.[107]

[102] Baogang Guo, 'Political legitimacy and China's transition', *Journal of Chinese Political Science*, 8, 1 & 2 (2003), pp. 1–25.

[103] Cheng Li, 'The battle for China's top nine leadership posts', *The Washington Quarterly*, 35, 1 (2012), pp. 131–145.

[104] Suisheng Zhao, 'China's pragmatic nationalism: is it manageable?' *The Washington Quarterly*, 29, 1 (2005), pp. 131–144.

[105] Yang Zhong, 'Legitimacy crisis and legitimation in China', *Journal of Contemporary Asia*, 26, 2 (1996), pp. 201–220.

[106] Pei, 'Corruption threatens China's future'.

[107] Zhu Lingjun, *Consensus and Conflict: Rethinking of Relations Between the People and the CCP* (Beijing: People's Publishing House, 2006).

Corruption can erode the CCP political legitimacy both in a direct and indirect manner. Directly, there are at least two ways through which the CCP's legitimacy could be negatively influenced by corruption. First, most government officials, and almost all senior officials, are CCP members and thus corruption scandals involving party officials will inevitably damage the CCP's image. Even if an official involved in a corruption scandal is not a party member, the party may still be blameworthy as government is not really separated from the party and non-party officials are actually accountable to superior party officials.

Second, as discussed earlier in this section, although CCP ideology is always changing under different leaderships, the Party consistently claims that it represents the common interests of the majority of the people and is dedicated to serving the people. Corruption is clearly a total deviation from the 'for its people' image of the party.

Indirectly, corruption has its own corrosive influences on legitimacy by undermining capacity and effectiveness.[108] Corruption can influence the government's ability to serve basic social needs such as security and healthcare and thus endanger China's economic development; however, the CCP's legitimacy, to a large extent, relies on its ability to supply basic social needs as well as general material and economic improvement, especially in food security, medicine security, and school building security in rural areas. Some cases of this type will be discussed below.

One case to illustrate this is the Zheng Xiaoyu case. Mr. Zheng is the former head of China's National Bureau of Food and Drug Administration. He received a bribe worth 6.5 million RMB and in return approved six fake drugs.[109] It is difficult to imagine how many people are actually victims of these fake drugs, but the number would not be small. This is not an isolated case. In 2003, fake baby milk powder in Fuyang City, Anhui Province, killed at least 12 babies and resulted in hundreds of cases of serious infant malnutrition.[110] Official corruption is a major reason behind the counterfeit products scandals in recent years – corrupt regulators usually neglect their responsibilities.[111]

---

[108] Holbig and Gilley, 'Reclaiming legitimacy in China'.

[109] 'China executes former Food and Drug Safety chief', *NewScientist*, 10 July 2007, available at www.newscientist.com/article/dn12230-china-executes-former-food-and-drug-safety-chief.html (last visited on 21 September 2009).

[110] Jim Yardley, 'Infants in Chinese city starve on protein-short formula', *New York Times*, 5 May 2004.

[111] Waikeung Tam and Dali Yang, 'Food safety and the development of regulatory institutions in China', *Asian Perspective*, 29, 4 (2005), pp. 5–36.

It is estimated that around 10,000 students were killed when their school buildings collapsed in the Wenchuan earthquake of 2008 – a collapse partly attributed to corruption between school constructors and local officials.[112] Though earthquakes are a natural phenomenon, the collapsed buildings might still have remained standing if they had not been constructed with substandard materials because most of the buildings surrounding the schools did not collapse.

Both the fake (or substandard) food scandals and the school building collapse scandal led to strong public resentment towards the party that seriously eroded its legitimacy. Zhao Lianhai, known as the 'Toxic milk protest father', organized parents whose children were poisoned by the tainted milk and milk products. He set up a blog to provide information on tainted milk to parents and allowed these parents to discuss the suffering of their children amongst themselves.[113] Mr. Zhao was charged with inciting social disorder and sentenced to two-and-a-half years' imprisonment.[114] However, according to Zhao's defence lawyer, what Mr. Zhao did is not more than what a regular citizen would do to defend their rights as a victim.[115] The conviction of and sentence on Zhao Lianhai aroused even stronger public criticism and resentment towards the government and many (even activists in Hong Kong) expressed their support for Mr. Zhao and urged the authorities to release him.[116] Zhao's supporters criticized the government for using its power to silence critics.[117]

With respect to the school building collapse scandal, the public was even angrier at the government. According to a Tsinghua University report on the Wenchuan earthquake, the number of collapsed school

---

[112] Carol Divjak, 'Corruption and shoddy construction behind school collapse in China earthquake', *World Socialist Web Site*, 16 October 2008, available at www.wsws.org/articles/2008/oct2008/chin-o16.shtml (last visited on 21 September 2009).

[113] See the website of Home for Kidney Stone babies (*Jieshi Baobao Zhi Jia*) www.bullogger.com/blogs/jieshibaobao/ (last visited on 3 January 2012).

[114] 'China jails tainted milk activist Zhao Lianhai', *BBC News*, 10 November 2010, available at www.bbc.co.uk/news/world-asia-pacific-11724323 (last visited on 3 January 2012).

[115] Ibid.

[116] Fanny W. Y. Fung and Tanna Chong, 'Legislators unite to urge justice for milk activist', *South China Morning Post*, 18 November 2010, available at http://topics.scmp.com/news/china-news-watch/article/Legislators-unite-to-urge-justice-for-milk-activist (last visited on 27 December 2011).

[117] Stephen McDonnell, 'Chinese outraged at activist's jailing', *ABC News*, 12 November 2010, available at www.abc.net.au/worldtoday/content/2010/s3064557.htm (last visited on 17 November 2011).

buildings was four times that of collapsed government office buildings,[118] indicating that the schools were poorly built. The local governments did not admit that the collapsed buildings were caused by poor quality materials but the parents of the students who died were not convinced. The parents accused the local government of fearing public investigation because the poor construction involved corruption.[119] This not only aroused strong resentment towards the government but also damaged public confidence in the government's ability to protect the people from avoidable disaster.

The CCP maintains its political legitimacy mainly through efforts on two aspects: building up an image of representing the people and improving living standards. This is also supported by Guo Baogang's observation. Guo observed that the CCP justifies its legitimacy in two respects: original justification (moral justification) and utilitarian justification.[120] Regarding moral justification, corruption can directly ruin CCP's moral legitimacy because corruption seriously damages the CCP's 'for the people' image. With respect to utilitarian justification, corruption can cause failures in providing social welfare such as food safety to its people and thus indirectly damage CCP's utilitarian legitimacy.

Although in the last two decades the CCP has successfully maintained its utilitarian legitimacy through rapid economic growth, according to conventional wisdom, claiming its legitimacy solely on economic performance 'implies that Communist one-party rule will immediately plunge into a serious legitimacy crisis should economic success one day falter'.[121] Economic growth in China is not likely to be sustained in the long run as it 'generates its own problems (inequalities, environmental degradation, etc.)' and 'creates rising expectations'.[122]

---

[118] Tsinghua University et al., *An Analysis of Wenchuan Earthquake Disaster Caused by Construction and Countermeasures for Building Design* (Beijing: China Architecture & Building Publishing House, 2009).

[119] 'Salt in their wounds: bereaved parents treated like criminals', *The Economist*, 14 May 2009, available at www.economist.com/node/13650027 (last visited on 17 November 2011).

[120] Baogang Guo, 'Political legitimacy and China's transition', *Journal of Chinese Political Science*, 8, 1 & 2 (2003).

[121] Heike Holbig, 'Ideological reform and political legitimacy in China: challenges in the post-Jiang era', in Thomas Heberer and Gunter Schubert (eds.) *Regime Legitimacy in Contemporary China: Institutional Change and Stability* (London and New York: Routledge, 2009), p. 13.

[122] Holbig and Gilley, 'In search of legitimacy in post-revolutionary China', p. 11.

Thus, for its own benefit, the CCP has a strong political will to fight against corruption. The next section will examine criminal approaches against corruption in China and its influence on CCP legitimacy.

2.4.2   Criminal approach against corruption and the CCP legitimacy

This section will first explore the features of criminal approaches against corruption in China, explain the underlying reasons behind the features, and then discuss how these features will influence the CCP's legitimacy. A key finding is that the CCP is facing a dilemma in fighting against corruption through criminal approaches: leaving corruption unchecked and serious criminal enforcement both pose legitimacy challenges to the CCP.

Two criminal enforcement features against corruption are worth noting. First, the punishments imposed on corrupt officials are lenient. The leniency is reflected both in criminal legislation and enforcement practice. According to criminal law, for example, a bribe-giver will not be subject to criminal liability if the amount offered is less than 5,000 RMB.[123] In practice, bribers are even exempted from punishment to a greater degree than stipulated in criminal law, which can be surmised through either our observation of how those who offered bribes were dealt with and through news articles concerning bribery crimes. In most cases, bribe-givers will not be charged. From January 1999 to June 2000, procuratorates in Jiangsu Province filed 1,010 bribe-taking cases, 1,022 bribe-takers involved.[124] During the same period, these procuratorates only filed eighty-seven bribe-giving cases with eighty-seven bribe-givers involved.[125] This is not isolated to Jiangsu. In 2000, procuratorates in Guangzhou City recorded eleven bribe-giving cases with thirteen bribe-givers involved; the record is 117 (125 bribe-takers involved) bribe-taking cases in the same year.[126] In 2001, thirteen bribe-giving cases (thirteen bribe-givers involved) were recorded, whereas 129 bribe-taking cases were recorded in the same city.[127]

These statistics are rather dated, but it seems this situation has not changed. In a recent news article by Shen Lijie, several prosecutors confirmed that bribe-givers are still being under-punished or exempted from punishment.[128] Zhou Kai, a prosecutor in the Huiji District

---

[123] Article 383, Chapter 8, Criminal law of the People's Republic of China (1997).
[124] 'Why are bribing bosses not sentenced?' *Yanzhao Wanbao*, B5, 19 October 2007.
[125] Ibid.   [126] Ibid.   [127] Ibid.
[128] Lijie Shen, 'How to deal with those who offer huge bribes?' available at www.hndjw.gov.cn/ Article/fazhijiaoyu/fazhi/fayan/2009-07-29/5938.html. (last visited on 14 April 2009).

Procuratorate, Zhengzhou City, said in most bribery cases, bribe-givers are not punished at all and in exceptional cases where bribe-givers are punished, they are actually under-punished. Ding Yuling, a prosecutor in the same procuratorates, expressed her concern that because bribe-givers are seldom punished the cost of committing the crime is very low, therefore businessmen choose to bribe without hesitation. Many times, the bribe-givers are not only exempted from punishment but also continue holding their official positions in governmental bodies. For example, He Tao offered fourteen bribes to Liu Jiayi (former chief judge of Fuyang Intermediary Court), but he is still the chief judge of Jieshou People's Court (a basic-level court) even after he was discovered to be offering a bribe.[129]

Bribe-takers and those who abuse their public power for private gain through embezzlement are also leniently punished. Li and Wu's research shows that sentences are often suspended and exemptions are often imposed on duty offenders (including embezzlement, bribery, and dereliction of duty offenders).[130] For example, Zhang Hongge from the Basic People's Court of Wugang City reported that 44 criminal penalties for duty offences were exempted or suspended by her court between January 2005 and August 2008, accounting for 85.1 per cent of the total of convicted duty offenders.[131]

However, casual observers might have an impression that punishment for corruptors is very harsh in China; it is not uncommon to read news that China's senior officials were executed for such crimes.[132] However, appearances are quite deceiving because only a very small proportion of corrupt party members and government officials actually received punishment.[133]

The second feature is that political campaigns are frequently adopted in the criminal enforcement against corruption. Political campaigns are

---

[129] 'Most corrupt officials involved in Fuyang Intermediate Court corruption cases are still in their positions', 31 March 2008, available at www.ah.xinhuanet.com/ahws/2008-03/31/content_12836550.htm (last visited on 14 April 2009).

[130] Li Li and Chonghao Wu, 'The application of sentence suspension and exemption for "duty offences" in China: special social status and ineffective legal techniques', in Michal Tomasek and Guido Muhlemann (eds.) *Interpretation of Law in China: Roots and Perspectives* (Prague: Karolinum Press, 2011), pp. 175–179.

[131] Hongge Zhang, 'Investigation and analysis of the application of sentence suspension and exemption for duty offences', available at http://hnwgfy.chinacourt.org/public/detail.php?id=33 (last visited on 10 August 2009).

[132] Data about death penalty in general and death penalty for corruption specifically is not available as China does not disclose such information.

[133] Pei, 'Corruption threatens China's future'.

one of the most common strategies in China's anti-corruption enforcement; there have been at least six anti-corruption campaigns since 1951: the 1951–1952 campaign, the 1982 campaign, the 1986 campaign, the 1989 campaign, the 1993 campaign, and the 1995 campaign.[134] Benjamin Van Rooij defined an enforcement campaign as:

> [A] set of political speeches, policy directives from central level politicians or bureaucracies defining a particular, targeted, stricter and swifter, form of law enforcement for a particular period of time, and especially centrally instituted processes to verify the outcomes; and the organized forms of local enforcement action and reports thereof following such central level speeches, directives and verification mechanisms within the specified period of time.[135]

Manion identified several characteristics of anti-corruption campaigns in China.[136] First, although campaigns were triggered by different factors, it is apparent that the anti-corruption campaigns are mainly a negative response to social protest/uprisings or serious corruption situations which has already raised public resentment rather than proactively fighting against corruption. Second, campaigns can achieve apparent and immediate deterrent result, but this has no long-term effect. Third, the leaders encourage people to report corruption; however, the Party is also worried about the possible negative effects of anti-corruption efforts on the Party itself as well as on society. For the Party, cases of corruption always involve Party members, some of them high-ranking officials,[137] which will damage the Party's legitimacy and reputation.[138] For society,

---

[134] Melanie Manion, *Corruption by Design: Building Clean Government in Mainland China and Hong Kong* (Cambridge, MA, and London: Harvard University Press, 2004); Benjamin Van Rooij, 'The politics of law in China: enforcement campaigns in the post-Mao PRC', (25 March 2009), p. 6. Available at SSRN: http://ssrn.com/abstract= 1368181; Zhengke He, 'Corruption and anti-corruption in Reform China', *Communist and Post-Communist Studies*, 33, 2 (2000), pp. 243–270; Hon S. Chan and Jie Gao, 'Old wine in new bottles: a county level case study of anti-corruption reform in the People's Republic of China', *Crime, Law and Social Change*, 49, 2 (2008), pp. 97–117; and Qianwei Zhu, 'Reorientation and prospects of China's combat against corruption', *Crime, Law and Social Change*, 49, 2 (2008), pp. 81–95.

[135] Van Rooij, 'The politics of law in China' p. 6.   [136] Manion, *Corruption by Design*.

[137] In 2008, according to the Supreme People's Procuratorate Work Report, there are 2,687 county level officials, 181 bureau level officials, and 4 ministry level officials involved in embezzlement, bribery, and dereliction of duty crimes. 'Annual work report of the Supreme People's Procuratorate 2008', available at www.spp.gov.cn/gzbg/201208/ t20120820_2496.shtml (last visited on 12 June 2012).

[138] Keyuan Zou, 'Judicial reform versus judicial corruption: recent developments in China', *Criminal Law Forum*, 11, 3 (2000), pp. 323–351.

these cases may lead to society's resentment of the Party and to social instability.[139]

Given that corruption seriously damages the CCP's political legitimacy and that the top authorities have motive to fight against corruption, it is difficult to understand the leniency imposed on corruptors. However, the CCP is facing a dilemma in fighting against corruption. If corruption is left unchecked, the CCP's legitimacy will be ruined. That is why anti-corruption campaigns were initiated periodically when corruption reached intolerable levels. However, a harsh criminal approach against corruption may also result in undesirable result. Prosecution for public corruption is an admission of systemic failure of the government. A large number of arrests and prosecutions do nothing to reinforce the public's belief in the fairness and legitimacy of government institutions.[140] That is why anti-corruption campaigns ended when peaks of exposition of corruption began to trigger popular resentment and anger against the Party regime.

In China, as discussed in this section, the criminal justice system against corruption may ruin CCP's legitimacy. Thus, criminal approaches against corruption have inherent limitations in China.

2.4.3   Regulatory approach against corruption and the CCP legitimacy

This section will explore the relationship between regulatory approaches against corruption and the CCP's legitimacy. It argues that contrary to criminal approaches, regulatory approaches can enhance the party's legitimacy and thus may be effectively enforced by the top echelons of the CCP if they realize its role in fighting against corruption.

The first feature of a regulatory approach is its minimal use of criminal sanctions which is used only as a last resort.[141] Actually, if a regulatory system has to largely rely on prosecution and criminal punishment, the regulatory regime has, to some extent, failed. With respect to the war against corruption, as discussed earlier, prosecution and criminal sanctions are frequently adopted as an indicator of the consequences of corruption: the higher the number of prosecution and sanction of corrupt officials, the more serious the consequences of corruption. Media reports on serious corruption scandal will also exaggerate the public's perception

---

[139] Ibid.   [140] Comstock, 'Maintaining government integrity'.

[141] Hazel Croall, 'Combating financial crime: regulatory versus crime control approaches', *Journal of Financial Crime*, 11, 1 (2003), pp. 45–55.

of the corruption level. Minxin Pei, for example, used both media reports and official anti-corruption enforcement data (mainly criminal enforcement) as two key ways to measure the level of corruption in China.[142]

The aims of a regulatory approach against corruption are securing and maintaining integrity standards, securing compliance, and preventing corruption rather than prosecuting and punishing corruption offenders and seeking justice and moral condemnation. Thus, regulatory enforcement against corruption will not damage CCP's political legitimacy and is more likely to strengthen its legitimacy. This is due to two reasons. First, tough enforcement against corruption, which involves mainly checking compliance of integrity standards and correcting misbehaviour if violations are found, will not necessarily ruin the public's confidence in the government. For example, if the Discipline Inspection Commissions (DICs), the CCP's anti-corruption agency, makes a rule that all civil servants must disclose the state of their family wealth and establishes institutions for each department to check compliance, the public is very likely to strengthen their confidence in the government. Second, a regulatory anti-corruption system, which is primarily against misconduct and maladministration, mainly identifies regulation violations involving corruption risks/potential such as conflicts of interest and appearance of corruption. Corruption risks are different from criminal corruption offences such as bribery and embezzlement: the latter will damage the CCP's ruling legitimacy as discussed in Section 2.3.1; the former, if identified and properly corrected, will prevent a possible risk of corruption from developing to criminal corruption offences. The public may have reasonable doubt about the official's integrity if violations are identified in regulatory enforcement against corruption. When these corruption risks are reduced or even eradicated through regulatory enforcement, the CCP's seriousness about fighting corruption will be evident.

2.5   Conclusion

This chapter has examined the role of the regulatory approach against corruption in relation to the criminal approach in a general to more specific context in China. It argues that the regulatory approach in the war against corruption should play a more important role than it does now in China due to both the features of regulatory approaches and China's political features.

---

[142] Pei, 'Corruption threatens China's future'.

By its nature, the effect of a criminal approach against corruption can only be improved by a higher detection rate and harsher punishment. It is difficult to improve either punishment magnitude or possibility of punishment in China because on the one hand punishment magnitude for corruption in China includes the death penalty and on the other hand the CCP only allows a low punishment rate for corruption for ruling legitimacy considerations. However, there is room for further development of the regulatory approach against corruption in China because much of the misconduct and maladministration has not yet been effectively regulated.

Criminal enforcement against corruption also faces serious political constraints in China. Criminal enforcement will damage the CCP's political legitimacy, which is against the Party's fundamental interest. Thus, the effect of criminal enforcement against corruption is negatively influenced. On the other hand, regulatory enforcement against corruption is likely to improve the CCP's legitimacy and thus the CCP will have an incentive to support a regulatory regime.

Although arguing for the great applicability of the regulatory approach against corruption in China, this research will not suppose that establishment of an effective regulatory regime against corruption will solve the problem of corruption. It is more appropriate to view a country as being at a certain level in terms of corruption or cleanliness rather than to view it as either absolutely corrupt or absolutely clean. It appears reasonable to argue that the level of integrity in China will be improved if its regulatory regime can be effectively designed and enforced. Actually, corruption control arrangements are not cost free and sometimes 'these costs outweigh any benefits as measured by reduced corruption'; the implication of this cost-benefit approach is that we should undertake optimal corruption control (rather than absolute integrity).[143]

A regulatory system against corruption can be examined from two aspects: rules governing government ethics per se and the enforcement of these rules. Chapter 3 will examine government ethics rules in China to identify patterns/features of existing government ethics rules (including CCP rules).

---

[143] James Jacobs, 'Dilemmas of corruption control', in Cyrille Fijnaut and Leo Huberts (eds.), *Corruption, Integrity and Law enforcement* (Kluwer Law international, 2002), p. 286.

3

Government ethics rules

3.1 Introduction

Chapter 2 argued that a regulatory approach against corruption has special applicability to China. This chapter will examine government ethics rules in China. However, before discussing China specifically, government ethics rules in several selected clean countries including the United States, the United Kingdom, and Hong Kong will be analyzed first. In doing so, the purposes are twofold: first, to gain a comprehensive picture of government ethics rules in these locations so that a baseline can be used to compare government ethics rules in China; and second, to develop an analytic framework so that research findings in different countries can be presented in a consistent manner.

Then it will move to the central focus of this chapter: government ethics rules in China. Discussion will mainly be based on a survey of government ethics rules/standards/requirements, real enforcement cases, and other scholars' relevant research findings including both theoretical and empirical findings. In China, the rules of the Communist Party of China (CCP) play a similar role to government regulations and national laws in regulating government ethics, and thus these rules will be included in the research.

The key argument of this chapter is that serious inadequacies and weaknesses exist in the government ethics rule system in China, although rules on the conduct of government officials at first sight may appear substantial. This impression is formed by the fact that China does have a large number of regulations/circulars (at least seventy) dealing with the integrity of government officials. However, evaluated against a framework of where government ethics are broken down into several key categories (some categories contain several subcategories), inadequacies and weaknesses become apparent. First, existing rules have not reflected certain government ethics aspects such as improper statements or actions that raise doubts on the basis of an official decision (a form of appearance of corruption) and assisting a third party in the party's dealing with the government (a form of conflicts of interest). Second, some aspects of government ethics are only weakly addressed. For example, the appearance of favouring one party in dealings involving official duties is touched on in China's rules, but relevant prohibitions are far from enough. And finally, technically speaking, government ethics rules per se are poorly made. For example, the country does not have a Code of Conduct which serves as the foundation of government ethics rules which set forth a framework of key categories of official conduct (mainly including conflicts of interest, the appearance of corruption, financial disclosure, and outside employment/activities).

The remaining part of this chapter is composed of six sections. Section 3.2 will systematically explore government ethics rules in the three selected countries. Section 3.3 will analyze the characteristics of government ethics rules in the selected jurisdictions. Section 3.4 will survey and analyze China's government ethics rules. Section 3.5 will present the key characteristics of government ethics rules in China as compared with that of the three selected jurisdictions. Section 3.6 will discuss the insights and implications of the findings for the improvement of China's government ethics rules. Finally, Section 3.7 will summarize the key findings of this chapter.

3.2   Government ethics rules in the United States, the United Kingdom, and Hong Kong

Although in any country it is superficial to assume that the system of regulatory rules against corruption is the same as the regulatory regime against corruption, written rules, without doubt, is one of the most important aspects of such a regime and is a starting point to researching the regulatory system. These regulations/rules/standards can be put into four groups: (1) regulating conflicts of interest, (2) regulating appearances of corruption, (3) regulating financial disclosure, and (4) regulating outside employment/activities. These four categories are not mutually exclusive but sometimes overlap. For example, most postemployment regulations are designed to avoid conflicts of interest. However, the core of conflicts of interest regulation lies not in postemployment prohibitions but in the prohibition of conflicts between a government official's individual private interests and his or her public duties.[1] On the other hand,

---

[1] Robert N. Roberts, *White House Ethics: The History of the Politics of Conflict of Interest Regulation* (New York: Greenwood Press, 1988).

as the development of regulations on employment issues become more and more systematic and comprehensive, a subsector of government ethics regulation is also included. Therefore, in this research outside employment/activities will be discussed separately from regulating conflicts of interest.

Before systematically analyzing specific rules governing government ethics, this section will briefly discuss the overall forms of government ethics rules in the United States, the United Kingdom, and Hong Kong. These conflicts of interest rules can be found in different forms of binding documents. In the United States, both the federal government and each state have their own public sector conflicts of interest rules and these rules vary from one state to another. Further, it must be noted that an agency (or a local-level government) may publish its own supplementary regulations. For example, in the United States about forty-eight agencies – for example, the Board of Governors of the Federal Reserve System, Commission on Civil Rights, and Commodity Futures Trading Commission – have published their regulations.[2] The purpose of this research is not to exhaustively list all relevant rules on conflicts of interest in the public sector but identify the major types of actions prohibited and the patterns or features of these rules in selected countries. Thus, the research mainly focuses on national-level rules.

These rules are mainly in the forms of criminal statutes, executive orders, and regulations. As pointed out in Chapter 2, regulatory offences incorporated into criminal law will be treated as a part of regulation although this research will not focus on the core of criminal corruption. In the United Kingdom, the Ministerial Code and Civil Service Code are the major sources of requirements on conduct. As all UK ministers are members of parliament (MPs) or Lords, with most coming from the House of Commons and a few from the House of Lords, ministers must also observe the Codes of Conduct of either the House of Commons or House of Lords. For the same reason, ministers must also comply with requirements set forth by the Independent Parliamentary Standards Authority. Although the Prevention of Bribery Ordinance (POBO) applies to various public officials, in Hong Kong senior officials, politically appointed officials and the civil service are each subject to different codes of conduct. Politically appointed officials have to comply with

---

[2] The United States Office of Government Ethics, 'Agency supplemental regulations', available at www.oge.gov/Laws-and-Regulations/Agency-Supplemental-Regulations/Agency-Supplemental-Regulations/ (last visited on 27 August 2013).

conflicts of interest requirements stipulated in the Code for Officials under the Political Appointment System. The civil service must comply with the Civil Service Code. Each of the three countries also has its own separate conduct requirements for its judiciary.

3.2.1   Regulating conflicts of interest

In any modern country it is expected that public offices serve the public and public office holders be independent from private influence. To achieve this aim, two significant values, identified by Beth Nolan, must be protected in designing conflicts of interest rules.[3] First, the integrity of the service must be protected; that is, private interests should not be allowed to influence public decisions. Second, every private person should have equal access to the government. Any conflicts of interest rule is expected to protect one or both the values.

Perkins provides a more specific structure for understanding conflicts of interest rules; he observed four principles emerging from statutes and regulations.[4] The first principle is *self-dealing by a public official.* Under this principle, a public official must *disqualify* himself from participating in an action related to his public office in case this action may affect his personal economic interests. The second one is *transfer of economic value to a government official from a private source.* The idea of this principle is that a public official should not be allowed to receive economic value from a private source even if this does not involve bribery. The third principle is *assisting a private party in dealing with the government.* Under this principle, a public official is not allowed to assist or represent a private person in this private person's dealings with government. The fourth principle is *private gain from information acquired in one's official capacity.* This principle does not allow a public official to use official

---

[3] Actually, Nolan identified three values. The third value is that appearance of conflicts must also be avoided. As pointed out in many different occasions, the appearance of corruption should be separated from a conflicts system and stand alone as one of the four groups of regulation against corruption. Thus, in the above, only two values are cited. See Beth Nolan, 'Public interest, private income: conflicts and control limits on the outside income of government officials', *Northwestern University Law Review*, 87, 1 (1992–1993), pp. 57–147.

[4] Perkins identified five principles. The fifth one is related to postemployment conflict of interest. As employment-related regulation in this book has been separated out as one of the four groups of regulations, I intentionally omitted this principle. See Roswell B. Perkins, 'The new federal conflict-of-interest law', *Harvard Law Review*, 76, 6 (1963), pp. 1113–1169.

information for private economic gain. This principle can be extended from misusing official information to misusing public office. That is *profiting from misusing one's official position.*

Government officials are paid from public funds and work for the common good of the public. If a government decision is affected by an official's personal interests, the public welfare may be damaged (or at least there is such a risk). For example, a government official may pay above market price to a company when purchasing items from a company in which the official holds shares. This is against the public common good as government funds from taxes are spent improperly. The official gets benefits at the expense of the public. Further, from the perspective of other competitors, conflicts of interest violate the basic value of fairness. In the above example, the company in which the official holds shares enjoyed an unfair advantage over other market competitors. Moreover, if an official's personal interests intervened in his or her public decisions, the public will lose their trust in these government decisions. Each of the four principles above can address one or more of the three problems (public common good, fairness, and public trust in government decision) caused by conflicts of interest.

Of course, the four principles are not mutually exclusive or exhaustive. Nevertheless, they shall capture the core part of regulating conflicts of interest. The remaining part of Section 3.2.1 will explore to what extent the four principles of conflicts of interest have been reflected in the government ethics rules in the three selected jurisdictions.

Conflict of interest rules are central to the United States' federal public integrity standards.[5] The same can be said for the United Kingdom and Hong Kong. In these three jurisdictions, conflicts of interest rules account for a large part of government ethics rules.

In the United States, senior government officials and other employees are subject to the same conflict of interest rule system in general with additional provisions which impose additional requirements for senior officers. In the United Kingdom and Hong Kong, ministers (or politically appointed officials) and the government bureaucracy are regulated by different systems of rules.

In all of the three jurisdictions, there are general principles requirements on conflicts of interest. In the United States, an official is generally

---

[5] Carol W. Lewis, 'Ethics codes and ethics agencies: current practices and emerging trends', in H. George Frederickson (ed.), *Ethics and Public Administration* (New York and London: M. E. Sharpe, 1993).

prohibited from holding financial interests which conflict with his or her official duties.[6] In the UK, government officials are generally required to avoid any conflict (or perceived conflict) between their public duties and their private interests.[7] In Hong Kong, similar rules can also be identified.[8] Government officials in these jurisdictions are also required to observe values such as selflessness, integrity, objectivity, and honesty, which all contain some requirements on avoiding conflicts of interest.[9]

An important feature of general conflict of interest rules in the three jurisdictions is that they not only concern actual conflicts of interests but also the *appearance* of conflict, which is separately addressed in Section 3.2.2.

Self-dealing

Self-dealing, as mentioned earlier, is a situation where an official participates in an action related to his or her official duties when this action may affect his or her personal economic interests. For example, an official may be involved in making a decision on whether a contract will be awarded to a company where the official's son is a director of the company board. The usual response to self-dealing is disqualification which in general concerns an employee's official action rather than his or her private action.[10]

In the United States, it will constitute a criminal offence if the prescribed person does not disqualify himself or herself from participating in a public office–related action in which he or she has a personal financial

---

[6] Subsection (b), section 101, Executive Order 12674.

[7] Paragraph 1.2, f, Ministerial Code (the UK) 2010; Paragraph 10, The Code of Conduct for Members of Parliament (approved by the House of Commons in 2012); Paragraph 3, Civil Service Code (the UK) 2010.

[8] Paragraph 3.4, Civil Service Code (Hong Kong); Paragraph 1.3 (6), Code for Officials under the Political Appointment System (Hong Kong).

[9] For example, the Committee on Standards in Public Life identified seven principles in public life, available at the committee's official website, www.public-standards.gov.uk/; see also Annex A of Ministerial Code 2010 (the UK).

[10] However, in certain situations an employee's private action may be regulated. For example, if an employee is a major shareholder of a bank and his or her agency is responsible for regulating banks. In this case, disqualification is not practical as the official's central responsibility is banking regulation. Disqualification will fundamentally impair the employee's ability to perform the duties of his or her position. In this case, diversion of personal interests which conflict with the official's duty is an alternative solution; all three selected jurisdictions have such diversion rules in place.

interest.[11] There are exemptions if the interest is too minor or too remote to 'affect the integrity of the services which the government may expect from the employee' or officer.[12]

An official must also disqualify himself or herself if their official action may bring interests to his or her prospective employer[13] or former employers (or clients).[14] A special type of appointee (registered lobbyists within two years before appointment) is subject to additional disqualification requirements: they must not participate in the particular matter on which they lobbied.[15] Ex-lobbyists may have personal interests in the matters they lobbied about before they joined the government and thus they should not be allowed to participate in that particular matter.

In the United Kingdom and Hong Kong, rules on self-dealing are made in a more general manner compared to that of the United States. In the United Kingdom, Part 7 of the Ministerial Code specifically addresses conflicts between a minister's public duty and his or her private interests. Ministers are required to 'ensure that no conflict arises, or could reasonably be perceived to arise, between their public duties and their private interests, financial or *otherwise*'.[16] This provision explicitly sets out that conflict prohibition includes noneconomic interests. In Hong Kong, politically appointed officials must disqualify themselves from handling cases in which their actual or potential interests might be affected.[17]

Transfer of economic value from a private source to a government official

Even if transfer of economic value to a government official from an outside government source does not form bribery, the compensation

---

[11] 18 U.S.C. 208 (especially 208[a]) and 216. This provision does not require the prescribed person to actually realize their financial interest. The key point is the official's public action may bring him (or his spouse, minor child, etc.) personal financial gain.

[12] 18 U.S.C. 208 (especially 208[b, c, and d]). This provision applies only to the executive branch not to the legislature. Nor is it applied to the president, vice president, a member of congress, or a federal judge as these persons are not included in the term 'officer' and 'employee'. This is not to say that judiciary and legislature staff members are not subjected to disqualification rules. Legislators and judges must observe their own ethics requirements.

[13] 18 U.S.C. 208; Paragraph (a), § 2635.606, 5 C.F.R. Part 2635; Subsection (a), 41 U.S.C. 2103.

[14] Paragraph 2, section 1, executive order 13490; Paragraph (a), § 2635.503, The Standards of Ethical Conduct for Employees of the Executive Branch (5 C.F.R. Part 2635).

[15] Paragraph 3, section 1, executive order 13490.

[16] 7.1, Ministerial Code 2010 (the UK).

[17] Paragraph 5.3, Code for Officials under the Political Appointment System (Hong Kong).

may affect the officer or employee's independence. Thus outside compensation from private sources inherently conflicts with an official's public office duty.

In the United States, such outside compensation may constitute a criminal offence.[18] The most typical case, according to Perkins, is 'where a corporate executive is asked to go to Washington, and his corporation offers to pay all or part of the difference between his present salary and his future government salary'.[19] Of course, there are exceptions such as money from an inheritance and sale of property.

Similar to the United States, in Hong Kong the Prevention of Bribery Ordinance (POBO) creates a criminal offence for accepting an advantage by public officers.[20] This offence is distinct from a bribery offence; for the latter offence, the advantage accepted should serve 'as an inducement to or reward for or otherwise on account of the official's performing or abstaining from performing any official act'.[21]

Just as pointed out by Nolan, a 'gift' is not judged on its name and a 'gift' may be a bribe, compensation, or a real gift depending on how a transfer of value functions.[22] In this sense, accepting something may commit a traditional bribery crime, a criminalized regulatory offence as discussed earlier, or a disciplinary violation.

More rules governing this issue are not in criminal form. In the United States, noncriminal rules extend outside compensation from salary to

---

[18] 18 U.S.C. 209, especially 209(a).

[19] Perkins, 'The new Federal Conflict-of-Interest Law', pp. 1113–1169, especially pp. 1137–1138.

[20] Section 3 of the Prevention of Bribery Ordinance set forth that '[a]ny prescribed officer who, without the general or special permission of the Chief Executive, solicits or accepts any advantage shall be guilty an offence'. The scope of criminal prohibitions in Hong Kong is greater than that in the United States. The latter is limited to compensation salary whereas the former includes all types of advantage. Advantage in the POBO includes a variety of benefits such as gifts, loans, fees, rewards or commissions, office; 'employment or contract; payment, release, discharge or liquidation of any loan, obligation or other liability'; service or favour; and the exercise of a certain right or power. It must be noted that entertainment is expressly excluded from favour as a type of advantage. Entertainment is defined as 'the provision of food or drink, for consumption on the occasion when it is provided, and of any other entertainment connected with, or provided at the same time as, such provisions' (Paragraph (1), section 2, POBO). Further, many other exceptions are permitted by the Acceptance of Advantages (Chief Executive's Permission) Notice 2010. For example, the acceptance of advantages from people with whom the official has relations such as a spouse, a regular union as if man and wife, fiancé and fiancée, etc.

[21] Paragraph (2), section 4, the Prevention of Bribery Ordinance.

[22] Nolan, 'Public interest, private income', pp. 57–147.

gifts (or other items of monetary value).[23] The Standards of Ethical Conduct for Employees of the Executive Branch prohibits two types of gift transfer: transfer related to an employee's official position or transfer from a prohibited source.[24] The test for official position-related transfer is whether or not the employee would have been offered the gift had he or she not held the official position.[25] President Obama signed Executive Order 13490 in 2009, which prohibits senior appointees from accepting gifts from lobbyists during the official's service in government in the form of contractual commitment. This can be understood as transfer from a prohibited source.

The United Kingdom and Hong Kong mainly addresses official position-related value transfer. In general they mainly prohibit acceptance of benefits from anyone which might reasonably be seen to affect their official judgement or compromise their integrity.[26] The prohibition scope is broad, including gifts, hospitality, or services.[27]

Ministers in Hong Kong must also not accept entertainment from any person if the entertainment might, or might appear to, arouse embarrassment of the official in carrying out his or her official duties or bring the public service into disrepute.[28] In 2012, the then chief executive was criticized in the media for traveling on private yachts and private jets of his friends and accepting a banquet in Macau offered by his friends.[29] As the chief executive is not subject to POBO provisions on accepting of advantages and only voluntarily observes the code for politically appointed officials, he is technically not violating criminal and disciplinary rules on conflicts of interest. However, the Independent Review

---

[23] Section 101 (d), Executive order 12674; § 2635.201and § 2635.203, 5 C.F.R. Part 2635. Gifts include any benefit having monetary value (such as gratuities, favours, discounts, entertainment, hospitality, etc.), but there are exceptions (e.g. items with little intrinsic values modest items of food, refreshments, etc.).

[24] § 2635.201, 5 C.F.R. Part 2635.

[25] Paragraph (e), § 2635.203, 5 C.F.R. Part 2635, stipulates that '[a] gift is *solicited or accepted because of the employee's official position* if it is from a person other than an employee and would not have been solicited, offered, or given had the employee not held the status, authority or duties associated with his Federal position'.

[26] 7.20 and 1.2 (g), Ministerial Code 2010 (the UK).

[27] 7.20 and 1.2 (g), Ministerial Code 2010 (the UK); Paragraph 6, Civil Service Code (the UK) 2010; Paragraph 5.9, Code for Officials under the Political Appointment System (Hong Kong).

[28] Paragraph 5.10, Code for Officials under the Political Appointment System (Hong Kong).

[29] 'Report of the Independent Review Committee for the Prevention and Handling of Potential Conflicts of Interests', 2012, available at www.irc.gov.hk/pdf/IRC_Report_20120531_eng.pdf (last visited on 15 May 2013).

Committee considered the chief executive as the chief servant of the Hong Kong People and recommended he or she shall 'observe rules at least as rigorous as those applied to PAOs and the Civil Service'.[30]

Assisting a third party in the party's dealing with governments

In the United States it is a criminal offence if a government official represents a person or an entity when this third party is dealing with the government whether the representational service is compensated or not; it will constitute a more serious offence if such service is compensated.[31] Executive order 12834, signed in 1993 by President Clinton, created additional prohibitions for senior appointees. Senior appointees are prohibited from lobbying government on behalf of a private party in this party's dealing with government within a certain period after the termination of the senior appointee's employment.[32] Similar prohibitions can also be found in Executive Order 13490.[33]

In Hong Kong, politically appointed officials are also not allowed to 'represent any person in connection with any claim, action, demand, proceedings, transaction or negotiation against or with the Government' within one year after leaving office.[34] However, a similar prohibition for officials during the term of office has not been identified. That does not mean officials are not prohibited from representing a third party when holding office as they 'shall avoid putting themselves in a position where they might arouse any suspicion of dishonesty, unfairness or conflict of interest'.[35] Nevertheless, an express prohibition for those in office is helpful in avoiding possible confusing consequences. This is a postemployment restriction, but it also addresses assisting a third party in

---

[30] Ibid., p. 44.   [31] 18 U.S.C. 203 and 205 (a).

[32] Subsection (a), Section 1, Executive Order 12834. However, President Clinton revoked Executive Order 12834 in 2001 when his presidential term ended by signing executive order 13184. In 2009, President Obama reintroduced similar ethics pledge by signing Executive Order 13490.

[33] Paragraph 4, Section 1, Executive Order 13490 stipulates that '[i]f, upon my departure from the Government, I am covered by the post-employment restrictions on communicating with employees of my former executive agency set forth in section 207(c) of title 18, United States Code, I agree that I will abide by those restrictions for a period of two years following the end of my appointment'. Paragraph 5 stipulates that '[i]n addition to abiding by the limitations of paragraph 4, I also agree, upon leaving Government service, not to lobby any covered executive branch official or non-career Senior Executive Service appointee for the remainder of the Administration'.

[34] Paragraph 5.16, Code for Officials under the Political Appointment System (Hong Kong).

[35] Ibid., Paragraph 5.1.

dealing with the government. The Leung Chin-man case is a good illustration of this prohibition.[36] Although these officials have already left office, their government influence may remain for a certain period afterwards.

Unlike the United States and Hong Kong, the United Kingdom only prohibits paid representational service by ministers and MPs.[37] The rule does not touch on representing a third party without receiving payment.

Profiting from misusing official position

In the three selected jurisdictions, officials are prohibited from furthering private gain from their public office in general.[38] Sometimes these prohibitions are stated in a positive way. In the United Kingdom, for example, civil servants are required to 'use public money and other resources properly and efficiently'.[39] Rewording this in a more negative way, they must not misuse their official positions to further their own interests or the interests of others.[40]

Specific forms of benefiting from a government position are also addressed. First, nonpublic government information for private gain is specifically prohibited in the United States and the United Kingdom.[41] Second, using official transport for private travel arrangements and travel costs is a key concern in both the United Kingdom and Hong Kong.

[36] Gary Cheung, Fanny W. Y. Fung, and Tanna Chong, 'Former housing chief in fresh controversy', *South China Morning Post*, 14 August 2012, available at www.scmp.com/ article/965115/former-housing-chief-fresh-controversy (last visited on 12 June 2013). Leung Chin-man, a former housing chief, left office in 2007 and after a one year post-office employment control period submitted an application to take up an appointment with New World China Land, a property developer. The Secretary for the Civil Service approved his application and this triggered strong criticism over a potential conflict of interest. He left his new job in New World after then Chief Executive Donald Tsang ordered a review of the decision-making procedure for post-office employment approval.

[37] The Code of Conduct for Members of Parliament (approved by the House of Commons in 2012), paragraph 11; Resolution of the House of 15 July 1947, amended on 6 November 1995 and on 14 May 2002.

[38] Subsection (g), Section 101, Executive Order 12674 stipulates that '[e]mployees shall not use public office for private gain'; Paragraph 3.4, Civil Service Code (Hong Kong); and Paragraph 1.3(8), Code for Officials under the Political Appointment System (Hong Kong).

[39] Paragraph 6, Civil Service Code (the UK) 2010.   [40] Ibid.

[41] Subsection (c), section 101, Executive Order 12674 stipulates that '[e]mployees shall not engage in financial transactions using nonpublic Government information or allow the improper use of such information to further any private interest'; § 2635.703, 5 C.F.R. Part 2635; paragraph 14 and 15, The Code of Conduct for Members of Parliament (approved by the House of Commons in 2012).

Third, in the United States, an employee is prohibited from giving a gift to his or her superiors and from accepting a gift from an employee receiving less pay than him or her.[42] Fourth, the United States also prohibits an employee from using his or her public office 'for the endorsement of any product, service or enterprise, or for the private gain of friends, relatives'.[43] This type of action, although may not bring benefits to the official themselves, can benefit the official's friends, and thus is still profiting from misusing public office.

There are also detailed rules on claim of official duty-related expenses. For example, the United Kingdom sets forth clearly the items which can be claimed, the items which cannot be claimed, the amount limit, the process to claim, and documentation needed to support the claim.[44] The Independent Parliament Standards Authority (IPSA) publishes a summary of the total amount of the claims of every MP each year. These detailed standards and guidance on public expense, to some extent, is a reform resulting from strong public criticism of the integrity of MPs caused by the parliamentary expenses scandal in 2009.[45]

Finally, it is worth pointing out that the above conflict refers to conflict between an official's public duty and his or her private interests. The conflicts of interest rules in the United Kingdom and Hong Kong also address another type of conflict, conflict between ministers' public office and ministers' party interests.[46] This type of conflicts of interest will not be discussed in detail in this book as the ruling party, CCP, in China is not separated from the government. However, this is not to say that this type of conflict should not be regulated in China.

3.2.2   Regulating appearance of corruption

It is widely accepted that in order to maintain a high standard for official conduct it is not enough to regulate only actual corruption but also the

---

[42] § 2635.301 and § 2635.302, 5 C.F.R. Part 2635.   [43] § 2635.702, 5 C.F.R. Part 2635.

[44] See the official website of the Independent Parliamentary Standards Authority, available at http://parliamentarystandards.org.uk/TheGuide/Pages/home.aspx (last visited on 15 June 2013).

[45] Alan Lawton, Michael Macaulay, and Jolanta Palidauskaite, 'Towards a comparative methodology for public service ethics', EGPA Conference, 2009, available at www.law .kuleuven.be/aap-bap/integriteit/egpa/previous-egpa-conferences/malta-2009/lawton.pdf (last visited on 15 June 2013).

[46] Section 6, Ministerial Code (the UK); and 4.4, Code for Officials under the Political Appointment System.

appearance of corruption or impropriety.[47] Concern with the appearance of corruption in the United States increased as public trust in the government experienced decline in the 1960s.[48] Thus, justification for the regulation concerning the appearance of corruption mainly rests on the grounds that appearance regulation can strengthen public trust in government.[49] Gray has identified six typical categories of appearance violation for judicial misconduct.[50] These categories can be generally applied to other public officers although specific requirements for the judicial sector may be different from other public officers.

First, behaving in a way which is perceived that the public official may have used his or her influence is a major type of appearance of impropriety. Take, for example, the Pastrick case. Pastrick, a Justice of the Corning Town Court, met with an officer in charge of general office management and human resource duties in a food company to discuss procedures in a bad cheque case involving this company. The Justice then asked the officer whether there were any positions available in the company as his daughter was seeking part-time employment. The officer told the Justice that his daughter should submit an application. The Justice picked up an application form and returned it to the company after the form was filled in by his daughter. He also inquired whether the company was hiring people. Later, his daughter was hired by the company. The New York State Commission on Judicial Conduct concluded that the Justice's misconduct was established. The commission pointed out that the Justice's intent was not important even if he had no intention to influence the company's employment decision: 'In that context, respondent's discussion of procedures in a bad check case involving the store could easily be perceived as an explicit reminder of his judicial power, intended to intimidate or influence the store's hiring decision'.[51]

---

[47] Ronald M. Levin, 'Fighting the appearance of corruption', *Journal of Law & policy*, 6, pp. 171–179; and Mark E. Warren, 'Democracy and deceit: regulating appearances of corruption', *American Journal of Political Science*, 50, 1 (2006), pp. 160–174.

[48] The American National Election Studies, 'The ANES guide to public opinion and electoral behavior', Center for Political Studies, University of Michigan, 2004.

[49] Mark E. Warren, 'Democracy and deceit: regulating appearances of corruption', *American Journal of Political Science*, 50, 1 (2006), pp. 160–174.

[50] Cynthia Gray, 'Avoiding the appearance of impropriety: with great power comes great responsibility', *University of Arkansas at Little Rock Law Review*, 28, 1 (2006), pp. 63–102.

[51] The New York State Commission on Judicial Conduct, 'Pastrick', available at http://scjc.state.ny.us/Determinations/P/pastrick.htm (last visited on 17 June 2013).

Second, a public official may create the appearance of favouritism in appointment, although in many cases actual favouritism cannot be proved. For example, state of Illinois Governor Pat Quinn's appointment of 1,000 board members was viewed as having the appearance of political favouritism even though the appointment was managed by a 'fair-minded, ethically centered governor'.[52] This appearance was created because of the facts that many other states such as Minnesota used a committee to select candidates and many appointed board members in Illinois had been political contributors (though this may be coincidence).[53]

The third group of acts related to the appearance of corruption is the appearance of favouring one party in official business. For example, a judge behaves in a manner in which he or she is perceived to favour the attorney or the other party. The fourth appearance of misconduct is mainly limited to judicial sectors: behaving improperly (e.g. associating with criminals) and raising the public's doubt on the overall justice system. An example of this category would be when a judge attended a party hosted by a criminal, who was a friend of the judge, before the criminal began his prison sentence.[54] A judge's improper association with criminals may be perceived as 'evidencing sympathy for the convicted individual or disagreement with the criminal justice system'.[55] Fifth, a public official's improper statement may raise doubts about the basis of an official decision, especially for a judicial officer. For example, an official publicly talking about media criticism of policies made by him and saying that he is trying to avoid similar criticism in the future may give the appearance that he would not consider policies on the basis of the situation's merits alone. Sixth, a public official may behave in a manner which creates the appearance of bias towards a certain person. For example, a government official saying 'good morning' and calling a white man 'Sir' or 'Mr' when he received the white man's application for a bar license but saying nothing to a black applicant might be perceived as though the decision was not made solely on the predetermined standard. The black applicant would have reason to suspect that he was treated with bias if his application was rejected.

---

[52] 'Appointments must avoid appearance of favoritism', *The Southern Illinoisan*, available at http://thesouthern.com/news/opinions/voice_southern/appointments-must-avoid-appearance-of-favoritism/article_2c3bd624-9c82-11e1-ae4c-001a4bcf887a.html (last visited on 15 September 2013).
[53] Ibid.   [54] Gray, 'Avoiding the appearance of impropriety', pp. 63–102.
[55] Ibid., p. 82.

In all three jurisdictions, there are general requirement rules on the appearance of corruption. These rules require government officials and court judges to avoid impropriety and the appearance of impropriety; the test for whether an appearance of impropriety has been created is from the perspective of a reasonable person.[56] These general requirements have an important advantage that they can catch loopholes in specific requirements which cannot exhaustively list every possible undesired situation. At the same time, these principles have inherent drawbacks in terms of rule enforcement as too much discretion will be left to government integrity monitors. In addition to the general rules, the three jurisdictions also have rules which specifically address the six types of appearance of corruption.

Appearance of using official influence and power

Specific prohibitions on the appearance of using official power are mainly found in judicial conduct codes. First, using official letterhead is a common concern. Judges are generally not allowed to use judicial stationery for private business as such conduct may create a reasonable perception that the judge is attracting attention to the fact of his or her judicial status to exert pressure.[57] An example in point is writing to complain about an insurance policy.[58] Further, improper use of judges' judicial office may create such appearance. In Hong Kong, judges are required not to use their judicial offices in any attempt or any reasonable perception of attempt to extricate themselves from legal or bureaucratic difficulties.[59] An example of such conduct is that a judge volunteers his judicial status to the police when he is stopped for an alleged traffic offence.[60]

Moreover, improper use of judges' residence may also create the appearance of using influence. The UK rules require a judge to 'avoid the use of the Judge's residence by a member of the legal profession to receive clients or other members of the legal profession'.[61] In doing that,

---

[56] Section 2365.101 (n) and Paragraph 14, Subsection (b), Section 2365.101, Standards of Ethical Conduct of the Executive Branch; Canon 1, ABA Model Code of Judicial Conduct 2007, especially Comment [1], Rule 1.2; Paragraph 5.1, Code for Officials under the Political Appointment System; Paragraph 19 and 24, Guide to Judicial Conduct (Hong Kong); and Guide to Judicial Conduct 2011 (The UK), 5.1 (1).

[57] Comment [2], Rule 1.3, ABA Model Code of Judicial Conduct 2007; and Paragraph 81, Guide to Judicial Conduct (Hong Kong).

[58] Paragraph 81, Guide to Judicial Conduct (Hong Kong)   [59] Ibid., Paragraph 79.

[60] Ibid.   [61] 5.1(5), Guide to Judicial Conduct 2011 (The UK).

a judge may be perceived to use his or her influence for the benefits of his or her friend in the legal profession or may be perceived to share some part of the benefits with the legal practitioner. This rule also reflects improper behaviour/action raising doubt on the basis of an official decision. If the judge later listens to a case in which the legal practitioner who used the judge's residence to receive clients represents a certain party in the case, an appearance of impartiality in judgement will likely be created.

Appearance of favouritism in appointment

Although the *appearance* of favouritism in appointments is not explicitly set out, general principles on public appointment can to a large degree reduce actual favouritism and *appearance* of favouritism in public appointments. In the United Kingdom, a general requirement is that public appointments shall not be abused for partisan purposes.[62] Hong Kong requires that the appointment and promotion of civil servants be based on the basis of merit, openness, and fairness.[63] In addition to these general principle requirements, there are also detailed rules on government recruitment.[64]

Appearance of favouring one party in dealing with official business

General requirements on the appearance of favouring one party in dealing with official business can be found in codes of conduct both for government officials and the judiciary. For example, in the United States a government employee is prohibited from participating in a relevant matter if he or she determines that 'the circumstances would cause a reasonable person to question his impartiality in the matter'.[65] For judges, the United Kingdom requires a judge to avoid situations which might create the *suspicion or appearance* of favouritism or partiality in his or her personal relations with those who regularly practice in the judge's court.[66]

---

[62] Paragraph 3.1, Ministerial Code 2010 (The UK).
[63] Paragraph 2.20, Code for Officials under the Political Appointment System.
[64] See, for example, Civil Service Commission, 'Recruitment principles', available at http://civilservicecommission.independent.gov.uk/civil-service-recruitment/ (last visited on 25 June 2013).
[65] Section 2635.502, Standards of Ethical Conduct of the Executive Branch.
[66] 5.1(3), Guide to Judicial Conduct 2011 (The UK).

Several specific forms of appearance of favouritism can also be found in the rules in the three jurisdictions. First, ex parte communication is a common concern. This may create an appearance that a government decision might be made unfavourably to the party who is absent in the communication.[67]

Second, a judge's social contacts within the legal profession may also create such an appearance. For example, a judge maintains direct social contact with members of the profession who are currently involved in cases before the judges.[68] This kind of contact, if not properly handled, might easily create the perception that the judge is favouring the party with whom he or she is keeping in contact.

A third specific requirement is about judges' intervention manner in hearing a case. Improper intervention such as interruption of the claimant's or defendant's words improperly by a judge may be perceived as favouring one party.[69]

Finally, nominations of individuals for awards by government officials may also raise the perception of favouritism. This will create an appearance that the government is favouring one party in a situation where the government should not take a stance.[70] This is slightly different from the above prohibitions which stress favouritism to one party in *official duties* such as awarding a judgement. The nomination prohibition requirement concentrates on situations where the government is expected not to involve itself in the matter. Maintaining a state of not intruding on some matter can be understood as a passive official duty.

Improper actions raising doubts on the overall justice system (only for the judiciary)

Several improper acts may give rise to a perception that the judge is disagreeing with the overall justice system and may lead to public doubts

---

[67] Subsection (d), 5 U.S.C. 557; Rule 2.9 (A) and (B), ABA Model Code of Judicial Conduct 2007; and Paragraph 30, Guide to Judicial Conduct (Hong Kong). For the judiciary, more requirements are imposed regarding this issue. In the United States and Hong Kong, a judge shall not only avoid initiating or permitting ex parte communication but also shall 'inform the other parties concerned fully and promptly' if he receives such an ex parte communication. The United States also requires a judge to 'provide the [absent] parties with an opportunity to respond'. In so doing, the perception of favouring the party who receives the private communication can be eliminated.

[68] Paragraph 94 (a), Guide to Judicial Conduct (Hong Kong).   [69] Ibid., Paragraph 29.

[70] Paragraph 7.18, Ministerial Code 2010 (The UK). In the UK, ministers are prohibited from sponsoring individual nominations for any awards as in doing so the ministers' support may be perceived by some people as government support for that specific individual nominated.

about the reliability of the judicial system. That may also diminish the authority of the court. In the United States, 'a judge must interpret and apply the law without regard to whether the judge approves or disapproves of the law in question'.[71] In the United Kingdom, a judge is required to avoid responding to public criticism of a judgement or decision and not to air disagreements over judicial decisions in the media.[72] In Hong Kong, judges are generally not prohibited from visiting pubs, bars, karaoke lounges, casinos, or similar places.[73] However, they are reminded to carefully consider, in the eyes of a reasonable person, the reputation of the place visited and any concern that the place might not be operated in accordance with law.[74] Such visits might be perceived as supporting unlawful activities and disagreeing with the justice system.

Improper statements or actions raising doubts about the basis of an official decision

First, improper statements, speech, or expressions may raise doubts about the basis of an official decision. For example, if a judge makes a public speech improperly it might reasonably be expected to affect the outcome of a matter pending.[75] A judge's views improperly expressed in public might also create a perception of 'bias or prejudgment in cases that later come before the judge'.[76]

Second, relationship or ties, or appearance of relationship or ties, with certain parties or organizations may raise suspicion on the basis of a judgement. For example, a judge attends political gathering or political fundraising events or participates in public demonstrations that associate the judge to a particular political stance.[77] Judges are at risk of creating a perception of bias in listening to subsequent cases which involves that political party or that political viewpoint if they participate in these kinds of political activities. The Hong Kong rules pay special attention to ties

---

[71] Comment [2], rule 2.2, ABA Model Code of Judicial Conduct 2007.

[72] 8.1.1, Guide to Judicial Conduct 2011 (The UK).

[73] Paragraph 96 and 98, Guide to Judicial Conduct (Hong Kong).   [74] Ibid.

[75] Rule 2.10 (A), ABA Model Code of Judicial Conduct 2007.

[76] 3.4, 3.10, Guide to Judicial Conduct 2011 (The UK). 'If a judge is known to hold strong views on topics relevant to issues in the case, by reason of public statements or other expression of opinion on such topics', the judge is suggested to consider disqualifying himself to avoid this kind of appearance of impropriety. If such improper statements or expression was made by a judge and he or she later does hear the case without disqualification, the basis of the judgement is in doubt.

[77] Ibid., 3.3,

with a judge's old chambers or law firms. Excessively frequent visits are considered inappropriate.[78] The reason is that these organizations will appear frequently before the courts and thus the basis of judicial judgements involving the chambers or firms as a party may be perceived as not sound. For the same reason, judges also must be careful in using clubs and other social facilities of organizations (e.g. Police and the ICAC) which appear frequently before the courts.[79]

Third, judges must give to and require similar courtesy from all those that appear before them. Further judges shall avoid unjustified reprimands of counsel or offensive remarks about litigants or witness.[80] This kind of behaviour may raise question on the basis of his or her judgement even if that is a fair decision. Improper blame or courtesy may also create a perception of bias towards a certain party. Finally, giving legal advice by a judge may also create such an appearance; the rationale is that a judge's legal opinion on legal advice, in the eyes of the public, might influence the judicial decision.[81]

Appearance of bias towards a party

Judges in all three of the jurisdictions examined are required to avoid prejudice or bias in judicial duties based on 'race, sex, gender, religion, national origin, ethnicity, disability, age', and so forth.[82] In the United States, a judge must also require court staff and lawyers 'in proceedings before the court to refrain from manifesting bias or prejudice'.[83] The requirement is not limited to actual bias: '[A] judge must avoid conduct that may reasonably be perceived as prejudiced or biased'.[84] Furthermore, the United Kingdom requires judges to make proper arrangements in cases involving a disabled party so that the disabled face no disadvantage.[85] Such a requirement is helpful in preventing the appearance of bias.

Rules on appearance of corruption for government officials are mainly made in a general manner. However, for the judiciary, all three jurisdictions

---

[78] Paragraph 94 (c), Guide to Judicial Conduct (Hong Kong).   [79] Ibid., Paragraph 95.

[80] Ibid., Paragraph 27.

[81] Ibid., Paragraph 84. This is, in general, not allowed in Hong Kong, though there are exceptions (for example, offering personal advice informally and without remuneration to his or her family members or close friends).

[82] Rule 2.3 (B), ABA Model Code of Judicial Conduct 2007; Paragraph 28, Guide to Judicial Conduct (Hong Kong); and 4.2, Guide to Judicial Conduct 2011 (The UK).

[83] Rule 2.3 (C), ABA Model Code of Judicial Conduct 2007.

[84] Ibid., Comment [2], Rule 2.3.   [85] 4.2, Guide to Judicial Conduct 2011 (the UK).

have specific rules on the six types of appearance of corruption. The reason is that among the three branches of government (executive, legislative, and judiciary), the judiciary requires the highest standard of appearance of impropriety/corruption regulation due to the nature of judicial work in which judges are required to make decisions that 'sometimes many members of the public will challenge and at all times at least one party will dispute'.[86] Furthermore, although judges can and should ignore public calls for a specific decision, they cannot afford public challenges on their impartiality and integrity in making judicial decisions.[87] Although the American Bar Association (ABA) Model Code of Judicial Conduct is not mandatory, it is actually followed to a large extent in practice; the 1972 Model Code was adopted by almost all states and became the model for the US Judicial Conference.[88]

3.2.3   Regulating financial disclosure

Financial disclosure is a very important part of public ethics regulation because it is an effective way of encouraging compliance with conflict of interest requirements.[89] Financial interests which might conflict with one's official duty are usually an important type of financial disclosure. If an official has disclosed such private interests to the public, he or she is more likely to avoid carrying out official duties which might be affected by these private interests as the public, especially the media, is sensitive to these stories. In addition, to avoid conflicts of interest, public financial disclosure requirements can also serve the purpose of ensuring public confidence in governments.[90] Although in the 1980s there were calls for abolishing financial disclosure based mainly on the grounds that financial disclosure fosters a perception that public officials are inherently corrupt, as of 1993 thirty-six US states require financial disclosure of some kind.[91]

---

[86] Gray, 'Avoiding the appearance of impropriety', p. 66.   [87] Ibid.

[88] Andrew J. Lievense and Avern Cohn, 'The federal judiciary and the ABA model code: the parting of the ways', The Justice System Journal, 28, 3 (2007), pp. 272–282.

[89] Carol W. Lewis, 'Ethics codes and ethics agencies: current practices and emerging trends', in H. George Frederickson (ed.), Ethics and Public Administration (New York and London: M.E. Sharpe, 1993).

[90] The US Office of Government Ethics, 'Purpose of financial disclosure', available at www.oge.gov/Laws-and-Regulations/Statutes/5-U-S-C-app-4-§§-101-111-Public-financial-disclosure-requirements/ (last visited on 12 May 2013).

[91] Joseph W. Little, 'Abolishing financial disclosure to improve government', Stetson Law Review, 16, 3 (1987), pp. 633–680; and Lewis, 'Ethics codes and ethics agencies'.

Three issues are central to financial disclosure: who shall disclose? What shall be disclosed? And how to disclose (disclose to the public or to a commission, mandatory disclosure or voluntary disclosure)?

Requirements for senior officials

Generally speaking, each selected jurisdiction has two disclosure schemes, one for senior officials and the other for other government officials/employees. Senior officials are subject to tougher requirements both in terms of disclosure items and disclosure means (whether to disclose to the public).

Each of the jurisdictions requires a variety of items to be disclosed. In the United States, the items of a disclosure report for senior officials include assets such as income, gifts, and properties; liabilities; transactions (purchase, sale, or exchange); outside positions (such as an officer, director, or consultant of any corporation); and terms of any agreement or arrangement for future employment.[92] In the United Kingdom, when a minister is newly appointed, he or she is required to submit a full list of all the interests that might appear to result in a conflict. Specifically speaking, UK ministers are required to disclose four types of interests: gifts (above 140 pounds), hospitality, overseas travel for business purposes, and meetings with external organizations.[93] As most Ministers are MPs, they, and other MPs, must also register interests such as remunerated directorships, remunerated employment (office, profession, etc.), 'all clients to which personal services are provided', sponsorships received, gifts, benefits and hospitality, overseas visits, land or property owned, shareholdings, and controlled transactions.[94] MPs must also register interests which are not included in any of the above categories 'but which they consider to be relevant to the definition of the Register's purpose'.[95]

In Hong Kong, politically appointed officials are generally required to report to the Chief Executive *any private interests* that might influence, or appear to influence, their official duties.[96] Due to their access to commercially sensitive information, politically appointed officials are

---

[92] Paragraphs (1)–(7), subsection (a), 5 U.S.C. 102.
[93] 7.22, 7.24, 10.3, and 8.14, Ministerial Code 2010 (the UK).
[94] Paragraphs 22, 24, 27, 33, 38, 19, 51, 52, 22, and 60, Guide to the Rules relating to the Conduct of Members.
[95] Ibid., Paragraph 63.
[96] 5.4, Code for Officials under the Political Appointment System.

required to declare their investments and interests for the purpose of securing public trust.[97] Politically appointed officials are also required to maintain a register of gifts, advantages, payments, sponsorship (including financial sponsorships and sponsored visits), or material benefits received from any person, organization, or government (excluding the government, in any manner, relating to their office as politically appointed officials).[98] Currently, it could be said that there is a practice in Hong Kong for very senior officials to disclose illegal property structures. This was a response of the then Chief Executive in 2011 to media coverage of illegal property structures of several senior officials.[99]

Regarding means of disclosure, all three jurisdictions have rules that implicitly set forth that these financial disclosure reports must be made available to the public for public inspection purposes.[100]

Requirements for other nonsenior officials

Nonsenior officials are mainly administrated by their own agency or departments for financial disclosure requirements. Disclosures made by nonsenior officials are generally not required to be made available to the public.

Regarding disclosure items, in the United States, each supervising ethics office can set forth rules governing the information to be reported. The scope of the report, determined by the supervising ethics office, can either be more or less extensive than the scope of public report for senior officers and employees.[101] In the UK, the Civil Service Code does not require civil servants to make financial disclosure. However, many ruling party MPs are actually serving as paid government civil servants and thus they must comply with the disclosure requirements for MPs as discussed above.

In Hong Kong, civil servants shall disclose interests which might indicate actual or appearance of conflicts of interest.[102] They must also declare investments, including but not limited to shareholding or direct or indirect interest in any company; undertaking such as company directorship; any interest in land or buildings; securities and future and

---

[97] Ibid., 5.6.   [98] Ibid., 5.14.

[99] 'Henry Tang denied concealing his illegal property structures', *am730*, 14 February 2012, p. 2, available at www.am730.com.hk/article_print.php?article=92234 (last visited on 10 June 2013).

[100] 5 U.S.C. 105; 5.6 and 5.14, Code for Officials under the Political Appointment System; 7.5, Ministerial Code 2010 (the UK); and Paragraph 18, Guide to the Rules relating to the Conduct of Members.

[101] 5 U.S.C. 107.   [102] Civil Service Regulation (CSR) 462 (3) and (4).

options contracts; and investment transactions (acquisitions and dis-posals) reaching a certain value per transaction.[103]

3.2.4 Regulating outside employment and activities

Most outside employment/activity restrictions are designed to avoid conflicts of interest. The reason not to discuss this in the conflicts of interest section is that these employment-related provisions have gradually developed to being a very important subpart of government integrity regulations. Restriction on outside employment for those who are holding government office can also be justified on the grounds that even if there are no conflicts of interest between an employee's outside employment and his or her public duties, the officer's performance may be influenced by his or her outside employment. For example, if a police officer does construction work after his work as a police officer every day, he may be too tired to concentrate on his police duties the next day.

There are some common considerations for governments to restrict its former employees' employment in private sectors.[104] First, a former government employee may use confidential government information for the benefits of a private client. Second, a former government employee may enjoy unfair advantages in dealing with the government due to their connections and influence within a government agency. And third, if a former government employee can enter into private employment without restrictions he or she may behave not properly when still in government to advance his or her future employment opportunities.

Rules for those holding government offices

Outside employment/activities is, in general, discouraged. For example, the Hong Kong Civil Service Code stipulates that 'where necessary, the Government has a prior call at all times on the abilities, energies, and attention of civil servants'.[105] In general, a civil servant needs to seek approval in advance before engaging in specific outside activities or employment.[106]

---

[103] Civil Service Regulation (CSR) 464 (e); and Civil Service Regulation (CSR) 463 (1) (a) and (b).

[104] Rachel E. Boehm, 'Caught in the revolving door: a state lawyer's guide to post-employment restrictions', *The Review of Litigation*, 15 (1996), pp. 525–550.

[105] 3.12, Civil Service Code (Hong Kong).

[106] Section 2635.803, Standards of Ethical Conduct for Employees of the Executive Branch (2009).

Outside earning is a specific concern of rules on outside employment/ activity in all of the three selected jurisdictions. Government employees in Hong Kong are generally prohibited from supplementing their income by outside work.[107] The United States sets a maximum limit for covered officials' outside earnings. Prescribed officials are not allowed to earn outside income exceeding 15 per cent of the annual rate of basic pay.[108] Outside earnings from certain activities (e.g. compensation involves fiduciary relationship) are prohibited absolutely even if the maximum limit is not reached.[109] In the United Kingdom, ministers are not allowed to accept payment from contributing to a book, journal, or newspaper.[110] Nor can they accept payment for speeches or media articles which is related to his or her official responsibilities or experience.[111]

Dual positions within government are also subjected to restrictions though strictly speaking this is not *outside* employment. In the United States, '[A]n individual is not entitled to receive basic pay from more than one [government] position for more than an aggregate of 40 hours of work in one calendar week'.[112] In the United Kingdom, ministers are required to drop other public appointments when they are appointed as ministers.[113] In the Hong Kong Government, officers may advise other governments or international organizations as an expert after receiving approval. However, permission will not be given if the officer will retain more than 50 per cent of the fee or honorarium offered for his consultancy service.[114]

Other prohibited outside activities include serving as a principal, agent, director or shadow director, employee or otherwise in any other trade, business, occupation, firm, company (private or public), chamber of commerce, public body, or private professional practice; participating

---

[107] Civil Service Regulation (CSR) 550 (c), (g), and (h).

[108] 5 U.S.C. 501. These provisions are not limited to earnings generated from outside employment. Thus, earning an amount exceeding the limit from writing a bestseller, or any other activity, will violate the prohibition.

[109] 5 U.S.C. 502; Section 2635.807, Standards of Ethical Conduct for Employees of the Executive Branch (2009). It is also absolutely prohibited to receive compensation from nongovernment sources for teaching, speaking, or writing related to the employee's official duties.

[110] Ministerial Code 2010 (the UK), Paragraph 8.6.

[111] Ibid., Paragraph 8.8 and 8.9. While still in office, ministers are not even allowed to make arrangements with publishers regarding the publication of books about their ministerial experience after leaving office.

[112] 5 U.S.C. 5533.   [113] Paragraph 7.11, Ministerial Code 2010 (the UK).

[114] Civil Service Regulation (CSR) 550 (i).

in fundraising in a personal capacity in which the employee 'use[s] his official title, position or any authority associated with his public office to further the fundraising effort'; and other outside activities which might negatively affect an official's official performance or distract his attention from his official duties must be avoided.[115]

It is worth pointing out that sometimes an official's government duty may be influenced by his or her expectations of outside employment. For example, an official may favour possible future employers in carrying out official duties. This is regulated in the United Kingdom where ministers are required to ensure their official actions are not 'influenced by the hope or expectation of future employment with a particular firm'.[116]

Postemployment restrictions

Postemployment restrictions are generally applied to senior officials and based on the principle that, within a control period, any outside employment is prohibited unless prior approval is granted. Even after the control period, some specific outside work is implicitly prohibited. These works/ activities, in Hong Kong, for example, include bids for 'government land, property, projects, contracts, or franchises'.[117] Further, they must not take up outside work which may 'cause embarrassment to the government or bring disgrace to the civil service'.[118] However, Hong Kong rules give blanket permission (e.g. working in charitable, academic, or other nonprofit organizations) as exceptions, but these permissions are only given to unpaid outside work.[119] Hong Kong also uses pension suspension as a threat to prevent former officials from taking up certain outside employment.[120]

With respect to the four key categories of government ethics rules, the specific requirements (such as the scope of covered officials) vary from one country to another. There is also discrepancy in the comprehensiveness of rules among the three countries. For example, the United States' rules are more detailed and specific than the United Kingdom's. That does not necessarily mean the US regulation is heavier; the United

---

[115] 5.5, Code for Officials under the Political Appoint System; Section 2635.808, Standards of Ethical Conduct for Employees of the Executive Branch (2009); and Civil Service Regulation (CSR) 550 (b).

[116] Paragraph 7.7t, Ministerial Code 2010 (the UK).

[117] Paragraph 9 (a), Civil Service Bureau Circular No. 10/2005 on 'Taking up outside work by directorate civil servants after ceasing active service'.

[118] Ibid., Paragraph 9(c).   [119] Ibid., Paragraph 15.   [120] Ibid., Paragraph 22 (a).

Kingdom relies more on traditional informal mechanisms such as non-statutory rules.[121] Nevertheless, if taking a macro view, an apparent common feature can be concluded: all the four key categories have been reflected in the rules in each of the three selected jurisdictions. Section 3.3 will discuss the patterns of the government ethics rules observed in the three jurisdictions in more detail.

3.3   Patterns observed in the three jurisdictions

This chapter has discussed the major regulatory requirements with respect to four key areas (conflicts of interest, appearance of corruption, disclosure of financial information, and outside employment/activity issues) in the United States, the United Kingdom, and Hong Kong. Although the writing is largely descriptive, its principle purpose is not merely to describe the requirements in the regulatory rules. Instead, it hopes to achieve two purposes. First, in Chapter 2 it has been shown that corruption can be seen as a continuum from minor corruption to major corruption. The criminal approach to corruption is mainly for 'traditional' corruption such as bribery, fraud, and embezzlement; whereas the fight against misconduct and malpractice and maintenance of integrity in the government are mainly achieved via a regulatory approach, where the emphasis would be on prevention. Thus, it is hypothesized that countries which rank higher in Transparency International's corruption perception index ranking will have comprehensive and systematic standards for minor corruption offences such as misconduct, malpractice, and integrity maintenance. In surveying the key regulatory requirements, this hypothesis can be tentatively accepted. All three countries studied have a large body of regulatory rules governing misconduct and malpractice, which can be grouped into the four main categories, and rules in each of the categories are not isolated and scattered but guided by certain values/principles.

Second, by describing and analysing these rules, the preceding part of this chapter and this section seeks to determine whether and how the requirements in the three countries can be viewed and understood as a framework which can serve as a meaningful tool in exploring these requirements in China.

---

[121] Gillian Peele and Robert Kaye, 'Regulating conflict of interests: securing accountability in the modern states' (2006), pp. 23–24, available at www.corrupcion.unam.mx/docu mentos/investigaciones/peelekaye_paper.pdf (last visited on 14 July 2013).

Chapter 2 argued that the regulatory approach in the war against corruption should play a more important role than it does now in China due to both the features of regulatory approaches and China's political features. Making government ethics rules is a key element of the regime. However, it must be pointed out that this book does not follow the logic that the rules in the United Kingdom, the United States, and Hong Kong are ideal and thus China must copy every specific provision in the three jurisdictions. But China must ensure that all the key categories (including subcategories) of government ethics regulation are reflected in its regime. These categories are the foundation of government ethics regulation. All three countries have such a system of rules which vary considerably in terms of specific provisions but follow similar patterns in terms of values/principles guiding these specific rules. Thus, a summary of the key features/patterns of government ethics rules in the three jurisdictions will shed light on China's rule making. The remaining part of this section will serve as a summary.

Indeed, each of the three selected countries' regulatory rules/standards has loopholes and/or limitations, or other drawbacks. For example, President Obama in the United States instituted new rules to limit the influence of lobbyists by prohibiting executive branch officials from engaging in oral conversations with registered lobbyists on certain matters. President Obama was criticized as having gone too far and affecting the fundamental rights of free speech in society.[122] There are also problems with the Ministerial Code (UK). One of the key problems is the vagueness of some of the provisions of the Code.[123] Section 7.1 and 7.2 of the Code are such examples of vagueness.[124] These rules point out that conflicts of interest or the perception of conflicts of interest shall be avoided by ministers and it is up to the minister in question to decide what steps need to be taken to avoid such a conflict. Some criticized that language like this will give a minister the opportunity to jump through loopholes if he or she wants.[125] Thus, it is suggested that the Code must be made much more rigid so that the standards are clear for enforcement.[126]

---

[122] Brian W. Schoeneman, 'The Scarlet L: have recent developments in lobbying regulation gone too far?' *The Catholic University Law Review*, 60, 2 (2011), pp. 505–532.

[123] Matthew Ashton, 'Comment: Fox scandal shows need to reform ministerial code', available at www.politics.co.uk/comment-analysis/2011/10/11/comment-fox-scandal-shows-need-to-reform-mini (last visited on 21 April 2013).

[124] Ibid.   [125] Ibid.   [126] Ibid.

In Hong Kong, recent former chief executive scandals had raised public concerns on some actions of the former chief executive, Donald Tsang. Against this background, an Independent Review Committee was set up to review the current regulatory system for conflicts of interest concerning the chief executive and politically appointed officials. The former chief executive was exposed by the media that he travelled on private yachts and private jets of his friends without paying his friends the market value of the travel costs, sold his personal wine collection with the money from the sale donated to charities, and accepted hospitality offered by his friends including a banquet in Macau.[127] After a three-month review, the committee concluded that the regulatory system for conflicts of interest concerning the civil service and politically appointed official are generally satisfactory.[128] However, a fundamental defect exists in the current system: the chief executive is not subjected to the acceptance of advantage requirements set forth in the Prevention of Bribery Ordinance.[129] The chief executive is not subject to any checks and balances regarding solicitation and acceptance of advantages.[130]

This book, however, will not discuss the details of the problems in the regulatory rules against corruption in the three jurisdictions. The remaining part of Section 3.3 will discuss the common characteristics of government ethics rules observed in the three countries.

First, every country's government ethics rule system is composed of four key components which are conflicts of interest, appearance of corruption, financial disclosure, and outside work issues. There are also additional rules within these four categories. For example, civil servants also have the responsibility to report corrupt and/or other illegal offenses of other colleagues if he or she knows of any such conduct.[131] All four key categories are necessary for a system of rules for government ethics to be valid and comprehensive. The four key components are not proportionate in any country's system. Conflicts of interest rules occupy a considerably large part of government ethics rules in any country; indeed, around half of the rules deal with conflicts of interest.

Before discussing the detail of the ethics rules in each country, the beginning of Section 3.2 discussed some general principles/values/purposes of each category of the rules, especially for conflicts of interest

---

[127] 'Report of the Independent Review Committee for the Prevention and Handling of Potential Conflicts of Interests'.
[128] Ibid.   [129] Ibid.   [130] Ibid.
[131] 7.1, Code for Officials under the Political Appointments System.

and appearance of corruption which are the two basic categories. The second pattern observed is that all three jurisdictions' ethics rules, to a large extent, reflect these basic principles/values/components of each category (see Appendix B).

Third, criminal enforcement is adopted to address certain kinds of regulatory issues. Although criminal law is mainly for traditional corruption offences such as bribery, embezzlement, and fraud, it can be used to combat certain misconduct. For example, the United States criminalized self-dealing and Hong Kong criminalized transferring economic value to public officials from private sources; both are two categories of conflicts of interest. In general, the nontraditional aspects of government integrity are still addressed by the regulatory system.

Finally, the rules in all three jurisdictions are composed of general principle requirements which set forth the core values of government and specific prohibition requirements which describe most common prohibitions in detail. The latter can capture most of the undesired behaviour in unambiguous language so that the regulated and the public can easily judge what is allowed or not allowed. For example, a government official shall not use frequent flyer miles earned from official travel for private travel purposes. These kinds of rules cannot capture every undesired action. General requirements can help the regulated to decide how to behave appropriately in situations where a certain behaviour is not described specifically in the rules. For example, a government official shall not use public resources for private purposes. Of course, general rules will leave a certain amount of discretion and different persons may have a different understanding of them.

3.4 Government ethics rules in China

In China, rules governing government ethics at the national level can be found in three forms. The first one is statutory rules which are laws passed by the National Peoples' Congress or its standing committee, China's legislative body at the central level. Laws in this form include the Criminal Law of the People's Republic of China 1997 (hereafter Criminal Law 1997); the Civil Servant Law of the People's Republic of China (Civil Servant Law hereafter); and the Administrative Supervision Law of the People's Republic of China (Administrative Supervision Law hereafter). In the appearance of corruption section of US, UK, and Hong Kong regulations, all the six forms of appearance of corruption are reflected in conduct requirements for judges. Requirements for judicial conduct will also be examined in this section. Unlike the other three jurisdictions where codes of conduct (rather than laws) are the most crucial guidelines for judges, the Judges Law of the People's Republic of China 2001(Judges Law 2001) is the most significant guidance for judges in China. The second form of rules is government regulations which include rules made by the State Council and some ministries (especially the Ministry of Supervision). Finally, the CCP also have its own disciplinary rules. The Constitution of the CCP is the most fundamental party document. However, it only contains a few provisions governing government/party ethics in general; it requires that party members must keep clean and honest and observe both party rules and national laws.[132] In addition to substantive provisions governing government ethics, the CCP Constitution also contains a chapter which deals with government ethics enforcers, the Discipline Inspection Committees (DICs).[133] However, Chapter 3 will only focus on government ethics rules; the enforcement of these rules will be discussed in Chapter 4.

Although in theory government regulations and party regulations have clear distinctions, they will be examined together as a single form for three reasons. First of all, most government officials are also Party members due to the lack of separation between government and the country's ruling Party, the CCP;[134] thus party rules can be applied to most government officials. Second, most of these regulations and regulatory documents are issued jointly by the General Office of the CCP Central Committee and the General Office of the State Council. A careful search of *Chinalawinfo*, a comprehensive China law database, yields around seventy regulations governing government official integrity. Of the seventy, thirty-eight regulations are jointly issued by the General Office of the CCP Central Committee and the General Office of the State Council. Third, in practice the Ministry of Supervision exists in name only and indeed it is a section of the CCP Central Commission for Discipline Inspection.[135] The current minister of the Ministry of Supervision, Ma Wen, is one of the vice secretaries of the CCP Central Commission for Discipline Inspection.

---

[132] Article 3 and Article 34, The Constitution of Chinese Communist Party.
[133] Ibid., Chapter 8.
[134] Flora Sapio, 'Shuanggui and extralegal detention in China', *China Information*, 22, No. 1 (2008), pp. 7–37.
[135] Ibid.

3.4.1 Regulating conflicts of interest

Self-dealing

As discussed earlier, there are four main subcategories of conflicts of interest. The first one is self-dealing. China has distinct types of self-dealing rules targeting party organs and government institutions rather than individual party officials or civil servants due to China's transformation from a planned economy to a market economy. Before the reform from planned economy to market economy, a majority of businesses were state owned and the government directly ran these businesses or intervened in the corporate governance frequently. This state is termed as *Zhengqi bufen* in Chinese. Through economic reform, China aimed to distance government from running businesses directly, in Chinese *Zhengqi fenkai*, so that corporate governance of state-owned enterprises could be improved and independent regulators as market referees be established.[136]

In order to achieve this, the General Office of the CCP Central Committee and the General Office of the State Council issued several circulars from 1984 to 1998. In 1984, a circular on prohibiting party organs and governments and their officials from setting up businesses was issued. It prohibited party organs and governments from setting up enterprises or jointly setting up enterprises with private persons, or economically linking with businesses set up by other private persons.[137]

In 1993, a circular on the disconnection between party organs/governments and the businesses run by them was issued. It restated the above 1984 prohibition and further stipulated that party organs, the People's Congress, judiciary organs, procuratorates, and government organs such as public security, state security, supervision, justice, audit, tax, business administration, land administration, custom, quality, and technique supervision above county level should not set up any form of business entity, invest in business entities in the name of the organization in which they working, or allow business entities to affiliate with their organizations.[138]

---

[136] Margaret M. Pearson, 'Governing the Chinese economy: regulatory reform in the service of the state', *Public Administration Review*, 67, 4 (2007), pp. 718–730.

[137] Article 1, Circular of the CPC Central Committee and the State Council on Prohibiting Party Organs and Governments and Their Personnel from Setting Up Enterprises.

[138] Article 2, Circular of the General Office of the CCP Central Committee and the General Office of the State Council for Issuing the Provisions on the Disconnection between Party Organ/Governments and Businesses Run by Them.

Some exceptions in extreme circumstances were allowed but had to be approved by state council or provincial government.[139]

In 1998 another circular was issued, which focused on prohibiting the army, the armed police, and politics-law institutions (*zhengfa jiaguan*) from running businesses.[140] Politics-law institutions include police, procuratorates, and courts in China. In the same year, a circular on settling the problem of the mixture of government functions and enterprise management (*zhengqi bufen*) was issued jointly by the two offices. This circular requires that, first, all party organs and government departments had to shut down companies which were previously set up; and second, except for a few companies which have been approved by the State Council to have both corporate governance functions and also administration powers, other companies with both functions must strictly separate corporate management functions from administration powers.[141]

China also has rules dealing with individual government officials with respect to self-dealing. In 2005 a Civil Servant Law was passed in China. Article 70, a general disqualification rule, requires:

> a civil servant to disqualify himself from handling his official duties in the following three circumstances: (1) When any of his personal interests is involved; (2) When any of the interests of his relatives is involved; or (3) Any other circumstance that may have any impact on the impartiality of duty performance.[142]

Self-dealing is also addressed by several party/government regulations. Unlike in the three selected jurisdictions discussed above where prohibition of official actions is a general principle and prohibition of private actions is exceptional, in China, specific prohibition requirements mainly address private actions. In other words, China relies more on the restriction of an official's personal interests when the official's private interests might be influenced by his or her official actions compared with the three selected jurisdictions. Though certain prohibitions of private interests, such as diversion of private interests, are also found in the three selected

---

[139] Ibid.

[140] Circular of the General Office of the CCP Central Committee and the General Office of the State Council on the Termination of Business Run by the Army, Armed Police, and Politics-Law Institutions.

[141] Circular of the General Office of the CCP Central Committee and the General Office of the State Council on Settling the Problems of Mixture of Government Functions and Enterprise Management (*zhengqi bufen*).

[142] Article 70, Civil Servant Law of the People's Republic of China.

jurisdictions, these are occasional consequences. In China, some private actions, such as running up private businesses by an official's family even if his official actions will not influence the business, are *in general* restricted by rules. In 2001, the General Office of the Central Committee of the CCP and the General Office of State Council jointly issued a circular on investment in securities by party/government officials. It prohibits:

> officials, including their spouse, parents or children, who are working in the department in charge of regulating any listed company, or in the department in charge of regulating the state-owned controlling entities of any listed company, from buying or selling stocks of such listed company.[143]

For example, Guangdong Investment limited, a Hong Kong Exchange listed company, is run by the Guangdong provincial government; thus according to the above circular, officials in the Guangdong Government are not allowed to buy or sell stocks in this company.

Article 5 of the circular further prohibits officials, their parents, spouses, and children of the securities regulatory department under the State Council or any agency thereof, or of any stock exchange or futures exchange to buy or sell stocks.[144] According to this rule, officials in the China Securities Regulatory Commission, Shanghai Stock Exchange, and Shenzhen Stock Exchange are prohibited from buying or selling stocks. Article 6 prohibits members of party organs or government officers (including their parents, spouse, or children), who hold a post in any securities company or fund management company, or works in any accounting (auditing) firm, law firm, investment consultancy agency, assets rating agency, or credit rating agency which are conferred by the Securities Regulatory Department of the State Council with the qualifications for engaging in securities and futures business, from buying or selling stocks of any listed company having business relations with any of the earlier-mentioned companies or agencies.[145] These three provisions continue to be binding on party organ and government personnel for three months after they leave office.[146]

In 2010, the Ministry of Supervision, the Ministry of Human Resources and Social Security, and the Ministry of Public Security jointly

---

[143] Article 4, Circular of the General Office of the CCP Central Committee and the General Office of the State Council for Issuing the Provisions on Party/Government Officials' Personal Investment in Securities.
[144] Ibid., Article 5.   [145] Ibid., Article 6.   [146] Ibid., Article 7.

issued Provisions on Disciplines for the People's Police of the Public Security Organs. Article 17 of the Provisions imposed punishments on the following activities: directly or indirectly investing in mineral enterprises or entertainment places, or engaging in any other profitable operations; or any of his or her near relatives engages in business operations in the area under the official's charge, which may affect his or her impartial performance of duties, but the relative refuses to quit after dissuasion or the police refuses to accept a new position.[147]

In addition to government employees who hold the special positions discussed above, personnel of party organs or governments are also generally prohibited from running businesses and setting up enterprises.[148]

Transfer of economic value from private sources to a government official

The transfer of economic value from private sources to a government official is different from bribery. For bribery, the value is an inducement for an official to do a certain act or omit to do something. Transfer of economic value from private sources to officials does not require the element of inducement. China's rules regulating this issue mainly address acceptance of gifts including coupons, banquets, and travel paid by a private source.

Criminal law makes it a criminal offence if 'state functionaries who accept gifts in the course of carrying out official duties at home or in intercourse with foreign countries fail to turn over the gifts to the state in accordance with state provisions, when the amount is fairly large'.[149] The punishment is comparable with that for embezzlement.

There are also several party/administrative regulations dealing with this issue. In 1986, a circular on prohibition of pursuing illegal interests in social or economic activities was issued. Article 1 prohibits officials from illegally accepting any form of monetary reward or gifts.[150] The use of the word 'illegally' implies that in general acceptance of a gift from a private source in the official's private capacity is not prohibited unless it is otherwise prohibited by other laws or regulations. Illegal acceptance

---

[147] Article 17, Provisions on Disciplines for the People's Police of the Public Security Organs.

[148] Article 2, Circular of the CCP Central Committee and the State Council on Prohibiting Party Organs and Governments and Their Personnel from Setting Up Enterprises.

[149] Article 394, Criminal law of the People's Republic of China (1997).

[150] Article 1, Circular of the General Office of the State Council on Prohibition of Pursuing Illegal Interests in Social or Economic Activities.

mainly refers to criminal offences (accepting bribes), accepting a value in carrying out official duties, or accepting economic value from expressly prohibited sources.

Transfer of economic value in connection to an official's government duties is a major focus. In 2010, the Central Committee of the CCP issued Provisions for Party Officials on honesty and cleanness in performing official duties. Article 1 prohibits party officials from demanding, accepting money, or gifts from companies or persons in carrying out official duties; accepting gifts, banquets, travel, or entertainment which might affect their performance in carrying out official duties; or accepting cash gift and coupon in carrying out official duties.[151]

The Ministry of Public Security also issued requirements addressing this issue. Police are barred from accepting treats from enterprises, public institutions, or individuals in any business trip or public service activity, or entering commercial entertainment places and joining entertainment activities under the arrangements of enterprises, public institutions, or individuals; or taking cash, negotiable securities, payment vouchers, or performance shares in violation of the provisions.[152]

An especially prohibited source is gifts (or other items of value) from foreigners. In 1987, the General Office of the CCP Central Committee and the General Office of State Council jointly issued a circular on tightening control of overseas visits of party and government officials. That prohibits officials from visiting foreign countries for business or private purposes which is economically supported by Hong Kong or Macau businessmen.[153] In 1993, the State Council issued a Regulation on Giving and Receiving Gifts in Official Functions Involving Foreigners. Article 7 stipulates that gifts received at 'official functions involving foreigners shall be disposed of properly.[154] Gifts in cash and negotiable securities offered by the foreign party at official functions shall be declined, or shall be handed over to the State Treasury if this proved impossible.'[155] These rules are issued since China became a recipient of

---

[151] Article 1, Provisions of the Central Committee of CCP on Integrity in Performing Official Duties for Party Officials.

[152] Article 17, Note 147 above.

[153] Article 1, Circular of the General Office of the CCP Central Committee and the General Office of the State Council on Tightening Control of Overseas Visit of Party/Government Officials.

[154] Article 7, Regulation of the State Council of the People's Republic of China on Giving and Receiving Gifts in Foreign-Related Official Activities.

[155] Ibid.

foreign direct investment for Hong Kong and Macau businessmen as well as foreign businessmen in recent years.

Officials are also prohibited from accepting Chinese New Year gifts or attending banquets provided by subordinate units or officials in these units.[156] If officials are invited to banquets or provided with gifts using the subordinate unit's budget, this is not transfer of economic value from private source to officials. However, if the gifts and banquets are offered by an employee using his or her own money, this is value transfer from a private source to a government official. Although the giver is also a government official he or she provided the gifts or banquet in a private capacity.

Transfer of economic value from private sources to officials can be grouped into two categories. The first category is accepting economic value which is connected to an individual's official duty. For example, an official may visit a company as part of his or her official duties and is invited for lunch. The second type is accepting economic value from a private source in a private capacity. For example, an official accepts a gift during certain social activities from a person other than whom he or she has a close relationship with. In the United States, the United Kingdom, and Hong Kong both types are generally prohibited especially for senior officials with certain exceptions. In China, existing rules as discussed above mainly address transfer of economic value in connection to government/party employee's official duties. For the second category (transfer of economic value not connected to an official's official duty), rules in China only expressly regulate gifts (or benefits) from certain sources (such as private travel financially supported by Hong Kong or Macau businessmen and accepting Chinese New Year gifts or attending banquets provided by subordinate units or officials in these units); that means unprescribed gifts accepted in the officials' private capacity is not prohibited.

Assisting a third party in dealing with governments

Although there are a large number of laws and regulations, around seventy, governing government/party ethics in China, rules regulating 'assisting a third party in dealing with governments' were not found. China does have rules which prohibit officials from using their influence or official convenience to create advantages or benefits for a third party.

---

[156] Article 2, Circular of the General Office of State Council on Prohibition of Waste and Acceptance of Gifts and Banquets.

For example, an official using his or her power to assist his or her friend to successfully get a government contract violates bidding principles. However, this kind of act is indeed a serious abuse of official power, which is not the essence of assisting a third party in dealing with a government. The latter means representing or assisting a third party in his or her dealings with a government without the intention to giving this person favourite treatment and thus violating no rules other than the 'assisting a third party in dealing with a government' principle per se.

Profiting from misusing government position

The fourth category of conflicts of interest is profiting from misusing one's government position. Rules governing this issue in China mainly include three types. The first type is receiving gifts from nonprivate sources. For example, an official receives gifts or cash from subordinate government units and the gifts or cash are covered by the budget of the subordinate government units. In 1988, the General Office of the State Council issued a circular on prohibition of giving and accepting gifts. Article 2 prohibits various departments of the central government from purchasing commodities for the Chinese New Year at a price which is lower than market rate in any of the provinces or cities.[157] The hidden meaning is the price difference covered by local governments and given to the central government officials as gifts. Article 3 prohibits central government officials from accepting commercial products and agricultural products given by localities and subordinate units and prohibits subordinate units from offering local agricultural products as gifts purchased using public funds to superior government officials.[158] In 1993, the Central Committee of the CCP and the State Council issued a circular on handling some recent issues in fighting corruption. Article 1 prohibits party/government officials above county/section level [xianchuji] from accepting credit cards as gifts given by subordinate party/government units or other nongovernment organizations which are financially supported by public funds.[159]

The second type is using government resources for private purposes. The focus is mainly on three aspects: first, travel, especially overseas

---

[157] Article 2, Circular of the General Office of the State Council on Prohibition of Giving Money or Gifts.
[158] Ibid., Article 3.
[159] Article 1, Circular of the Central Committee of CCP and the State Council on Some Recent Issues on Handling the Fight against Corruption.

travel, with public funds;[160] second, public cars for private use;[161] and third, using public funds to purchase various club memberships and pay entertainment bills.[162] For example, it is required that any organization shall not organize overseas travel in the name of 'training', 'internship', 'seminar', and 'exchange'.[163] Travel costs are also a key concern in the three selected jurisdictions. In the United Kingdom, it is expressly stipulated that a minister is generally not allowed to pay the expense of his spouse with public money when he is accompanied by the latter on the minister's official travel.[164] Both in the United Kingdom and Hong Kong, officials are prohibited from using earned air miles through public-funded business travel for private purposes.[165] Compared with prohibitions on this issue in China, these are more subtle consequences of profiting from misusing government office.

Another form of using government resources for private purposes is claiming a private expense as a public expense. This was addressed in a circular issued in 2009. Article 7 stipulates that officials shall not put a private expense into the list of expenses related to official duties and

---

[160] Article 7, Provisions of the General Office of State Council on Sending Officials to Receive Overseas Training; Article 15, Provisions of the Central Committee of CCP and the State Council on Spending Frugally and Prohibiting Waste in Party Organs and Government Departments; Article 7, Circular of the General Office of the CCP Central Committee and the General Office of the State Council on Issuing Provisions on the Integrity for Officials of State-owned Enterprises; Article 1, Circular of the General Office of the CCCPC and General Office of the State Council on Several Issues Concerning the Frugal Spending by the Party and Government Organs; Article 6, Circular of the General Office of the CCCPC and the General Office of the State Council on Firmly Preventing Overseas Travel with Public Funds; article 5, Provisions of the General Office of the CCP Central Committee and the General Office of the State Council on Domestic Business Reception for Party Organs/Government Departments; and Article 4, Provisions on Punishment for Officials Using Public Funds to Travel Abroad.

[161] Article 6, Provisions of the General Office of the CCP Central Committee and the General Office of the State Council on Allocation and Management of Government Cars; and Government Car Reform Policy for the CCP Central Committee and the Central Government.

[162] Article 1, Note 159 above; Article 4, Circular of The General Office of CCP Central Committee and the General Office of State Council on Seriously Checking the Enforcement of Relevant Regulations on Prohibitions of Using Public Funds for Private Banquets, Gifts Giving, etc.; and Article 4, Circular of the State Council on Enforcement Opinions on the Recent Fight against Corruption.

[163] Article 7, Provisions of the General Office of State Council on Sending Officials to Receive Overseas Training.

[164] 10.17, Ministerial Code 2010 (the UK).

[165] 10.16, Ministerial Code 2010 (the UK); Paragraph 6.6, Code for Officials under the Political Appointment System.

claim the private expense.[166] Compared with China, in addition to prohibitions, the three selected jurisdictions tend to have detailed guidelines on the claim of public duty-related expenses. For example, the United Kingdom set forth clearly the items which can be claimed, the items which cannot be claimed, the amount limit, the process to claim, and the documentation needed to support the claim.[167] These guidelines would be helpful to officials and avoid possible confusion that might result from ambiguous or overly general rules or principles.

Another variety is that officials unnecessarily or luxuriously use public funds in performing their official duties. In 1994, a circular was issued on reception standards in business. It requires that party organ/government officials in conducting their business, including inspection work by a higher level official to a subordinate units and mutual visits between different government departments, shall not exceed local reception (meals and accommodation) standards.[168] In 2001, it is further required that 'accommodation shall be arranged in prescribed hotels; meals shall not exceed standards; and entertainment with public funds shall not be arranged'.[169] In 2013, more detailed reception standards were made: for example, meal cost for foreign guests at minister level is limited to 500 RMB per person per day.[170] In the three selected jurisdictions, in addition to detailed guidance on business reception standards, there are also positively worded principle requirements. For example, the UK requires government officials must make efficient and cost-effective use of government resources.[171]

The third type is misusing office-related information/influence for private gain such as using sensitive commercial information to gain

---

[166] Article 7, Circular of the General Office of the CCP Central Committee and the General Office of the State Council on Issuing Provisions on the Integrity for Officials of State-owned Enterprises.

[167] Independent Parliamentary Standards Authority, 'Guidance for MPs' business costs and expenses', October 2012, available at http://parliamentarystandards.org.uk/IPSAMPs/Guidance/Documents/Guidance%20for%20MPs%20Business%20Costs%20and%20Expenses%20updated%20(April%202013).pdf (last visited on 15 March 2013).

[168] Article 1, Circular of the General office of the Central Committee of CCP and the General Office of the State Council on That Reception Standards Shall Not Exceed Local Standards.

[169] Article 1, Circular of the General Office of the Central Committee of CCP and the General Office of the State Council on Frugal Spending in Domestic Business Receptions.

[170] Article 11, Circular of Ministry of Finance on Issuing Provisions on Reception of Foreign Guests by Central Committee of CCP and Central Government.

[171] 10.1, Ministerial Code 2010 (the UK).

economic value. In 2001, the Provisions on Party Organ and Government Personnel's Personal Investment in Securities were issued. Article 3 stipulates that officials shall not directly or indirectly buy or sell stocks or securities investment funds or to suggest others to buy or sell stocks or securities investment funds by exploiting inside information and to buy and sell stocks or securities investment funds in office time by using office equipment.[172] Officials are not allowed to profit from official information unavailable to the public.[173] This requirement extends inside information concerning the stock market to any government information not available to the public. This specific requirement is also reflected in the rules in the three selected jurisdictions.

Prohibitions gradually expanded from non-public information to other official government position for private benefits. In 2011, provisions on integrity in conducting business for basic-level officials in villages were issued that prohibit such officials from gaining benefits for themselves or their relatives and friends by taking advantage of their official influence or convenience.[174] Certain actions in the management and use of public funds and property are also prohibited: borrowing government funds or other government properties illegally or lending government funds or properties in control to others; illegally using public funds or properties or acquiring state properties by paying below-market prices.[175]

In general, rules in China addresses more apparent forms of profiting from misusing government office, whereas rules in the three selected jurisdictions also address certain subtle consequences.

3.4.2   Regulating appearance of corruption

As discussed in Section 3.2.2, there are six types of appearance of corruption: (1) appearance of using influence; (2) appearance of favouritism in appointment; (3) appearance of favouring one party in official duties; (4) associating with criminals or behaving otherwise improperly creating a perception that the official is in disagreement with the overall justice system (this is only for the judicial sector); (5) improper statements (or action/behaviour) raising doubts about the basis of an official decision;

---

[172] Article 3, Note 143 above.   [173] Article 5, Note 151 above.

[174] Article 2, Circular of the General Office of the CCP Central Committee and the General Office of the State Council on Issuing Provisions on Integrity in Conducting Business for Basic Level Officials in Villages.

[175] Article 1 and 3, Note 151 above.

and (6) appearance of bias towards a certain person. The judicial sectors in the three selected jurisdictions are all subjected to more stringent appearance requirements. In the United States, the United Kingdom, and Hong Kong, in addition to practices within government, special attention was given to the requirements on appearance of corruption in the judicial branch. The reason is that the judiciary sector demands the highest standards of appearance of corruption (especially impartiality). Thus, appearance of corruption rules for nonjudicial sectors and the judicial sectors in China will be discussed separately so that the comparative analysis between China and the three jurisdictions is meaningful and fair. The remaining part of Section 3.4.2 will examine government ethics rules (with special attention to government ethics rules for the judiciary) in China against the framework of the six categories.

The requirements for governments and party organs will be examined first. In terms of appearance of using influence, there are no relevant rules for governments and party organ officials in China. China does have rules which address using influence improperly by officials. For example, Article 13 of the Provisions on Disciplines for the People's Police of the Public Security Organs stipulates that the following two acts will be punished: first, taking advantage of one's position to interfere with any law enforcement activity or the handling of a case or to order the illegal handling of a case; and second, taking advantage of one's position to interfere with any economic dispute or to claim debts on behalf of anyone else.[176] Article 17 further punishes the following acts: selling or designating firefighting, security, traffic, or insurance products by taking advantage of one's official position; taking advantage of or intervening in project bidding, government procurement, or personnel arrangements for the purpose of seeking for illicit benefits for the official or any other person who is in a specific interest relationship with that official; or collaborating with any other policeman in providing advantages and seeking illicit gains for each other's interested parties in terms of investment, business operations, or business start-ups.[177]

However, all these type of rules deal with *actual* acts of using official influence rather than only the appearance of such acts. The nature of these acts is fundamentally different from that of appearance of using influence in the United States, the United Kingdom, and Hong Kong discussed earlier in Section 3.2.2. The latter mainly refers to the acts

---

[176] Article 13, Note 147 above.   [177] Ibid., Article 17.

which might cause a person to reasonably perceive the official is using influence even if the official actually does not have any intention to take advantage of his or her influence. A typical example set forth in the Hong Kong rule is that it is not proper for a judge to use judicial stationery when writing to complain, for instance, about a disputed claim on an insurance policy.[178] In China, this kind of act has not been discouraged by any form of ethics rules although there is a large body of existing rules regulating actual abuse of official influence.

The second category of regulation on the appearance of corruption is appearance of favouritism in appointment. Article 68 of the Civil Servant Law prohibits certain situations where civil servants have close relationships with others working in the same department. These close relationships include 'husband and wife, lineal descent, collateral consanguinity within three generations or close affinity between civil servants'.[179] The persons concerned are not allowed to take up posts 'immediately subordinate to the same leading member in the same organ or hold posts with a relation of immediate superior and subordinator, or take such work as organization, human resource, disciplinary investigation, supervision and inspection auditing and finance in the organ where one party concerned holds a leading post'.[180] Apparently, this rule can avoid the appearance of creating benefits including favouritism in appointments for officials by leading members in the same organ/department. However, the appearance of favouritism not only happens between those with close relationships; indeed an appointment decision made to any official in an improper manner may arouse suspicion of appearance of favouritism. It would be better if, in addition to addressing the specific concern, the rules can stress the basis of merit, openness, and fairness in appointment and promotion, similar to the rules in the three selected jurisdictions.

Relevant rules on the third category of appearance of corruption (appearance of favouring one party in dealing with official duties), in China are not found. In both the United States and the United Kingdom, there are specific rules dealing with this kind of appearance. For example, the United States expressly prohibits officials from making ex parte communications.[181] This is a very common consequence where an appearance of corruption is created. In the United Kingdom, ministers are prohibited from sponsoring individual nominations for any awards

---

[178] Paragraph 81, Guide to Judicial Conduct (Hong Kong).
[179] Article 68, Civil Servant Law of the People's Republic of China.   [180] Ibid.
[181] Subsection (d), 5 U.S.C. 557.

as this may be perceived as government support for the individuals nominated.[182]

For nonjudicial sectors, a systematic study of existing government ethics rules fails to identify rules on the fifth category (improper statement or action/behaviour raising doubt on the basis of an official decision); and the sixth category (appearance of bias towards a certain person). The fourth category (associating with criminals or behaving otherwise improperly which creating a perception that the official is in disagreement with the overall justice system) is exclusively for judicial sectors and will be examined below. Though the three selected jurisdictions also do not have rules addressing these three categories of appearance of corruption, that does not mean they are not regulated for nonjudicial sectors. There are principle rules in the three jurisdictions which can address appearance of corruption generally. For example, the US Standards of Ethical Conduct for Employees of the Executive Branch (2009) created fourteen general principles of ethical conduct. The last one stipulates that 'employees shall endeavour to avoid any actions creating the *appearance* that they are violating the law or the ethical standards'.[183] Similarly, in Hong Kong politically appointed officials are required to avoid situations in which they might arouse *any suspicion* of dishonesty and unfairness.[184] However, China does not have this kind of general principle on appearance of corruption.

Moving to rules regulating the appearance of corruption for the judicial sector, rules in the three selected jurisdictions have both general principles and specific provisions addressing all the six categories of appearance of corruption (see Section 3.2.2 for a detailed discussion), whereas rules in China only address two categories of appearance of corruption. Firstly, judges in China are not allowed to take advantage of their judicial influence to gain benefits for themselves or for others. For example, Article 32 of the Judges Law prohibits judges from 'taking advantage of the functions and powers to seek gain for himself or herself or other people'.[185] Just as discussed in rules for government/party officials above, this is *actual* abuse rather than simply the appearance

---

[182] Paragraph 7.18, Ministerial Code 2010 (the UK).
[183] Paragraph 14, Subsection(b), Section 2365.101, Standards of Ethical Conduct of the Executive Branch.
[184] Paragraph 5.1, Code for Officials under the Political Appointment System.
[185] Article 32, Judges Law of the People's Republic of China (2001).

of using influence. Thus, rules addressing the first category (appearance of using influence) for the judicial sector have not been identified.

The second category is appearance of favouritism in appointment. Article 16 of the Judges Law prohibits judges with certain close relationships from holding the following posts at the same time:

> (1) the president, vice-presidents, members of the judicial committee, chief judges or associate chief judges of divisions in the same People's Court; (2) the president, vice-presidents, judges or assistant judges in the same People's Court; (3) the chief judge, associate chief judges, judges or assistant judges in the same division; or (4) presidents or vice-presidents of the People's Courts at the levels next to each other.[186]

'Judges who are connected by a husband-wife relationship, or who are directly related by blood, collateral related within three generations or closely related by marriage' are considered to have close relationships.[187] This requirement can to some extent address the appearance of favouritism in appointments.

The third category is appearance of favouring one party in dealing with official duties. Article 32 of the Judges Law prohibits judges from 'meeting the party concerned or his or her agent without authorization or attending dinners or accepting presents given by the party concerned or his or her agent'.[188] This rule is designed to address the appearance of favouring one party in making judicial decisions. However, this rule is too specific and thus covers only a few acts which may arouse the appearance of favouring one party in adjudication. For example, making a telephone call to a certain party lies outside the scope of the prohibition. This rule can be improved if it prohibits ex parte communication, like that in the United States, the United Kingdom, and Hong Kong.

Rules addressing the fourth category (associating with criminals or behaving otherwise improperly which creates a perception that the official is in disagreement with the overall justice system), the fifth category (improper statement [or action/behaviour] raising doubt on the basis of an official decision), and the sixth category (appearance of bias towards a certain person) cannot be identified in ethics rules for the judiciary in China.

In conclusion, ethics rules in China for party/government officials only address the second category of the appearance of corruption (appearance of favouritism in appointment) and the other five key categories have not

---

[186] Ibid., Article 16.   [187] Ibid.   [188] Ibid., Article 32.

been dealt with. For judges who are expected to be subject to the highest standards of appearance of corruption regulation, existing ethics rules address the second category and the third category and leave the other four categories unregulated.

3.4.3   Regulating financial disclosure

This section will summarize the features of the rules with respect to 'who shall disclose', 'what to disclose', and 'how to disclose (disclose to the public or to a commission)'.

In terms of who discloses, the scope includes three groups of people: state personnel (also termed state functionaries),[189] officials at or above vice county/division level,[190] and core leaders in state-owned enterprises.[191] State personnel refer to all personnel of state organs.[192] 'Personnel engaged in public service in state-owned corporations, enterprises, institutions, and people's organizations; and personnel whom state organs, state-owned corporations, enterprises, and institutions assign to engage in public service in non-state-owned corporations, enterprises, institutions, and social organizations; as well as other working personnel engaged in public service according to the law' are treated as state personnel according to the Criminal Law.[193] Thus, state personnel is the widest scope of group which includes officials at or above the vice county/division [fu xianchuji] level, and core leaders in state-owned enterprises. Thus, the scope of who shall disclose is comparable to the three selected jurisdictions (or even broader than that in the United Kingdom where junior civil servants are not covered by mandatory financial disclosure system). Each group needs to disclose different items.

Regarding what to disclose, state personnel (or state functionaries) are required to disclose only overseas deposits. Article 395 of the Criminal Law requires state functionaries who have savings deposits in foreign countries to declare their deposits according to state provisions.[194] Those who hide their deposits of this nature by not declaring them will be punished by fixed-term imprisonment.[195] Many other items which are as

---

[189] Article 395, Criminal Law of the People's Republic of China (1997).
[190] Article 3, Circular of the General Office of the Central Committee of the CCP and the General Office of the State Council on Provisions on Reporting Personal Matters for Officials.
[191] Article 14, Note 166 above.
[192] Article 93, Criminal law of the People's Republic of China (1997).   [193] Ibid.
[194] Ibid., Article 395.   [195] Ibid.

important as overseas deposits such as domestic deposits and property are not included in the disclosure list; the other two groups who need to disclose account for only a very small portion of the make-up of state personnel. That means most government servants only need to disclose foreign deposits.

Senior officials (officials above or at vice county/division level) have to disclose three types of financial information: (1) income including outside employment income such as teaching and writing; (2) house property; and (3) investments including investments in partnerships or sole individual enterprises.[196] They also need to report these items held by their spouses and children. They are also required to report certain information such as marriage status change, private travel documents, private overseas travel records, marriage of their children to foreigner(s), or stateless person(s), etc.[197] This article requires a wide variety of personal information but it is mainly nonfinancial information. Core management officials in state-owned enterprises have to disclose four items: (1) outside employment; (2) investment; (3) wealth in foreign countries; and (4) employment and foreign residence information of their spouse and children.[198]

Like in the three selected jurisdictions, senior officials in China are subject to a broader scope of disclosure items. However, the difference between senior and non-senior officials in the three selected jurisdictions is not big. Nonsenior officials in the three countries also have to disclose common items (e.g. in Hong Kong they must disclose investment, shareholding in any company, positions such as company directorship, properties, and traded securities[199]). Compared with the three selected jurisdictions, China only requires nonsenior officials disclose savings deposits in foreign countries. Another distinction is that the scope of disclosure items for senior officials in the three selected countries is considerably broader than that in China; many items (such as hospitality, controlled transactions, liabilities, agreements, or arrangements for future employment, etc.) are not required to be disclosed for senior officials in China.

With respect to whom to disclose, all disclosures are submitted to certain units of governments or party organs depending on the ranking status of the reporting official. The information is not available to the public. Though relevant rules requires the information reported by

---

[196] Article 3, Note 190 above.   [197] Ibid.   [198] Article 14, Note 166 above.
[199] Civil Service Regulation (CSR) 462 (3), (4) and 463 (1) (a).

officials of state-owned enterprises shall be made available to a certain scope of people in a proper manner[200]; there are no further rules specifying the scope and the proper disclosure manner. Thus, in practice, this information is not available to the public. In the three selected jurisdictions, though nonsenior officials are in general not required to disclose financial information publicly, senior officials' disclosures are available to the public for inspection.

Throughout the book the focus is mainly on national/federal level in terms of rules examined. However, it is worth outlining some important local-level rules with respect to financial reporting as some new financial disclosure requirements are being conducted as a trial in three counties. Many reforms in China started first as trials at the local level and then were promoted nationwide. For example, Shenzhen was set up as the first trial for market economy reform in 1978, and gradually, market economy reform was established throughout the country. Thus, discussion of these local rules may shed light to future developments regarding financial disclosure for government officials in China.

In 2009, Aletai district in Xinjiang introduced official financial disclosure institutions voluntarily. Since then, various local regions have designed their own financial disclosure system for local officials. The first three local regions that have trialled financial disclosure regulations will be discussed. Besides Aletai, the other two districts are Cixi in Ningbo City, Zhejiang Province, and Liuyang in Hunan Province. Ting Gong refers to this local level reform as an institutional turn from top-down rectification to local innovations in anticorruption.[201]

In May 2008, the DIC of the Party Committee in Aletai, Xinjiang, issued Provisions of Aletai District on Financial Disclosure for Officials at County/Division Level (under trial). This was described as 'the first person to eat crabs in China'.[202] Although the title of the provisions indicates that the rules are for officials at county/division level, the application scope of the provisions goes beyond that. The following three groups of officials are required to disclose: (1) core leaders in party organs, governments (or government departments), courts, procuratorates, and

---

[200] Article 14, Note 166 above.

[201] Ting Gong, 'The institutional logic of local innovation: an analysis of anticorruption initiatives in Guangdong Provinces', International Conference on Public Management Research: Seeking Excellence in a Time of Change, 2012, Shanghai.

[202] Jie Heng (ed.), 'Aletai "eating crabs", breakthrough in financial disclosure for officials', Honesty Outlook (February 2009), pp 16–17.

other county/division level officials[203]; (2) officials who are below county/
division level but have law enforcement powers such as police and tax
administration department officials, and judges and prosecutors who can
handling cases independently[204]; and (3) persons in charge of local state-
owned enterprises.[205] Compared with national rules, the scope of officials
covered addressed a new element: those with actual administrative powers
(not necessarily those at senior positions). For example, a police officer
patrolling on a street can be very powerful as they can issue traffic tickets.
This progress is also observed by Heng Jie.[206]

The items subject to disclosure are considerably wider than the
national requirements. They include the following types of financial
interests: (1) official position income and outside income including
teaching and writing income[207]; (2) gifts and gifts of cash received by
the prescribed officials, their spouses, and children from individuals or
organizations in connection with the official's duties[208]; (3) advantages,
such as meals, accommodation, travel, and entertainment received by
officials, their spouse, and children, which is connected to the official's
duties in either a direct or indirect way and may affect the impartiality of
his or her official duties[209]; (4) profits of officials, in charge of state-
owned enterprises, from contracting the enterprises of which they are in
charge[210]; (5) property transactions of a value beyond 0.1 million RMB
such as purchase or lease and the sources of the money used to make
these transaction[211]; (6) gains from securities transaction and sources of
funds used to make these transaction[212]; (7) assets inherited or given to
the official as a gift[213]; and (8) credit or debts of more than ten thousand
with persons or organizations who, directly or indirectly, relate to the
official's official duties.[214] Among the eight types, the national requirements only cover type (1) and (2); the other six types of items are
innovations in terms of financial disclosure.

A great step forward of the rules in Aletai is it first made the disclosure
of some items, though not all, available to the public. That was referred to
as the 'principle of limited disclosure to the public'; types (1) and (2) are

---

[203] Paragraph 1–4, Article 4, Provisions of Aletai District on Financial Disclosure for
Officials at County/Division Level (Under Trial).
[204] Ibid., Articles 5 & 6.   [205] Ibid., Article 7.
[206] Heng (ed.), 'Aletai "eating crabs"', pp. 16–17.
[207] Paragraph 1–3, Article 8, Note 203 above.   [208] Ibid., Paragraph 4, Article 8.
[209] Ibid., Paragraph 5, Article 8.   [210] Ibid., Paragraph 6, Article 8.
[211] Ibid., Paragraph 7, Article 8.   [212] Ibid., Paragraph 8, Article 8.
[213] Ibid., Paragraph 9, Article 8.   [214] Ibid., Paragraph 10, Article 8.

made available to the public on the Aletai Integrity web whereas types (3) through (8) will not made available to the public.[215]

In December 2008, the DIC and Organization Department of the party committee of Cixi City in Zhejiang Province jointly issued Provisions on Financial Disclosure for Officials in Cixi City (Under Trial). In terms of who discloses, Cixi's scope is narrower than that in Aletai discussed above. In terms of what to disclose, the scope in Cixi is comparable with that in Aletai. Finally with respect to whom to disclose, the information is posted in certain places in the departments where the officials are working. Thus disclosure is not reported to an organ in the city but handled by each entity/bureau.[216] One feature worth pointing out is that each disclosure report will be peer reviewed by the official's colleagues and a disclosure report will be scrutinized closely if more than one-third of colleagues think the official's disclosure is incomplete.[217]

In 2009, Liuyang City Hunan Province, issued Ten Provisions on Establishing and Improving Prevention and Punishment Mechanisms for Corruption. Its disclosure items and the scope of officials to which it is applicable largely follow the relevant rules in Aletai District and Cixi City; there has not been any breakthrough in the two aspects compared with the other two regions.[218] Regarding whom to disclose, Liuyang made the disclosed information available to the public via popular channels such as newspapers, the Internet, and TV/radio.

Thus, for all the three aspects of financial disclosure, compared with national requirements, selected local rules, taken as a whole, have been greatly tightened by requiring more to make financial disclosures and making this information more available to the public. Compared with the three selected countries, the local requirements on financial disclosure have largely covered most common disclosure items in the three countries (e.g. gifts, investments, company directorships, hospitality, controlled transactions, debts, etc.). However, a few items (e.g. terms of arrangements for future employment) still have not been regulated. Nevertheless, it must be noted that the three places cover only a very small part of the geographic area and the population of the country; nor are the three places important in terms of economic development.

---

[215] Ibid., Article 16.
[216] Provisions on Financial Disclosure for Officials in Cixi City (Under Trial).   [217] Ibid.
[218] Ten Provisions on Establishing and Improving Prevention and Punishment Mechanisms for Corruption in Liuyang City.

3.4.4   Regulating outside employment/activity

Outside employment/activities during holding office

Civil Servants are generally prohibited from undertaking or participating in any profit-making activity or holding 'a concurrent post in an enterprise or any other profit-making organization'.[219] If a civil servant has to take up outside work due to his or her official work needs, he or she shall seek approval from the 'relevant organs and shall not collect any reward from his or her outside job'.[220] In 2010, the Central committee of CCP set forth five forms of such outside profit-seeking activities: first, setting up personal business or enterprises or setting up business in the name of others; second, holding shares or securities of nonlisted enterprises in a manner violating relevant rules; third, buying or selling securities in a manner violating relevant rules; four, setting up companies or investing in securities in foreign countries or outside mainland China; and five, taking up remunerated outside employment in business entities, NGOs, or doing intermediary business.[221]

Police have stricter prohibitions imposed on them by the Provisions on Disciplines for the People's Police of the Public Security Organs. According to Article 17, a police officer is subject to serious punishment (a demerit or a special demerit, being demoted or removed from office if the circumstances are rather serious, or being expelled if the circumstances are serious) if he or she is hired by any organization or individual.[222]

For senior officials (officials at or above county/division level), in addition to prohibitions on profit-seeking activities/employment such as setting up enterprises, carrying out remunerated intermediary activities, and taking up positions in various business entities,[223] they are also prohibited from taking up certain unpaid outside activities/employments. In 1998, the General Office of the CCP Central Committee and the General Office of the State Council issued a circular which prohibits officials at or above county/division level in various party organs/government departments from holding leadership positions in NGOs.[224]

---

[219] Article 53, Civil Servant Law of the People's Republic of China.   [220] Ibid., Article 42.
[221] Article 2, Note 151 above.   [222] Article 17, Note 147 above.
[223] Article 1, Note 159 above.
[224] Article 1, Circular of the General Office of Central Committee of CCP and the General Office of the State Council on Prohibition of Leaders of Party Organs/Government Departments from Taking up Leadership Positions in Non-Government Organizations.

In summary, civil servants holding office are only subjected to restrictions on paid outside work/activities. Although senior officials are subject to certain prohibitions on unpaid outside work, the scope of the restrictions is very narrow.

Requirements on post-office outside employment/activity

Rules on post-office outside employment/activity in China are mainly restricted to conflicts between outside employment/activity (conflict between a former official's government duty and his or her outside employment) and profit-making employment. Former civil servants are not allowed to 'take any post in an enterprise or any other profit-making organization that is directly related to his original post, or engage in any profit-making activity directly related to his or her prior work within two years after he or she leaves his or her post'.[225] For those who held leadership posts before retirement, the control period is three years.[226] Similar requirements were restated in the Provisions of the Central Committee of CCP on honesty and cleanness in performing official duties for party officials.[227]

Retired officials in various party organs/government departments above county level are also not allowed to set up commercial enterprises or take up positions in such companies for their entire lifetime.[228] However, they can earn income from consulting, teaching, writing, and translating and other similar activities.[229]

A former judge is not allowed to represent a party in a lawsuit as a lawyer within two years after he or she left their post at the People's Court; nor shall he or she represent a party in the cases handled by the court where he or she was working.[230] This is a considerably low requirement compared with the United Kingdom, where a judge is not allowed to return to practice law as a solicitor or barrister for the rest of his or her life.

There are also restrictions for former officials in state-owned enterprises. Former officials in leadership positions in state-owned enterprises, within three years after leaving office, are not allowed to take up positions

---

[225] Article 102, Civil Servant Law of the People's Republic of China. [226] Ibid.

[227] Article 2, Note 151 above.

[228] Provisions of the General Office of the CCP Central Committee and the General Office of the State Council on Issues Related to Setting Up Business by Retired Officials in Party Organs or Government Departments above the County Level.

[229] Ibid. [230] Article 17, Judges Law of the People's Republic of China 2001.

in private companies, foreign companies, or intermediary entities which have business with the state-owned enterprise where he or she was working; nor shall he or she invest in these prescribed companies.[231]

3.4.5   Unjustified restrictions

Ethics requirements imposed on government officials will restrict an official's certain aspects as an average citizen. However, government officials are put in a special situation where they tend to abuse their office if they are not watched closely. It has been correctly pointed out by Lord Acton that 'power tends to corrupt and absolute power corrupts absolutely'.[232] Based on this logic, government officials should be regulated. Nevertheless, they should be regulated properly and wisely; that means restrictions imposed on government officials shall be reasonably justified. There are mainly two aspects of justifications. Firstly, in terms of performance, the requirements imposed on government officials can help improve government integrity. Simply speaking, these requirements work. Secondly, these prohibitions and requirements should not impose an unfair burden on government officials either while they are in office or after they leave office. A reasonable test is that the restraint imposed on an official should not be greater than is necessary to protect legitimate government interests.[233]

Thus, restraints are inherently unjustified if they play no (or a little) role in protecting government interest or if they impose more burden than necessary on the official. Further, restraints created by ethics rules for government officials not only impose burdens on government employees but also the price which the public has to pay. Unnecessary and unfair restraints on officials may discourage excellent people with skills and experience from joining public service. This was a particular concern of the US Federal Government recruitment in the 1950s, which brought the federal ethics rules under critical review by many persons.[234] If public services, provided by government directly or indirectly, such as

---

[231] Circular of the General Office of the CCP Central Committee and the General Office of the State Council on Issuing Provisions on the Integrity for Officials of State-owned Enterprises.

[232] Lord Acton, *Essays on Freedom and Power* (Boston, MA: Beacon Press, 1949), p. 364.

[233] Boehm, 'Caught in the revolving door', pp. 525–550.

[234] Perkins, 'The new Federal Conflict-of-Interest Law', pp. 1113–1169.

security, healthcare, waste management, and environment protection, are managed by unqualified government officials, the public will suffer.

Two restraints on officials in China will be presented to illustrate their unfairness. The first burden is about prohibition of setting up businesses by an official's family members. Since 1985, a variety of regulations were issued to prohibit the children and spouses of senior party organ/ government department officials from setting up businesses.[235] In 2001, the DIC of the CCP central Committee issued provisions on issues related to setting up businesses by children and spouses of core leaders of party committees and governments at provincial and city levels. It prohibits children and spouses of the prescribed officials from carrying out a variety of actions: (1) developing real estate or providing consultancy services; (2) setting up advertisement agencies; (3) setting up law firms; (4) setting up discos, night clubs, sauna massages, and similar entertainment businesses.[236]

The limited scope of the first restraint cannot be justified from the viewpoint of performance of the rule. It is true that many officials' spouses and children make profits through officials' influence. However, the core of the problem lies in abuse of power by the official; restriction of doing business by the official's spouse and children only cannot address this kind of public office abuse for private gain. According to the rule, the prohibition applies only to the official's spouse and children. The official can continue profiting through preferential treatment given to his or her family members such as brothers, sisters, parents, in-laws, and other close friends. Thus, the design cannot address the real problem. What should be addressed is using power to create competitive advantages by an official to any business. If conflicts of interest and appearance of corruption principles were properly reflected in well-designed prohibitions, the problem of running a business will be solved. In this sense,

---

[235] Provisions of the General Office of the CCP Central Committee and the General Office of the State Council on Issues Related to Setting Up Business by Retired Officials in Party Organs or Government Departments above the County Level; Circular of CCP Central Committee and the State Council on Prohibition of Setting Up Businesses by the Children and Spouses of Leadership Position-holding Officials; and Circular of Discipline Inspection Committee of the Central Committee of CCP on Issuing Provisions on Issues Related to Setting Up Businesses by the Children and Spouses of Core Leaders of Party Committees and Governments at Provincial and City Levels.

[236] Circular of Discipline Inspection Committee of the Central Committee of CCP on Issuing Provisions on Issues Related to Setting Up Businesses by the Children and Spouses of Core Leaders of Party Committees and Governments at Provincial and City Levels.

restriction on the setting up of businesses by officials' spouses and children cannot achieve its expected purpose even if this rule receives full compliance because it allows the officials to abide by the letter of rule but at the same time violate its spirit.

The first restraint also imposes more burdens on officials (more specifically, the spouses and children of prescribed officials) than necessary. Running businesses by officials' children and spouses as well as other close friends is not wrong as long as there are no conflicts between the business and the official duties of the party/government official. If conflicts of interest and appearance of corruption principles are followed by officials, their children and spouses should be able to run their own businesses and at the same time compete fairly with their competitors. Officials' children and spouses should not be constrained by such heavy burdens just because of their status as the official's spouse or children.

The second restraint imposed on officials was not a nationality rule at the beginning. This was first initiated in Shenzhen, well known as the window of China's reform and opening-up to the world. In 2009, the Shenzhen Party Committee and the Shenzhen Government jointly issued Provisions on Tightening Supervision of Heads in Party Organs/Government Departments. Article 6 stipulates that to strengthen the supervision of officials whose children and spouses have migrated to foreign countries or regions outside mainland China, all officials whose spouses and children have resided in foreign countries or regions outside mainland China not for Chinese government work-related purposes or who have obtained foreign nationality or permanent residency outside mainland China, shall not serve as head of a party organ or government department nor take up a core leadership position in important departments.[237] The Organization Department of the CCP put in place similar provisions to make this a national restraint in 2014.[238] These officials are termed 'naked officials' (luo guan) because they live alone in China without their family. Justification of this restraint on officials has been shown by statistics that from 1992 to 2007 around 16,000 officials had fled to

---

[237] Article 6, Provisions of Shenzhen Party Committee and Shenzhen Government on Tightening Supervision of Heads in Party Organs/ Government Departments.

[238] Article 3, Provisions of the Organization Department of CCP on Supervision of Party/ Government Officials Whose Children and Spouse Have Migrated to Foreign Countries or Regions outside Mainland China.

foreign countries with a total of 1 trillion RMB corruptly gained; and most of the officials who had fled were said to be 'naked officials'.[239]

This restraint cannot achieve the purpose of preventing officials from fleeing to foreign countries as officials who decide to flee can easily bypass the rule. This rule does not allow an official to serve as head positions in party organs and government departments if, and only if, both his or her spouse and children (1) have resided in foreign countries or regions outside mainland China not for Chinese government work-related purposes; or (2) have obtained foreign nationalities; or (3) have obtained permanent residency status in foreign countries or in regions outside mainland China. That means the official can take up head posts if either his or her spouse or child(ren) live in foreign countries. Thus, an official can first send only his or her spouse to a foreign country while the official himself and his children still stay in China. After his or her spouse receives nationality or permanent residency in that foreign country, the official can then flee to that foreign country with his or her children with any corrupt gains. Because the official's spouse has obtained the nationality of that country, he or she and his or her children will usually be granted a stay visa in that country. Another loophole of this rule is that the official can still take up a head position if his or her spouse and children are all in foreign countries for China's public work-related purposes (e.g. working in an overseas representative office of a state-owned enterprise). As a head of a party organ/government department, the official can use his or her influence to send his or her spouse and children to a foreign country in the name of working for the state-owned enterprise. Thus, this rule is not an effective rule and it cannot be justified from this perspective.

This rule can also be challenged from the perspective of the fairness of the burden. Immigration to a foreign country by an official with his or her family per se should not be regulated. A clean official should not be deprived of the opportunity of being promoted to a head position if they are qualified to take up that position just because their spouse and children have resided in a foreign country. Take the following analogy as an example. If some people are killed by a kitchen knife, it is not justified to pass a rule which prohibits people from owning kitchen knives. People who decide to kill others can still kill persons with other

---

[239] Xiujiang Li, 'Converging attack "naked officials"', *Insight China* (September 2010), pp. 100–101; Hu Yi, 'Early warning supervision for naked officials', *People's Court Daily* (27 July 2007); and Shuoliang Jiang, 'Moral risk for naked officials and its prevention', *Journal of China National School of Administration*, 6 (2011), pp. 99–102.

items; hence, this rule will not achieve its purpose of preventing murder. And of course it disproportionately affects those who use knives for legitimate purposes such as food preparation.

3.5   Patterns of government ethics rules in China

Based on the description of government ethics rules in China compared with that in the other three selected countries, some general features can be observed. Firstly, the quantity of laws/regulations/circulars/documents governing government ethics in China is considerably greater than that in any of the selected three countries. All the three jurisdictions examined have no more than ten major laws/regulations governing government ethics at the national level; whereas China has more than seventy such binding documents.

However, that does not mean rules in China are more comprehensive. On the contrary, many issues addressed in the four key groups of ethics rules (conflicts of interest, appearance of corruption, financial disclosure, and outside employment) in the selected three countries have not been reflected in China's government ethics rules. This can be illustrated in many aspects. Section 3.3 has outlined the pattern of ethics rules in the three countries (see Appendix B for the pattern). A similar table (Appendix C) also summarizes the key issues addressed in China's government ethics rules. If the two tables are read together, several observations will flow from the comparative analysis; these conclusions will form a picture of the weakness and inadequacy of China's ethics rules.

In respect to conflicts of interest, an apparent observation is that an important conflict of interest principle – assisting or representing a third party in this person's dealing with the government – has not been addressed in China's government ethics rules (the second observation). China does have rules which prohibit officials from using their official influence to bring up illegal benefits for a third party (e.g. an official using his or her power to assist his or her friend to successfully bid for a government contract in a manner violating the bidding principles or procedure). However, this kind of act is indeed a more serious official power abuse (which may constitute a criminal offence) than assisting a third party in the sense of conflicts of interest. The latter means representing or assisting a third party in his or her dealing with the government without the intention to giving this person favourite treatment and thus violate no laws other than the 'assisting a third party in dealing with government' principle per se.

The inherent nature of a civil servant's official duties requires that equal access to the government is provided to the public. Apparently, assisting a third party (even if preferential treatment is not offered to that person) inevitably conflicts with that nature of a civil servant's official duties. Without restraints on this aspect in China, it is common to see government/party officials representing a third party in that person's claim, action, demand, proceedings, transaction, or negotiation with the government.

This is supported by my field study interviews with regulated government officials and government ethics regulatory officials. In the interviews, the author designed a story about representing a third party in dealing with government by a government official: Mr Ma is an official of the Legal Affairs Office of the Government of Y City. His wife's college classmate, Miss Liu, was running a restaurant in Y City. Miss Liu's restaurant license was revoked recently by Y City's Administration for Industry and Commerce on the grounds that she sold expired food. Miss Liu thinks that the punishment is too heavy and asked Mr Ma to assist her in appealing to the Y City Bureau for Letters and Call (responsible for receiving complaint letters and calls, termed *xin fang ju* in Chinese) and to Y City Administration for Industry and Commerce. Mr Ma agreed to help Miss Liu to prepare a letter of complaint, and challenged the basis of the punishment before Y City Bureau for Letters and Call and to Y City Administration for Industry and Commerce on behalf of Miss Liu.

This story was told to thirty interviewees to elicit their response. Among the interviewees, none identified this as improper behaviour. Thirteen participants think Mr Ma's act is good as a government official on the ground that he helped the person in need without breaking any rule; ten think Mr Ma's act is neutral (the act of the official has nothing to do with position ethics as a civil servant).

A third finding is that requirements on the transfer of economic value from a private source to a government official focus mainly on economic values related to official duties in China. In the selected three jurisdictions, government officials (especially senior officials) are generally prohibited from accepting any gift or advantage (even if the gift is not connected to the civil servant's official duty) that might, or might appear to, bring the public service into disrepute or compromise the government official's integrity. For example, the former chief executive, Donald Tsang of Hong Kong, was strongly criticized by the public and media in that he accepted hospitality offered by his friends including a banquet in Macau.[240] In this case, the transfer of economic value was not connected to the Chief Executive's official duties. But it did arouse the public's doubt on the probity of the chief executive's actions.

Acceptance of advantages from a private source while carrying out official duties may be more problematic than acceptance in an official's private capacity. A typical instance of the former is when an official accepts a lunch/dinner at lunch/dinner time with business managers while visiting these businesses for official duty purposes such as inspections, licensing, tax collection, and so on. A typical example of the latter is accepting meals offered by business people or other persons in private settings. The latter type is also problematic because this can easily arouse public controversy just as the Hong Kong former chief executive case demonstrated. Restrictions only on official duty-related economic value transfer from private sources to officials, as China's government ethics rules do, cannot effectively minimize the potential of conflicts of interest or its appearance caused by economic value transfer in private settings.

A fourth observation is about self-dealing: the United States, the United Kingdom, and Hong Kong generally prohibit officials from participating in certain official duty–related actions such as official decisions when there is a conflict or potential conflicts of interest, whereas China generally disqualifies officials from participating in certain private actions such as setting up businesses or investing in securities. For example, as shown in Appendix B, the United States prohibits government appointees from participating in official activities involving their former employers or former clients within a certain period from the date of their appointment; whereas, as shown in Appendix C, China restricts certain officials from purchasing or selling securities.

Broadly speaking, there are two basic ways of dealing with conflicts of interest between official duties and an official's private interests. The rules can disqualify an official from participating in certain official actions where his or her private interests may be affected by the official action; instead, rules can also restrict the official from carrying out certain private activities or prohibit the official from retaining certain private interests when his or her official duties conflict with his or her personal interests. The former is self-dealing regulation which restricts official activities rather than private activities. The basic idea of self-dealing is

---

[240] 'Report of the Independent Review Committee for the Prevention and Handling of Potential Conflicts of Interests'.

that 'a public official should not be in the position of acting for the Government where his private economic interests are involved'.[241] The self-dealing prohibition expresses a principle of disqualification that does not forbid the government official from acquiring private interests.[242]

Of course, there are exceptions: for example, the Hong Kong chief executive has the right to ask a politically appointed official to divest himself of all or any of his investments or interests if there is (or there may be) a conflict of interest between this official's investments or interests and their official duties. The central focus of self-dealing, however, shall always be the regulation of official duties while sometimes private activities may be touched upon. In this sense, rules governing self-dealing in China (other than general disqualification requirements) discussed in the beginning of Section 3.4.1 are not really self-dealing regulations because these rules forbid officials from acquiring certain private interests. The latter is outside activity regulation which restricts a government official's private activities. The regulation of outside activities and outside employment is one of the four key components of government ethics. The rationale of the outside activities and outside employment restrictions is not limited to conflicts of interest; the government also is concerned about the diversion of its employees' energy, time, and commitment. Thus, restrictions imposed on government officials in light of outside activities and outside employment are designed on the basis of the rank of the official (usually senior officials and other civil servants) rather than on the basis of conflicting interests between official duties and private interests. These arrangements in China's self-dealing regulation suggest that the rules were drafted without a comprehensive understanding of the principles of self-dealing regulation.

A fifth finding is that the three selected countries' rules regulating self-dealing are armed with more enforcement mechanisms than in China. In the US, in addition to general disqualification (the principle requirement that an official shall disqualify himself from participating in an official activity where this action may affect his or her personal interests), it also has specific disqualification requirements for former lobbyists and officials whose former employers or clients are involved. Further, the United States introduced a tax on self-dealing transactions. This is an innovative enforcement tool for dealing with conflicts of interest. Moreover, the United States has a diversion mechanism that requires an official to

---

[241] Perkins, 'The new federal conflict-of-interest law', pp. 1113–1169, p. 1129.   [242] Ibid.

divert certain investment or interests. The United Kingdom and Hong Kong rules also have specific disqualification and diversion mechanisms. In China, rules governing self-dealing only deal with general disqualification. While it forbids certain outside activities, these activities are not self-dealing. The reason has been discussed above.

There are two other interesting findings about misusing official positions for private purposes (the fourth type of conflicts of interest). One is that all three selected countries' government ethics rules explicitly prohibit officials from using earned air miles on official travel for private purpose use, whereas a similar prohibition cannot be found in China's rules (the sixth observation). At first sight it seems that this prohibition is just a specific rule about public transportation resources for private purposes. China has rules against private travel using public funds and public (official) cars for private use; both rules address government transportation resources for private purposes. However, the nature of earned miles is somewhat different from other prohibitions on the use of public transportation for private gain. Prohibitions on using government cars or other resources for private purposes targets resources directly funded by the government. On the other hand, earned air miles in official travel is a benefit derived from government funds but not a benefit directly at the expense of the government. Thus, rules on earned miles have expanded the scope of profiting from misusing government office. An example of the same nature is about the former chief executive of Hong Kong, Donald Tsang. Tsang was implicated by the Hong Kong Audit Commission to pay accommodation expenses using his own credit card (and thereby earning personal reward points) and claim reimbursements after duty visits.[243] This was questioned by public media.[244]

The other observation about misusing official positions for private purposes is that China does not restrict the conflict between government duties and political party interests, whereas the three selected countries all prevent conflicts between government interests and political party interests (the seventh observation). This difference reflects the political discrepancy between the three selected jurisdictions and China. In the three selected jurisdictions, political parties are separated from governments,

---

[243] Hong Kong Audit Commission, 'Hotel accommodation arrangements for the Chief Executive's duty visits outside Hong Kong' (May 2012), available at www.aud.gov.hk/pdf_e/hotele.pdf (last visited on 19 May 2013).

[244] Wayne Chung, 'What the local media says', *South China Morning Post* (9 June, 2012), CITY2.

whereas in China the CCP and the government cannot be separated. The members of the Standing Committee of the Politburo of the CCP are the leaders of the Party and the country. The 'principle that the CCP assumes the administration of cadres' is assured by law.[245] All party organ officials are paid in the same way as civil servants at the expense of the government treasury. However, this political state does not mean that China shall leave this conflict between government and party interests unsolved. However, this issue is not the key focus of this research and thus will not be discussed in detail.

In terms of appearance of corruption, China's government ethics rules do not consciously embrace the 'appearance of corruption' idea; as one of the four key components of government ethics rules, this has only been reflected in a few scattered and isolated requirements in China. First of all, four of the six categories of appearance of corruption cannot be found at all in China's government ethics rules (the eighth observation). These four categories are: behaving in a way that creates a perception of how the official may use his influence; association with criminals or behaving improperly, creating a perception the judge is in disagreement with the overall justice system; improper statement (or action/behaviour) raising doubts about the basis of an official decision; and appearance of bias towards a certain person (see Appendix C). Second, appearance of favouritism in appointment is not regulated in general while a few prohibitions exist (acceptance of gifts or cash from subordinate government officials is prohibited and civil servants with close relationships are not allowed to take up posts with the immediately subordinate – the ninth observation). An appearance of favouring assistants to leaders and their children at various levels of government/party organs seems to be firmly rooted in government appointments in China.[246]

Third, the appearance of favouring one party when carrying out official duties is not prohibited in general although two scattered restraints are relevant (the tenth observation). Judges are not allowed to meet a concerned party or their lawyer privately without authorization; nor can they accept banquets or gifts offered by a party concerned. Both requirements can help prevent the impression of favouring a party. However, without a general prohibition – officials shall avoid behaviour which might be perceived as favouring one party in carrying out an official duty – officials may create such an appearance without violating

---

[245] Article 4, Civil Servant Law of the People's Republic of China.
[246] Song Li, 'Problems of promotion of leaders' assistants', *Outlook*, 45 (2010), pp. 12–14.

the two specific prohibitions. For example, a judge makes a phone call to one of his or her concerned parties or, in the court, uses a more friendly tone to speak to one party than the other. A very common practice in China's criminal trials is that prosecutors wear suits in the court and the defendant has to wear a special vest with words like 'X city detention house'. The defendant appears in the court, in terms of image, which at least gives the impression to a court audience that the defendant is in the court to be punished rather than to defend himself or herself. This can create an appearance that the judge is favouring the prosecutors. This impression is also confirmed by McConnell's empirical research *Criminal Justice in China*.[247]

In addition to the six categories of appearance of corruption, the lack of the notion of appearance of corruption in China's government ethics rules is also reflected in its conflicts of interest rules. In the selected three countries, all four types of conflicts of interest rules prohibit both *actual* conflict as well as *appearance* of conflicts, whereas conflicts of interest rules in China mainly focus on actual conflict (the eleventh observation). In any of the three selected jurisdictions, appearance of conflicts of interest is expressly regulated. For example, the Civil Service Code of Hong Kong stipulates that 'civil servants shall ensure that no actual, perceived or potential conflict of interest shall arise between their official duties and private interests'.[248]

With respect to financial disclosure, three further findings have been observed. First of all, the scope of disclosed items for the three examined jurisdictions is considerably greater than that in China, especially for nonsenior officials (the twelfth observation). For nonsenior officials in China, the only item that needs to be disclosed is overseas deposits; by contrast, investments, interests, transactions, outside positions, assets, and liabilities all need to be disclosed in the other three jurisdictions. For senior officials, many items needing to be disclosed in the United States, the United Kingdom, and Hong Kong have not been reflected in ethics rules in China. These items include transactions, liabilities, and arrangements for future employment after leaving office.

Another observation is about whom to disclose: in the three selected jurisdictions, all senior officials' disclosure must be made available to the public; whereas in China all disclosures are made to certain party organs/

---

[247] Mike McConville, *Criminal Justice in China: An Empirical Enquiry* (Cheltenham: Edward Elgar, 2011).
[248] Paragraph 3.4, Civil Service Code (Hong Kong).

government departments (the thirteenth observation). True, in the three experimental cities, Cixi, Liuyang, and Aletai, discussed earlier in this chapter, disclosure is made available to the public; but this serves the public in three isolated small regions in relation to the big country.

Moving to outside employment and outside activities, the regulation of this in China, both during office and on leaving office, focuses mainly on profit-making activities and paid employment; by contrast, the three jurisdictions pay equal attention to nonprofit activities/unpaid employment (the fourteenth observation). For example, dual public appointment is forbidden in the United Kingdom, whereas in China this is very common. China only restricts former officials from taking up paid employment or carrying out profit-making activities which directly relate to their previous official duties; whereas the three jurisdictions restrict lobbying government, representing a third party in dealing with the government regardless of whether it is paid or unpaid. Furthermore, in Hong Kong and the United Kingdom, former senior officials must seek prior approval before taking up any outside employment regardless of whether it is paid or unpaid.

In addition to observations related to the content of government ethics regulation in China contrasted with that in the three selected jurisdictions, some findings about the regulation techniques have been found. First, in all three selected jurisdictions a code for government officials (with different titles such as Civil Service Code and Code for Officials under the Political Appointment System, Ministerial Code, etc.) is the most critical document of their government ethics regulation rule system[249]; China, however, does not have such a document of fundamental position in its government ethics rule system (the fifteenth observation). In China, although a large body of government ethics rule documents in the form of statutes, regulations, and circulars have been identified, there is no one code-like document which sets out the basic framework for government officials' behaviour in a comprehensive and coherent manner. Conversely, rules are scattered in various documents in China. For example, there are more than twenty documents addressing the receiving and giving of gifts alone.

---

[249] Stuart C. Gilman, who surveyed more countries, also thinks that codes are the ultimate terms of reference for public servants. See Stuart C. Gilman, 'Ethics codes and codes of conduct as tools for promoting an ethical and professional public service: comparative successes and lessons' (2005), World Bank Research Reports, available at www.oecd.org/mena/governance/35521418.pdf (last visited on 19 April 2013).

Secondly, ideally a code should be composed of values, principles, and specific standards of behaviour. Values are general moral obligations such as integrity, impartiality, and honesty; principles are general guidance or expectations of behaviour (such as government officials should avoid conflicts of interest and the appearance of corruption). Although principles derived from values contain certain prohibitions, principles are too general to guide officials' behaviour, especially in unclear or difficult situations. Specific standards are rules which articulate the values and principles expected of government officials when confronting unclear or ambiguous ethical circumstances through setting forth the majority of circumstances that confront government officials.[250]

The codes of the three selected countries are devised in a way that contain values, principles, and specific standards whereas China's government ethics rules contain mainly values and specific behaviour standards but are short on principles (the sixteenth observation). Take transfer of economic value from a private source to a government official as an example. Rules in China set forth values such as clean and upright and list many specific forms of prohibited benefits such as money, coupon, securities, meal, etc. (specific standards). However, there is not a principle prohibition which in general restricts value transfer from a private source to a government official. Principles are important because specific standards cannot exhaust every specific form of benefit. Thus, without these principles the regulated officials can creatively accept things which have not been captured by existing rules.

The US Standards of Ethical Conduct for Employees of the Executive Branch sets out fourteen general principles; the Hong Kong Civil Service Code requires that civil servants follow the following core values: commitment to the rule of law, honesty, integrity, objectivity, impartiality, political neutrality, etc., with principles deprived from these values; and the UK Civil Service Code and Ministerial Code set forth seven values, which are selflessness, integrity, objectivity, accountability, openness, honesty, and leadership. Each of the values has been accounted for by principles covering a broad group of prohibited activities. For example, under the integrity value of the Code for Officials under the Political Appointment System in Hong Kong, conflicts of interest (including the appearance of conflict) and its subcategories such as transfer of economic value from private sources to a public official and profiting from misusing

---

[250] Ibid.

government office have been covered. In China's government ethics rules, although some general values are also mentioned such as 'being honest and clean, just and upright',[251] they have not been developed to guiding principles like that in the other three jurisdictions.

Thirdly, in addition to observations at the macro level of the codes, at the micro level (individual provisions of government ethics in China), rules in general are drafted not as clearly as that in the three selected jurisdictions (the seventeenth observation). Gift acceptance–related provisions in Hong Kong and in China will be compared to illustrate this point. In Hong Kong, acceptance of an advantage is prohibited in general. 'Advantage' is defined to include almost any benefit (monetary or nonmonetary, tangible or intangible) and excludes entertainment and election donations. The general prohibition, then, is given exceptions in case of general or specific permission from the chief executive. Then, a special document was made to set forth various permissions given, such as for advantages from relations, advantages from tradesmen, and advantages from close personal friends. In both the general prohibition and the Chief Executive's Permission, definition is a frequently used tool to avoid unambiguous situations. The use of a separate Chief Executive's Permission is an effective way of maintaining the stability of the prohibition of acceptance of advantages framework and at the same time giving flexibility for some specific exceptions.

Moving to China, there are a variety of binding circulars dealing with gifts acceptance. However, clear definitions, which set forth the scope of what constitutes a 'gift' or a broader word such as advantage, or benefit, are not given. Different circulars just focus on different forms of gifts including gifts of cash and securities, coupons, banquets, entertainment, and travel. Apparently, the scope of gifts is considerably narrower than that in Hong Kong. Thus, in practice, many officials and businesspeople in China can bypass the gifts prohibitions easily. For example, an official can borrow a car from a businessperson for a long time, eg, several years, because such a benefit has not been specifically prohibited.

3.6   Insights and implications for the improvement of government ethics rules in China

The previous section has identified certain characteristics and patterns of China's government ethics rules differing from the rules in the selected

---

[251] Article 12, Civil Servant Law of the People's Republic of China.

three jurisdictions. Some insights and implications for China's government ethics rules reform will naturally flow from the findings observed. These seventeen findings can be put into three groups.

The first group is composed of findings that identify important government ethics regulation aspects/elements which are absent in China's rules. This group can be shortly described as the 'nonexistent aspects' group. Five observations among the seventeen belong to this group include:

- Assisting or representing a third party in this person's dealing with government (the second observation).
- Frequent flyer miles (the sixth observation).
- Conflict between government official duties and political party interests (the seventh observation).
- Behaving in a way that creates a perception of how the official may use his influence; association with criminals or behaving improperly creating a perception the judge is in disagreement with the overall justice system; improper statement (or action/behaviour) raising doubts on the basis of an official decision; and appearance of bias towards a certain person (the eighth observation).
- Appearance of conflicts of interest (the eleventh observation).

The second group includes observations that identified government ethics regulation aspects/elements which have only been very weakly reflected in China's rules. This group can be termed as the 'weak aspects' group. Six observations of the seventeen belong to this group:

- Value transfer not related to official duties (the third observation).
- Appearance of favouritism in appointment (the ninth observation).
- Appearance of favouring one party in dealing with official duties (the tenth observation).
- The scope of disclosed items (the twelfth observation).
- Disclosure to the public (the thirteenth observation).
- Unpaid outside employment and nonprofit outside activities (the fourteenth observation).

The third group includes observations that show the downside of government ethics rules per se (legislative technique). This group can be described as the 'rule-making technique' group. Six observations can be grouped into this category:

- A large number of government ethics rule documents (the first observation).
- Generally disqualifying officials from participating in certain private actions involving conflicts of interest (the fourth observation).
- Self-dealing rule not equipped with enforcement tools such as tax on controlled transactions and diversion of investments (the fifth observation).

- Nonexistence of a code of conduct as the foundation of government ethics rules (the fifteenth observation).
- Nonexistence of principles in the government ethics rules (the sixteenth observation).
- The rules are ambiguous (the seventeenth observation).

Each of the three groups of observations of the pattern and characteristics of China's government ethics rules will shed specific light on how to improve the rules. The 'nonexistent aspects' group indicates that a variety of crucial aspects about conflicts of interest and appearance of corruption are missing in China's government ethics rules. The notion of appearance of corruption is nearly foreign to China's government ethics regulation. The necessity of these aspects for a government's ethics rule system is not simply based on the observation that all three selected countries have them, but on the logical reasoning that any government cannot afford to miss these ideas/notions such as appearance of corruption and assisting a third party in dealing with the government if it wants to achieve success in fighting corruption. This can be understood by applying common sense. The fact that all three selected jurisdictions have these ideas, however, provides an empirical basis for justification. All the three countries rank at the top in Transparency International's Corruption Perception Index ranking. Thus, it is self-evident that China should introduce these ideas and notions into its government ethics rules as soon as possible. Of course, due to political reasons, it is not possible for China at this stage to adopt conflict between official duties and political party interests. Fortunately, all other missing aspects are not inherently incompatible with China's political condition.

The 'weak aspects' group shows that weaknesses of key aspects/components exist in all four categories of government ethics rules (conflicts of interest, appearance of corruption, financial disclosure, and outside employment/activities). The implications are apparent: these weak aspects must be strengthened so that the loopholes are filled. Although the implications of the 'nonexistent aspects' group and the 'weak aspects' group both point to improvement through more prohibitions of undesired behaviour, the former introduces totally new notions while the latter just supplements existing ideas.

The 'rule-making technique' group presents problems identified at the technique level in government ethics rule making. The implications are twofold: at the macro level, the government ethics rule system in China shall be designed in a coherent, systematic, and comprehensive manner. Most of the requirements can be integrated in a well-designed foundation document, such as a code for government officials. At the micro level, the provisions should consist of values, principles, and specific prohibitions which are written in an unambiguous manner. Techniques such as definitions and other specific enforcement tools (such as transaction tax and diversion of interests) shall be effectively used in rules design.

Further, unjustified rules discussed in Section 3.4.5 also have concrete government ethics rule-reform implications. As pointed above, both rules prohibiting officials' spouses and children from running businesses and rules prohibiting 'naked' officials (officials whose children and spouses are not residing in China) from serving as heads of party organs or government departments cannot be justified in terms of both effect-iveness and fairness of the burden of these rules. Indeed, the focus of rules prohibiting officials' spouses and children from running businesses is using official power to profit from private businesses and the focus of the rules on 'naked officials' is their fleeing China with corrupt gains. Thus, the solution should be on preventing the abuse of government office and on preventing the officials from gaining money corruptly in the first place. These purposes should be achieved through effective criminal anti-corruption enforcement against mainly embezzlement, bribery, and fraud as well as well-designed government ethics enforce-ment (mainly conflicts of interest, appearance of corruption, financial disclosure, and outside employment). These unjustified rules failed to achieve these purposes and thus shall be repealed.

3.7   Conclusion

Regarding anti-corruption legislation/regulations in China, there are two mainstream opinions in the academic debate. Some scholars argue that China needs an anti-corruption law. They have accurately observed that China's party/government regulations are scattered, repeated, and ambiguous.[252] However, they failed to find that many important govern-ment ethics components are missing and that some of these components are weak in China, although they noticed the importance of financial disclosure and disqualification in certain circumstances (e.g. the involved official is dealing with his relatives).[253] Further, they did not realize the

---

[252] Yiqian Feng (ed.), *Public Ethics* (Guangzhou: South China University of Technology Publishing House, 2010).

[253] Zhe Lin, 'What kind of anti-corruption law shall we have?' *Honesty Outlook*, 3 (2011), pp. 44–45.

regulatory approach against corruption for government ethics is quite different from the criminal approach for traditional corrupt offences; they suggested that the anti-corruption law should aim at establishing and empowering anti-corruption agencies and setting forth enforcement mechanisms such as reporting, investigation, prosecution, and adjudication.[254]

The other argument is that China's problem with corruption lies mainly in enforcement rather than a lack of laws/rules against corruption. Scholars point out that China has already passed criminal laws and civil servant laws and has issued many texts governing corruption. They further argue that since existing anti-corruption criminal provisions (such as provisions against bribery and embezzlement) cannot play an effective role in reality due to enforcement problems, it is not logical to expect that a new anti-corruption law will play a different role.[255] Thus, they conclude the point is better law enforcement rather than better law/ rule making. This argument is only partially true. Anti-corruption problems in China can be attributed to ineffective law enforcement to a certain degree. However, that does not mean that rules against corruption are not problematic in themselves. Government ethics rules also contain many problems as demonstrated in the seventeen findings.

This chapter has discussed the fundamental components of government ethics rules and applied these standards to the rules as they currently stand in China in contrast with that in three selected countries which rank at the top in Transparency International's Corruption Perception Index ranking. Although this chapter contains a large part of the discussion of rules in China and in the three countries which in itself may seem largely descriptive, the purpose is to identify patterns and characteristics based on which interesting findings can be observed.

These findings clearly show the problems of China's government ethics rules at both the macro- and micro-levels. These findings provide fresh knowledge on China's anti-corruption picture as well as insightful implications for the country's regulation reform.

Chapter 4 will explore key elements of regulatory enforcement against corruption in the three selected countries and apply these elements to government ethics enforcement in China to form a more thorough picture of government ethics regulation in China.

---

[254] Hongtai Yang, 'Legislative thoughts on the National Anti-corruption Law', *Law Science*, 9 (1998), pp. 23–25.

[255] Duola Pan, 'Do not hurry to be optimistic about the anti-corruption Law', *China National Conditions and Strength*, 7 (1999), p. 35.

Enforcement of government ethics rules

4.1 Introduction

Chapter 3 showed the inadequacy and weakness of some aspects of government ethics rules in China. The focus in this chapter will now turn to enforcement of these rules. Despite the proliferation of government ethics codes in many countries since the 1970s, how these codes function and how they are enforced are still not well known.[1] Knowledge on enforcement of government ethics is even worse in China's case.

In general, government ethics 'enforcement is not a black or white issue, but a matter of the degree of enforcement'.[2] While it is apparent that various enforcement efforts such as enforcement tools are crucial factors for effective government ethics enforcement, it is also important to understand that enforcement degree, to a certain extent, is determined by ethics rules *per se*. There are at least three circumstances in which government ethics rules themselves can influence their enforcement. First, the scope of requirements imposed by rules on government officials' behaviour is the basis of enforcement scope. Second, rules written in ambiguous language will create difficulties for enforcement. And third, preventive enforcement tools and enforcement authority granted to enforcement bodies are also critical for effective enforcement. While this chapter focuses on enforcement, government ethics rules will also be touched on where they relate to enforcement.

Enforcement broadly involves two dimensions: first, enforcement agencies (including officials in these agencies); and second, actual actions performed by government ethics regulatory officials in order to encourage compliance with ethics requirements through various means such as

---

[1] J. Patrick Dobel, 'The realpolitik of ethics codes: an implementation approach to public ethics', in H. George Frederickson (ed.), *Ethics and Public Administration* (Armonk & London: M. E. Sharpe, 1993), pp. 158–174.

[2] Robert W. Smith, 'Enforcement or ethical capacity: considering the role of State Ethics Commissions at the millennium', *Public Administration Review*, 63, 3 (2003), pp. 283–295.

rule making, rule interpretation, counselling, sanctions, and referrals to other agencies including prosecution departments. This is the broad meaning of enforcement. Enforcement is also used narrowly to refer to formal activities involving investigation, prosecution, conviction, and punishment. In the book, when regulation regime generally or government ethics regulation specifically is discussed, enforcement is used in a broad sense. When criminal corruption enforcement is discussed, enforcement is here narrowly defined. Thus, the meaning of the term enforcement depends on the specific context. When the term is broadly used, it has a similar meaning with the word regulation which, for the purpose of this research, means various actions taken by government ethics regulators in manipulating the behaviour of those regulated towards the desired direction (see Chapter 2 for a detailed discussion of the meaning of regulation). These two aspects of the enforcement of government ethics are the chief concern of this chapter.

The key argument of this chapter is that government ethics should be enforced by a regulatory regime which focuses on setting standards, monitoring compliance, and correcting misdeeds rather than apprehending violators and punishing them. The three selected countries all take such a compliance-oriented approach in regulating government ethics in their own countries, whereas in China, the enforcement of government ethics is largely dealt with in the same way as criminal corruption enforcement, which focuses on investigation and punishment (the difference between deterrence-oriented and compliance-oriented will be examined in detail in Section 4.2.3). This chapter further argues that China's deterrence-oriented enforcement of government ethics mainly results from the fact that a single agency, the DIC, is both a criminal corruption enforcer and a government ethics enforcer. The enforcers are dominated by their criminal enforcement responsibilities.

The remainder of this chapter is composed of three parts. Section 4.2 will consider five basic regulatory enforcement elements (including enforcement agencies, authorities and responsibilities, enforcement styles, enforcement tools, and enforcement resources) in order to form a conceptual framework against which the enforcement of government ethics in the three selected countries and in China can be assessed. As there is only a small body of existing literature on the specific enforcement of government ethics whereas research on regulatory enforcement in general is rich, this part will review both the former and the latter. Research has shown that regulation of business and regulation of government are highly similar in many aspects; generic regulatory approaches and styles cut across the regulation of business and the regulation of government.[3] In so doing, a by-product contribution of this chapter is to offer an additional test of the applicability of general regulatory enforcement knowledge to regulatory enforcement of government ethics. After a general discussion of each enforcement element, specific enforcement actions in reality in the United States, the United Kingdom, and Hong Kong will be explored.

Section 4.3 will examine the features of enforcement of government ethics in China. Rich empirical data retrieved from interviewing regulatory officials and actual enforcement cases will serve as the basis for analysis. As research on this issue in China is exploratory, these findings themselves are an important contribution to understanding government ethics enforcement in China. These findings, in contrast to enforcement in the three selected countries, may also offer some fresh explanations for the consequences of corruption in China. Section 4.4 will summarize the key findings and arguments of this chapter.

4.2   Key elements of government ethics rules enforcement: the United States, the United Kingdom, and Hong Kong

4.2.1   Enforcement agencies

A natural starting point for examining enforcement is to consider the bodies in charge of enforcing government ethics rules. Existing studies on government ethics regulatory agencies/bodies centre mainly on the following dimensions: authorities (functions or duties), enforcement strategies, enforcement styles, and enforcement tools. For example, it has been repeatedly observed that regulatory enforcement is compliance oriented in contrast to deterrence oriented. Take banking regulation as an example; banking regulators mainly set detailed operation standards and guidelines (e.g. capital requirement, reserve requirement, and large exposure restrictions) and constantly monitor banks compliance with these standards. This is compliance oriented. Whereas the approach against banking related crimes, such as credit card fraud, is mainly addressed via investigation and prosecution, which is largely deterrence oriented (see Section 4.2.3 for detailed discussion about enforcement style). This finding can be applied to both regulation of private

---

[3] Christopher Hood, et al., *Regulation inside Government: Waste-Watchers, Quality Police, and Sleaze-Busters* (New York: Oxford University Press, 1999).

businesses – such as banking, environment, and child care centres[4] – and regulation of government ethics.[5] Theoretical frameworks, such as deterrence versus compliance enforcement, developed by previous studies, can provide important insights for this research.

These enforcement dimensions can be gauged by carefully and systematically studying the enforcement actions performed by regulatory agencies. Usually, an enforcement agency's authority will be expressly granted by statute and regulations.

Many ethics agencies are given the power to oversee conflicts of interest, lobbyist registration, and financial disclosure forms; ethics education and training are also crucial missions of ethics bodies.[6] Authorities derived from statutes and regulations are the basis of the everyday enforcement actions for government ethics bodies. However, actual enforcement actions do not necessarily overlap with an agency's formal powers because some formal authorities may not be performed in reality or only occasionally performed for various reasons. For example, lack of recourse has led to a serious inadequate review of financial disclosure forms submitted to most ethics commissions in the United States.[7] On the other hand, an agency may extend its enforcement action boundaries gradually even if their legal authority is still the same. For example, the US Office of Government Ethics (OGE) was suddenly taken seriously in 1992 after Stephen D. Potts, the then head of the OGE, restructured its operation and sought increased funding and staff.[8]

All these dimensions will be discussed in relevant sections in this chapter; this section mainly focuses on the existence of an agency and its form. As certain unethical behaviour may be regulated by criminal law, the investigation and prosecution departments dealing with these offences are not considered as government ethics enforcement agencies for the purpose of this book. For example, the Independent Commission Against Corruption (ICAC) in Hong Kong is in charge of investigating the transfer of economic values from private sources to public officials; in

---

[4] William T. Gormley, Jr, 'Regulatory enforcement: accommodation and conflict in four states', *Public Administration Review*, 57, 4 (1997), p. 285.

[5] Hood et al., *Regulation inside Government*.

[6] Robert W. Smith, 'A conceptual model for benchmarking performance in public sector ethics programs: the missing link in government accountability?' *International Journal of Public Administration*, 30, 12–14 (2007), pp. 1621–1640.

[7] Smith, 'Enforcement or ethical capacity', pp. 283–295.

[8] Robert N. Roberts and Marion T. Doss, *From Watergate to Whitewater: The Public Integrity War* (Westport, CT and London: Praeger, 1997).

the United States, the Federal Bureau of Investigation (FBI) and the Public Integrity Section of the Department of Justice are responsible for identifying and prosecuting public officials who violate criminalized government ethics rules.[9] However, these agencies are not the mainstream of government ethics enforcement agencies as only a few government ethics rules have been criminalized as shown in Chapter 3.

The most crucial agencies are those with noncriminal government ethics responsibilities. Specifically, this research focuses on the agencies overseeing conflicts of interest, financial disclosure, appearance of corruption, and outside employment/activities at the national level in the United States and the United Kingdom, and across the region of Hong Kong. These agencies are usually named boards, commissions, or offices.

Regardless of the names of these enforcement bodies, their existence is crucial for government ethics enforcement. As Herrmann has pointed out, the importance of such agencies to the management of government ethics cannot be exaggerated because 'there is a critical relationship between the effectiveness of any law and the police that enforce it'.[10] It should not be assumed that all jurisdictions have such agencies though it is true that almost every country has a government department/agency combating traditional corruption.

In the United States, the entity at the federal level in charge of government ethics is the US OGE, which was established in 1978 by the Ethics in Government Act. The primary responsibilities of the OGE include ethics education, interpretation and enforcement of government ethics regulations, and management of financial disclosure programmes.[11] It also regulates conflicts of interest, outside employment, and appearance of corruption because these issues are covered in government ethics regulations enforcement by the OGE. For example, in 2011 three instances regarding contact with former employers by covered appointees were reported to the OGE.[12] This involves the appearance of corruption. The jurisdiction of the OGE covers federal government

---

[9] Ibid.

[10] Frederick M. Herrmann, 'Empowering governmental ethics agencies', *Spectrum: Journal of State Government*, 77, 3 (2004), pp. 33–35.

[11] Roberts and Doss, *From Watergate to Whitewater* .

[12] The United States Office of Government Ethics, 'Annual report pursuant to Executive Order 13490' (2011), available at www.oge.gov/displaytemplates/searchresults.aspx?query=annual%20report%20of%20executive%20order%2013490 (last visited on 15 December 2012).

officers in the executive branch. The legislative and judicial branches have their own ethics enforcement bodies.

The overall regulator (OGE) for the executive branch in the United States oversees ethics both for political appointees and federal civil servants though the political appointees may be subject to more stringent requirements (e.g. they are required to sign a Pledge Consent), whereas in the United Kingdom and Hong Kong, ministers (politically appointed officials in Hong Kong) and the bureaucracy are overseen by different ethics enforcement entities. Ministers and politically appointed officials as senior officials in the executive branch are regulated by the Ministerial Code and Code for Officials under the Political Appointment System in the United Kingdom and Hong Kong, respectively.[13] In the United Kingdom when a minister's conduct is questioned with respect to a breach of the Code the prime minister is the person, and the only entity, who ultimately judges the standards of behaviour expected of a minister and the final consequence of a violation of the Code.[14] Similarly, in Hong Kong the chief executive, the head and representative of the Hong Kong Special Administrative Region, and the head of the government of the Region enforces the Code for Officials under the Political Appointment System and manages the ethics of politically appointed officials through a variety of enforcement means. For example, He or she gives advice and guidance on the acceptance and retention of gifts, advantages, or other benefits.[15] In this sense, there is no independent regulator who oversees the ethics of ministers (politically appointed officials in Hong Kong) as the prime minister (the chief executive in Hong Kong) is indeed the

---

[13] The ethics of politically appointed officials are mainly subject to the Code for Officials under the Political Appointment System though the Prevention of Bribery Ordinance which also covers politically appointed officials.

[14] Paragraphs 1.3 and 1.5, Ministerial Code.

[15] Paragraphs 5.4–5.8, 5.11 and 5.12, Code for Officials under the Political Appointment System. For more examples, he or she requires them to report to him or her any conflicted interests. He or she also reviews these officials' applications for outside employment while they are holding office and decides whether to grant them permission or not. He or she also gives approval to outside sponsored visits and private use of earned miles from duty travel. He or she also can require any official suspected to have conflicts of interest to 'divest all or any of the investments or interests, to refrain from acquiring or disposing of the investments, to freeze any investment transaction for a specified period, to place the investments or interests in a blind trust; to refrain from handling cases with actual or potential conflict of interest; or to take other actions as directed by the Chief Executive'. The Chief Executive's Office manages the declaration of investments made by these officials.

colleague of his or her ministers and thus he or she may not be eager to enforce these rules rigorously.

The bureaucracy in the United Kingdom is regulated by the Civil Service Code which is enforced by the Civil Service Commission. The Civil Service Commission is comparable to the OGE in the United States in many ways. Both agencies are independent nonpublic regulators which have the overall responsibilities in ethics regulation in the executive branch of their governments at the national level. Further, both agencies largely focus on monitoring and guiding ethics policies at the government department/agency level though they also oversee individual officials. The OGE regularly offers training programmes to the Designated Agency Ethics Officials (DAEOs) in all government departments and agencies. The Civil Service Commission also meets Link Commissioners in the main government departments and large agencies regularly help these departments to promote the Civil Service Code. It also conducts regular audits of departments to identify the vulnerability of a department to ethical risk.[16] Both regulators delegate each agency and give each department the power to make department-tailored ethics standards.

The OGE in the United States and the Civil Service Commission in the United Kingdom vary in two aspects. First, the former is a special government ethics regulator solely responsible for government ethics regulation, whereas the latter has two primary functions: ensuring merit-based civil service recruitment and enforcing the Civil Service Code.[17] Further, the OGE is not an investigatory body for specific violations, whereas the Civil Service Commission can consider and investigate specific offences. It should be noted that the Civil Service Commission only consider appeals brought to it by civil servants.[18] If a complaint is raised about the civil servants' violation of the Civil Servants Code by a member of the public, this should in most cases be done through the Parliamentary and Health Services Ombudsman.[19]

Similar to the United Kingdom, in Hong Kong the bureaucracy is regulated by the Civil Service Code which is enforced by the Civil Service Bureau (CSB). Like the Civil Service Commission in the United Kingdom, the CSB is responsible for the overall management of the civil service, and is not solely focused on government ethics. The Public

---

[16] Civil Service Commission, 'Civil Service Commission annual report and accounts 2011–12'.
[17] Ibid.   [18] Ibid.   [19] Ibid.

Service Commission also plays an advisory role in issues regarding the appointment, promotion, and discipline of senior officials in the civil service. In addition to deliberating on the appropriate level of punishment in each case submitted to it for advice, the Commission also oversees the operation of the disciplinary mechanism.[20]

In addition to managing the disciplinary proceedings for the civil service, the CSB also works with departments and agencies to carry out educational activities aiming to foster an integrity culture in the civil service.[21] These programmes mainly include induction, training, and seminars. It also issues policies and guidance to officials to enhance understanding and awareness of integrity standards. However, generally speaking, compared with the other two jurisdictions, especially the OGE in the United States, the CSB in Hong Kong is less active in regulating departments and agencies in a systematic and focused approach. The Civil Service Commission in the United Kingdom has programmes such as auditing departments to regularly and systematically evaluate the level of risks of working practice vulnerable to misconduct. The US OGE has mandatory ethics training programmes and special programmes to review financial disclosure reports. The CSB in Hong Kong's interaction with the departments and bureaus mainly include visiting departments and agencies officials and issuing guidance.

Each government agency/department itself is a government ethics regulator in all the three jurisdictions. Agencies and departments are granted the power by their respective primary government ethics regulators to make individual agency ethics standards. Further, the primary regulators work closely with agency/department ethics officials. In the United States the actual day-to-day management of the ethics programmes in each government agency or department is vested to the DAEO.[22] The OGE regularly reviews agency ethics programmes and

---

[20] Public Service Commission, 'Annual report 2011', available at www.psc.gov.hk/english/ann_rep/files/11rep.pdf (last visited on 13 February 2012).

[21] Civil Service Bureau, 'Legislative council panel on public service: promotion of integrity in the civil service', 2005, available at www.csb.gov.hk/english/admin/conduct/files/paper050412e_2.pdf (last visited on 12 June 2013).

[22] § 2638.203 and § 2638.202, 5 C.F.R. Part 2638 –Office of Government Ethics and Executive Agency Ethics Program Responsibilities. Each US federal government agency or department head must appoint a qualified individual as the DAEO in his or her agency or department and 'an individual to serve in an acting capacity in the absence of the primary designated agency ethics official (alternate agency ethics official)'. DAEOs coordinate and manage the agency's ethics programmes and maintain a close liaison with the OGE in developing and maintaining its agency's ethics programmes.

provides counselling, advice, and training programmes to the DAEOs.[23] In the sense that the DAEOs work under, and follow in practice, the OGE guidance, DAEOs can be seen as the extension of the enforcement commitment of the OGE. In the United Kingdom the Civil Service Commission also meets Link Commissioners in main government departments and large agencies regularly help these departments to promote the Civil Service Code. It also conducts regular audits of departments to identify the vulnerability of a department to ethical risk.[24] Moreover, agencies/departments have the power to impose disciplinary sanctions. In Hong Kong, each government department and agency is responsible for conduct of officials in its own agency and can issue verbal or written warnings directly for minor misconduct without recourse to formal proceedings.[25] In the United States and the United Kingdom, the agency concerned can also initiate disciplinary or corrective actions.[26]

In addition to the above government ethics regulators, other agencies also play certain roles in regulating government ethics. For example, in the United States the General Accounting Office can audit federal programmes; the Federal Elections Commission is responsible for regulating public financing; the Office of Personnel Management is in charge of general personnel management; the General Services Administration is responsible for proper use of government property and vehicles; and the Office of Special Counsel is responsible for regulating political activities of the employees. Both in the United Kingdom and Hong Kong the ombudsman considers complaints related to government ethics in the government. However, these agencies do not primarily focus on the four key areas of government ethics: conflicts of interest, appearance of corruption, financial disclosure, and outside employment/activities. Their responsibilities are related to but go far beyond government ethics. For example,

---

[23] The United States Office of Government Office, 'OGE conference', available at www.oge.gov/Education/National-Government-Ethics-Conference/OGE-Conference/ (last visited on 28 December 2012). For example, since 1991 the OGE has been holding an annual conference for DAEOs which serves to provide guidance to DAEOs on the application of ethics laws and regulations and to discuss common ethics issues in the federal executive branch.

[24] Civil Service Commission, 'Civil Service Commission annual report and accounts 2011–12'.

[25] Civil Service Bureau, 'Updated overview of civil service conduct and discipline', 2007, available at www.csb.gov.hk/english/info/files/panel070618e.pdf (last visited on 12 June 2013).

[26] § 2635.106 (b), 5 C.F.R. Part 2635 – Standards of Ethical Conduct for Employees of the Executive Branch.

the ombudsman, though it considers government ethics–related complaints, mainly considers complaints in which individuals have been treated unfairly or have received poor public service.[27] Issues such as financial disclosure, outside employment activities, and conflicts of interest of the civil servants do not lie in the remit of the ombudsman. In order to have a clear research boundary, this research concerns the entities which primarily regulate one or more of the four key categories of government ethics. Thus, in the book some times when the term 'government ethics' is mentioned, it actually means the four key categories of government ethics.

In all the three jurisdictions, the judiciary systems have their own separate ethics regulatory agencies. In the United States and the United Kingdom, ethics matters in the judicial systems are regulated by the Judicial Conference of the United States and the Office for Judicial Complaints, respectively.[28] In Hong Kong, the ethics of judges is managed by the Chief Justice and the Court Leader of the particular Court where the concerned judge is working.[29] There is no special committee or similar entities responsible for judicial ethics; this is, perhaps, because of the small number of judiciary in Hong Kong.[30]

The legislative systems in the three jurisdictions also have their own separate ethics regulatory agencies. The US federal legislative system consists of two houses: the House of Representatives (the lower house) and the Senate (the upper house). Each of the houses has its own ethics regulator.[31] The United Kingdom's legislative system is very similar to

---

[27] Parliamentary and Health Services Ombudsman, 'The Ombudsman', available at www.ombudsman.org.uk/about-us/who-we-are/the-ombudsman (last visited on 4 January 2013).

[28] However, it should be pointed out that the functions of the Judicial Conference are considerably broader than simply ethics regulation. The Conference is designed to make policy regarding the management of the US courts. The Office for Judicial Complaints was established in 2006 as an associated office of the Ministry of Justice.

[29] Paragraph 5, Guide to Judicial Conduct (Hong Kong); and The Hong Kong Judiciary, 'Complaints against a Judge's conduct', 3rd edition, 2010, available at www.judiciary.gov.hk/en/crt_services/pphlt/pdf/complaintsjjoleaflet.pdf (last visited on 24 April 2013).

[30] The Hong Kong Judiciary, 'List of judges and judicial officers (position as at 7 January, 2013)', available at www.judiciary.gov.hk/en/organization/judges.htm#HC (last visited on 24 April 2013). As of 2013, the number of judges in the three levels of courts, various tribunals, and magistrates' courts was 182, which is considerably smaller compared to the size of the executive branch.

[31] The Committee on Standards of Conduct in the House of Representatives is responsible for the ethics of its representatives and its counterpart in the Senate is the Select Committee on Ethics.

that in the United States.[32] In Hong Kong, ethics of the legislature, the Legislative Council, is overseen by a seven-member committee, the Committee on Members' Interests, which is elected by the members of the Legislative Council.[33]

4.2.2   Legal authorities and responsibilities

Each of the three jurisdictions has an enforcement system for officials' ethics and several agencies may be involved in enforcement in the executive branch alone. In this section, the focus is primarily on the formal authorities and responsibilities of the key enforcement agencies for the executive branch. The reason is that the agencies for the executive branch are the most systematic mainly because that branch is larger and most vulnerable to misconduct. These agencies are the US OGE, the UK Civil Service Commission, and the Hong Kong CSB.

Enforcement agencies have to 'operate under the confines of the ethics statutes'.[34] Statutes usually delegate immense enforcement powers and authorities, many times including quasi-lawmaking powers and quasi-adjudication powers, to regulatory agencies.[35] Sometimes, an enforcement agency is given legal standing by a law. For example, in the United States, the OGE was created by the Ethics in Government Act in 1978. It is apparent that these powers (enforcement powers, quasi-lawmaking powers and quasi-adjudication powers) are crucial to an enforcement agency as these powers are the basis of the agency's regulatory activities.

A variety of powers are absolutely necessary for an agency to be effective. The first type is investigatory powers. Even for compliance-oriented enforcement agencies, having the legal power to receive and consider third-party complaints and the power to initiate investigations

---

[32] Members in the House of Lords are overseen by a committee of peers with respect to ethics issues such as register of on-going employment and their consultancy services. Ethics allegations of MPs in the House of Commons are heard and investigated by a Parliamentary Commissioner for Standards. Investigation findings of the Commissioner will be reported to a Select Committee that will impose a sanction if the allegation is proved.

[33] Legislative Council, 'Annual report 2011–2012', p. 39, available at www.legco.gov.hk/general/english/sec/reports/a_1112.pdf (last visited on 15 September 2013).

[34] Robert W. Smith, 'Enforcement or ethical capacity'.

[35] Gary C. Bryner, 'Trends in social regulation', in David H. Rosenbloom and Richard D. Schwartz (eds), *Handbook of Regulation and Administrative Law* (New York, Basel, and Hong Kong: Marcel Dekker, 1994), pp. 73–90.

is crucial.[36] During an investigation, empirical research through interviews by Smith revealed that agencies need the power to issue subpoenas and the ability to require assistance from other government departments in investigations.[37] An agency must also be vested the power to impose either positive or negative sanctions on the regulatees. Although compliance enforcement agencies tend not to use formal sanctions, being able to use these sanctions is a very useful bargaining chip.

Though the OGE, in balance, is not an investigatory entity, it does have investigation powers. It can investigate officials' compliance with requirements and standards relating to financial disclosure.[38] Further, it can also investigate 'possible violations of any rule, regulation, or Executive Order relating' to conflicts of interest or standards of conduct applicable to individual executive branch officials.[39] If the OGE director suspects an official is violating, or has violated, any conflicts of interest rule or standards of conduct, it can recommend the head of the agency of that official to investigate the violation.[40] This recommendation power is not soft but in practice is usually followed up by the agency head because the director of the OGE can notify the president if he or she finds the agency head has not conducted an investigation as recommended.[41] The UK Civil Service Commission also shares investigation powers.[42] In Hong Kong, minor offences are investigated by the suspected violator's department or bureau; repeated minor offences or more serious misconduct will trigger formal disciplinary action where the department or bureau may carry out a preliminary investigation and then transfer the case 'to the Secretariat on Civil Service Discipline ('SCSD') under the Civil Service Bureau for consideration of formal disciplinary action'.[43]

The second type is compliance monitoring powers which are enforced usually through conducting random audits,[44] requiring register of conflicted interests and gifts, collecting and reviewing financial disclosure

---

[36] Robert M. Rhodes, 'Enforcement of legislative ethics: conflict within the conflict of interest laws', *Harvard Journal on Legislation*, 10, 3 (1973), pp. 373–406; Herrmann, 'Empowering governmental ethics agencies'.

[37] Smith, 'Enforcement or ethical capacity'.

[38] (b) (3), §402, Ethics in Government Act of 1978.   [39] Ibid., (f)(2)(B)(i), §402.

[40] Ibid., (f)(2)(A)(ii), §402.   [41] Ibid.

[42] 9 (5) and (6), Constitution Reform and Governance Act 2010.

[43] Civil Service Bureau, 'Legislative council panel on public service: disciplinary mechanism and related procedures for disciplined services and civil grades', 2009, available at www.csb.gov.hk/english/info/files/20090420_panel_discipline_eng.pdf (last visited on 20 June 2013).

[44] Herrmann, 'Empowering governmental ethics'.

forms, and so forth. These powers can allow enforcement agencies to monitor compliance in a proactive and systematic manner. These powers can be divided into two subgroups: one is the power to monitor compliance at the agency/department level and the other is at the individual official level. In the United States, the OGE enjoys powers at both levels. At the agency level, the OGE can monitor compliance with financial disclosure requirements by agency officials who are responsible for receiving and reviewing financial statements.[45] The OGE can also require each executive agency/department to submit to it an annual report about the agency's ethics programme.[46] At the individual official level, the OGE can monitor compliance with financial disclosure requirements by officers and employees of the executive branch[47] and conduct a review of financial statements.[48] The UK Civil Service Commission does not monitor individual compliance with government ethics standards though it does consider specific individual allegations. At the agency level, it can work with departments to help them with their promotion of the Code.[49] It usually conducts audits concerning the Civil Service Code.[50] But these measures are not comparable to the OGE's power to review financial statements. The latter is more systematic and more focused. Further, it is also a responsibility of the OGE, not only its power, to review these financial statements to monitor compliance. In Hong Kong, relevant laws and regulations do not explicitly vest monitoring compliance powers to the CSB at both levels. However, it has the overall responsibility to manage civil servants including their ethics and conduct. Thus, in practice it does have the power to take necessary measures to check compliance with ethics standards by individual civil servants and the various departments/bureaus. For example, in 2005 alone, the CSB visited thirty departments under the Civil Service Integrity Entrenchment Programme in order to promote and entrench integrity culture in the civil service.[51]

The third type is quasi-lawmaking powers. Many agencies have the power to make binding rules or codes. The government ethics regulators in the three jurisdictions all have such powers. In the United States, the

---

[45] (b) (3), § 402, Ethics In Government Act of 1978.   [46] Ibid., (e) (1), § 402.

[47] Ibid., (b) (3), § 402.   [48] Ibid.,(b) (4), § 402.

[49] Civil Service Commission, 'What we do', available at http://civilservicecommission .independent.gov.uk/about-us/what-we-do/ (last visited on 20 January 2013).

[50] Civil Service Commission, 'annual report and accounts 2011–2012'.

[51] Civil Service Bureau, 'Legislative Council panel on public service: promotion of integrity in the civil service', 2005, available at www.csb.gov.hk/english/admin/conduct/files/ paper050412e_2.pdf (last visited on 12 June 2013).

OGE has the power to develop rules and regulations about conflicts of interest and ethics in the executive branch.[52] It must also make sure that 'each executive agency has written procedures' regarding 'how the agency is to collect, review, evaluate, and, if applicable, make publicly available, financial disclosure statements filed by any of its officers or employees'.[53] Similar to the United States, the Hong Kong CSB can issue and revise regulations, rules, and guidelines governing, among other subjects, the 'avoidance of conflicts of interest, acceptance of advantages and entertainment, declaration of private investments', and outside work during service and for a specified period after leaving the civil service.[54] Compared with the United States and Hong Kong, the Civil Service Commission in the United Kingdom does not enjoy formal legal authority to issue regulations. In the United Kingdom, regulations regarding the civil service are made by the minister for the Civil Service, who is the prime minister since the creation of the ministry, and the Civil Service Code is published by the Ministry for Civil Service.[55] In practice, the Civil Service Commission usually issues guidance on the enforcement of the Code.

Further, it is also important for agencies to write advisory opinions.[56] These opinions also play an important role in guiding the regulatees' behaviour. They can serve as case law.[57] This is a similar power to regulations making when the regulator issues opinions regarding matters of general applicability. The regulator can also issue opinions on matters for the parties concerned and this function cannot be carried out by the regulation making power. Advisory opinions can also provide the regulator with the opportunity to respond to the ever-changing behaviour trend of officials in a fast and frequent manner. The OGE in the United States has responsibility to establish 'a formal advisory opinion service whereby advisory opinions are rendered on matters of general applicability or on important matters of first impression after, to the extent practicable, providing interested parties with an opportunity to transmit written comments with respect to the request for such advisory opinion, and whereby such advisory opinions are compiled, published, and made available to agency ethics counsellors and the public'.[58] In contrast, its

[52] (b) (1), § 402, Ethics In Government Act Of 1978.   [53] Ibid., (d) (1), § 402.
[54] 4.1, Civil Service Code.
[55] 5, Civil Service Code; and 3 (1) and 5 (1), Chapter 1, Part 1, Constitutional Reform and Governance Act 2010.
[56] Herrmann, 'Empowering governmental ethics agencies'.
[57] Smith, 'Enforcement or ethical capacity'.
[58] (b) (8), § 402, Ethics In Government Act of 1978.

UK and Hong Kong counterpart regulators do not have the responsibility to issue advisory opinions.

Finally, government ethics may involve different government bodies, so collaboration and sharing of information between these departments is important. Thus, it is important to vest the primary government ethics regulatory agency the role in making overall enforcement policies and coordinating or collaborating different agencies which play a role in the enforcement. Otherwise the regulatory policies may lack coherence. In the United States, the OGE is responsible for providing 'overall direction of executive branch policies related to conflicts of interest'.[59] In the United Kingdom and Hong Kong, relevant laws and regulations do not clearly vest the Civil Service Commission and the CSB the function to play an overall directive role regarding government ethics policies. However, based on their broad civil service management power, they can play such a role in practice. For example, both regulators have meetings on ethics policies regularly with ethics officials in each government agency and department.[60]

4.2.3   Enforcement approaches/styles

According to Lesley K. McAllister, 'Enforcement style describes how regulators interact with regulated entities as they seek to gain compliance with the law'.[61] Different terms – approach, method, style, and strategy – have been adopted as synonyms to conceptualize enforcement actions of enforcement officials and enforcement agency–level decisions.[62] The concept of enforcement style is very useful in examining regulatory enforcement differences and it has been a major theme for academic research in Western literature for more than two decades; however, the concept has not received wide attention in regulatory studies of developing countries[63]: 'Enforcement style has most often been conceived as a spectrum between the legalistic style and the conciliatory style'.[64]

---

[59] Ibid., (a), § 402.

[60] Civil Service Commission, 'Annual report and accounts 2011–12', especially p. 12; Civil Service Bureau, 'Update on integrity enhancement initiatives for civil servants', especially p. 3, available at www.csb.gov.hk/english/info/files/20100222_panel_integrity_eng.pdf (last visited on 15 September 2013).

[61] Lesley K. McAllister, 'Dimensions of enforcement style: factoring in regulatory autonomy and capacity', Law & Policy, 32, 1 (January 2010), pp. 61–78, p. 62.

[62] Peter J. May and Soren Winter, 'Reconsidering styles of regulatory enforcement: patterns in Danish agro-environmental inspection', Law & Policy, 22, 2 (April 2000), pp. 143–173.

[63] McAllister, 'Dimensions of enforcement style', pp. 61–78.   [64] Ibid., p. 62.

The legalistic style is largely relied on coercion and punishment to deter law violators and potential violators. Enforcement agencies employing compliance strategies are concerned with securing conformity to rules or standards and they tend to think of rule-breaking as a problem.[65] They prefer to use techniques such as education, advice, persuasion, or negotiation. These two contrasting enforcement strategies have been given different names, such as persuasion versus deterrence;[66] compliance versus sanctioning;[67] and the penalty model versus the compliance model.[68] Studies of enforcement style are helpful in understanding the relationship between these styles and their effectiveness.[69]

It appears that compliance strategy is the primary system of enforcement in regulatory control.[70] Though regulatory enforcement covers a very broad area (such as consumer protection, housing, industrial health and safety, pollution, conservation, and the financial industry), enforcement agencies from different areas all display a clear preference for compliance style enforcement.[71] It is found that regulatory enforcement officials seldom perceive themselves as 'policemen' but as seeking compliance.[72] Empirical research in a variety of regulatory enforcement areas, such as occupational safety and health administration enforcement[73] and environmental regulation,[74] has shown that compliance-oriented enforcement style is more effective than deterrence-based strategies in improving compliance state. The improved compliance may be

---

[65] Keith Hawkins, 'Bargain and bluff: compliance strategy and deterrence in the enforcement of regulation', *Law & Policy Quarterly*, 5, 1 (January 1983), pp. 35–73.

[66] William T. Gormley, Jr., 'Regulatory enforcement: accommodation and conflict in four states', *Public Administration Review*, 57, 4, pp. 285–293.

[67] Hawkins, 'Bargain and bluff', pp. 35–73.

[68] Albert J. Reiss and Albert D. Biderman, *Data Sources on White-Collar Law-breaking* (Washington, DC: National Institute of Justice, 1981).

[69] Robert A. Kagan, 'Regulatory enforcement', in D. H. Rosenbloom and R. D. Schwartz (eds.), *Handbook of Regulations and Administrative Law* (New York: Marcel Dekker, 1994), pp. 383–422.

[70] Hawkins, 'Bargain and bluff', pp. 35–73.   [71] Ibid.

[72] W.G. Carson, 'Some sociological aspects of strict liability and the enforcement of the factory legislation', *The Modern Law Review*, 33, 4 (1970), pp. 396–412; A. J. Reiss, 'Selecting strategies of social control over organizational life', in K. Hawkins and J. Thomas (eds), *Enforcing Regulations* (The Hague: Kluwer-Nijhoff, 1984).

[73] John T. Scholz, 'Cooperative regulatory enforcement and the politics of administrative effectiveness', *American Political Science Review*, 85, 1 (1991), pp. 115–136; Steven Kelman, *Regulating America, Regulating Sweden: A Comparative Study of Occupational Safety and Health Policy* (Cambridge, MA: MIT Press, 1981).

[74] Hawkins, 'Bargain and bluff', pp. 35–73.

attributed to the following reasons. While deterrence-enforcement strategies may sometimes be appropriate for dealing with a few 'bad apples',
these strategies in a very large number of cases create 'resistance and
resentment' that will divert the energy of both regulatory agencies and
the regulated into 'dispiriting legal routines and conflicts'.[75] On the other
hand, a compliance strategy can strengthen trust between the regulators
and the regulated, and thus, the regulatee is more likely to commu-
nicate with the regulators about his compliance difficulties and seek
advice or help from the regulator.[76] Unlike the deterrence enforcer,
the compliance-oriented enforcer will usually not impose sanctions for
minor deviations if the regulatee is willing to correct his misbehaviour.

In addition to regulatory enforcement in general, there is also evidence
that in government ethics regulation, the compliance-oriented enforcement style has been widely adopted by government ethics agencies. In his
empirical research on government ethics commissions in New York and
Connecticut, Smith found, through interviewing government ethics
administrators, that staff of these government ethics enforcement agencies described their 'enforcement of ethics as somehow loftier than the
police' who strive to identify 'bad apples' and impose punishment on
them; all of the staff interviewed 'placed themselves on the end of the
[police-consultants] continuum as consultants'.[77]

Though there is clear evidence that compliance-oriented enforcement
practices are widely used in government ethics enforcement, enforcement
styles of government ethics regulation have not been examined in a
systematic way compared with regulation in other areas such as environmental regulation, occupational health and safety, and childcare centre
regulation. Put simply, there is a research gap in studies on government
ethics enforcement. Furthermore, the majority of research on enforcement of government ethics is focused on the United States. This kind of
research is almost absent in China.[78] Thus it is worthwhile to explore the
enforcement style of government ethics against the framework of key
features of compliance-oriented enforcement – especially for China, as
'the concept [of enforcement style] has not been widely employed in the

---

[75] Eugene Bardach and Robert A. Kagan, *Going by the Book: the Problem of Regulatory Unreasonableness* (Philadelphia, PA: Temple University Press, 1982), p. 119.
[76] Hawkins, 'Bargain and bluff.'   [77] Smith, 'Enforcement or ethical capacity', p. 288.
[78] Robert W. Smith, 'A comparison of the ethics infrastructure in China and the United States: should public servants be executed for breaches of ethics—or is a $150 fine enough?' *Public Integrity*, 6, 4 (2004), pp. 299–318.

study of regulatory behaviour in developing countries'.[79] The remaining part of Section 4.2.3 will identify the key features of compliance-oriented regulatory enforcement and examine the enforcement styles of government ethics in the United States, the United Kingdom, and Hong Kong against these features.

Nine features of compliance-oriented enforcement style, in contrast to deterrence enforcement styles, can be summarized as shown in Table 4.1 below.[80] The summary of these nine features are mainly based on Reiss' research on 'Selecting strategies of social control over organizational life'[81] and Hawkins' work on 'Bargain and bluff: compliance strategy and deterrence in the enforcement of regulation'.[82] Though almost three decades have passed since the publication of their research, the basic model of compliance versus deterrence enforcement is now still adopted to examine enforcement styles in different regulation areas. For example, Stewart, in 2001, used this framework to examine the US environment regulation.[83] May and Wood, in 2003, adopted a similar thinking framework in researching street-level inspectors' enforcement styles in safety of building regulation.[84] Although they introduced certain new indicators of enforcement styles (such as asking the regulatees to decide whether the inspectors are less knowledgeable or more knowledgeable), most indicators they adopted to conceptualize enforcement styles (such as 'less trustworthy versus more trustworthy', 'less helpful versus more helpful', 'hard to work with versus easy to work with', 'less threatening versus more threatening', 'less rigid versus more rigid', etc.) are the same or similar to the features summarized in Table 4.1.[85]

First, the compliance-enforcement style can be distinguished from deterrence-enforcement styles in the means of prevention adopted.

---

[79] McAllister, 'Dimensions of enforcement style', p. 61.

[80] It should be stressed that some of the features such as the fifth and the eighth are identified in a sub-area of regulation, environmental regulation; hence, the features shall be viewed as a thinking framework rather than definite conclusions.

[81] Albert J. Reiss, Jr, 'Selecting strategies of social control over organizational life', in Keith Hawkins and John M. Thomas (eds.), *Enforcing Regulation* (Boston, The Hague, Dordrecht, and Lancaster: Kluwer-Nijhoff Publishing, 1984) pp. 23–26.

[82] Hawkins, 'Bargain and bluff'.

[83] Richard B. Stewart, 'A new generation of environmental regulation?' *Capital University Law Review*, 29, 1 (2001), pp. 21–182.

[84] Peter J. May and Robert S. Wood, 'At the regulatory front lines: inspectors' enforcement styles and regulatory compliance', *Journal of Public Administration Research and Theory*, 13, 2 (2003), pp. 117–139.

[85] Ibid., especially p. 126.

Table 4.1 *Key features of compliance enforcement as contrasted with deterrence enforcement.*

	Compliance Enforcement	Deterrence Enforcement
Means of prevention	Premonitory: fostering conditions that induce conformity	Postmonitory: apprehending violators and penalizing them to prevent future violations
The role of penalties	Penalties as threats to induce compliance and thus when compliance is demonstrated sanction will usually be suspended or withdrawn	Penalties are integral to a deterrence system
	Manipulate rewards such as money grants, subsidies, privileges, licensing, and limited liability	Manipulate punishments
When facing potential violation	Prevent its occurrence	Wait for the occurrence of the violation so that violators can be caught and punished
When actual violation identified	Punishments (threats to impose penalties; Threats to withdraw, or actual withdraw, of rewards) are more directly linked to compliance and the prevention of noncompliance	Punishment is more generic in nature and less likely to be connected to offenders' conduct
Relationship between enforcement agency and the regulated parties	A continuing relationship	One-off punishment
Organization for the mobilization of law	Proactive mobilization: to induce conformity either by providing incentives or by using preventive means	Reactive mobilization: although deterrence system also contains reactive mobilization forms, on balance it is largely reactive

Table 4.1 (*cont.*)

	Compliance Enforcement	Deterrence Enforcement
The way of recognizing violations	Creates technic standards to monitor compliance and noncompliance; core offences violating these standards are thus largely technical	Core violations are immediately harmful
Working basis	Exchange relationship: the regulated party can offer ultimate compliance, cooperation and compliance cost in return for the enforcement agency's forbearance and free advice on compliance	General deterrence and specific deterrence effect
The way of interpreting rules	Flexible in interpreting the rules in dealing with the regulated parties	Relatively rule bound

Source: The summary of these nine features are mainly based on: Albert J. Reiss, Jr., 'Selecting strategies of social control over organizational life', in Keith Hawkins and John M. Thomas (eds), *Enforcing Regulation* (Boston, The Hague, Dordrecht, and Lancaster: Kluwer-Nijhoff Publishing, 1984) pp. 23–26; and Keith Hawkins, 'Bargain and bluff: compliance strategy and deterrence in the enforcement of regulation', *Law & Policy Quarterly*, 5, 1 (January 1983), pp. 35–73.

Both aim to prevent violations, but they adopt different means: compliance enforcement tends to foster conditions that encourage obedience, thus it is, borrowing Reiss's words, 'premonitory'; deterrence enforcement is 'postmonitory' in the sense that it prevents violations through its general and specific deterrence effect (detecting and punishing violators for past misconduct).[86]

Each of the three selected jurisdictions adopts both the premonitory (fostering conditions that induce conformity) and the postmonitory (apprehending and penalizing violators) means in preventing ethics

---

[86] Reiss, Jr, 'Selecting strategies of social control over organizational life'.

violations. For the US OGE, most of its programmes and commitments are dedicated to creating a compliance-inducing condition. For example, it manages a financial disclosure programme which covers both current and certain prospective employees in the federal government in order to prevent conflicts of interest.[87] It offers many training programmes to agency ethics officials. It also frequently issues advisory opinions either on its own initiative or in response to government officials' requirements. This can help to shape a system which induces compliance to ethics rules and standards. Though it is vested with investigatory powers in certain circumstances, the OGE seldom investigates specific ethics violations of individual officials. Thus, the OGE mainly adopts a premonitory means, rather than postmonitory means, in preventing violations.

In both the United Kingdom and Hong Kong, government ethics regulators rely more heavily on preventing violations through means of apprehending and disciplining offenders than the OGE. In addressing government ethics, though the UK Civil Service Commission does use investigation as an important means to prevent violations of its code of ethics, it actually only processes a very small number of cases each year. It investigated twenty-five cases in the year 2009–2010, twenty-five cases in the year 2010–2011, and sixteen cases in the year 2011–2012.[88] Further, it only considers complaints from civil servants. Nor does it conduct investigation on its own initiative. On the other hand, it has committed much energy to premonitory means. It conducts audits of departments regularly and provides detailed department-tailored responses to these departments regarding potential risks and possible improvement recommendations.[89] It also conducts a Civil Service Staff Survey to examine staff's awareness of the Civil Service Code. Moreover, it holds meetings to raise and discuss ethics issues that may challenge civil servants.[90]

---

[87] The United States Office of Government Ethics, 'Financial disclosure', available at www.oge.gov/Financial-Disclosure/Financial-Disclosure/ (last visited on 23 January 2013).

[88] Civil Service Commission, 'Annual report and accounts 2010–2011', available at http://civilservicecommission.independent.gov.uk/wp-content/uploads/2012/04/Annual-Report-10-11.pdf; and Civil Service Commission, 'Annual report and accounts 2011–2012', available at http://civilservicecommission.independent.gov.uk/wp-content/uploads/2012/07/CSC-Annual-Report-2011-12.pdf (last visited on 23 January 2013).

[89] Civil Service Commission, 'Annual Report and Accounts 2011–2012', available at http://civilservicecommission.independent.gov.uk/wp-content/uploads/2012/07/CSC-Annual-Report-2011-12.pdf (last visited on 23 January 2013).

[90] Ibid.

All these means can prevent ethics violations through fostering a condition which induces compliance. Thus, in balance, the Civil Service Commission in the United Kingdom relies more on premonitory means than on postmonitory means in preventing ethics violations.

Postmonitory prevention through apprehending and penalizing violators in Hong Kong plays a more important role than that in the United States and the United Kingdom in preventing government ethics violations. The CSB in Hong Kong processed more than 300 disciplinary cases per year in the civil service during 2010 and 2012 (minor cases imposed summary disciplinary actions investigated by bureaus/departments are not included in the above number).[91] However, it is still difficult to decide whether postmonitory or premonitory means plays a more important role in preventing ethics violation as the CSB also adopts a serial of means to foster conformity-inducing conditions. For example, it conducts integrity checks for almost every civil servant before they take up government employment. It also visits and meets department/ agency ethics management officials to discuss new challenges and issues in ethics regulation.

Second, the roles of penalties are different in the two enforcement styles. Compliance enforcement agencies demonstrate an unwillingness to apply formal sanctions such as prosecution.[92] However, that does not mean sanctions are not important for compliance enforcement. Sanctions still play an important role as the ultimate response if all other bargaining measures fail to bring the violators into compliance.[93] Thus, when compliance is demonstrated, sanctions will usually be suspended or withdrawn.[94] Although they tend to avoid actual punishment, the threat of legal sanctions, 'bluff' in Hawkins' words, is a frequently used and very useful tactic where uncooperative or potentially uncooperative regulatees are concerned even if the enforcement official has no intention to use it.[95] Bluffs are mainly concerned with legal sanctions available or the risk of prosecution.[96] In contrast, penalties are integral to deterrence enforcement style. Furthermore, another difference regarding punishment is that compliance enforcement agencies principally employ positive sanctions such as money grants, subsidies, and privileges

---

[91] Civil Service Bureau, 'Disciplinary cases in the civil service', available at www.csb.gov.hk/ english/stat/annually/553.html (last visited on 20 January 2013).
[92] Hawkins, 'Bargain and bluff.'   [93] Ibid.
[94] Reiss, Jr, 'Selecting strategies of social control over organizational life'.
[95] Hawkins, 'Bargain and bluff.'   [96] Ibid.

(e.g. license and limited liability) whereas deterrence enforcement system principally resorts to penalties.[97]

The regulators in the three countries mainly use disciplinary penalties to improve compliance though they do not heavily rely on punishments compared with criminal enforcers. Furthermore, none of the three regulators manipulate positive sanctions to induce ethics compliance in their respective governments.

Perhaps the reason is that government department/agencies are in general less sensitive to positive sanctions such as rewards, money grants, and privilege than private businesses. Officials as individuals in government departments will not benefit directly from these rewards, whereas the owners of private businesses can benefit from these rewards. Further, license renewal as a reward in private business is common, whereas there is no identical reward for government departments. However, that does not mean positive sanctions are not applicable to government ethics regulation. A government ethics regulator may, for example, exempt mandatory ethics training programmes offered by the regulator if this agency's own training programmes are effective. The regulator can conduct an annual audit and review to decide whether a department/agency satisfies the requirements or not. It can issue the department/agency a certificate if it is satisfied with this agency/department's training programmes. But again the inducement is not as strong as license-like reward for private businesses.

Third, a compliance-enforcement system differs from the deterrence-enforcement style in their response when facing potential violations.[98] Facing a potential violation, compliance enforcement agencies will attempt to prevent the occurrence of the violation. In contrast, deterrence enforcement agencies will wait for the occurrence of the violation so that it can catch and punish the violators or step in immediately to punish an inchoate violation. Thus, the two different enforcement styles differ in intervention time. Compliance enforcement tends to intervene when risk is identified and the deterrence system generally intervenes when harm has been caused or is imminent.[99]

Fourth, they also behave differently when actual violations are detected. As compliance enforcement agencies tend to manipulate positive sanctions, they usually threaten to, or actually withdraw, rewards.

[97] Reiss, Jr, 'Selecting strategies of social control over organizational life'.   [98] Ibid.
[99] Arie Freiberg, *The Tools of Regulation* (Leichhardt, NSW: The Federation Press, 2010), especially pp. 49–56.

The punishment thus is more directly linked to compliance and the prevention of noncompliance. Deterrence enforcement agencies tend to impose actual punishments such as fines and prosecution which are less likely to be directly connected to the behaviour change of the violators.

The third and the fourth features are how a regulatory agency responds to potential violations and actual violations. The three government ethics regulators all demonstrate a tendency to prevent the occurrence of the ethics violations rather than to punish the violators when facing potential and actual violations. The US OGE will recommend appropriate action to correct possible conflicts of interest or ethical problems if it identifies possible violations in reviewing financial statements submitted by executive branch officials.[100] For violations at the department level, it can also order corrective action. In the United Kingdom, the Civil Service Commission usually recommends policies, process, and practices to the department or agency concerned if its official's action conflicts or have the potential to conflict with stated ethics values and rules. For example, from 2009–2010, the Civil Service Commission considered a press release issued by a department for a book written by one of its staff as inappropriate based on the grounds that public resources have been misused for private interests.[101] Instead of imposing punishment, the commissioners made recommendations on the policy, process, and practice of drafting and approving press releases in these circumstances and the department has since acted upon these recommendations.[102] In Hong Kong, the CSB will usually impose appropriate disciplinary action against individual government ethics standard offenders; officials violating criminalized conflicts of interest rules will be processed by the ICAC. However, the CSB and the ICAC are also active in revising working procedures and practice which may be conducive to ethics violations and corruption.

Fifth, the relationship between enforcement agencies and the regulated parties are different for the two contrasting enforcement styles. Compliance enforcement agencies usually 'maintain a continuing relationship with the regulated' community.[103] In practice, regulatory agencies adopt various negotiating and bargaining tactics organized over a continuous

---

[100] (b) (4), § 402, Ethics in Government Act of 1978.
[101] Civil Service Commission, 'Annual report 2009-2010', available at http://civil servicecommission.independent.gov.uk/wp,content/uploads/2012/03/Annual%20Report %2009-10.pdf (last visited on 23 June 2013).
[102] Ibid.   [103] Hawkins, 'Bargain and bluff'.

period to secure and maintain compliance.[104] Deterrence enforcement agencies mainly perform one-off punishment in dealing with violators.

The three government ethics regulators all demonstrate a continuing relationship with government departments/bureaus through various means, such as educational programmes, training, visits, meetings, disclosure reports review, and department ethics audits.

Sixth, the two styles mobilize enforcement in a different manner. Compliance enforcement agencies are proactive in the organization of mobilization of enforcement in that they attempt to induce conformity either by providing incentives or by using preventive means. For the deterrence enforcement style, though the mobilization of enforcement uses both reactive and proactive forms, on the whole it is principally reactive.

Although each of the three jurisdictions is both proactive and reactive in enforcement, on balance enforcement is largely proactive. These proactive enforcement mobilization commitments take many forms, such as a review of financial statements; issuance of ethics guidance and advisory opinions; educational programmes; improvement of working procedure, policy, and practice in government departments and bureaus; audit of departments, regular meetings with department ethics officials to discuss newly emerging trends, and issues in government ethics, and so forth.

Seventh violations in the two enforcement styles are recognized differently.[105] A compliance system creates technical standards to monitor compliance and noncompliance; core offences violating these standards are thus largely technical and do not cause immediate harmful consequences. In contrast, in deterrence-oriented enforcement systems, core violations are immediately harmful.

Most ethics violations are technical offences rather than immediately harmful. For example, financial disclosure standards are a technique used to prevent conflicts of interest and other ethical problems; failure to disclose or incorrect disclosure, though violating ethics standards, will not lead to an immediate practice of corruption. Each of the three countries mainly uses this kind of technique standard to regulate government ethics.

Eighth, the two enforcement styles are based on different efficacy bases.[106] The compliance enforcement style works based on an exchange

---

[104] Ibid.   [105] Reiss, Jr, 'Selecting strategies of social control over organizational life'.
[106] Hawkins, 'Bargain and bluff'.

relationship between the regulator and the regulated parties. The regulated can offer cooperation and ultimate compliance and a willingness to share compliance costs. For enforcement officials, two important commodities can be offered to the regulated in return. One is free advice and information about compliance; the other is forbearance: 'Forbearance helps generate a sense of trust that enhances the agency's ability to . . . detect rule breakers'.[107] The regulated 'who trust their field officers are willing to alert them on the first sign of trouble and will not seek to play problems down'.[108]

Compared with regulated sectors such as businesses, banks, and factories in the private sector, it seems that government departments are less sensitive to compliance costs compared with their counterparts in the private sector. Thus, free compliance advice may not be very important for government departments as regulated parties. But the working basis of an exchange relationship can still partly be applied to government departments because the additional compliance cost may result in a budget shortage for its other functions. Though general deterrence and specific deterrence from apprehending and penalizing offenders are considered the working basis for deterrence-oriented enforcement, they are also the partial working basis for government ethics enforcement. Furthermore, government ethics regulators in the United States can recommend, or even force, the government department concerned to improve or revise its working procedure, policy, and practices which are vulnerable to corruption. This is a third source of the working basis of government ethics regulation.

Ninth, they also differ in their manner of interpreting rules. Compliance-oriented enforcement officials are quite flexible in interpreting rules in dealing with the regulated parties. Put in Hawkins's words, 'they will not enforce the law in the manner in which they are theoretically entitled to enforce the law'.[109] In contrast, deterrence enforcement agencies tend to be 'rule-bound' in interpreting rules and regulations.[110]

In dealing with the regulatees at the entity level (government departments/bureaus/agencies), all three government ethics regulators demonstrate a high level of flexibility and discretion in rule interpretation and application. Each of the three regulators has tailored guidance on policy, procedure, and working practice for each department. They also have great discretion in deciding whether a specific department has adequate

---

[107] Ibid., p. 49.   [108] Ibid., p. 50.   [109] Ibid.
[110] Reiss, Jr, 'Selecting strategies of social control over organizational life'.

and effective mechanisms in preventing ethics misconduct. At the individual official level, they demonstrate considerable differences in terms of the level of flexibility in rule interpretation. The CSB in Hong Kong is more rule-bound in its disciplinary actions. Since 2000, the disciplinary procedure has been streamlined, and a new independent secretariat has been created to centrally process formal disciplinary cases.[111] The Public Service Commission was set up to 'ensure that the principle of broad consistency in punishment is maintained' throughout the civil service.[112] The CSB processes more than 300 cases per year[113] and many of which may require a high degree of uniformity in rule application to maintain efficiency. Compared with Hong Kong, the Civil Service Commission only processes less than thirty ethics cases each year and the OGE in the United States seldom processes disciplinary cases involving individual government officials.

Though each of the three government ethics regulators has demonstrated some features of deterrence-oriented enforcement style, in balance, if the nine features are viewed as a whole, all can be placed close to the compliance-oriented enforcement style pole in the compliance-deterrence continuum.

The compliance versus deterrence enforcement styles discussed earlier are understood from a single dimension perspective. Based on that, multidimensional conceptualizations of enforcement styles have been developed to capture the dynamic of enforcement styles. For example, a two-dimensional analytical framework has been adopted by Braithwaite et al.,[114] May and Winter,[115] and Kagan[116] in their discussions of the regulatory style. McAllister further expanded the

---

[111] Civil Service Bureau, 'Information note for the LegCo panel on public service: disciplinary mechanism in the civil service – supplementary information', available at www.csb.gov.hk/english/admin/conduct/files/LC_Disciplinary_Mechanism__Eng_.pdf (last visited on 31 January 2013).

[112] Public Service Commission, 'Aims and function', available at www.psc.gov.hk/english/aboutus/aim_fun.html (last visited on 31 January 2013).

[113] Civil Service Bureau, 'Disciplinary cases in the civil service', available at www.csb.gov.hk/english/stat/annually/553.html (last visited on 31 January 2013).

[114] John Braithwaite, John Walker, and Peter Grabosky, 'An enforcement taxonomy of regulatory agencies', *Law & Policy*, 9, 3 (1987), pp. 23–51.

[115] Soren Winter and Peter May, 'Reconsidering styles of regulatory enforcement: patterns in Danish agro-environmental inspection', *Law & Policy*, 22, 2 (2000), pp. 143–173.

[116] Robert A. Kagan, 'Regulatory enforcement', in David H. Rosenbloom and Richard D. Schwartz (eds), *Handbook of Regulation and Administrative Law* (New York, Basel, and Hong Kong: Marcel Dekker, 1994), pp. 383–422.

ENFORCEMENT OF GOVERNMENT ETHICS RULES

two-dimensional framework of enforcement styles by introducing additional dimensions.[117]

Nine key features of compliance versus deterrence enforcement have been identified earlier. Indeed, each can be viewed as a separate dimension. If a framework of enforcement styles is based on all nine dimensions, the framework will be too complicated to be used. Thus, it is not the more, the better. Furthermore, while each of the nine features can be analyzed separately, some of these features may be correlated. Thus, it is not proper to regard each feature as an independent dimension. For example, a regulator that maintains a long-term continuing relationship with those regulated may tend to be more flexible in rule interpretation, whereas a regulator maintaining one-off punishment relationship with the regulated may tend to be more rule-bounded in interpreting the rules. Thus that means the two dimensions, relationship and the way of interpreting rules, may be correlated to a certain degree.

Moreover, while an expanded model of enforcement styles with more dimensions may shed more light on enforcement behaviour, the focus of this section is not on the conceptualization of enforcement styles itself in general. Instead, this section aims to extend knowledge of basic enforcement styles to a specific new enforcement area, government ethics enforcement, especially that found in China. Therefore in this chapter, the single dimensional compliance versus deterrence enforcement model has been adopted as a tool to organize thinking about enforcement styles.

4.2.4   Enforcement techniques: tactics, methods, and tools

This section is related to legal authorities as a specific enforcement technique which are both backed and restrained by formal legal authorities and responsibilities. Some enforcement authorities themselves are also enforcement tools. For example, investigation is both a broadly vested power and a common enforcement tool. However, they are different concepts. Enforcement agencies can create specific tactics to perform a legal power. For example, they can take different detection measures in investigation (either encourage third-party whistle-blowing or strengthen frontline investigatory resources). They can develop customer-tailored educational programmes to improve compliance. They can also generate social pressure through disclosing violator information. Enforcement

---

[117] McAllister, 'Dimensions of enforcement style'.

agencies may also leave some legal powers unused or underuse them because of constraints on enforcement resources or enforcement policies. This section will examine various techniques and tools adopted by regulators in government ethics enforcement in the three selected jurisdictions.

The regulation process comprises three continuous stages: setting standards, information gathering, and behaviour manipulation.[118] Setting standards have been discussed in Chapter 3; enforcement concerns the last two stages. Thus, enforcement tools and techniques can be examined and evaluated from two aspects: information-gathering tools and behaviour-modification tools.

Tools and tactics for compliance/noncompliance information gathering

An agency can rely on its own investigatory and monitoring methods to acquire needed information. Inspections and audits are typical tools widely adopted in compliance-oriented regulatory enforcement. By inspection, an agency visits the regulated organization, observes its operation, and checks whether its staff, equipment, and other resources on the books exist in reality and function well.[119] Audit, which originated in financial bookkeeping examination but has been increasingly used in other areas including government ethics auditing, involves examination of documentary records.[120] Thus, the two tools overlap to a certain extent and can be replaced by each other in the context of government ethics regulation. Audit and inspection can be performed in different manners and with a different scope. If some specific officials are suspected of behaving unethically, audit work is more focused on these people and on the suspected aspects. Regular or random and undisclosed audit/inspections can take the form of a compliance audit to monitor overall compliance (consistence with rules and standards) in some organizations. The agency can even audit the ethical climate and ethical system (e.g. review the willingness to seek advice when facing confusion and difficulties over ethics) of an organization.[121]

The US OGE's review of financial disclosure statements submitted by federal executive branch officials is a specific ethics audit method.

---

[118] Hood et al., *Regulation inside Government.*, especially p. 49.

[119] Hood et al., *Regulation inside Government.*

[120] Ibid.; and Donald J. Hardman, 'Audit of ethics in government', *International Journal of Government Auditing*, 23, 2 (April 1996), pp. 11–12.

[121] Smith, 'Enforcement or ethical capacity'.

The OGE manages both confidential and public financial disclosure pro-grammes. Although these financial disclosure reports, both public and confidential, are submitted to the ethics office in each government agency, 'agencies do forward reports of Presidential appointees confirmed by the Senate and certain other reports to OGE for additional review and certification'.[122] The OGE also has developed close guidelines for agency ethics officials regarding whether an official is required to submit such a report[123] and how to review these financial disclosure reports.[124]

In addition to financial disclosure audits, each government agency is also required to submit to the OGE a detailed 'semiannual report of payments for travel, subsistence, and related expenses received from non-Federal sources'.[125] The OGE also reviews and audits the effectiveness of agencies' ethics programmes designed to prevent government ethical problems. It has audited 231 ethical programmes and issued detailed reports for its review work.[126] All these audit means are key mechanisms for the OGE to gather information on the compliance/noncompliance of various agencies/departments with ethics standards.

The UK Civil Service Commission also has similar audit tools, though its audit tools are not as rich as the US OGE. The Civil Service Commission has conducted two audits of departments' efforts in preventing ethics violations and promoting ethical values in the Civil Service Code in 2009 and 2011 respectively. Its audit focuses on four aspects:

---

[122] The US Office of Government Ethics, 'Public financial disclosure', available at www.oge .gov/Financial-Disclosure/Public-Financial-Disclosure-278/Public-Financial-Disclosure/ (last visited 30 January 2013).

[123] The US Office of Government Ethics, 'Confidential financial disclosure: OGE Job Aid – a tool for ethics officials', 2009, available at www.oge.gov/uploadedFiles/Education/Educa tion_Resources_for_Ethics_Officials/Resources/450_FilersJobAid.pdf (last visited 30 January 2013).

[124] The US Office of Government Ethics, 'Guidance for reviewers of the OGE Form 450, Part I (Assets and Income)', 2008, available at www.oge.gov/Financial-Disclosure/Docs/ Guidance-for-Reviewers-of-the-OGE-Form-450,-Part-I/ (last visited on 16 April 2012); and the US Office of Government Ethics, 'Public financial disclosure: a reviewer's reference', second edition, 2004, available at www.oge.gov/Financial-Disclosure/Docs/ Financial-Disclosure-Guide/ (last visited on 16 April 2012).

[125] The US Office of Government Ethics, 'OGE Form 1353: semiannual report of payments accepted from a non-federal source', available at www.oge.gov/Forms-Library/OGE-Form-1353-Semiannual-Report-of-Payments-Accepted-from-a-Non-Federal-Source/ (last visited on 29 January 2013).

[126] The US Office of Government Ethics, 'Program review reports', available at www.oge .gov/Program-Management/Program-Review/Program-Review-Reports/Program-Review-Reports/ (last visited on 29 January 2013).

leadership (clear policy from senior leaders on ethics procedures and practice), clear routes to raise concerns about ethics, nominated officers in the department to provide assistance to department staff with ethics concerns, and induction.[127] The Civil Service Commission also conducts regular Civil Service Staff Surveys which is designed to know to what extent the civil service staff are aware of the Code and the procedures to raise a concern.[128] This can be considered as a component of the ethics climate audit.[129] The UK Civil Service Commission lacks audit programmes targeted at specific items of ethics regulation such as financial disclosure audits or audits of payments for travel, subsistence, and related expenses received from nongovernment sources.

In Hong Kong, the CSB is more dependent on its investigatory function. It also visits different government departments and bureaus to discuss ethics issues with department leaders. However, it seems it does not have ethics review programmes at the government department/ agency level in as systematic a manner as the US OGE and the UK Civil Service Commission. Nor does it produce a detailed review/audit report.

It should be noted that the financial disclosure form, conflicted interests form, gift registers, and so forth, submitted to relevant departments/ bureaus or other agencies, are also constant and systematic tools for information gathering. Although these programmes may not be directly managed by the key government ethics regulators, the key regulator can still review these programmes. Now, thanks to the development of the computer and Internet technology, this information can be now gathered electronically.

Furthermore, an agency can gather needed information from third parties. The most common practice is to encourage whistle-blowing. For government officials, it is a legal responsibility to report learned unethical conduct by other official(s) within the same department in most jurisdictions. In the United States, federal government employees are required to disclose waste, fraud, abuse, and corruption to the appropriate authorities.[130] The United Kingdom and Hong Kong also have similar legal requirements.[131] For other persons, while reporting is not a mandatory

---

[127] Civil Service Commission, 'Annual report and accounts 2011–12'.   [128] Ibid.
[129] Smith, 'Enforcement or ethical capacity'.
[130] b (11), § 2635.101, 5 C.F.R. Part 2635 – Standards of Ethical Conduct for Employees of the Executive Branch.
[131] Paragraph 18, Civil Service Code (the UK); 3.2, Civil Service Code (Hong Kong); 7.1 and 7.2, Code for Officials under the Political Appointment System.

requirement, some legal tools can definitely encourage their willingness to blow the whistle. An important point is whistle-blowing must be legally designed as a right for any third party. That means a government ethics regulatory agency shall not be allowed to selectively put complaints on record (though they can dismiss a complaint according to certain standards). Otherwise, the agency may simply ignore certain complaints.

Whistle-blowers must be protected from retaliation. If this cannot be guaranteed, those who have clues are more likely to keep silent. This is especially true for corruption and government ethics violations because the violators are those who have power to negatively influence the life of the whistle-blowers. The United States, the United Kingdom, and Hong Kong all take retaliation against whistle-blowers very seriously. In addition, after an enforcement agency has made a decision on a reported case (whether to dismiss it or conduct a formal investigation), the person or body who reported the case must be informed of the progress of the case. In so doing, the whistle-blower will know that their voice has been heard. In return, this can encourage further reporting.

Another form of third-party information gathering is cases/complaints transferred from another government agency/department. Even if the government has designed a clear jurisdiction for each enforcement agency, it should not be assumed that whistle-blowers will always report to the right agencies. Indeed, whistle-blowers in reality do frequently make complaints to the wrong agency. For example, the ICAC referred 234, 161, and 170 noncriminal corruption cases to relevant bureaus/ departments for consideration of disciplinary or administrative action in 2003, 2004, and 2005, respectively.[132] These departments/bureaus will transfer the cases to the CSB if former disciplinary action is taken. Thus, coordination between government ethics enforcement agencies and other government departments/agencies is important for information gathering.

Tools and tactics for behaviour manipulation

Broadly speaking, behaviour modification in government ethics enforcement involves mainly three weapons. The first weapon is advisory opinions which can either take the form of published opinion about the

---

[132] Civil Service Bureau, 'LCQ13: Government remains vigilant to fortify the culture of integrity in the civil service', available at www.csb.gov.hk/english/info/269.html (last visited 1 February 2013).

interpretation of a rule or about the application of a rule to a specific circumstance or the form of one-to-one private communication or telephone communication. Another weapon is education which focuses on not only getting the regulated officials to know the requirements and the do's and don'ts but also enabling them to understand the values that underlie these specific requirements. The third weapon is punishment-related tools which are either positive or negative. Punishment tools will not be discussed not because they are not important for compliance enforcement, but because these tools are integral to the deterrence-enforcement style. Thus, in the three selected jurisdictions and in China, punishment tools have already been almost fully developed and more or less take the same forms (informal warning, formal warning, administrative punishments, and criminal punishments).

Advisory opinions   Advisory opinions have been widely adopted in, to mention only a few, healthcare fraud enforcement,[133] antitrust regulation (the Federal Trade Commission's programme of advisory opinions),[134] and food and drug regulation.[135] This means advisory opinions of themselves can prevent numerous technical violations.[136] It is also one of the most commonly and frequently used tools in government ethics enforcement. It works because it helps to define grey areas. This is important for the regulated, the enforcement staff, and for the public. Government officials may find it easier to commit an ethics offence when facing confusing grey circumstances than facing clear prohibitions. Just as Rhodes has observed, 'not knowing clearly what is properly expected of them in concrete situations, they allow themselves to be led into compromising acts which gradually wash away a large part of their original idealism.'[137] It is also a useful tool to avoid violations if an official seeks opinions on his or her own initiative when facing unclear conditions. In this sense, it is also a protection for the regulated parties: 'It cannot be expected that every employee will have a full knowledge of ethics laws or

---

[133] Joan H. Krause, 'A conceptual model of health care fraud enforcement', *Brooklyn Journal of Law and Policy*, 12, 1 (2003), pp. 55–147.

[134] Spencer Weber Waller, 'Prosecution by regulation: the changing nature of antitrust enforcement', *Oregon Law Review*, 77, 4 (1998), pp. 1383–1450.

[135] Peter Barton Hutt, 'Philosophy of regulation under the Federal Food, Drug and Cosmetic Act', *Food and Drug Law Journal*, 50, 5 (1995), pp. 101–110.

[136] Ibid.

[137] Paul H. Douglas, *Ethics in Government* (Cambridge, MA: Harvard University Press, 1952), p. 102.

financial disclosure provisions, and hence there is an opportunity to request clarification'.[138]

For government ethics agencies, advisory opinions can also guide their enforcement actions.[139] They can determine what constitutes a violation and whether an enforcement action will be taken by the agency in certain circumstances. Without these opinions, enforcement officials may take different actions when facing similar circumstances.

For the public, these opinions, if available to them, will allow them to have another means by which to judge what actions are expected from government officials and what are not expected, especially under confusing circumstances. This may also help improve public reporting of unethical behaviour and generate social pressure towards these officials.

In the United States, both at the state and at the federal level a very important enforcement function of ethics commissions is to issue advisory opinions: 'The US OGE has built a detailed body of advisory opinions to cover the US executive branch'.[140] It is observed that in the first decade of the Massachusetts State Ethics' operation, the number of formal advisory opinions issued by the commission declined substantially.[141] This is because previously issued opinions have formed general guidelines which can guide government officials when ambiguities occur.[142] On the other hand, seeking advisory opinions by government officials on their own initiative reflects government officials' ethics awareness and commitment to compliance. The US OGE adopts three kinds of ethics advisories: legal advisories, education advisories, and programme management advisories. They provide advisory opinions on substantive ethics issues (e.g. guidance for implementing requirements regarding post-government employment negotiations[143]); training and education matters (e.g. publishing of special editions of Federal

---

[138] Smith, 'Enforcement or ethical capacity', p. 290.

[139] Smith, 'Enforcement or ethical capacity'.

[140] Andrew Stark, 'Public-sector conflict of interest at the federal level in Canada and the U.S.: differences in understanding and approach',' in H. George Frederickson (ed.), *Ethics and Public Administration* (New York: M.E. Sharpe, 1993), p. 58.

[141] Carol W. Lewis, 'Ethics codes and ethics agencies: current practices and emerging trends', in H. George Frederickson (ed.), *Ethics and Public Administration* (New York and London: M. E. Sharpe, 1993).

[142] Ibid.

[143] The US Office of Government Ethics, 'LA-12-01: Post-employment negotiation and recusal requirements under the STOCK Act', 2012, available at www.oge.gov/OGE-Advisories/Legal-Advisories/LA-12-01–Post-Employment-Negotiation-and-Recusal-Requirements-under-the-STOCK-Act/ (last visited on 15 December 2012).

Ethics Laws[144]), and managing an ethics programme (e.g. Ethics Pledge Assessment[145]) respectively.[146] In 2012 alone, the OGE issued twenty advisory opinions, of which ten were legal advisories, five were education advisories, and five were programme management advisories.[147]

Unlike the US OGE, both the UK Civil Service Commission and the Hong Kong CSB have not developed a formal and systematic advisory opinion programme. The US OGE developed three categories of advisories: legal advisory, education advisory, and programme management advisory. The legal advisories are substantive advisories of government ethics rules in order to provide guidance for government employees. The last two types of advisories are designed for agency ethics officials to help them manage training programmes and other ethics management skills such as skills needed to review financial reports. Compared with the OGE, the regulators in the United Kingdom and Hong Kong mainly carry out the legal advisories. However, they do interpret ethics standards when necessary, which can play a similar role, at least to some extent, as advisory opinions. For example, the UK Civil Service Commission added special guidelines on policy and procedure to the Civil Service Code.[148] The Hong Kong CSB also issued a large body of advisory guidelines on substantive ethics issues,

---

[144] The US Office of Government Ethics, 'EA-12-03 GPO rider for special edition CFR and compilation books', 2012, available at www.oge.gov/DisplayTemplates/ModelSub.aspx? id=2147488657 (last visited on 13 December 2012).

[145] The US Office of Government Ethics, 'PA-12-01: ethics pledge assessment', 2012, available at www.oge.gov/displaytemplates/modelsub.aspx?id=2147485555 (last visited on 13 December 2012).

[146] The US Office of Government Ethics, 'OGE advisories', available at www.oge.gov/OGE-Advisories/OGE-Advisories/ (last visited on13 December 2012).

[147] The US Office of Government Ethics, 'All advisories – 2012', available at www.oge.gov/OGE-Advisories/All-Advisories/Index/?id=2147488083&LangType=1033&y=2012 (last visited on13 December 2012).

[148] The Civil Service Commission, 'The Civil Service Code: a guide to bringing a complaint to the Civil Service Commission', 2010, available at http://civilservicecommission .independent.gov.uk/wp-content/uploads/2013/08/Guide-to-bringing-a-complaint-to-the-Commissioners-Civil-Service-Code-March-2012.pdf (last visited on 13 December 2012); The Civil Service Commission, 'Policy and procedures to the Civil Service Code', 2010, available at http://civilservicecommission.independent.gov.uk/wp-content/ uploads/2013/03/Policies-and-Procedures-Guide-to-the-Civil-Service-Code-Feb-12.pdf (last visited on 13 December 2012); The Civil Service Commission, 'A guide for departments subject to a complaint to the Civil Service Commission', 2010, available at http://civilservicecommission.independent.gov.uk/wp-content/uploads/2013/07/Code GuideforDepartmentsApril2013.pdf (last visited on 13 December 2012); and The Civil Service Commission, 'Complaints handling procedure', available at http://civilservice

such as *Guidelines on Avoiding or Reporting Conflict of Interest*[149]and *Declaration of Investments by Civil Servants.*[150]

Educational programmes Incompetence may be a minor cause or even a major cause of regulatory violations;[151] educational programmes are thus a necessary response to these violators. In the context of government ethics, it has been recognized that government ethics should be part of an educational process, and therefore the role of the ethics officer should be more like an educator than an enforcer (enforcer used in a narrow sense here).[152] These programmes are essential parts of the broader prevention system of government ethics offences.[153] The regulated must be informed about what constitutes compliance and noncompliance and how to avoid violations: 'Part of education in government ethics, of course, involves instruction in how to fill out forms, and part requires interpretations of the fine points of the many regulations (what counts as a gift or how to avoid a conflict of interest)'.[154] Further, covered officials need to be taught key ethics principles (especially regarding conflicts of interest and the appearance of corruption); ethics officials in government departments and agencies also should be taught enforcement policies so that 'creative' compliance is minimized, if it cannot be eliminated. A regulatory system should not be understood as a pure technical system consisting of only specific standards, though technical violation is one of its main features.

The US OGE's survey showed that a majority of various government agencies and departments' DAEOs, who are appointed within every department and agency in the US government, rank 'understanding

commission.independent.gov.uk/wp-content/uploads/2012/04/Complaints-Handling-Procedure-Jan-2012.pdf (last visited on 13 December 2012).

[149] The Civil Service Bureau, 'LCQ19: guidelines on avoiding or reporting conflict of interest', available at www.csb.gov.hk/english/info/1610.html (last visited on 23 April 2013).

[150] The Civil Service Bureau, 'Declaration of investments by civil servants 2000', available at www.csb.gov.hk/english/info/813.html (last visited on 23 April 2013).

[151] Robert A. Kagan and John T. Scholz, 'The "criminology of the corporation" and regulatory enforcement strategies', in Keith Hawkins and John M. Thomas (eds.), *Enforcing Regulation* (Boston, The Hague, Dordrecht, and Lancaster: Kluwer-Nijhoff, 1984), pp. 67–95.

[152] Dennis F. Thompson, 'Paradoxes of government ethics', *Public Administration Review*, 52, 3 (1992), pp. 254–259.

[153] Stuart C. Gilman, 'The U.S. Office of Government Ethics', *The Bureaucrat*, 20, 1 (1991), p. 13.

[154] Thompson, 'Paradoxes of government ethics', p. 255.

standards of conduct' as the second most important programme goals among nine ranks, ranging from most important to least important. The chief job of DAEOs, the US OGE believes, is to provide counselling and training on ethics. The South Carolina State Ethics Commission see the number of training sessions held and number of officials trained as a measurement of its performance.[155] The OGE also offers a variety of education programmes to agency ethics officials. It shares with every agency model practices so that each agency can meet the annual requirements in training employees on ethics rules. It has created an online resource centre including job aids, brochures, pamphlets, and web-based training for ethics officials. It has been hosting an annual conference for ethics officials in the executive branch since 1991.[156] The conference serves to 'inform ethics officials about the application of ethics-related laws and regulations'.[157] In addition to the annual conference, it also organizes workshops and seminars on various ethics topics such as *Fundamentals of Public Financial Disclosure Pre-Course Self Assessment* for agency ethics officials.[158] The OGE's education programmes offered to federal executive branch employees include various compulsory training sessions, online training resources, and self-education resources. Every year each government agency of the US government must provide mandatory ethics training to its covered employees. The agency training programmes are supported and directed by the OGE that provides assistance to agency's educational programmes through the periodic review and assessment of individual agency ethics training programmes.

Hong Kong CSB and the UK Civil Service Commission have similar ethics education tools including publications, training sessions, and other education programmes. For example, the *Civil Servants' Guide to Good Practices*[159] issued by the Hong Kong CSB are educational materials

---

[155] Smith, 'Enforcement or ethical capacity'.

[156] The US Office of Government Ethics, 'OGE conference', available at www.oge.gov/Education/National-Government-Ethics-Conference/OGE-Conference/ (last visited 24 April 2013).

[157] Ibid.

[158] The US Office of Government Ethics, 'Workshops & seminars', available at www.oge.gov/Education/Education-Resources-for-Ethics-Officials/Workshops-and-Seminars/Workshops–Seminars/ (last visited 24 April 2013).

[159] The Civil Service Bureau, 'Civil servants' guide to good practices', 2005, available at www.csb.gov.hk/hkgcsb/rcim/pdf/english/publications/civilservant_e.pdf (last visited 24 April 2013).

provided to regulated government officials; 'A guide to departments subject to a complaint'[160] issued by the UK Civil Service Commission is a guidebook for agency ethics officials. There are also training activities on ethics both for government employees and agency officials with ethics responsibilities. The Hong Kong CSB encourages government departments/bureaus to hold briefings/seminars for their staff.[161] The UK Civil Service Commission regularly meets agency ethics officials to discuss common ethics issues.

4.2.5   Enforcement resource allocation

Any given enforcement agency's enforcement resources such as staff and budget are finite. On the other hand, an agency usually faces infinite enforcement work, especially for agencies that regulate a huge number of regulated entities or individuals. A government ethics agency is a typical example as it has to oversee a large number of government officials. Therefore, it is an age-old question for an enforcement agency on how to allocate limited resources to different enforcement actions and different organizations/individuals regulated.

At the macro level, the resource allocation of an agency can be evaluated against the overall government income and spending (the percentage of the total income and spending) and compared with resources allocated to other law enforcement agencies. On the other hand, the resource of an agency must be allocated to different enforcement functions such as investigation and education. As government ethics regulators vary greatly in their roles and responsibilities, it is difficult, if not impossible, to make a meaningful comparison of resource allocation at the macro level. Furthermore, the examined jurisdictions also vary considerably geographically and demographically, which will further damage the reliability of the macro-level comparison. Thus, this section mainly focuses on resource allocation among different enforcement activities within a given government ethics regulator.

---

[160] The Civil Service Commission, 'A guide for departments subject to a complaint', 2010, available at http://civilservicecommission.independent.gov.uk/wp-content/uploads/2012/03/CS%20Code%20-%20Guide%20for%20departments.pdf (last visited 24 April 2013).

[161] Jennifer Mak, 'Opening remarks', Seminar on Integrity Programme Implementation, 2001, available at www.csb.gov.hk/hkgcsb/rcim/pdf/english/conference_meterials/speech_d3-2001_11_13_a.pdf (last visited 24 April 2013).

The US OGE has 'a staff of 80 full time equivalent positions and a current budget of less than $14 million'[162] and '[s]alaries, rent and basic operating expenses comprise approximately 96% of OGE's annual expenditures'.[163] It consists of four divisions: General Counsel and Legal Policy Division, Program Counsel Division, Compliance Division, and International Assistance and Internal Operations Division. Among which, the International Assistance and Internal Operations Division is a logistic and support division with nine staff. The General Counsel and Legal Policy Division is in charge of ethics laws and policy and presidential nomination with fifteen staff. The Program Counsel Division, with 26 staff, is mainly responsible for developing training programmes and assisting government agency/departments in ethics regulation. The Compliance Division is mainly responsible for financial disclosure and reviewing ethics programmes, and has eighteen staff. It can be concluded that most of the personnel resources have been allocated to education, review of ethics programmes, financial disclosure, and guidelines for agency ethics officials. This can serve as supplementary evidence of its compliance-oriented enforcement style.

The UK Civil Service Commission is composed of twelve civil service commissioners and another thirteen staff on secondment from the civil service. It seems the commissioners work like a board and there is no separation of responsibilities between each of these commissioners. Among the thirteen staff, five are performing administrative and logistic functions while the rest perform three functions (civil service recruitment, complaints cases, and monitoring compliance to the Civil Service Code). Compared with the United States, fewer resources are allocated to compliance-oriented enforcement activities.

The Hong Kong CSB is responsible for the overall management of the civil service including 'such matters as appointments, pay and conditions of service, staff management, manpower planning, training, discipline and use of official languages in the Civil Service'.[164] Thus it has many divisions not directly related to government ethics regulation.

---

[162] The US Office of Government Ethics, 'Legislative affairs & budget', available at www.oge.gov/About/Legislative-Affairs-and-Budget/Legislative-Affairs–Budget/ (last visited on 27 July 2012).

[163] The US Office of Government Ethics, 'Budget and appropriations', available at www.oge.gov/About/Legislative-Affairs-and-Budget/Budget-and-Appropriations/ (last visited on 27 July 2012).

[164] Civil Service Bureau, 'Introduction', available at www.csb.gov.hk/english/aboutus/org/intro/355.html (last visited on 21 May 2013).

Three divisions (conduct and discipline division, secretariat on civil service discipline, and civil service training and development institute) regulate government ethics directly. There is no information on resource allocation such as staff allocation between these divisions available on its official website. These divisions both focus on handling disciplinary cases and compliance monitoring.

4.2.6   Common features of government ethics enforcement in the three jurisdictions

With respect to enforcement agencies, all the three examined jurisdictions have relevant bodies which regulate government ethics, specifically on conflicts of interest, appearance of corruption, financial disclosure, and outside employment and activities. The US OGE is different from the UK Civil Service Commission and the Hong Kong CSB in that the US OGE is a body which is solely responsible for government ethics and the latter two bodies have other responsibilities such as overall management of the civil service and public service recruitment.

Another distinction is that the US OGE oversees the ethics of all the federal executive branch employees regardless of rank. The Hong Kong CSB does not regulate politically appointed officials and the UK Civil Service Commission does not regulate ministers. Instead, officials under the political appointment system in Hong Kong and ministers in the United Kingdom are monitored by the chief executive in Hong Kong and the prime minister in the United Kingdom, respectively. This is inherently problematic as they are basically regulating their own colleagues. In recent years, both in Hong Kong and in the United Kingdom, there have been a number of ethics scandals involving these senior officials. In Hong Kong, the former financial secretary Antony Leung Kam-chung's purchase of a car in 2003 involved conflicts of interest. In 2012, regarding the allegation of the conflicts of interest of Mr Leung Chun-ying's involvement as a member of the jury in the West Kowloon Reclamation Concept Plan Competition, the Legislative Council's report considered 'that Mr LEUNG Chun-ying should endeavour to avoid possible conflict of interests ... and considers that Mr LEUNG Chun-ying had unshirkable responsibility'.[165] Take a case from the United Kingdom. In 2010, British

---

[165] Legislative Council of The Hong Kong Special Administrative Region, 'Report of the select committee to study Mr Leung Chun-ying's involvement as a member of the jury in the West Kowloon Reclamation Concept Plan competition and related issues',

Defence Secretary Liam Fox was reported to maintain a strange relationship with a businessman, Mr Werritty, and the secretary admitted that 'I made a mistake blurring the line between my interest and my government activities'.[166]

The government ethics regulatory agencies in the three jurisdictions share several common features regarding legal authority/responsibilities. First, the three agencies all have investigative authority with respect to government ethics violations though in practice the Hong Kong CSB investigates several hundred cases a year and the US OGE rarely investigates individual violations. Second, compliance monitoring is an important power in all three jurisdictions. The compliance monitoring authority is performed at individual official level and government department level; even more stress is given to the department/agency level monitoring. Specified monitoring mechanisms including audits, register of conflicted interests and gifts, and financial disclosure are set forth expressly for the US OGE. Third, each of the three regulators has quasi-law-making power. These government ethics regulators can make ethics rules in the forms of regulations, guidance, and advisory opinions. Finally, all three regulators have the authority to cooperate and collaborate with other bodies which have a role in government ethics regulation (especially government departments/agencies/bureaux). This cooperation and collaboration function is crucial for information sharing and coherent enforcement of ethics policy and rules.

In terms of enforcement style, if enforcement is portrayed as a continuum with one pole as compliance enforcement and the other as deterrence enforcement, all three regulators' enforcement style could be described as compliance enforcement though they may be put at different places on the continuum closer to the compliance pole. This observation is based on nine aspects of enforcement as discussed in Section 4.2.3.

As far as enforcement tools and methods are concerned, there are two broad categories of tools: tools for gathering compliance information and tools for manipulating the regulated behaviour. These regulators usually rely on audits, investigation, third parties' whistle-blowing and

pp. 163–164, available at www.legco.gov.hk/yr11-12/english/sc/sc_lcy/report/lcy_rpt-e.pdf (last visited on 27 May 2013).

[166] Tim Shipman, Ian Drury, and Rupert Steiner, 'Secret cash trail that meant Fox had to go: defence secretary resigns after claim he "personally asked Tory donor to fund his best man"', *Daily Mail Online*, 15 October 2011, available at www.dailymail.co.uk/news/article-2049222/Liam-Fox-resigns-Defence-Secretary-finally-quits-Adam-Werritty-scandal.html (last visited on 27 May 2013).

information sharing with other government bodies as tools to gather compliance information. Advisory opinion and educational programmes are the most adopted behaviour modification enforcement tools.

For all three ethics regulators, a considerable part of their resources (mainly in the form of human resources) are allocated to educate, monitor, counsel, and guide government officials with respect to government ethics. This adds further support to the observation that a compliance-oriented enforcement style is adopted by these regulators. Regarding resource allocation, another common feature is that guidance and education for ethics officials as well as compliance monitoring at the government agency/departments level needs more commitment on the part of the regulators than that at the individual official level.

4.3   Enforcement of government ethics rules in China

4.3.1   Enforcement agencies

This section will focus on the following questions: is (are) there an agency (agencies) which oversee(s) conflicts of interest, financial disclosure, appearance of corruption, and outside employment (activities) of government officials in China? If yes, what are they? Are they solely responsible for government ethics regulation? Or do they have multiple responsibilities in addition to government ethics regulation? In order to answer the above questions, and since these agencies, especially those set up within CCP organs, are not well known in the West, it is necessary to first survey various government/party bodies which have a broad anti-corruption role and then rule out the agencies which are not government ethics regulators.

In Chapter 3, a detailed comparison of Chinese ethics rules in the three selected jurisdictions has shown that China has abundant rules governing certain aspects of government ethics. However, some aspects of conflicts of interest and the appearance of corruption have not been regulated by existing ethics rules and standards, such as assisting a third party in dealing with governments, behaving in a way that creates a perception that an official may be using his or her influence, and improper statements or action/behaviour that raises doubts about the basis of an official decision. There are also many aspects which have only been weakly reflected in China's rules, such as transfer of economic value from a private source to a public official (not bribery). Readers may find it helpful to re-read Sections 3.5 and 3.6 to recall the key characteristics of government ethics rules in China. The current section will also examine each government ethics agency against this question: whether, and to what extent, are the existing rules governing conflicts of interest, appearance of corruption, financial disclosure, and outside employment/activities being enforced by China's anti-corruption agencies? Having rules does not mean they are effectively enforced. It has been widely observed that weak law enforcement is a common issue in China even if well-designed laws are in place. For example, formal contracts in China are only weakly enforced.[167] 'Formal law and law enforcement' is believed to be only playing 'a marginal role in China's market development'.[168] In the area of environmental protection, China has made great improvement in establishing environmental laws and regulations, but weak and slow enforcement remains the problem.[169] Thus, it is necessary to examine whether the existing government ethics rules have been effectively enforced.

However, enforcement, although closely relying on rules, does not entirely depend on rules. Therefore, even if much undesired behaviours have not been prohibited by current government ethics rules, it is possible that government ethics agencies in China can still regulate these activities. Thus, another question must also be addressed: whether in practice anti-corruption agencies regulate activities which have not been governed, or only weakly governed, by ethics rules?

Party Disciplinary Inspection Committees

The most well-known anti-corruption agency in China is the Party's Disciplinary Inspection Committees (DICs) at various levels of the Party Committee;[170] the central-level agency is called the Central Commission for Discipline Inspection (CCDI). However, 'in Western scholarship, no systematic study has been devoted to the CCP's discipline inspection system in recent years, and little is known on its latest development'.[171]

---

[167] Mingming Duan, 'The role of formal contracts with weak legal enforcement: a study in the Chinese context', *Strategic Organization*, 10, 2 (May 2012), pp. 158–186.

[168] Katharina Pistor and Gangxu Cheng, 'Governing stock markets in transition economies: lessons from China', *American Law and Economics Review*, 7, 1 (2005), pp. 184–210, p. 185.

[169] Benjamin van Rooij, 'Implementation of Chinese environmental law: regular enforcement and political campaigns', *Development and Change*, 37, 1 (2006), pp. 57–74.

[170] Yufan Hao, 'From rule of man to rule of law: an unintended consequence of corruption in China in the 1990s', *Journal of Contemporary China*, 8, 22 (1999), pp. 405–423.

[171] Ting Gong, 'The party discipline inspection in China: its evolving trajectory and embedded dilemmas', *Crime, Law and Social Change*, 49, 2 (2008), pp. 139–152, p. 139.

We often read in newspapers that some official is being investigated by the DICs[172]. For example, the *China Daily* (Hong Kong edition) reported in early 2013 that 'Wu Yongwen, deputy head of the Standing Committee of the People's Congress of Hubei Province, is being investigated by the Central Commission for Discipline Inspection'.[173] It investigates and disciplines officials who violate party rules. The committees are also responsible for promoting integrity education.[174] It also has a leading role in overall anti-corruption policies and strategies. It set out four key points for anti-corruption work at the beginning of 2013 at its annual conference.[175] It regularly launches five-year anti-corruption plans.[176]

Party DICs are largely more of a criminal enforcement agency than a government ethics regulatory enforcement agency for two reasons. First, they play an initial investigatory role for party officials and transfer the officials to Procuratorates for further criminal investigation. From January 1993 to October 1998, 28,900 officials received disciplinary or administrative punishment; 42.7 per cent of these cases were later transferred to the People's Procuratorates.[177] For the transferred cases, the procuratorates are mainly responsible for preparing the evidences collected by DICs (procuratorates may also supplement more evidences through their further investigation) to successfully have the officials convicted. For the 57.3 per cent of the cases which were first investigated by the Party DICs and were not transferred to the People's Procuratorates, it is difficult, if not impossible, for the People's Procuratorates to initiate a separate investigation; even if they believe the un-transferred officials are subject to criminal sanctions.[178] Putting in other words, DICs can refuse to transfer the cases which constitute criminal corruption.

---

[172] DICs, when mentioned in a general setting, refer to DICs at various levels including CCDI. When the term CCDI is used it stresses the highest level of DIC.

[173] Lei Zhao, 'Hubei official investigated', *China Daily* (Hong Kong edition), p. 3, 19 January 2013.

[174] Qishan Wang, 'Report at the second plenary meeting of the Eighteenth Central Commission for Discipline Inspection of the CCP', 21 January 2013, available at http:// cpc.people.com.cn/n/2013/0226/c64094-20597121.html (last visited 27 February 2013).

[175] 'The 2nd plenary meeting of the 18th Central Commission for Discipline Inspection of the CCP held and four key anti-corruption works decided', available at http://fanfu .people.com.cn/n/2013/0123/c64371-20302846.html (last visited 27 February 2013).

[176] Keith Zhai, 'Watchdog to launch 5-year war on graft', *South China Morning Post*, EDT6, 24 January 2013.

[177] Yong Guo, 'Historical evolvement and future reform of the China Communist Party Discipline Inspection Commission', The Opening Ceremony of the Centre of Anti-corruption Studies and Seminar, ICAC, Hong Kong, 2 April 2009.

[178] Ibid.

This means they, to a large extent, decide whether to prosecute an official or not. This is an important part of criminal enforcement.

Second, party DICs (and administrative supervision departments) handle a large number of 'administrative or party disciplinary' cases which do not constitute criminal corruption according to the corruption laws in China. However, these cases are of a criminal nature if they are viewed from a comparative law perspective. Accepting bribes below 5,000 RMB, or accepting gifts, does not constitute criminal corruption in China, and thus are subject only to administrative or/and party discipline. These 'administrative' and 'party disciplinary cases' are criminal cases in the three selected jurisdictions and many other countries. That means party DICs are enforcing criminal corruption when viewed from a comparative perspective.

Party DICs' supervisory scope largely exceeds the government ethics regulated by the US OGE, the UK Civil Service Commission, and the Hong Kong CSB. They have a broad ideological and political education function. They are responsible for party members' 'political discipline (adhering to the party's basic line, principles, policies, and decisions)'[179] and the party's style of work. All these authorities/powers conferred on DICs go beyond a purely anti-corruption function and related to maintaining the supremacy of party leadership and its ruling legitimacy. Political education only slightly and abstractly involve government ethics element: it encourages government carders to live a proletarian way of life and work hard to serve the people and to avoid materialism. These are not comparable to government ethics education in the three selected jurisdictions where priorities are given to ensuring officials to know the requirements of rules and reminding them of various confusing and difficult consequences.

The broad political discipline and political education functions of the DICs is confirmed by interviewing officials in several DICs. Officials from three provincial level DICs interviewed all said that their commissions have a department which specifically supervises the execution of the party's basic line, principles, policies, and decisions.[180] These provincial DICs also regularly send inspection work teams to ascertain how key leaders execute the party's basic line, principles, policies, and decisions,

---

[179] Gong, 'The party discipline inspection in China', p. 146.
[180] Interviewee 01, interviewee 02, interviewee 11, interviewee 12, interviewee 21, and interviewee 22.

and other political discipline.[181] However, some city-level and county-level DIC officials agree that in practice, they just forward higher-level commissions' circulars and provisions regarding political discipline to regulated party officials, though they also have the authority for inspecting the delivery of broad political discipline.[182]

DICs regularly enforce only a few regulated activities of party/government officials. In order to learn the situation of the enforcement of the existing government ethics rules as it occurs in practice for the purpose of this study, a questionnaire was designed and sent to 72 officials working in two provincial DICs, one city-level DIC, and one county-level DIC. This questionnaire contained thirty behaviours which are regulated by existing party/government ethics rules, as discussed in Section 3.5.[183] These officials were asked to judge whether their DIC in practice enforced these rules or not. For each behaviour regulated by existing ethics rules, the officials are asked 'have you (or a colleague) ever handled (opened a file, or investigated, or punished the violator) of such a case?' They are reminded that, in words that are bolded, 'you tick the yes box *only* when you yourself *indeed* handled such a case or you 100% sure that your colleague handled such a case'. Thirty-nine completed questionnaires were successfully completed. The response is shown in Table 4.2. All thirty-nine respondents have never handled a case concerning rules regulating twenty undesired activities; this is indicated by the '0' item in the 'No. of "yes" ticking participants' column in Table 4.2. Only five regulated behaviours are regularly enforced. They are: civil servants running a prohibited business; gifts including cash gifts, coupons, banquets, entertainment (especially connected to official duties); private travel with public funds; unnecessarily or luxuriously use public funds in the performance of official duties; and accepting gifts or cash from subordinate government officials. This reflects an enforcement practice: DICs' enforcement is largely focused on activities involving monetary gain.

DICs only occasionally enforce existing rules such as using a public car for private gain and disclosure requirements. This is reflected in the small number of participants who ticked 'Yes' in Table 4.2. Such cases are more likely to be handled when they attract public concern mainly due to media reports. DIC officials seldom deal with these cases on their own

---

[181] Ibid.   [182] Interviewee 05, interviewee 17, and interviewee 18.
[183] See Appendix F for the questionnaire.

Table 4.2 *Actual enforcement of existing rules governing government ethics in several DICs.*

Behaviour regulated by existing party/government rules			No. of 'Yes' ticking participants
Conflicts of interest	Self-dealing	General disqualification requirements	0
		Disqualified from buying or selling securities for officials who may have inside information	0
		Setting up businesses by party organs and governments prohibited	0
		Running businesses by civil servants prohibited	6
	Transfer of economic value from private source to a public official (not bribery)	Gifts including cash gifts, coupons, banquets, entertainment (especially connected to his or her official duties)	11
		Travels paid by private source	0
	Profiting from misusing official position	Private travel with public funds	23
		Claiming private expenditure in the name of official expenditure	0
		Public car for private use	1
		Using public funds to purchase various club memberships	0
		Unnecessarily or luxuriously use public funds in performing official duties	13

Table 4.2 (*cont.*)

Behaviour regulated by existing party/government rules			No. of 'Yes' ticking participants
		Misusing office related information/influence for private gain	3
Appearance of corruption	Appearance of favouritism in appointment even if actual favouritism cannot be proved	Accepts gifts or cash from subordinate government officials	16
		Civil servants with close relationships not allowed to take up posts with immediately subordinate or supervisory relations in the same organ	0
		(For judges) Meeting the party concerned or his agent without authorization	0
	Appearance of favouring one party in dealing with official duties	Attending dinners or accepting presents given by the party concerned or his agent	0
Financial disclosure	Disclosing scope	Overseas deposits, wealth in foreign countries	0
		Income including outside employment such as teaching and writing	0
		House property	0
		Investment including investment in partnerships or sole individual enterprises	3
		Outside employment	0
		Employment and foreign residence information of their spouse and children	0

Table 4.2 (*cont.*)

Behaviour regulated by existing party/government rules			No. of 'Yes' ticking participants
Outside employment and activities	While holding office	Outside profit-making activity	0
		Paid outside employment	0
		Outside leadership positions at NGOs (only applies to senior officials)	0
	After leaving office	Take up outside employment or profit-making activity directly related to his or her prior work within the control period	0
		(For former judges) Practicing law as a lawyer within the control period	0
		Invest in companies which has business related to his or prior work in the control period	0

Note: This table is designed to present the response of the participants of the questionnaire only. In the questionnaire, only specific regulated activities described in the third column were presented to participants; the categories of these behaviours are not presented to the participants to avoid any possible contamination of their ideas by these categories' names such as conflicts of interest, appearance of corruption, and so forth.

initiative even if there are applicable rules in place. It seems regulated officials also recognize the enforcement agencies' ignorance of most government ethics offences. Regulated officials generally make no attempt to conceal their offences. One feature of 'small corruption [*xiaofubai*]' (referring to government ethics offences and other corruption with a minor nature) is committed in an open manner.[184] Officials even compare and show off the benefits they achieved through violating ethics rules to show their smartness in thumbing their nose at officialdom.[185] This is also indicated in recent media coverage of several corruption scandals.

The first scandal is the so-called 'Property Uncle [*fang shu*]' case. On 8 October 2012, a poster in the Tianya Forum[186] disclosed that Cai Bin, the former political commissar of the Bureau of City Management in Panyu district, Guangzhou, and his family owned twenty-two properties worth around 35.5 million RMB. This soon attracted heated discussion and many Internet users said that they were shocked about this revelation and requested relevant government entities to investigate Cai Bin. The next day, 9 October, Liu Hu, a journalist, forwarded the poster's comment to his Sina Weibo (mini-blog) account. Cai's property registry information and the picture of his properties were also posted on Sina Weibo. On 10 October 2012, the *Southern Metropolis Daily* reported this scandal; the newspaper made a tentative audit which confirmed Cai Bin, and his family owned twenty-one properties worth at least 40 million.[187] On 11 October, local authorities confirmed that Cai and his family owned twenty-two properties and on 22 October he was sacked and detained on corruption charges.[188]

Interestingly and unbelievably, Cai did not make any attempt to disguise his ownership of these twenty-two properties.[189] All twenty-two properties were registered under his, his wife's, and his son's names. The whistle-blower simply compiled the information from the city's property registry. Cai Bin declared only two apartments to the authority. Just as questioned by state media, the problem reflected in this scandal is that the current official property disclosure system includes only declarations to the authorities; there is no audit and no rule that property declarations be made to the public in the disclosure system.[190] The media

---

[184] Daosheng Shao, *China: Anti-corruption Campaigns* (Beijing: Social Sciences Academic Press, 2009).
[185] Ibid.
[186] Tianya Forum (www.tianya.cn) is the most visited online forum in mainland China.
[187] 'Net citizens ask 'Property Uncle' in Panyu to 'sun himself', *Southern Metropolis Daily* (Guangzhou), AII02, 10 October 2012.
[188] Xiangwei Wang, 'Homing in on the corrupt "uncles"', *South China Morning Post*, EDT/EDT5, 17 December 2012.
[189] Ibid.
[190] Yizhu Mao, 'Will official property disclosure become a sharp anti-corruption sword?' *China Youth Daily*, p. 06, 11 December 2012.

described the existing official property declaration institution as 'the blind's eyes or the deaf's ears'.[191] Put in other words, the DICs are not enforcing the rules governing official property declarations though the Provisions on Reporting Party Cadre's Personal Affairs, which was made in 2006, and in 2010 the revised provisions required party cadre to report house properties, investments, and children's employment.

It only took the Guangzhou DIC less than two weeks to investigate this case. That means this kind of ethics rule violation is easy to be investigated. Thus, it is reasonable to conclude that enforcement of these rules is not placed in the DICs regular enforcement schedule. During its investigation of Cai Bin's property holdings, the Guangzhou DIC unexpectedly also found that Cai Bin allegedly took bribes and operated a private business since 2000.[192] From Cai Bin's position, he must have clearly known the rules governing setting up businesses and declaration of property holdings. He probably also knew investigations into these matters were lax, otherwise he would have taken steps to disguise his property holdings.

Internet users quickly nicknamed Cai Bin 'Property Uncle [*fangshu*]' after the scandal was exposed.[193] Sadly, this scandal is not an isolated case, but merely the tip of the iceberg.[194] More and more similar scandals have been disclosed such as, to mention just a few, Zhang Xin (former deputy chief of Hangzhou's Housing Management Bureau) owned twenty properties,[195] and Zhai Zhengfeng (former head of Erqi District Bureau of Land Resources and Housing Administration in Zhengzhou City) and his family owned thirty-one properties.[196]

Another case in point is the He Haichang case. He Haichang was the director of the Food Bureau in Luliang, Shanxi Province. On 17 February 2013, several photographs of rooms in He's office were posted on the Tianya forum. The room was furnished with a luxury queen-sized bed,

---

[191] Ibid.
[192] Fiona Tam, 'Exposing loopholes and lax oversight', *South China Morning Post*, EDT/ EDT6, 27 October 2012.
[193] Ibid.
[194] Xiangwei Wang, 'Homing in on the corrupt "uncles"', *South China Morning Post*, EDT/ EDT5, 17 December 2012.
[195] Pinghui Zhuang, 'Housing official ted to big assets', *South China Morning Post*, EDT/ EDT6, 14 December 2012.
[196] Baijie An, 'Officials whose family owns 31 houses arrested', *China Daily (Hong Kong Edition)*, p. 5, 15 January 2013.

an LCD television and a number of leather sofas.[197] This post attracted more than 148,000 hits within a short time and was reposted by many Internet users on other social media networks.[198] Immediately following this, many state media outlets reported this scandal.[199] Given the strong social concern resulting from Internet and newspaper reports on the scandal, the DIC in Luliang, Shanxi soon carried out an investigation and announced that He Haichang had violated the provisions regarding office size and furnishing standards of officials' offices. The DIC then imposed a demerit [*jiguo*] as a penalty on the disgraced official.[200]

This case further reflected that this kind of government ethics rules are largely laws on paper only. Any of He's colleagues or supervisors could easily discover He's total disregard for the relevant ethics rules by simply visiting the official. Just as observed by a news article, failure to adhere to standards on the use of officials' cars and offices is almost a normal phenomenon; without other causes, few officials will be disciplined for using luxury cars or offices.[201] In He Haichang's case, Internet and media reporting are the 'other causes'.

Interviews with DIC officials also provide further support to the finding that certain existing government ethics rules are not regularly enforced. Thirty officials working in three provincial-level DICs, three city-level DICs, and three county/district-level DICs were interviewed. In each of the interviews, the question was asked:

> Some party/government rules on anti-corruption and government integrity promotion [*fanfu changlian*][202] (such as rules prohibiting officials from running a business, rules on assets/property declaration, rules prohibiting a public car for private use, rules prohibiting luxury office furnishing, and rules prohibiting certain outside employment) have

---

[197] Laura Zhou, 'Large bed in official's office stirs talk', *South China Morning Post*, EDT/ EDT8, 22 February 2013.

[198] Ibid.

[199] See, for example, 'Head of food bureau in Luliang City, Shanxi Province, was exposed having a luxury queen-sized bed in his office' *Nanguo Zaobao*, p.22, 21 February 2013; and 'Luxury office of a head of food bureau in Shanxi was exposed', *Bao'an Daily*, p. A14, 21 February 2013.

[200] 'Around China', *China Daily*, p. 2, 23 February 2013; 'Head of Luliang bureau of food was recorded a demerit', *Beijing Daily*, p. 13, 22 February 2013.

[201] 'A thorough investigation is needed for the luxury office case', *Beijing Times*, p. A02, 22 February 2013.

[202] In the interview, I used the expression 'party/government rules on anti-corruption and government integrity promotion' instead of 'government ethics rules' because the former is better understood by the DIC officials.

already been issued. But my review of media scandal handled by DICs and certain DICs' case files shows that officials are seldom disciplined for violating these rules giving the background that these kinds of rule violations are very common. Do you agree with my finding?[203]

Twenty-one of the thirty interviewees responded to this question, and twenty agreed with the finding though three of the twenty did not fully agree. They were asked a follow-up question: 'why, in your opinion, are they seldom held responsible for violating these rules?'[204] A city-level DIC chief's response is most comprehensive and is quoted in full below:

> I feel that the reasonableness and practicality of some rules can be further discussed though these rules are rational. For example, using a public car for private use is even common in the commission which has the duty to monitor this problem. A widespread saying is that one third of an official's car is used by him, one third by his driver, and the final one third by the official's family. In recent years some cases have been handled because the car was used to drive the whole family to another city for family travel and was exposed by the media. But, generally speaking, using public cars for private purposes in an unpretentious manner is still common and will usually not catch our attention.
>
> From a practical perspective, I think this kind of violation is too minor and common to deserve punishment; after all, a lot of more important cases are waiting to be handled by us. Another example is accepting gifts/banquets from businessmen. Sometimes, to attract investors, I do need to meet businessmen. Sometimes, businessmen treat me and sometimes I treat the businessmen using public money. Attracting investment is a key job of the city's leadership. As a city leader, I must perform the city party committee's strategy on investment attraction and economic development. ... Another reason is both the city Party Committee and the provincial DIC expect that we can tackle some big cases and important cases [da'an yao'an]. We are expected to handle more cases in the important areas such as government project tendering, work safety, and estate development. After all we have limited capacity and we should focus on these areas. Further, both the public and the media are more interested in cases involving high-ranking officials, large sums of illegal gains or sex affairs.[205]

---

[203] See Appendix D for more detail about interview questions.

[204] I intentionally avoid using the sentence, 'Why do DICs not regularly enforce these laws?' This may be considered offensive by some officials.

[205] Interviewee 23 (the head of X City DIC in H Province, the highest ranking official interviewed in my research.).

The official's response suggests two important and usually ignored explanations for the weak enforcement or lack of enforcement of some of the existing ethics rules. First, a DIC is both a criminal corruption enforcement agency and a government ethics regulator. This is inherently problematic. Criminal enforcement relies more on deterrence through investigation whereas regulatory enforcement relies more on setting standards and monitoring compliance. Further, criminal corruption enforcement generally has clearly separated investigatory, prosecutorial, and adjudicatory departments, whereas government ethics regulators are usually charged with quasi-rule making, investigating, and quasi-adjudication powers. In all three selected jurisdictions (the United States, the United Kingdom, and Hong Kong), criminal corruption enforcement and government ethics regulation are separated though there is collaboration between them. Second, there is a conflict between the DICs' anti-corruption and government ethics regulation role and the heads of these agencies' role in economic development and attracting investment as key leaders of local party committees.

A review of DICs' case files also confirmed that the existing rules on government ethics such as using a public car for private use, property declaration requirements, and government officials running a business are not regularly enforced. A review of cases handled by three DICs (one city-level DIC and two county/district-level DICs; see Tables 4.3, 4.4, and 4.5) have found that cases concerning existing government ethics rules (cases described in Table 4.2) handled by the DICs only account for a small part of the total number of cases handled.[206]

All three DICs' case statistics show that traditional criminal corruption account for a very large percentage of the total number of cases handled (from 58 per cent to 77 per cent). Cases concerning activities regulated by existing party/government ethics rules only account for a very small percentage of the total number of cases handled (from 4 per cent to 6 per cent).

---

[206] It is difficult to gain permission to review the details of cases involving higher-level officials handled by the DICs at city or province levels perhaps because higher-level officials generally concern more serious abuses of power. As case statistics in all the three DICs are categorized in a way not compatible with this research, these statistics cannot be used directly for this research. For example, buying or selling official posts (买官卖官; *maiguan maiguan*) is categorized by DICs as a major type of corruption case. For the purpose of this research this group of cases is treated as the same as other bribery cases. Case reviewing is quite time-consuming; thus only a single year in each DIC was reviewed.

Table 4.3 *Cases handled by N County DIC in 2009.*

Category	No.	Percentage
Bribery	24	44
Embezzlement	18	33
Political discipline cases	1	2
Cases involving existing ethics rules as listed by the thirty activities in Table 4.2	3	5
Dereliction of duty cases	3	5
Others	6	11
Total	**55**	**100**

Table 4.4 *Cases handled by R District DIC in 2008.*

Category	No.	Percentage
Bribery	39	42
Embezzlement	22	24
Political discipline cases	4	4
Cases involving existing ethics rules as listed by the thirty activities in Table 4.2	4	4
Dereliction of duty cases	11	12
Others	13	14
Total	**93**	**100**

Table 4.5 *Cases handled by X City DIC in 2008.*

Category	No.	Percentage
Bribery	39	36
Embezzlement	24	22
Political discipline cases	6	6
Cases involving existing ethics rules as listed by the thirty activities in Table 4.2	6	6
Dereliction of duty cases	15	14
Others	17	16
Total	**107**	**100**

Different sources of evidence have shown that existing government ethics laws in China are generally not enforced, or at least are largely weakly enforced. Attention here is paid to behaviour which is not covered by existing government ethics rules in China but regulated in the other jurisdictions examined in Chapter 3. The focus is on whether DICs in practice enforce unwritten rules on activities that are not covered. These not-covered activities, which are mainly sub-categories of conflicts of interest and appearance of corruption, include: assisting a third party in dealing with the government; behaving in a way and creating the perception that the official may use his or her influence; association with criminals or behaving improperly creating a perception that the judge is in disagreement with the overall justice system (for judges only); improper statement (or action/behaviour) raising doubts about the basis of an official decision; and the appearance of bias towards a certain person (see Appendices B and C).

Evidence from these three sources suggests that these activities are not regulated by DICs in their anti-corruption enforcement. First of all, in reviewing more than 250 cases in three DICs, no case was found which lies in the five sub-categories of conflicts of interest and appearance of corruption.

Second, these kinds of activities occur frequently and apparently the DICs never consider these activities as improper with respect to public ethics. In interviews with party/government officials under regulation by the DICs, officials agreed that they 'helped their friends' many times in dealing with governments. Ten officials (five from Z city, S province, and the other five from X city, H province) were interviewed.[207] The ten officials were reached through contacts in Z city party college, S province and X city party college in H province. They are government/party cadres undergoing training courses at party schools and agreed to be interviewed. They all 'helped' their friends or relatives in various interactions with governments such as applying for a business license, applying for a tax cut, or enquiring certain matters such as recruitment to a public post. Interestingly, they all think that these are legitimate activities because they 'helped' their friends and, at the same time, fully abided by relevant party/government rules and principles. Interviewee 32 from Z city, S Province said that:

---

[207] Interviewee 31, Interviewee 32, Interviewee 33, Interviewee 34, and Interviewee 35 in Z city, S Province; and Interviewee 41, Interviewee 42, Interviewee 43, Interviewee 44, and Interviewee 45 in X city, H Province.

A high school classmate's son loses his job in the privatization of state-owned enterprises in our city and is in financial difficulty. He has just started a small business, a makeup store. His father asked me whether there is any policy supporting those who have served in a state-owned enterprise but recently lost their jobs. I said that I was not sure but agreed to enquire relevant departments about this. Finally, I learned that his son can enjoy tax-free support for three years and I applied for that support on behalf of his son. The application will be approved soon.

For my classmate, he appreciated my help. For his son, his difficulty is alleviated. For the government, it is a supporting policy being put into practice. For me, I am just doing something that I am able to do. Thus, from any angle, this is good. Why not help them ... Reform of state-owned enterprises has resulted in unemployment, which is one of the causes of social instability. Thus, in some sense, what I did is good for social stability.[208]

The problem of interviewee 32 lies in that he applied for the tax exemption support for his classmate's son. Submitting an application to the government for certain approval is dealing with government by a third party. A government official who does this for a private party may create the appearance, in the eyes of the public or another applicant, that the application assisted by the official will be treated preferentially or will be processed earlier. Further, every member of the public shall have equal access to the government. An application submitted by an official on behalf of a third party will enjoy easier access, or at least a perception of easier access, in dealing with government. For interviewee 32, it would be all right if he only enquired about the issue, informed his friend, and let the son make the application instead of handing in the application on behalf of the son.

Another example is interviewee 45 from X city in H Province. This interviewee is an official in this city's education bureau, which is responsible for regulating schools. His daughter told him that the school is selecting five students for a joint middle school chorus and she is interested in taking part. He made a call to the headmaster of the school and enquired about the selection of chorus members. The next day the headmaster faxed him an application form for the chorus. He completed the form and sent it to the headmaster and his daughter was eventually selected as one of the five members. He said that:

---

[208] Interviewee 32.

I also helped many of my friends in selecting appropriate schools for their children in this city. But in all of these cases including my daughter's case, I never require that relevant school staff give special treatment to the students I mentioned. The schools have their own standards in admitting students; the students I mentioned to them must also pass their evaluation. I never intervene in these schools evaluation. Just like my daughter's case, I only expressed the interests of my daughter. My daughter experienced all the same evaluation process for the chorus selection as other applicants. There are also many friends asking me to ask the school to reconsider their children who were rejected by the school. I did not help these friends. If I help them, it is clear that I use my public position to influence the student admission fairness.[209]

Although interviewees 32 and 45 both think their behaviour was not improper, interviewee 32 was apparently assisting a third party in dealing with the government and interviewee 45 was behaving in a way that created the perception that the official may use his influence. Other interviewees also expressed very similar experiences in 'helping' their friends similar to interviewees 32 and 45. All of the ten interviewees were certain these activities were neither prohibited by party/government rules nor by enforcement practice. In their minds, these activities should not be prohibited.

Third, observation has shown that many government working practices involve improper statements (or action/behaviour) raising doubts about the basis of an official decision and appearance of bias towards a certain person. Three criminal trials in three basic courts (W District court, in X City, H Province; and N County Court and M County Court, in Z City, S Province) were observed. The reason to observe courts trials is twofold. First, in court trials, judicial staff will deal with different parties at the same time; this provides a good opportunity to observe whether they show bias towards a certain party. Second, most of the court trials are open to the public. Thus, no consent is needed to attend and observe proceedings. This allows for unobtrusive observation where judges' behaviour is not influenced. In all the three criminal trials, defendants are presented in a humiliating fashion. The defendant is forced to wear a yellow uniform jacket. On the back of the jacket, a number and several Chinese characters saying 'such and such detention centre' are printed. His hair is shaved short. His hands are in handcuffs and placed behind his back; this makes him bend low and makes his head

---

[209] Interviewee 45.

bend down. This is a position of repentance in Chinese culture. This improper practice in criminal trials was also observed by McConville in his empirical study of criminal justice in China.[210] This way of presenting defendants in court trials is likely to raise doubts on the basis of judicial judgments.

Further, it is observed that in all three trials the defendants and their lawyers are frequently stopped or interrupted by the judges, whereas the prosecutors were seldom stopped or interrupted. The judges usually use the expression 'please talk about key points' to stop defendants and their lawyers when the latter talk for a long time (e.g. more than ten minutes). Sometimes judges say to the lawyers 'do not repeat your ideas' in an impatient manner to urge them to hurry up and finish. This is bias towards defendants and their representative lawyers as the judges never speak to prosecutors in such a manner.

Another improper behaviour observed is that prosecutors and judges usually greet each other before and after the trial in a friendly manner. Usually, to avoid being late, prosecutors will arrive at the court ten to thirty minutes earlier than the formal starting trial time. The court hall for a trial is usually opened in advance before the trial. Defendants' representatives or lawyers, other audiences before their time usually stay in the trial hall. Prosecutors usually wait in the judges' office. They enter into the trial hall together with the judges. It is also common that, before the formal start of the trial, if a judge smokes he will give all his fellow judges in the court and all the prosecutors a cigarette. A prosecutor will also offer each judge or his prosecutor colleagues a cigarette if he wants to smoke. It seems prosecutors and judges see each other as colleagues. Usually, lawyers of defendants also offer cigarettes to prosecutors and judges, and prosecutors and judges usually accept the cigarettes. But, judges and prosecutors seldom offer cigarettes to lawyers. This apparently raises doubts in the minds of defendants' relatives and friends on the basis of the judgment. This kind of behaviour occurs very frequently and without being perceived improper by the judges. Though this is observed only in criminal process in three basic level courts, the judges' lack of sense of appearance of impartiality is apparent. It seems they are not reminded by the regulators to avoid such improper practices. These examples observed in courts, together with internal document review and

---

[210] Mike McConville, *Criminal Justice in China: An Empirical Enquiry* (Cheltenham: Edward Elgar, 2011).

interviews with ten government officials, indicate that DICs in practice do not enforce rules on assisting a third party in dealing with the government; behaving in a way and creating the perception that the official may use his or her influence; association with criminals or behaving improperly, creating a perception that the judge is in disagreement with the overall justice system (for judges only); improper statement (or action/behaviour) raising doubts about the basis of an official decision; and the appearance of bias towards a certain person.

In conclusion, the DICs are responsible for supervising government ethics in China. However, they are not solely responsible for government ethics; they are mainly criminal corruption enforcers. They are also charged with political discipline and political education responsibilities. Regarding their government ethics regulatory role, they only regularly enforce a small portion of existing government ethics rules. Many behaviours that are widely practiced (mainly in the sub-category of conflicts of interest and appearance of corruption), which are regulated by rules in the three selected jurisdictions are not covered in China.

Ministry/Bureau of Supervision

Ministry/Bureaus of Supervision at various levels of government are described as being the parallel of DICs in government. For example, in comparing the anti-corruption infrastructure in the United States and China, Smith has stated that 'the anti-corruption agencies that were established [in China] included disciplinary inspection committees at the party level and the Ministry of Supervision at the governmental level'.[211] He further pointed out that the Ministry of Supervision is responsible for disciplinary action against administrative wrongdoing in the government and the DICs supervise party members and leaders on party discipline.[212]

For the reasons given in this section, it is suggested that it is better to see DICs and government supervision departments as a single agency rather than as two separate ethics agencies. First, the DICs and government supervision departments are composed of the same staff at various levels. Since 1994, the DICs and the supervision authorities both at the national level and local level have been carrying out a working mechanism of 'one single working team, two organizational labels (*yitao renma,*

---

[211] Smith, 'Enforcement or ethical capacity', p. 305.
[212] Smith, 'Enforcement or ethical capacity'.

liangkuai paizi)'.[213] This is similar to the relationship between the CCP Military Committee and the Central Military Commission of the People's Republic of China. In this sense, separate administrative supervision authority only exists in theory.

Second, in the field study of the N County DIC in Z city, S Province, it was found that the official stamp of N County DIC and the stamp of N County Bureau of Supervision are kept in the same office. They use different stamps according to different situations.

> Provisions and circulars [of N County DIC] in most cases will be stamped with both stamps. For disciplinary cases, even if a case involves a non-party official, it is a discipline decision and is made in the same way as other cases. Actually we do not distinguish government officials from party officials. Further most government officials, more than 95 per cent of senior officials and more than 80 per cent of junior government officials are party members.[214]

Thus, there is no reason to view Ministry/Bureaus of Supervision as separate anti-corruption agencies in governments. Practically, it is also not possible to distinguish government administrative supervision from party discipline by the DICs.

Anti-corruption bureau within various levels of procuratorates

An anti-corruption bureau established within each procuratorate is responsible for investigating and prosecuting criminal corruption cases. It may deal with government ethics cases only if an ethics rule has been criminalized. Thus, it is mainly a criminal law enforcer. In handling corruption cases, anti-corruption bureaus are guided by the DICs in term of both policy and specific cases.

National Bureau of Corruption Prevention

The National Bureau of Corruption Prevention is a relatively new agency which was established in 2007. Its responsibilities focus on corruption prevention, especially: first, the overall design of corruption prevention policies, collaboration of corruption prevention work across different anti-corruption agencies, and supervision and guidance of corruption

---

[213] Anthony B. L. Cheung, 'Combating corruption as a political strategy to rebuild trust and legitimacy: can China learn from Hong Kong?' *Research in Public Policy Analysis and Management*, 17 (2008), pp. 55–84, p. 77.

[214] Interviewee 09.

prevention work; and second, international cooperation and aid in corruption prevention according to the requirements of the UN Convention
Against Corruption for signed Parties.[215] The news media have also
reported that the National Bureau of Corruption Prevention was charged
with a wide range of anti-corruption powers including cadre education,
institution building, and international cooperation.[216]

The National Bureau of Corruption Prevention has posted its activities
since its establishment in 2007 on its official website. It mainly does the
following: (1) organizing or attending corruption-prevention related
seminars and conferences; (2) visiting foreign anti-corruption or corruption prevention agencies or receiving foreign visitors; (3) organizing
corruption prevention-related study tours for various government
departments, state-owned enterprises, or provinces; and (4) helping to
establish provincial bureaus of corruption prevention.[217] It is more of a
research than an enforcement entity. It does recognize the role of instilling an integrity culture through education but it never educates cadres
or public employees on how to comply with the ethics rules and principles and how to deal with challenging ethical situations or difficulties.
Government ethics regulators' education (the OGE in the United States,
Civil Service Commission in the United Kingdom, and CSB in the Hong
Kong) is more about the rules and principles and their educational
communication has an informal rule interpretation function as following
their advice can usually mean avoiding committing an offence. The
National Bureau of Corruption Prevention does regularly visit various
government departments/agencies but it does not audit these agencies'
corruption prevention effectiveness. It mainly aims at examining various
corruption prevention mechanisms through study tours and it does not
have the power to issue mandatory advisory opinions. It was only
involved in a few government ethics regulation activities. For example,
it, together with Ministry of Finance, Ministry of Foreign Affairs,
Ministry of Supervision, and the National Audit Office, issued a joint
circular of Provisions on Strengthening Management of Fund for

---

[215] National Bureau of Corruption Prevention, 'Responsibilities of the National Bureau of
Corruption Prevention', available at www.nbcp.gov.cn/article/zzjg/ (last visited on 26
April 2012).

[216] 'National Bureau of Corruption Prevention's personnel composition is modelled on
Hong Kong's ICAC', *Wen Wei Po*, p. A9, 21 March 2007.

[217] See the entries under the title 'Recent work' on the Bureau's official website, available at
www.nbcp.gov.cn/article/English/RecentWork/ (last visited on 17 April 2013).

Overseas Business Travel.[218] Though the national bureau claims it is responsible for the overall design of corruption prevention institutions, policy making, and corruption prevention collaboration, it achieves this role through research and collecting information, and it then provides policy opinions to the Central Commission for Discipline Inspection.

Like the Ministry of Supervision, the National Bureau of Corruption Prevention is not really a separate agency though it was given a ministry rank. This new agency is led by the Minister of Supervision and its two deputy directors also concurrently hold senior posts in the Ministry of Supervision. By October 2011, thirteen provincial Bureaus of Corruption Prevention have been established.[219] These newly established provincial bureaus also take the same staffing structure as the national bureau – the heads and deputy heads of the provincial bureaus of supervision concurrently hold the leaderships of the provincial bureaus of corruption prevention. That means, at the national level, the head of the Minister of Supervision, the Head of the National Bureau of Corruption Prevention, and the deputy head of the party's CDIC is the same person; the local levels have copied this arrangement.

Further, the bureau does not distinguish government ethics from criminal corruption. That means the bureau does not have a notion of government ethics regulation centred on conflicts of interest, appearance of corruption, financial disclosure, and outside employment. Its concept of corruption is the same as the CDIC and Ministry of Supervision. Its focus is mainly on criminal corruption just as the CDIC and Ministry of Supervision, but it concentrates on developing preventive institutions. Focusing on criminal corruption does not necessarily mean prevention is ignored. The ICAC in Hong Kong is a criminal corruption enforcer which is also active in preventive measures. However, it mainly concerns prevention of bribery, fraud, and some criminalized government ethics offences (such as non-bribery gift giving). In Hong Kong, conflicts of interest and appearance of corruption are regulated not by ICAC, but by CSB. However, the National Bureau of Corruption Prevention in China,

---

[218] Joint Circular of Ministry of Finance, Ministry of Foreign Affairs, Ministry of Supervision, National Audit Office, and the National Bureau for Corruption Prevention on Issuing 'Temporary rules on strengthening management of government spending on overseas visits for business for party and government officials'.

[219] National Bureau for Corruption Prevention, 'Seminar on "Fighting corruption: theories and practice for preventing conflict of interests" and the fourth integrity forum were held in Hangzhou', available at www.nbcp.gov.cn/article/gzdt/201110/20111000014851 .shtml (last visited on 21 May 2013).

though focusing on criminal corruption, does not have the power to enforce these preventive measures. Thus, it can be viewed as the research and policy advice department within the CDIC. This is not a government ethics regulator comparable with the OGE in the United States, the Civil Service Commission in the United Kingdom, or the CSB in Hong Kong. The three agencies in the United States, the United Kingdom, and Hong Kong make rules, monitor compliance with these rules, and deal with violations, whereas the National Bureau of Corruption Prevention in China only occasionally is involved in rule making together with major rule making agencies (CDIC, Ministry of Supervision). It mainly works on developing new preventive institutions in anti-corruption and advising the CDIC to adopt these institutions. However, it cannot formally introduce these preventive institutions; neither can it enforce them.

In conclusion, government ethics enforcement agencies are the DICs and Ministry/Bureaus of Supervision. As they are indeed 'one team with two labels,' they can be viewed as a single agency. The relationship in practice among the several government ethics enforcers is shown in Figure 4.1. Unlike the OGE in the United States, the CSB in Hong Kong,

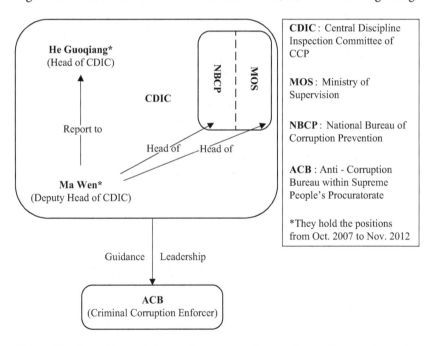

Figure 4.1   The relationship in practice among anti-corruption enforcement agencies in China.

and the Civil Service Commission in the United Kingdom, the DICs are both criminal corruption enforcers and government ethics enforcers with more commitment to the former. The government ethics regulators in the three selected jurisdictions are not involved in the criminal corruption enforcement, whereas DICs are active in investigation and guidance of prosecution in criminal corruption. On the other hand, the regulators in the three selected jurisdictions constantly monitor officials' compliance with government ethics rules and intervene early if they identify even minor deviations. Interviews and other evidence suggest that the DICs only regularly enforce a few categories of existing rules on government ethics and their enforcement activities are mainly centred on punishment of violations. The deficiencies in enforcement further weakens China's government ethics regulations which already suffers from inadequacy and weakness in government ethics rules as discussed in Chapter 3.

4.3.2   Legal enforcement power and responsibilities

As discussed in Section 4.2.2, government ethics regulators generally have the following four types of powers: investigatory power, compliance monitoring powers (e.g. conducting random audits, requiring register of conflicted interests and gifts, collecting and reviewing financial disclosure forms), rule-making powers, and the power for coordination of enforcement across different government agencies. These powers have generally been identified as existing in all of the three selected government ethics regulators.

Given the Communist Party's supremacy in the country's political system, the DICs, generally speaking, have all the powers they need to fight corruption even if these powers do not always have a legal basis. For example, the DICs (including administrative supervision agencies) widely use *shuanggui*, a form of extralegal detention in which a party member is asked to confess to wrongdoing at a stipulated time and place, to restrict the freedom of suspected corruptors. However, *shuanggui* itself has no legal basis because limitation of freedom is one of the matters which can only be regulated by laws made by the National People's Congress, rather than by party rules.[220] Thus, the DICs have

---

[220] Flora Sapio, 'Shuanggui and extralegal detention in China', *China Information*, 22, 1 (2008), pp. 7–37.

no barriers in exercising the identified four types of powers, at least from a practical perspective.

In Chapter 3, government ethics-related regulations in China were analyzed. Most of these rules are jointly made by the CCDI and the Ministry of Supervision. Most media reports on the DICs (including administrative discipline supervision entities) involve their investigatory activities, for example, the above-mentioned 'Property Uncle' case investigated by the Guangzhou DIC. It can be said that rule making and investigation are the most often exercised powers of the DICs in their anti-corruption and government ethics enforcement. Due to the DICs' dominant position in anti-corruption work, it occupies a coordinating position among all the anti-corruption and government ethics regulatory agencies. Even if the National Bureau of Corruption Prevention claims it is responsible for the overall design of corruption prevention institutions and policies, this power is indeed in the hands of the DICs. Interviewee 11 in G Province DIC confirmed this:

> For anti-corruption-related affairs (including government ethics, corruption prevention), the most important decisions are made through the DICs' secretary meetings [*shuji bangonghui*] or standing committee meetings [*jiwei changweihui*]. In our provincial DIC, we have one secretary, who is also a member of the standing committee of the G Province's Party Committee, and four deputy secretaries. DIC secretary meetings are held usually once a week and the five secretaries can make various decisions at the meetings. The head of the Bureau of Supervision of G Province, who is also the head of the G Province Bureau of Corruption Prevention, is one of the four deputy DIC secretaries. This leadership arrangement ensures that the DIC can coordinate other anti-corruption agencies.[221]

DICs also enjoy compliance monitoring powers and the power of issuing advisory opinions. However, in the practice of enforcement, both powers are considerably under exercised. In Section 4.3.1, the 'Property Uncle' case and the 'luxury queen's size bed in office' case have been discussed as notable examples. These cases are not isolated cases. There are also officials, who were implicated in corruption by wearing expensive watches,[222] wearing belts worth 15,000 RMB,[223] and many similar luxury lifestyles. This demonstrates that the DICs seldom monitor officials'

---

[221] Interviewee 11.

[222] 'Internet exposes corruption', *China Daily* (Hong Kong Edition), p. 8, 27 November 2012.

[223] Keith Zhai, 'Watch that watch: officials' displays of wealth scrutinized', *South China Morning Post*, EDT17, 14 October 2012.

wealth. The other form of monitoring identified in government ethics regulation is at the government agency/departmental level. The DICs have two regular monitoring programmes at the agency level. The first one is its inspection teams [*xunshi gongzuozu*] set up in the CCDI and provincial-level DICs. The other is working teams sent out to various government agencies/departments [*jijian jiancha paizhu gongzuozu*]. However, in practice these two kinds of monitoring mechanisms cannot perform monitoring power effectively. The inspection team is more focused on the leaderships' governance as a whole than on integrity/government ethics. An official in R County government, O City, G Province, said that:

> The provincial DIC inspection team mainly focus on the execution of party's line, policies, and decisions (such as improving the industrial structure, changing GDP growth), democratic centralism (collective decision-making for important issues), rules on integrity for party cadres, party style (such as maintaining a close relationship with public, and solving problems which concerns the public the most), and party and government officials' appointment and promotion principles and procedures. The inspection teams usually stay for a short time (from one day to several days). They focus on such broad a scope within a short time period. They do not have time to make an in-depth investigation into the integrity of the leadership of a locality such as my district. Further, they make the party line, party policies, and economic development as their top priority.[224]

This official also said that for integrity inspection, the inspection team focuses on whether these members of the leadership in this district have done any activity violating anti-corruption or government ethics rules. This is not the typical government ethics regulation at the agency/department level. The inspection team does not systematically evaluate the risk of violation of ethics rules in a specific agency/department based on the agency's prevention mechanisms and its enforcement of these mechanisms such as agency supplementary rules, resources, and educational programmes.

   DICs' working teams are sent out to various government agencies/departments and play a very limited role, at best, in monitoring the agency where they are sent to. Their monitoring role is restricted by their strong subordination to the departments where they are sent.

---

[224] Interviewee 38.

This is reflected in an interview with the head of discipline inspection office of F Bureau of Z City Government in S Province.

> Though I am the discipline inspection officer accredited to this bureau, I am, at the same time, a member of the leadership of this bureau. I draw my salary and other benefits from this bureau, rather than from the DIC or administrative supervision entity. In addition to overseeing party and administrative discipline (including anti-corruption and government ethics), I was also assigned other leadership responsibilities to this bureau. These two roles are in conflict to some degree. I cannot supervise the bureau where I myself am a member of the leadership of the bureau. Indeed I am more a leader of the bureau than a discipline inspection official of the DIC.[225]

Though the DICs have no barriers to exercise the common powers given to government ethics regulators, they seldom exercise the power to monitor compliance with ethics rules. Having 'power' means having the right or the authority to do something. Having 'responsibility' means having the burden of doing something. If an agency is under-performing an important power, it is helpful to make the power also a responsibility. For example, in the United States, an ethics official is explicitly required to ensure each financial disclosure report filed with him or her is reviewed within sixty days after the filing date. The ethics official must also state his or her opinion – whether or not the individual submitting the report has complied with applicable laws or rules – and signs the report.[226] This is a good practice to ensure that the ethics regulator properly monitors compliance. Furthermore, DICs may also be charged with the power/responsibility to review and certify the financial reports of an official above a certain level before the official formally takes up a position. This is widely practiced in the US OGE's enforcement. China may consider adopting these practices so that the under-exercised monitoring power can then play a greater role in government ethics regulation.

4.3.3   Enforcement styles

In Section 4.2.3, nine features of compliance enforcement style were summarized and contrasted with the deterrence enforcement style. The three selected countries' government ethics regulators in general adopt a compliance-enforcement style in their dealings with regulated

---

[225] Interviewee 03.   [226] § 106, Ethics in Government Act of 1978 (5 U.S.C. app. 4 § 106).

government agencies and officials. This section will explore the DICs' dealings with regulated government agencies/departments and officials in regulating government ethics against the framework of the nine features of compliance enforcement style. However, it must be borne in mind that, in practice, an ethics enforcer often uses a mix of both compliance features and deterrence features. Thus, there is not a neat division between the two. However, after taking into account all the nine features as a whole, an ethics enforcer can be described as leaning more towards either a compliance or deterrence style. A careful analysis of the nine features shows that DICs demonstrate a clear tendency towards the deterrence end of the compliance versus deterrence continuum in their government ethics enforcement.

The first feature is that a compliance enforcer uses premonitory means to prevent violations through fostering conditions that induce conformity, whereas a deterrence enforcer uses postmonitory means through apprehending violators and penalizing them to prevent future violations. DICs carry out only a few monitoring programmes at the agency/department level. This has been discussed in Section 4.3.2 above. Compared with enforcement activities for individual officials, government agency/department-level monitoring programmes are inherently more premonitory especially when these programmes are agency tailored. That is why agency-level programmes are widely exercised not only in the United States, the United Kingdom, and Hong Kong government ethics regulation but also in other regulatory enforcement areas such as environment regulation and food and drug regulation. The DICs in China largely rely on investigation and punishment enforcement activities. In reviewing internal documents from two county/district-level DICs (N county DIC in Z City, S Province and W District DIC in X City, H Province), two city-level DICs (Z City DIC in S Province and X City DIC in H Province) and one province-level DIC (G Province DIC), it was found that in response to their next higher level DICs' call to fight travel using public funds, four DICs stress that the key is to investigate and punish some officials who travel using public funds in a strict and quick manner.[227] This is similar to DICs' campaign-style enforcement in criminal corruption enforcement in which DICs mobilize agencies such as procuratorates and courts to apprehend and punish corrupt officials as soon and as severely as possible.

---

[227] Internal documents in DICs.

In interviewing DIC officials regarding their commitment in fighting against private travel with public funds, the interviewees were invited to discuss various efforts they had made and their comments on the effectiveness of these efforts. Their discussion centred mainly on quick investigation and serious punishment.

In the conversation below, the involved DIC wanted to improve the probability of catching violators through strengthening investigation capacity (i.e. setting up a special work team).

> We have set up special working group to investigating public funds for travel cases, especially those cases which may lead to strong undesired social effects (eg, increasing public resentment towards the party/government). We pay more attention to large scale travel cases (eg, a department/agency organizes all its members to travel using public funds), travel with a high profile (eg, using government cars with government car identity such as police vehicle, posting the agency/department title on the charted coach for travel, and so on), and luxury travel cases (eg, staying in villas or suites in luxury holiday hotels). Once such a case is found, we will first suspend or remove the involved officials from their positions.[228]

Some DICs increase the probability of catching violators through increasing the number of investigators and encouraging whistleblowing.

> We recently made the investigation of travel with public fund our work priority. We have temporarily drawn thirty officials from other entities/departments to join us. We also encourage the public to tell us about any instances of this that they know about. And, these measures do work; we have identified 27 cases within fifty days since taking these measures.[229]

The words of the interviewee below show that some DICs emphasize the high probability of punishment and magnitude of punishment once the violator is caught.

> The secretary of the DIC has stressed in this Monday's meeting that we must dig out all the officials who dare to violate the prohibition of travel with public funds during the crackdown and punish them more heavily than before. Otherwise, this unhealthy tendency may become even more rampant.[230]

The second feature involves the role of punishment. A compliance-oriented enforcement regulator usually manipulates positive sanctions such as rewards, money grants, privileges, licensing, and limited liability.

---

[228] Interviewee 06.   [229] Interviewee 15.   [230] Interviewee 22.

Further, such enforcement tends to use penalties only as threats to induce compliance and thus when the regulatee demonstrates compliance the regulator will usually suspend or withdraw penalties.[231] In contrast, penalties are integral to a deterrence system and the enforcer tends to manipulate negative punishments. As the discussion about the first type showed, the DICs see punishments as integral to their enforcement of government ethics. Different sources of data have shown that the DICs attach great importance to the deterrence role of punishment in government ethics enforcement.

The third and fourth features concern the regulator's reaction when learning of a potential violation and an actual violation respectively: a compliance enforcement agency tends to take measures to prevent the occurrence of the violation whereas a deterrence enforcement agency usually waits for the violation to happen (or about to happen) so that it can apprehend and punish the violator or violators. The DICs, especially county-level and township-level DICs, have a strong incentive to investigate a large number of cases, especially major and influential cases [da'an yao'an], because their performance is evaluated, at least partly, by higher-level DICs based on the numbers of cases they settle. In three city-level DICs, interviewees mentioned that the number of corruption cases (including government ethics cases) settled by county-level DICs (the next level of DICs) for their localities is one of the factors assessing county-level DICs performance and they are also assessed by provincial DICs (city-level DICs' immediately higher-level DICs) in the same way.[232]

This work performance assessment method practiced by the DICs is also confirmed by several DICs' documents posted on their official websites. Douyun DIC, in Guizhou Province, made an 'Assessment measures for discipline inspection and administrative supervision agencies' cases investigation in Douyun City' in 2013.[233] Article 8 of this

[231] Miles Goodwin and Glenda J. Maconachie, 'Redesigning the inspection blitz in the post Work Choices environment', in Barnes, Alison, Balnave, Nikola, and Lafferty, George (eds), Proceedings of the 24th Association of Industrial Relations Academics of Australia and New Zealand Conference – Work in Progress: Crises, Choices and Continuity, Association of Industrial Relations Academics of Australia and New Zealand (AIR-AANZ), Sydney Trades Hall, Sydney, 2010, available at http://eprints.qut.edu.au/31736/ (last visited on 26 May 2012).
[232] Interviewees 03, Interviewee 04, Interviewees 14, Interviewee 23, and Interviewee 25.
[233] Douyun Discipline Inspection Committee, 'Assessment measures for discipline inspection and administrative supervision agencies' cases investigation in Douyun City',

assessment measure stipulates that 'each township level DIC shall settle at least one case each year. A DIC will get a score of 80 if it accomplishes this basic one case requirement. Each additional case will bring a further score of 10. A DIC will earn a score of 0 for this item if it puts no cases on record in a year.' The overall score of each DIC will affect the DIC's honour and the promotion of the key officials in this DIC. Article 13 stipulates that 'the assessment result shall be circulated in the city in a ranking in which every DIC will be ranked according to their overall score. The result will serve as an important factor in selecting good entity in anti-corruption work and appointing and promoting discipline inspection officials in the city.' The Rong County DIC[234] and Tongchuan City DIC[235] also adopted similar assessment measures. Tongchuan DIC's case investigation assessment measures require that each county-level DIC must investigate at least two cases per year. It assesses the next level DICs' performance every half a year. According to its assessment in the first half of 2012, there was a huge difference of the results among the DICs assessed; the highest score was 153.5 while the lowest score is only 8.4.[236]

Undoubtedly, these assessment practices will lead to a result that the DICs will not likely prevent a potential violation but wait till the violation takes place so that they can apprehend the violators and thus improve their work performance since they are assessed by their higher-level DICs based on the number of cases they have investigated and settled.

The fifth feature concerns the relationship between the enforcement agencies and the regulated parties. Compliance enforcement agencies usually maintain a continuing long-term relationship with the regulated community; in contrast, deterrence enforcers usually make a one-off response (mainly punishment). In the selected three jurisdictions, government ethics are maintained through a continuing relationship through educational programmes, training, visits, meetings, disclosure reports review, providing ethics consulting to government employees,

---

available at www.dyjjjc.com/zcfg/ShowArticle.asp?ArticleID=440 (last visited on 12 April 2013).

[234] Zigong DIC, 'Rong County takes four measures to put into practice the spirit of the basic level DICs case investigation promotion conference', available at www.zgjw.gov.cn/News/show/play/3488 (last visited on 9 April 2013).

[235] Tongchuan DIC, 'Tongchuan made new breakthrough in case investigation by adopting six measures', available at http://jjw.tongchuan.gov.cn/structure/jjxx/jjxxzw_64808_1.htm (last visited on 10 April 2013).

[236] Ibid.

and department ethics audits. In China, the DICs' contact with regulated officials is mainly in the form of investigation and punishment. This is reflected in all the interviews with DIC officials though some interviewees mentioned that preventive institutions are important and they will put more and more attention to prevention in the future.

When asking interviewees to describe the types of interactions with government officials/government departments under their regulation, they mainly mentioned four major means of contact with the regulated: first, handling cases (including criminal corruption cases, government ethics cases, and political discipline related cases); second, carrying out warning education [*jingshixing jiaoyu*] (which usually involves circulating certain typical cases and punishments related to these cases, sometimes circulating the punished officials' confessions in the form of interview by a journalist or the criminal's writing confession letters); third, meeting with government department officials responsible for discipline inspection; and fourth, sending discipline inspection teams [*xunshi gongzuozu*] to prefectures and cities to learn the local leaderships' compliance to discipline rules.

Seventeen DIC officials from five DICs (one province-level DIC, two city-level DIC, and two county-level DICs) were invited to judge the workload of each means of contact with the regulated as a percentage of their DICs' total workload in dealing with the regulated. Sixteen interviewees believed that the investigation and punishment of violators account for at least half of their DICs' total workload in dealing with the regulated. Twelve of the sixteen thought that investigation and punishment accounted for more than 60 per cent of their total work load, while eight of the twelve believed that the percentage was more than 70 per cent. That means one-off contact is the major means that DICs deal with the regulated. This is a striking contrast with the three selected jurisdictions, especially the OGE in the United States and the Civil Service Commission in the United Kingdom, examined above in Section 4.2.3. Apart from the Hong Kong CSB which investigates several hundred government ethics cases each year, government ethics regulators in the United Kingdom and the United States only play a marginal role in investigation. Interviews show that though the DICs in China also employ several means which can help maintain a continuing relationship with the regulated these means only account for a small part of their total workload in dealing with regulated officials.

Further, the DICs' educational programmes and meeting with government department ethics officials are not counterparts to what occurs in the three selected jurisdictions examined. The DIC gives out punishment results and violators' confessions to regulated officials (to act as warnings to behave appropriately); whereas programmes in the three selected jurisdictions mainly involve educating the regulated about the detailed requirements of ethics rules, ethics values, and principles as well as how to avoid violations in confusing or difficult consequences. The DICs' meeting with government departments/agencies ethics officials mainly involves assessing their performance largely based on case investigation work whereas in the selected jurisdictions ethics regulators hope to help the departments develop department-tailored ethics programmes through visiting government departments. Thus, even if DICs had adopted some continuous means in dealing with regulated officials, these are still largely focused on one-off results, rather than instilling the condition which induces compliance over the long term. Undeniably, these DICs' programmes have deterrence effects. But many times an official may commit an offence just because of an ignorance of the rules or a failure to realize a complicated and confusing ethics circumstance. This is especially true for young government employees who newly join the government. Without knowing the details of the requirements, especially in confusing and difficult situations, these new staff may easily commit an offence.

However, some continuous contact means identified in the three jurisdictions have not been adopted by the DICs. These include advisory opinions, regular reviews of financial disclosure, and government department audits. The DICs also issue advisory opinions, but these opinions are either opinions on specific rules or enforcement guidance for government ethics officials. Government ethics regulators in the three jurisdictions frequently provide opinions directly to regulated officials with respect to ethics issues, especially what to do under a specific confusing ethics situation, and many of these opinions are made in an informal manner; this is more like an expert consultancy service. This is useful in establishing a continuing and positive relationship with the regulated as the regulated can take advantage of this service to avoid unnecessary punishment.

In addition to the above four types of interactions, in-house supervisory offices/officials [*jijian jiancha paizhu gongzuozu*] are also established in various Ministries/government departments. This tends to be an ongoing relationship between the regulators and the entities they regulate, at least in its form. However, in practice the supervisory offices sent out by DICs play a poor role in monitoring the agencies where they are sent. The reason is that they are strongly subordinated to the agencies they are to monitor. This has already been discussed in Section 4.3.2 regarding legal enforcement power and responsibilities.

These supervisory offices are also established in state-owned enterprises (SOEs). However, their supervisory roles are even weaker than those sent to government departments. Zhuang Deshui, a journalist, observed that few corrupt cases in SOEs in recent years were found and investigated by offices/officials sent to the SOEs.[237] This is confirmed by the recent Sinopec corruption scandal in 2013 in which at least forty-five officials were involved. Just as Wang Yukai, a professor at the Chinese Academy of Governance, pointed out that the Discipline Inspection Offices in Sinopec appeared to play no role in anti-corruption, as the oil giant had more than 100 senior discipline inspection officials but they did not find anything corrupt until the scandal was disclosed.[238] Indeed, in SOEs, the discipline inspection officials seldom challenge the unethical conducts of key SOE officials. The head of a discipline inspection office within a SOE usually sees himself as an official inferior to the top management officials in the SOE. Further, the supervisory officials' benefits, such as bonus, are decided by the top management officials whom the supervisory officials are expected to monitor. Thus, it is not unusual to see the supervisory offices set out in SOEs become just a mere formality. They do develop an on-going relationship with the managers they are to monitor, but the nature of the relationship is not regulatory in any strict sense.

In summary, though the DICs in China have adopted several means which can help shape a long-term continuing relationship with regulated officials, their role in achieving this relationship is quite weak. Furthermore, many means adopted in other jurisdictions have not been used in the DICs in China in dealing with the regulated. Thus, the DICs' contact with regulated officials is largely a one-off punishment-based relationship.

The sixth feature is that compliance enforcement agencies are proactive in the organization of mobilization of enforcement in that they

---

[237] Deshui Zhuang, 'Discipline inspection offices sent out to SOEs must break through the power constraints of the SOEs', *ChinaNet*, 22 April 2014, available at http://opinion .china.com.cn/opinion_94_96894.html (last visited on 15 May 2014).

[238] Qiao Chen, 'At least 45 officials were involved in the Sinopec corruption scandal', *Beijing Times*, 14 April 2014, available at www.chinanews.com/gn/2014/04–14/6058232.shtml (last visited on 15 May 2014).

attempt to induce conformity either by providing incentives or by using preventive means whereas, for the deterrence-enforcement style, though the mobilization of enforcement may use both reactive and proactive forms, on the whole it is principally reactive. As already discussed previously, the above five features as well as in Section 4.3.1, the DICs rely heavily on investigation and punishments and, at the same time, lack the sense of monitoring compliance. Though they do have preventive programmes, these programmes are quite limited. That is why the 'Property Uncle'–type of cases can happen again and again. Thus, it is safe to say that the DICs' government ethics enforcement is reactive. Their enforcement actions are especially sensitive and reactive to issues which attract major social concern and media coverage, such as the recent Party Chief Xi Jinping's call to the fight against having lavish banquets with public funds and the call for a 'clean plate' campaign.

The seventh feature involves the method of violation recognition. A compliance system creates technical standards to monitor compliance and noncompliance; core offences are thus largely technical and do not cause immediate harmful consequences. Thus, it requires systematic ethics rules (usually a code of conduct as the key document) and constant monitoring by the regulator. DICs still have not made such a code. Though more than seventy CCDI/Ministry of Supervision circulars (provisions or documents) covering some aspects of conflicts of interest, financial disclosure, appearance of corruption, and outside employment/activities have been made, they are mainly abstract principles or prohibitions rather than systematic standards. Take the DICs' asset disclosure rules as an example. As pointed out by Zhu Lijia, a professor at the Chinese Academy of Governance, 'the most important is not income declaration, because it was just a "task" that civil servants must do under the guiding principle. Instead, the key of the declaration lies in the accuracy of its contents and the transparency of its processes'.[239] Zhu stresses the importance of clear and specific requirements on items that need to be disclosed and making the disclosure reports available to the public. If the items that need to be disclosed are not clear and specific it would be difficult to identify problematic items. Abstract and principle requirement on financial disclosure thus becomes a task of filling in a disclosure form.

---

[239] Yinan Zhao and Yin Cao, 'Officials voluntarily give up 771m Yuan in questionable gifts', *China Daily* (Hong Kong Edition), p. 3, 23 October 2012.

After these systematic standards are made, regulators must constantly monitor regulated officials' compliance with these standards, rather than passively react only to serious violations as in criminal enforcement. Unfortunately, the DICs do not pay much attention to deviation from ethics standards per se which are of a minor nature compared to criminal corruption in terms of both harm and culpability. For example, in Section 4.3.1, the questionnaire survey has shown that they only occasionally enforce ethics rules on gifts acceptation, public cars for private use, and financial disclosure, and that some rules such as outside employment rules are almost never enforced. In many cases, a violation is learned from, and the enforcement is triggered by, media report. Further, the DICs tend to ignore ethics violations and pay more attention to criminal corruption. Take the exposed 'Property Uncle' case once more. After confirming that Cai Bin, the so-called 'Property Uncle', and his family members owned twenty-one properties, the Guangzhou DIC's enforcement focus was on corruption crimes such as bribery behind these properties. This is not saying that these crimes should not be investigated. But, the Guangzhou DIC should also review its monitoring system against the fact that why, as an expert government ethics regulator, it could not discover that the official had so many properties. For another example, in May 2013, Zeng Haokong, a section chief of Administration of Quality and Technology Supervision of Hengyang City, Hunan Province, fought with Wang Xianming, the section chief, for the reason that his request of using a government car for private purposes was declined by Wang.[240] However, Wang declined Zeng's request not because he want to uphold government ethics rules prohibiting a government car for private use, but because Wang want to make it difficult for Zeng because of his personal enmity for Zeng.[241] Zeng is not happy because it is common for staff in the section to use a government car for private purposes but his request was declined.[242] The two cases show that DICs in China have not established standard-based violation recognition for government ethics offences.

The eighth feature is about the working basis of compliance enforcement. It is observed that an exchange relationship is the working basis of

---

[240] Xinwu Yan, 'An government official in Hunan fought with his section chief for the reason that his request of using government car for private purpose was declined', *CCP News Net*, 13 May 2013, available at http://fanfu.people.com.cn/n/2013/0513/c64371-21457460.html (last visited on 15 October 2013).
[241] Ibid.   [242] Ibid.

compliance-oriented enforcement where the regulated party can offer ultimate compliance, cooperation, and pay compliance cost, and in return, the regulator can offer forbearance and free advice on compliance. In contrast, deterrence (both general and specific deterrence) is the working basis of the deterrence-enforcement style. Both interviews and reported DICs enforcement news indicate that the DICs believe the deterrence role is most important for fighting corruption (including government ethics regulation). In its fight against corruption including government ethics offences such as travel with public funds, some interviewees from the DICs expressed their strategies clearly. They hoped they could at least control the problem through increasing the likelihood of punishment, the magnitude of punishment, and the swiftness of punishment. They especially stress the punishment of higher-ranking officials; they call this 'fighting tigers'. After party secretary Xi Jinping took office in 2013, he stated at the plenary session of the Central Commission for Discipline Inspection that:

> on one hand we are resolute in investigating the party's leading figures when they are found to be involved in violations of party discipline and the laws of the country. On the other, we keep effectively tackling malpractices and solving bribe-taking issues, which have plagued the general public in their daily life.[243]

He used the analogy that 'we should persist in beating tigers in tandem with the flies'.[244] According to an article in the CCP's news network, 'flies' refer to those officials who violate ethics rules or other minor corruption offences [xiaofubai], such as eating meals paid for with public funds, using government cars for private purposes, and receiving 'red envelopes'.[245] Though tougher measures have been adopted to fight against government ethics offences especially eating meals paid out of public funds since Xi Jinping's speech, these measures are still mainly investigation and punishments, or to use their words, 'beating flies'.

It is worth pointing out that the new party chief also stressed that a regulatory system should be established in the future so that officials'

---

[243] Chi-yuk Choi, 'Xi urges officials' power to be 'confined in a cage', *South China Morning Post*, EDT1, EDT3, 23 January 2013.

[244] Ibid.

[245] Fusheng Gao, 'Beating both tigers and flies shows progress in anti-corruption', *CCP News Net*, available at http://cpc.people.com.cn/pinglun/BIG5/n/2013/0124/c241220-20314541.html (last visited on 14 April 2013).

power can be confined within the cage of regulation.[246] But so far, a regulatory system based on constant and effective monitoring of power is still absent in the war against corruption in China. Earlier, Jiang Zemin and Hu Jingtao, the former party heads, both made speeches on anti-corruption generating expectations that something more would be done to fight corruption, but the status quo regarding corruption remained largely unchanged. It is still early to judge whether President Xi and his administration is willing, or able, to build up such a regulatory system within his ten-year term of office. However there are signals that there will be no changes in the near future. Wang Qishan, a Politburo member and the head of the party's CCDI, the country's top anti-corruption official, tried to play down public expectations spurred by Xi's speech.[247] Wang said to the media that his agency would pursue the policy of treating the symptoms first by investigating and punishing corrupt officials.[248] Thus, the evidence suggests that the working basis of the DICs is deterrence based.

The final feature is about how rules are interpreted. Compliance-oriented enforcement regulators tend to be flexible in the interpretation of rules which allows discretion and situational factors in rule application. In contrast, the deterrence-oriented enforcement regulator is rule bound when interpreting rules and seeks uniformity in rule application. Rule application tends to be tightly controlled for local level DICs (including provincial, city, and county DICs) that follow the rules of the Central Commission for Discipline Inspection (CCDI). A deputy division chief in X city DIC, H province said that:

> We are required to highly follow the rules and internal guidance of the CCDI and seek further interpretation for a specific rule if we are not confident about the real meaning of that rule. We also require lower level DICs under our supervision must keep in line with both CCDI rules and rules made by us.[249]

However, that does not necessarily mean all similar cases are handled by DICs in a uniform way. Though all local-level DICs must follow the CCDI's rules and rule interpretations, they can make rules which are applicable in their own jurisdiction given that these rules are not in

---

[246] Baijie An, 'Power within cage of regulations', *China Daily* (Hong Kong Edition), p. 1, 23 January 2013.
[247] Xiangwei Wang, 'Xi gets off to good start but drastic reforms unlikely', *South China Morning Post*, EDT5, 25 February 2013.
[248] Ibid.   [249] Interviewee 24.

conflict with their higher level DICs. For example, X city DIC in H province and Z city DIC in S province are quite different in dealing with gifts. X city DIC prohibits officials from accepting any gifts worth more than 200 RMB; whereas Z city DIC only prohibits officials from accepting cash, securities, or other types of gifts of great monetary value.[250] But, this is a rule-making authority issue. With respect to rule interpretation per se, for ethics matters governed already by the CCDI, local-level DICs have little discretion in applying these rules to specific cases. Higher-level DICs also frequently use internal notices or files to guide lower-level DICs to uniformly and regularly carry out crackdowns on certain corruption matters or government ethics offences such as travel using public funds and having meals paid with public funds.

Among all the nine features of the compliance versus deterrence enforcement style, the DICs present some weak compliance enforcement features only with respect to their relationship with the regulated officials. For all the other eight dimensions, the DICs show clear deterrence enforcement features.

4.3.4   Enforcement techniques: tools and tactics

Tools and tactics for compliance/noncompliance information gathering

In the study of the enforcement tools in the three selected jurisdictions in Section 4.2.4, government ethics regulators gather compliance/noncompliance information mainly through monitoring tools (such as audit and review programmes both at the government department level and at the individual official level). They also rely on tools such as encouraging whistleblowing and case referral from other government agencies to gather information from a third party. Though investigation is also used, it only plays a small role in gathering information, especially for the US OGE and the UK Civil Service Commission.

All the three kinds of tools (monitoring, investigation, and third party referral/whistleblowing) have been adopted by the DICs. However, the importance and the scope of each differ greatly in the three selected countries. Investigation tools play a dominant role in the DICs' information gathering. Investigation is violation-information focused rather than compliance-monitoring oriented. DICs investigation of government

---

[250] Internal documents in X city DIC in H province and Z city DIC in S province.

ethics violation takes the same form as criminal corruption investigation. The most-used investigation methods are arranging talks [*yuetan*] with the suspected officials and other officials who may know the case.[251] *Shuanggui* is usually not used for cases of a minor nature.

Interviews with officials in several DICs suggest that third-party reporting is an important source for DICs for gathering case information. However, reporting with real names only account for no more than 10 per cent for all the interviewed officials' DICs. This greatly limits the power of this tool. The DICs will generally ignore anonymous reporting:

> We receive reports mainly made in two forms, letters and phone calls; the former is even more popular as letters are more anonymous. We will ignore anonymous reporting first because they are very difficult to follow up. Only very occasionally will anonymous reporting be followed up. Unfortunately, the number of reports mentioning real names is very low. We receive reports almost every week, but we receive no more than ten real-name reports most years. Whistle-blowers are afraid of retaliation and they have cause to worry. Both in my city and in other cities, retaliation of whistle-blowers are not uncommon.[252]

Recently due to the growth of Internet users in China, the Internet has become an important channel for DICs to glean information about corruption. Some place great expectations on anti-corruption campaigns by Internet users, especially after several corrupt officials such as 'Property Uncle' Cai Bin and Yang Dacai were investigated soon after they were exposed on the Internet.[253] However, its role may be overestimated. As Internet whistleblowing is not made to the DICs or other government authorities and DICs seldom take the initiative to learn this information, Internet exposure of corruption or government ethics issues will usually not attract DICs' attention until the exposed case has generated major social concern or is covered by newspapers. The DICs see online corruption exposure more as a pressure or a challenge than as an information-gathering tool. A DIC official expressed his concern on corruption exposed on the Internet:

> In most cases, corruption exposed online will give our DICs a hard time or difficulties. Though a case has been hotly discussed by the public or has

---

[251] Interviewee 08, Interviewee 11, Interviewee 17, Interviewee 23, and Interviewee 27.
[252] Interviewee 24.
[253] Yingying Shi, 'Internet anti-graft effort debated', *China Daily* (Hong Kong Edition), p. 4, 22 December 2012; 'Internet exposes corruption', *China Daily* (Hong Kong Edition), p. 8, 27 November 2012.

raised strong social sentiment towards the involved official, we often know nothing about the case. In order to maintain social stability, we usually have to punish the involved officials before we make a thorough investigation. Thus, corruption exposed online should be carried out in an orderly way. That means the information disclosure on internet should be regulated.[254]

In opposition to the three selected jurisdictions, the DICs generally have very limited monitoring tools for compliance information gathering. There are provisions requiring officials to declare personal matters such as ownership of property, investments, and employment status of family members. However, just as the 'Property Uncle' case demonstrates, these rules are just a general requirement and there is no detailed procedure regarding how these standards should be constantly monitored. Further, the DICs in China do not have monitoring tools such as audits or reviews at the government department level which plays an important role in the United States and the United Kingdom, though the DICs sometimes also visit government departments. These visits mainly involve investigation or study tours [*diaocha diaoyan*], but not audit or review of the department ethics system. Audits are carried out by the Audit Office. But these audits are focused on budgets, expenditure, and other pure financial items; this is not comparable with audits of government departments made by government ethics regulators such as the OGE in the United States which focuses on whether an effective ethics system (such as ethics programmes and ethical culture) exists in a department to prevent ethics violations and how to improve the system if weaknesses are identified.

Tools and tactics for behaviour manipulation

In the three selected jurisdictions, government ethics regulators mainly adopt three tools (advisory opinions, educational programmes, and punishment) to get the regulated officials to act in the desired way. Advisory opinions take three forms: first, opinions on ethics laws or rules; second, opinions on enforcement matters for ethics officials; and third, opinions responding to officials' enquiries about how they should behave in certain confusing circumstances. The third type of advisory opinion can guide the officials in what to do in a certain situation. The DICs in China do not provide this service to regulated officials.

---

[254] Interviewee 13.

The DICs do have educational programmes. These programmes are different from those carried out by government ethics regulators in the United States, the United Kingdom, and Hong Kong. Educational programmes in these three jurisdictions are more focused on making sure regulated officials have a clear understanding of the ethics principles and the rules, making clear what is allowed and what is not allowed, and guiding the officials on specific issues (how to fill in a gifts register, financial disclosure form, etc.). The DICs' educational programmes can be divided into two groups. The first type is political/ideological education in which officials are urged to maintain the credo of a Marxist party, that is, live a simple life, and serve the people. The government has introduced and promoted many model party/government cadres since the establishment of the PRC. For example, Jiao Yulu, party secretary of Lankao County, Henan province from 1962 to 1964, who died at his post, was described by the media as a real communist and died for the people. In 1990, an ideological film, entitled Jiao Yulu, was produced to praise the Jiao Yulu spirit. In March 2014, president Xi Jinping visited the Jiao Yulu Memorial Hall in the Lankao County to honour the 'model of county party secretaries'.[255] Xi told the audience 'to have people in their hearts, disregard self-interest, always seek truth and maintain a heroic and daring spirit despite any difficulties'.[256] This has been proved to be ineffective in ensuring that officials behave in the desired manner as although this kind of education has been carried out for many decades, the corruption problem has become even worse. For example, in August 2013 Wang Guoyan, former party secretary of Nanchang Aviation University, was sentenced to fifteen years in prison for taking bribes totalling 6 million yuan; ironically, he had been teaching Marxist Ideology Education in the university for many years.[257] The comparison of the educational programmes in China and in the three jurisdictions suggests that appeal to Marxist ideology, at least with respect to government ethics regulation, do not work, whereas appeal to professional values and standards do work.

The other type is so-called 'warning education' [jingshi jiaoyu]. This has already been touched on in Section 4.3.3 above. This mainly involves

---

[255] 'Xi Jinping revisits Lankao', Xinhua Net, available at http://news.xinhuanet.com/politics/2014-03/17/c_119810080.htm (last visited on 10 June 2015).

[256] 'Beijing's Facts and Fictions', New York Times, www.nytimes.com/2014/04/17/opinion/beijings-facts-and-fictions.html?_r=1 (last visited on 20 May 2015).

[257] 'An analysis of Wang Guoyan corruption case', CCP News, available at http://fanfu.people.com.cn/n/2015/0507/c64371-26961961.html (last visited on 20 May 2015).

circulating punishment results for certain typical cases to regulated officials. Sometimes these corrupt officials' confession in video interviews or
in other forms will also be circulated to regulated officials. For example,
in January 2015, CCDI listed the main anti-corruption tasks for 2015 and
one of the key anti-corruption tasks is collecting and compiling the
confessions of corrupt officials to warn potential offenders; in March
2015, CCDI has published some officials' confessions in its official
website.[258] This kind of education purports to enlarge the deterrence
effect of DICs' enforcement.

DICs educational programmes appeal to abstract political/ideological
values as well as deterrence, whereas programmes in the United States,
the United Kingdom, and Hong Kong aim to prevent government ethics
offences through manipulating officials' behaviour with respect to specific ethics issues. Though individual government departments have their
own anti-corruption training programmes, these programmes still largely
follow the style of the DICs' educational programmes. For example, after
party chief Xi Jinping and CCDI head Wang Qishan launched 'clean
plate' campaign in early 2013, ministries and local governments carried
out similar programmes.

4.3.5 Enforcement resources

This section will examine the resources, mainly human resources, allocated to government ethics enforcement and this will be compared with
the resources for criminal enforcement as well as total resources available
to the DICs. Three DICs (one provincial DIC, one city DIC, and one
county DIC) have been examined to learn the human resources allocated
to government ethics enforcement. Through interviews with officials in
the three DICs and examining the available internal documents, the
major offices/departments of the DICs and the specific work of each
office/division is as follows. Higher-level DICs usually have more offices/
divisions and staff than lower-level DICs. For the three DICs, S province
DIC composes around 20 offices/divisions and employs 203 staff;[259]

---

[258] 'Corrupt officials' confessions will be published as an anti-corruption tool to warn other
officials', *CCP News*, available at http://theory.people.com.cn/n/2015/0325/c49150-
26745816.html (last visited on 20 May 2015).

[259] Its offices include: General Office [*bangongting*], Secretariat [*mishuchu*], General Office
for Discipline Inspection [*jiancha zonghechu*], Logistics Department [*houqing fuwu
zhongxin*], General Office for Administrative Supervision [*jiancha zongheshi*], Research
Office for Policies and Regulations [*zhengce fagui yanjiushi*], Office for Propaganda and

O city DIC in G province has around 12 offices and employs 75 staff; and W District DIC in X city, H province have 8 offices and employs 23 staff. However they all have the following key offices/divisions (the title of the offices may be slightly different) (see Table 4.6).[260]

Among all these offices, the work of the Office for Party Style and Integrity Building [*dangfeng lianzheng jiansheshi*] is most relevant to government ethics enforcement, though this office still processes many traditional corruption cases. This office's enforcement focus mainly includes: first, using official power or influence to further personal benefits; second, various profit-making activities by officials; third, furthering private benefits through violating provisions on government property management; fourth, appointing or promoting cadres without observing the relevant rules; fifth, using official power or influence to benefit one's relatives or friends; sixth, squandering or wasting public funds; seventh, intervening in market economy activities illegally to gain private benefit; and eighth, making decisions based on false information or impractical assumptions and thus harming the public's interests. Though some of this office's work scope is criminal corruption (such as accepting gifts of cash at festivals or birthday ceremonies) at least in the United States, the United Kingdom, Hong Kong, and many other countries, some aspects of government ethics enforcement such as conflicts of interest and financial disclosure are also within the scope of this office. Hence, using the human resources allocated to the Office for Party Style and Integrity Building is not an exact measurement of DICs' resources spent on government ethics enforcement. But it is a useful indicator as long as we realize that the resources are over-estimated.

Education [*xuanchuan jiaoyu shi*], Office for Party Style and Integrity Building [*dangfeng lianzheng jianshe shi*], Office for Correcting Industrial Illegal Practice [*jiuzheng hangye buzhengzhifeng bangongshi*], Office for Law Enforcement Supervision [*zhifa jiancha shi*], First Discipline Inspection Office [*diyi jianjian jiancha shi*], Second Discipline Inspection Office [*dier jianjian jiancha shi*], Third Discipline Inspection Office [*disan jianjian jiancha shi*], Office for Case Management and Supervision [*anjian jiandu guanli shi*], Case Investigation Office [*anjian shenli shi*], Office for Letters and Visits [*xinfangshi*], Personnel Office [*ganbushi*], Warning and Admonition Office [*jingshi xunjie shi*], DIC Party Committee [*jiguan dangwei*], Information Centre [*xinxi zhongxin*], Service Office for Retired Employees [*lituixiu renyuan guanlichu*], and Cadre Education Centre [*ganbu peixun zhongxin*].

[260] A county-level DIC may combine with the First Discipline Inspection Office [*diyi jianjian jiancha shi*], the Second Disipline Inspection Office [*dier jianjian jiancha shi*], and the Third Discipline Inspection Office [*disan jianjian jiancha shi*] into one single Office.

Table 4.6 *DICs' internal offices/divisions and each office's major work.*

Departments/Offices	Major responsibilities
General Office [*bangong ting*]	Administrative matters
General Office for Administrative Supervision [*jiancha zongheshi*]	Investigating cases or administrative supervision work arranged by the government, people's congress, or Political Consultative Conference at the same level with the DIC concerned
Research Office for Policies and Regulations [*zhengce fagui yanjiushi*]	Planning and making party discipline and administrative supervision related rules/circulars/documents
Office for Propaganda and Education [*xuanchuan jiaoyushi*]	Propagandizing the party's policy and line of discipline inspection work; educating party cadres and government officials on party style and integrity; professional training for officials in charging of discipline inspection
Office for Party Style and Integrity Building [*dangfeng lianZheng jianshe shi*]	Supervising and analyzing party style and integrity building up work; carrying out inspection of party style and integrity building programmes in the DIC's locality; implementing special programmes on cadres' integrity building arranged by the CCDI or other higher level DICs
Office for Correcting Industrial Illegal Practice [*jiuzheng hangye buzhengzhifeng bangongshi*]	Analyzing illegal industrial practice (such as medicine manufacturers and retailers provide commission to buyers in hospital) and providing suggestions for correcting them
Office for Law Enforcement Supervision [*zhifa jiancha shi*]	Supervising law enforcement
First Disipline Inspection Office [*diyi jianjian jiancha shi*]	Investing cases involving officials in Various party organs and government departments
Second Discipline Inspection Office [*dier jijian jiancha shi*]	Investing cases involving officials in public institutions (e.g. hospitals, schools, etc.) and state owned enterprises

Table 4.6 (*cont.*)

Departments/Offices	Major responsibilities
Third Discipline Inspection Office [*disan jijian jian cha shi*]	Investing cases involving key officials in immediate next level locality (e.g. a provincial DIC investigates the key officials in the cities within the Province).
Office for Case Management and Supervision [*anjian jiandu guanli shi*]	Managing case records; analyzing case statistics to put forward work recommendations; following and supervising important cases (e.g. cases which party/government leaders pay close attention to)
Office for Letters and Visits [*xinfang shi*]	Accepting public letters, visits, and handling reporting and complaints
Personnel Office [*ganbu shi*]	Personnel management

For S province DIC, the Office for Party Style and Integrity Building has 12 staff. The number of staff for the O city DIC in G Province and the W District DIC in X city, H province are five and three respectively. Thus, the human resources allocated to government ethics enforcement in the three DICs is 6–13 per cent of the agency's total staff. Therefore, even if the figure is over-estimated, the human resources allocated to government ethics enforcement is still very small.

4.4   Conclusion

In Chapter 3 government ethics rules were discussed. This chapter focused on the enforcement of these rules. It has explored government ethics enforcement in China from five key dimensions (enforcement agencies, enforcement authority and responsibility, enforcement style/ approach, enforcement techniques and tools, and enforcement resources). Empirical data derived through interviewing DIC officials and regulated officials, examining available DIC internal documents, and question-naires, together with published materials, allows a thorough analysis of DICs' enforcement practice. Just as government ethics rules in Chapter 3 were analyzed, this chapter compared mainland China's enforcement features with that of the three selected jurisdictions (the United States, the United Kingdom, and Hong Kong). In doing so, several interesting enforcement features have been identified.

Regarding enforcement agencies, several interesting features have been observed. Each of the three selected jurisdictions has a government ethics enforcement agency which is separate from its criminal corruption enforcement mechanism. Strikingly, China does not have a separate government ethics enforcement agency (the first finding). DICs are both a criminal corruption enforcer and a government ethics enforcer, and with the former occupying a more important position. Further, the DICs have a broader work scope than its counterparts in the United States, the United Kingdom, and Hong Kong. DICs' work includes political/ideological-related discipline, criminal corruption enforcement, and government ethics enforcement; whereas in the United States, the OGE is solely responsible for government ethics regulation while the CSB in Hong Kong and the Civil Service Commission in the United Kingdom mainly has two tasks (government ethics regulation and recruitment – the second finding). A third finding is about the conflicted role of the heads of the DICs. The head of a DIC is at the same time a key leader of his or her locality. As a member of the leadership he or she may consider attracting investment for his or her locality and promoting the economy, a role that may conflict with anti-corruption work, at least from a short-term perspective.

Another finding is DICs only regularly enforce some regulated behaviour of existing government ethics rules (a fourth finding). These enforced rules are mainly about businesses that are run by officials, private travel using public funds, and accepting gifts. DICs only occasionally enforce existing rules on certain matters such as using public cars for private gain and disclosure requirements.

A fifth finding is that from a practical perspective, the CCDI, Ministry of Supervision, and National Bureau for Corruption Prevention can be viewed as a single entity. This is the same for local-level DICs and administrative supervision entities.

With respect to legal authorities and responsibility, the apparent feature is that DICs seldom exercise compliance monitoring powers (e.g. conducting random audits, requiring register of conflicted interests and gifts, collecting and reviewing financial disclosure forms, department audits, etc.); in contrast, monitoring power is the most relied authority in the three selected jurisdictions' government ethics enforcement, especially monitoring power at the government department level (sixth finding).

For enforcement style, a careful analysis of the nine enforcement dimensions clearly suggests that the DICs' enforcement style is deterrence oriented, whereas the three government ethics enforcers in the United States, the United Kingdom, and Hong Kong generally adopts a compliance-oriented enforcement approach (seventh finding).

Regarding compliance information-gathering tools, both the DICs and enforcement agencies in the three selected countries mainly rely on three tools (monitoring, investigation, and third party referral/whistleblowing). However, investigation plays a major role for the DICs and monitoring tools only play a marginal role; in contrast, monitoring plays a major role for the three selected jurisdictions and investigations only play a small role for them (eighth finding). With respect to tools for behaviour manipulation, the three selected jurisdictions (especially the US OGE) use advisory opinions very effectively to respond to regulated officials' confusion regarding ethics in an informal and 'customer'-tailored manner, whereas, the DICs have not adopted this tool (ninth finding).

Finally, human resources directly involved in government ethics enforcement in the three selected agencies account for a considerable part of the overall human resource allocation of their agencies; whereas only not more than 10 percent of DICs' human resources are allocated to government ethics enforcement (tenth finding). Further, this small figure is probably over-estimated.

The findings have important implications for China's government ethics enforcement. First, the importance of separate enforcement systems for criminal corruption and government ethics offences should be recognized. Key government ethics offences can be categorized into four general groups: conflicts of interest, appearance of corruption, financial disclosure, and outside employment/activities, each with several sub-categories. This has been covered in Chapter 3. The core areas of criminal corruption are the 'traditional' crimes such as bribery, theft of government assets, and fraud. The former requires a monitoring-based compliance enforcement system, whereas the latter is addressed with criminal enforcement. It is better to have the two systems functioning separately, just like the role of banking regulation cannot be replaced by, or combined into the police department which investigates financial crimes. China is dealing with both through a single system which is mainly a criminal-enforcement system. Though, theoretically, China has several anti-corruption agencies including the DICs, anti-corruption bureaux within procuratorates, the Ministry of Supervision and its local bureaux, the National Bureau of Corruption Prevention and its local bureaux, in practice, due to the DICs dominance in anti-corruption enforcement, all other agencies can be viewed as internal departments of the DICs.

Ideally, an agency solely dedicated to government ethics regulation (such as the US OGE) should be established in China to take over government ethics regulation from the DICs. More importantly, the new agency should not be led or guided by the CCDI in any manner so that the new agency can develop a compliance-oriented enforcement style, otherwise it may still be influenced by the CCDI's deterrence-oriented criminal corruption enforcement style.

A second implication is a newly established government ethics regulatory agency must adopt a compliance-oriented enforcement style which consist of the nine aspects as discussed in Section 4.4.3. Though recently the top authority in China alleged that more focus would be given to corruption prevention institution building and everyday graft,[261] it would mainly achieve this by making more rules on government ethics such as assets disclosure and punishing violators more heavily. However, all these new rules or institutions are still enforced by the DICs in a criminal enforcement manner. For example, an enforcement campaign, a regular enforcement tool in criminal corruption, has been adopted to enforce government ethics rules (e.g. the recent crackdown on eating meals paid for out of public funds). A political campaign starts from 'a set of political speeches ... from central level politicians ... defining a particular, targeted, stricter and swifter, form of law enforcement for a particular period of time'.[262] Then local-level law enforcer will take organized enforcement action and the central level authority will verify the local enforcement results within the specified period of time.[263] In the crackdown on eating meals paid out of public funds, all these political campaign features apply. More detailed discussion of political campaigns against corruption in China was given in Section 2.4.2.

A separate government ethics agency will offer institutional support for a compliance-enforcement style. However, establishment of a new agency solely for government ethics regulation (or transferring

---

[261] Nick Macfie, 'China's Xi urges swatting of lowly 'flies' in fight on everyday graft', *Reuters*, 22 January 2013, available at www.reuters.com/article/2013/01/22/us-china-corruption-xi-idUSBRE90L0AA20130122 (last visited on 21 April 2013).

[262] Benjamin Van Rooij, 'The politics of law in China: enforcement campaigns in the post-Mao PRC', p. 6, *SSRN*, 2009, available at http://ssrn.com/abstract=1368181 (last visited on April 23 2013).

[263] Ibid.

government ethics regulation responsibilities from the DICs to an existing agency) does not necessarily mean a compliance-oriented enforcement style will be formed. The agency must truly realize that it is designed to monitor compliance of government ethics rules and manipulate the regulated officials' behaviour towards a desired direction rather than apprehending violators and punishing them. Enforcement tools, resources, and authorities/responsibilities must be utilized with this key enforcement purpose in mind. Otherwise, simply superficially introducing various tools in forms identified in other jurisdictions is not likely to make real changes in enforcement style.

Third, some findings show that many existing government ethics rules are simply not enforced, or at least not constantly or regularly enforced. The implication is that this enforcement gap must be filled. The lack of enforcement (or weak enforcement) is closely connected to the lack of separation of criminal corruption and government ethics enforcement due to the DICs' criminal- and political-centred enforcement practice. Lack of enforcement, or under-enforcement, of some existing government ethics rules cannot be avoided when a criminal corruption enforcer is at the same time a government ethics enforcer and the enforcer views itself mainly as a criminal corruption enforcer. Though recently, the party's secretary-general Xi Jinping alleged that the party will crack down on corruption through 'confining power into the cage of regulations'[264] and beating 'tiger and flies together'.[265] Wang Qishan, China's top anti-corruption official, said on 25 February 2013 that the DICs would pursue a policy of treating the symptoms first by *investigating* and *punishing* corrupt officials. This was said almost one month after party chief Xi's speech concerning a crackdown on corruption.[266] Given that the key focus of the DICs is on criminal corruption, it is natural that government ethics is under-enforced. Thus, a separate enforcement system for government ethics will help solve this enforcement gap. On the other hand, enforcement resources for government ethics must be strengthened. Empirical data shows that resources allocated to government ethics enforcement in China are considerably inadequate. And, since regulated

---

[264] Baijie An, 'Power within cage of regulations', *China Daily* (Hong Kong Edition), p. 1, 23 January 2013.

[265] Baijie An, 'Tougher measures on corruption studied', *China Daily* (Hong Kong Edition), p. 3, 24 January 2013.

[266] 'Xi gets off to good start but drastic reforms unlikely', *South China Morning Post*, China Briefing, EDT5, 25 February 2013.

officials have perceived that there is a lack of enforcement, they commit these offences in an open manner.

The fourth implication concerns enforcement techniques. A working knowledge of the wide range of instruments available can provide regulators with a creative choice of interventions to achieve their desired policy outcomes. Monitoring techniques such as audits of government department/agencies' ethical programmes, a systematic review of financial disclosure forms, and conflicted interests disclosure and monitoring, and so forth, are effective ways in gathering compliance/non-compliance information as demonstrated in the three selected jurisdictions. A new government ethics regulatory agency in China should take advantage of these techniques and make a transition from its investigatory centred information-gathering practice. In influencing regulated officials' behaviour China's government ethics regulators should rely on a mix of tools such as educational programmes and advisory opinions (especially opinions responding to individual official's confusing in specific conditions either made formerly or informally), and punishments. Currently, the DICs mainly rely on punishment tools and educational programmes, with more stress on the former. Now, DICs' educational programmes mainly focus on political/ideological aspects (party members should maintain a simple lifestyle and serve the people) and warning education (DICs circulate punishments results imposed on violators to the regulated officials). Educational programmes shall also be reformed so that they are prevention and guidance oriented. For example, the regulatory agency can guide the officials regarding how to fill in financial disclosure forms. It can also regularly educate the officials on how to deal with ethical difficulties common for a specific department/agency; this requires department-tailored educational programmes.

Fifth, human resources allocated to government ethics enforcement within DICs are considerably inadequate. In terms of percentages, it accounts for only 5–10 per cent of the total human resources of a DIC. For a county-level DIC, the number of personnel is around three. Establishing a new agency can help solve this resource problem as this agency would be solely responsible for government ethics regulation.

Separating government ethics regulation from the DICs will help improve the overall regulatory system as many aspects of the system (such as regulatory style, regulatory technique, and resources) are shaped by the DICs' stress on criminal corruption and political/ideological aspects. The DICs have been prevented from carrying out enforcement tasks related to government ethics regulation with their focus on criminal corruption and political/ideological matters. A criminal enforcement style is by its nature investigation and punishment based as well as deterrence oriented. It is difficult, if not impossible, to solve the problem through simply strengthening government ethics enforcement within the DIC system. That is why China should consider separating government ethics enforcement from the DICs system as the starting point of reform.

One question that needs to be considered is this: whether and to what extent can reform proposals regarding government ethics enforcement will be adopted in China? Reforms, depending on their nature, will encounter different levels of resistance from either the top party authorities or the regulated officials.

Though in order to fight against corruption the party is embracing certain reforms, the leadership still lacks the courage to make fundamental political reforms and institute the rule of law to fight corruption.[267] The reason is that reforms such as legislative and judicial checks and balances on the party or the government will erode the supremacy of the party as the country's political regime. Yu Zhengsheng, 'the newly-elected leader of the Chinese People's Political Consultative Conference (CPPCC) and a member of the CCP Politburo', pledged on 12 March, 2013 that 'at the closing meeting of the first session of the 12th CPPCC National Committee [w]e need to more strictly follow the socialist path of political development with Chinese characteristics, not imitate Western political systems under any circumstances, always adhere to the correct political orientation, and strengthen the CPPCC's ideological and political foundations of collective struggle'.[268] Thus, anti-corruption reforms involve things that are difficult to be put into practice. Fortunately, almost all of the above proposed reforms for government ethics regulatory agencies, enforcement style, tools, and resources do not involve serious political aspects.

The only exception is the proposal for strengthening the enforcement of rules on financial disclosure. 'The party fears mandatory disclosure could further damage its image' and erode its ruling legitimacy (see

---

[267] Xiangwei Wang, 'Learn from the West on how to curb graft,' *South China Morning Post*, China Briefing, 22 April 2013.

[268] Zhengsheng Yu, 'Speech at the closing meeting of the first session of the 12th CPPCC national committee', available at www.cppcc.gov.cn/zxww/2013/03/12/ARTI1363071765408886.shtml (last visited 30 April 2013).

Section 2.4.1 for details on the party's concern about its image and legitimacy).[269] Just as the 'property uncle' case showed, a junior official can accumulate a huge amount of wealth, say more than 50 million RMB, which does not match the amount of an official's legal income. A mandatory national level disclosure of assets system will unavoidably expose many such cases due to rampant corruption in China. That will arouse the public's resentment towards the party. Thus, there is reluctance, or at least hesitation, from the top authorities who are the people having the final say on anti-corruption reforms. However, the signs are not totally negative. After party chief Xi Jinping took office in 2013, there has been experimental verification of assets declaration made by officials in selected areas of Shanghai and Guangzhou.[270] Now the CCDI is planning to start random checks on asset declarations made by officials at the national level.[271] It seems that the top party authorities are not intentionally resisting the enforcement of assets disclosure but is not confident in promoting it without damaging the party's legitimacy. Several recent scandals, such as the 'Property Uncle' scandal, the 'queen-size bed in office' scandal and the 'watch uncle' scandal as discussed in Section 4.3.1 were exposed by social media, and this trend is expected to enlarge due to the fast development of micro-blogs and smart phone in China. Exposed by the net users is even worse than exposed by the government ethics regulator through its regular enforcement. Thus, though this reform involves sensitive political aspect, the top authority may be forced to enforce the assets disclosure rules.

Other reform proposals will not face resistance from the top leadership because these measures do not involve political reforms. However, that does not mean there will not be any resistance at all, especially for the proposed agency reform (establishing a separated agency). As mentioned earlier, the obstacle for the country is downsizing and streamlining its party/government agencies. Reform on enforcement style and enforcement techniques will require the enforcement agencies to cast aside its familiar enforcement practice and adopt a new enforcement philosophy and new instruments, which means more commitment from the

---

[269] 'To fight corruption, China must push to disclose leaders' wealth', *South China Morning Post*, 19 April 2013.

[270] Alice Yan, 'Sites unveiled for Guangdong anti-graft pilot', *South China Morning Post*, EDT6, 10 December 2012.

[271] Mei Peng, 'The CCDI is now planning to start random checks on asset declarations made by officials', *Nandu Daily*, A17, 30 April, 2013.

regulators as they would be required to familiarize themselves with the new instruments. Thus, regulators may show their resistance.

It is also proposed that more ethics rules should be made to cover the unregulated aspects of government ethics, especially conflicts of interest and appearance of corruption (see Chapter 3) and change the weak enforcement (and lack of enforcement) situation. From the perspective of regulated officials, these reforms will greatly reduce their benefits as a government official. For example, they will not be able to use public cars or funds for personal purposes like they are doing now. Hence, it is natural that officials will not welcome these reforms. However, all this resistance is mainly at the personal, managerial, and technical levels, rather than the political level. Resistance can be overcome if the party wants these changes to happen.

Another issue related to the effectiveness of government ethics regulation in China is the independence of the proposed new government ethics regulatory agency. Currently DICs' government ethics enforcement is seriously dominated by its criminal enforcement function as discussed earlier. The establishment of a new agency will allow the government ethics regulation function to become independent from the criminal enforcement function. This will create a *more* independent government ethics regulatory agency. However, under China's current one party ruling system, the new agency cannot fully get out of hand of the Communist Party, especially the top party leaders. But, if the party realized that government ethics enforcement will in general not damage the party's legitimacy, it can at least allow the *local* government ethics agencies to function independently from the local party leaders at the province, city, and county levels. This is demonstrated by the Chinese military system: though the army is fully controlled by the party, in general local military command is not subject to local government or CCP committee control. Surely, enjoying this level of independence, the new agencies cannot effectively regulate the conduct of the top party/government officials. But, these new agencies shall be able to function independently in its everyday work at various local levels.

Most countries in their early development stages relied on deterrence to deal with undesired social behaviour. For example, death penalty, or even public hanging, were once widely practiced in many countries to achieve visible deterrent effect. This is partly related to enforcement cost. Regulatory enforcement is a much more resource-demanding enforcement method than deterrence oriented criminal enforcement.

A regulator has to watch every regulatee under its jurisdiction. For example, even if most officials are honest and clean, they still are asked to submit regular financial disclosure reports to the government ethics regulator, and the regulator has to review all the reports. However, a criminal enforcer in general targets at violators or the officials suspected to be corrupt. Thus more resources are needed for the regulatory enforcer, which is a relatively more expensive method than the deterrence method.[272]

Given that China is still a developing country, a question needs to be considered: does China have necessary resource to ensure at least a decent level of effectiveness in enforcing its government ethics regulation? In terms of GDP per capita, China is $6,091, while the United States, the United Kingdom, and Hong Kong are $51,749, $38,920, and $36,796 respectively in 2012.[273] The gap of the development level between the three developed countries and China is still very huge. However, GDP per capita is more an indicator of the people's living standard of a country than an indicator of the adequacy of a country's law enforcement resources. A better indicator of enforcement resources is government revenue because government ethics enforcement resource is largely determined by law enforcement personnel. In 2013, the revenue for the central government in China was 6,017.4 billion RMB (around $965 billion).[274] To simplify the discussion, only the United States is compared here with China. For the United States, federal government revenue was $2,775 billion.[275] Though the US federal government revenue is still 2.87 times more than that of China's central government, salary for government ethics enforcement agency personnel in China is considerably cheaper than that in the United States. The average salary for the US federal government employee is $78,500 per year in 2012,[276] whereas the figure is around

---

[272] This paragraph is partly based on Professor David Donald's comments on an early draft of the book.

[273] The World Bank, 'GDP per capita', available at http://data.worldbank.org/indicator/NY .GDP.PCAP.CD (last visited on 15 October 2014)

[274] 'Government revenue and spending in 2013', available at http://gks.mof.gov.cn/zheng fuxinxi/tongjishuju/201401/t20140123_1038541.html (last visited on 15 May 2014).

[275] 'Government revenue in the US', available at www.usgovernmentrevenue.com/fed_rev enue_2013US (last visited 17 May 2014).

[276] United States Office of Personnel Management, 'Common characteristics of the government', 2013, p. 6, available at www.opm.gov/policy-data-oversight/data-analysis-documentation/federal-employment-reports/common-characteristics-of-the-government/ common-characteristics-of-the-government-2012.pdf (last visited 17 May 2014).

$10,000 for China in 2012.[277] That means a regulatory agency in China can hire more government ethics enforcement staff than the United States with even less budget. The United Kingdom and Hong Kong need to pay a similar level of salary with the United States for their government ethics enforcement staff though, to simplify discussion, relevant data in the two jurisdictions is not included in the comparison.

Moreover, many Chinese cities (e.g. Shenzhen, Guangzhou, Beijing, and Shanghai) and areas (e.g. the Yangtze River Delta and the Pearl River Delta) are gradually catching up to developed economies. Thus, in general the effectiveness of government ethics enforcement in China, especially in some relatively developed cities, will not be seriously constrained by a lack of enforcement resources.

The regulatory regime first takes shape in financial and business sectors and is then gradually introduced to areas such as food and drug safety regulation, environmental regulation, government ethics regulation and other areas. For example, the idea of license and audit is first created in business and financial industry regulation. In Hong Kong, a directorate-level civil servant must seek prior approval if he or she would like to take up outside work within the control period; this is an example of introducing idea of licensing from business regulation to government ethics regulation. The US OGE's financial disclosure report review is an example of introducing the audit idea from business and finance regulation to government ethics regulation. Another reason for heavy reliance on punishment-centred deterrence enforcement style in a country's early development stage is that business and finance sectors were still not highly developed at that time. In China, due to rapid development of finance and business sectors in the last three decades, banking regulation and business regulation in China now become mature. Thus, China now has the basis and potential to develop a regulatory enforcement regime in enforcing government ethics.

---

[277] China does not disclose the statistic of average salary for government employees. However, it is estimated by researchers that the salary for government employees are comparable with the average salary level for private sectors in the same city. See, for example, Guang Zhang, 'Estimating government employees' salary based on official data in China', *Financial Times Online (Chinese version)*, available at http://m.ftchinese.com/ story/001054761 (last visited on 15 May 2014). In Beijing, the average salary is 62,677 RMB (around $10,000) for 2012. See 'Notice of Beijing Statistics Bureau on publishing average salary data for the Beijing City in 2012', available at www.bjstats.gov.cn/zwgk/ ystg/201306/t20130608_250285.htm (last visited on 15 May 2014).

It must be pointed out that though regulatory government ethics enforcement and criminal enforcement against corruption have been compared and contrasted throughout the book. They are not contradictory enforcement methods. Instead, they are complementary enforcement systems against corruption, just as pointed out earlier in Chapter 2. Though punishment is not the purpose of regulatory enforcement, it has shown that regulatory enforcement in general and government ethics enforcement in the three jurisdictions in specific both have to rely on punishments (including criminal punishments through referral of cases to the criminal justice system) as back-up at certain stage where the regulated party decline to cooperate with the regulator. Thus, government ethics enforcers in China should not mechanically resist or avoid punishments just in order to satisfy the characteristics of regulatory enforcement style discussed in Section 4.2.3.

5

Conclusion

5.1 Summing up: key findings and policy implications

Corruption can cause great harm. It can distort the market and under-mine a government's ability to deliver security and order.[1] It can also hinder economic development through a variety of channels. These channels are 'reduced domestic investment, reduced foreign direct investment, overblown government expenditure, distorted composition of government expenditure away from education, health, and the maintenance of infrastructure, towards less efficient but more manipulatable public projects'.[2] Corruption in certain sectors can be even more detrimental, for example in the judicial sector; when courts are corrupted, they can no longer serve their so-called role as the watchdogs of social justice.[3]

Many factors, such as the political system, a free media, anti-corruption laws and their enforcement, and civil society, are connected to the government integrity of a given country. Thus, anti-corruption efforts involve many aspects. Efforts in a single aspect may only mean limited improvement. Therefore, though the book argued that a government ethics regulatory system in China should be strengthened, it by no means argued that criminal enforcement and other anti-corruption measures should be replaced by government ethics enforcement. However, it is difficult to address every aspect in a single research project due to word limitations and the scope of this researcher's knowledge. This

---

[1] Alexandra Addison Wrage, *Bribery and Extortion: Undermining Business, Governments, and Security* (Westport, CT and London: Praeger Security International, 2007), pp. 50–56.

[2] Shang-jin Wei, 'Corruption in economic development: grease or sand?' *Economic Survey of Europe*, 2 (2001), pp. 101–112, available at www.online.bg/coalition2000/eng/bilb/Wei .pdf (last visited on 23 September 2009); and Paolo Mauro, 'Why worry about corruption?' *IMF Economic Issues*, 6, 24 February 1997, available at www.imf.org/external/pubs/ft/ issues6/index.htm (last visited on 23 September 2009).

[3] Ting Gong, 'Dependent judiciary and unaccountable judges: judicial corruption in contemporary China', *China Review*, 4, 2 (2004), pp. 33–54.

research addresses the legal aspects only. However, it does not focus on the criminal laws and their enforcement (criminal laws against corruption and their enforcement are discussed in the research mainly for comparative purposes). Instead, it focuses on government ethics rules and their enforcement *in China* (government ethics rules and their enforcement in three other jurisdictions are also examined for comparative insights). The research has important and practical policy implications for China's government ethics rules and enforcement though it is too ambitious to expect the application of these suggested policy reforms can eradicate corruption in China.

The reason for focusing on government ethics rules is that as long as the CCP remains the ruling party in China it is less likely to make improvements in fundamental political reform, freedom of the media, and bolstering civil society, as these reforms are perceived as being potentially damaging to the party's supremacy in China's political system. On the other hand, regulation of government ethics can help strengthen the public's trust in the government and the ruling legitimacy of the CCP. The reason is that regulation of government ethics involves mainly checking compliance of integrity standards and correcting misbehaviour if violations are found. This reflects an early intervention in the government officials' public conduct involving corruption risks/ potential rather than actual corruption. It will prevent a possible corruption risk from developing to full-blown criminal corruption if the risk is identified and properly corrected in a timely manner. When these corruption risks are reduced or even eradicated through regulatory enforcement, the public will gain more confidence in the government (see Chapter 2 for a detailed discussion on anti-corruption strategies and CCP ruling legitimacy).

Another good reason to focus on government ethics regulation in China is that in terms of both the rules governing government ethics and their enforcement, there is a significant room for improvement when compared with 'clean' countries (or regions) such as the United States, the United Kingdom, and Hong Kong. In other words, the function of government ethics regulation to fight against corruption has not been fully realized. However, the role of government ethics enforcement in China should also not be overstated as it is only one of many mechanisms against corruption. Though government ethics covers a large variety of behaviour, this research has focused on four categories: conflicts of interest, appearance of corruption, financial disclosure, and outside employment/activities, which cover a dominant part of the government ethics field. However, these categories are not mutually exclusive but overlap to some extent. This category and sub-category framework provides a very helpful structure in understanding government ethics.

Three important observations regarding the pattern of government ethics as compared with other jurisdictions have been made. First, though China has more than seventy party/government circulars/documents at the national level dealing with government ethics, some subcategories of conflicts of interest and appearance of corruption have not been reflected in these texts. That means many government ethics violations have not been regulated by China's government ethics rules at all. These unregulated subcategories include: assisting or representing a third party in this person's dealing with government; behaving in a way creating a perception the official may use his or her influence; association with criminals or behaving improperly creating a perception that a judge is in disagreement with the overall justice system; improper statements (or action/behaviour) raising doubts about the basis of an official decision; and appearance of bias towards a certain person. It is apparent that several subcategories of appearance of corruption and a subcategory of conflicts of interest are missing in China's rules. This is a striking loophole in the rules because all unregulated issues, though they are not criminal corruption, are apparently unethical conduct either from a commonsense perspective or if viewing ethics rules in other jurisdictions such as the United States, the United Kingdom, and Hong Kong. Many of China's party rules prohibit government officials from exerting the power of their position to gain private benefits (*actual* use of influence), but they do not take the further step of prohibiting activities which may reasonably be regarded as officials using their influence (the *appearance* of using influence). Taking this further step concerning appearance is important in building the public's confidence in the government.

Second, many aspects, although they have been touched by China's government ethics rules, are only regulated weakly by the rules compared with that in the United States, the United Kingdom, and Hong Kong. These aspects are, first, value transfer from a private source to a government official; second, appearance of favouritism in appointment; third, appearance of favouring one party in official duties; fourth, the scope of disclosed items; and fifth, disclosure to the public. An aspect is weakly reflected in the rules because the prohibitions and sanctions are either not comprehensive enough or inadequate. Take value transfer from a private source to a government official as an example. Value transfer by a private source to a government official not related to that official's official duty is not severely prohibited in China, whereas in the United States, the United Kingdom, and Hong Kong rules prohibit transfers both made in the official's public and private capacity. As another example, the scope of items that one has to disclose in China is considerably narrower than that of other jurisdictions.

Third, some government ethics rules in China are poorly made in terms of legislative technique. This is reflected in the following observations. First, a large number of documents concerning government ethics rules exist but many aspects have not been regulated. Second, the rules generally disqualify officials from participating in certain private actions involving conflicts of interest. However, the principle of disqualification is to disqualify an official from participating in an official activity which conflicts with his personal interests. Personal activities can be handled by 'outside activity/employment' rules. Third, self-dealing rules are not equipped with enforcement tools such as taxes on controlled transactions and diversion of investments. Fourth, China does not have a code of conduct–like document, which is the most important document concerning government ethics. Fifth, government ethics rules are mainly composed of three types of rules – values (general moral obligations such as integrity, impartiality, honesty, etc.), principles (guidance or expectations of behaviour such as that government officials should avoid conflicts of interest and the appearance of corruption), and specific standards (rules which articulate the principles expected of government officials when confronting unclear or ambiguous ethical circumstances through setting forth the majority of circumstances that confront government officials). Rules in China lack provisions about ethics principles. And six, many rules are ambiguous and too abstract.

In addition to these findings, it is also found that some rules in China are unjustified as they play only a marginal role in achieving the purpose of improving government integrity and at the same time impose unnecessary burdens on the regulated officials. Both rules prohibiting officials' spouses and children from running businesses and rules prohibiting 'naked officials' (officials whose children and spouses are not residing in China) from serving as heads of party organs or government departments are examples of this problem (see Section 3.4.5 and Section 3.6 in Chapter 3 for detailed discussion). Take rules prohibiting the spouse and children of covered officials from running business as an example. These rules cannot effectively prevent officials from abusing power for private gains as they can still benefit private businesses controlled by their other relatives or close friends. On the other hand, officials' spouses and children suffer an unnecessary burden as running a business by officials' spouses and children is not wrong as long as they do not profit from official power.

These findings have important implications for rule reform. China must review its government ethics rules against the four categories framework (including the subcategories for each) systematically so that the loopholes can be filled. Further, rule-making techniques must be improved to advance the current scattered, repeated, and ambiguous rules into a coherent, comprehensive, and clear system. Moreover, the unjustified rules shall be repealed. The most important implication of the unjustified rules is that rule-making shall not merely respond to corruption/unethical phenomena but shall address the core problem underlying these phenomena.

The enforcement of government ethics rules in China have been explored from five key dimensions (enforcement agencies, enforcement authority and responsibility, enforcement style/approach, enforcement techniques and tools, and enforcement resources). Empirical data derived through interviewing DIC officials and the regulated officials, examining available DIC internal documents, and questionnaires, together with published materials, have shown interesting features of DICs' enforcement practices. Regarding enforcement agencies, several interesting features have been observed. First, China does not have a government ethics enforcement agency separate from its criminal corruption enforcement; DICs are both a criminal corruption enforcer and a government ethics enforcer, with the former being in a more important position. Though China does have several anti-corruption agencies, from a practical perspective, the CCDI, Ministry of Supervision, and National Bureau for Corruption Prevention can be viewed as a single entity. This is the same for local-level DICs and administrative supervision entities. Further, the head of a DIC is at the same time a key leader of his or her locality. As a member of the leadership he or she may consider attracting investment for his or her locality and promoting its economy which may conflict with anti-corruption work, at least from a short-term perspective. Another finding is that the DICs only regularly enforce a few of the existing government ethics rules (mainly including running a business by officials, private travel using public funds, and accepting gifts); rules on certain aspects such as using a public car for private gain and disclosure requirements are only enforced occasionally.

Indeed, the DICs do not distinguish government ethics enforcement from criminal corruption enforcement. Nor do they realize the systematic difference between them. From the perspectives of enforcement authorities/responsibilities, enforcement style, and enforcement tools and techniques, the DICs enforce government ethics rules in the same manner as they enforce criminal corruption. Their style is deterrence-oriented in contrast to being compliance-oriented. Their powers mainly involve investigation and punishment, and they seldom exercise compliance-monitoring powers (e.g. conducting random audits, requiring register of conflicts of interest and received gifts, collecting and reviewing financial disclosure forms, department audits, etc.). In information gathering, investigation plays a major role for the DICs and monitoring tools only play a marginal role; in contrast, monitoring plays a major role for the three selected jurisdictions and investigation only plays a small role. The DICs have not adopted tools such as advisory opinions in behaviour manipulation, whereas the three selected jurisdictions (especially the US OGE) use these tools very effectively in dealing with regulated officials' confusion about ethics in an informal and 'customer-tailored' manner.

These findings have shed important light on and have straightforward implications for how government ethics enforcement can be achieved in China. China should transfer from the deterrence-enforcement style to the compliance-oriented enforcement style in regulating government ethics. This transfer requires China to make changes in its enforcement agencies, enforcement powers, and enforcement tools accordingly. Separating government ethics regulation from the DICs will help improve the overall regulatory system as many aspects of the system (such as regulatory style, regulatory technique, and resources) are shaped by the DICs' stress on criminal corruption and political/ideological concerns. The DICs have been preempted on this matter by having to focus on enforcement tasks related to criminal corruption and political/ideological matters. And a criminal enforcement style is by its nature investigation and punishment based as well as deterrence oriented. It is difficult, if not impossible, to solve this problem through simply strengthening government ethics enforcement within the DIC system. That is why China should consider separating government ethics enforcement from the DIC system as the starting point of reform.

In general, the recommendations suggested in government ethics rule making and enforcement of these rules in China will not encounter fierce resistance because almost all of the above proposed reforms do not involve serious political aspects. However, there might be reluctance, or at least hesitation, from the top authorities for certain reforms. For example, a mandatory national level disclosure of asset systems will unavoidably expose many corruption cases in China; that may arouse the public's resentment towards the party. It seems that the top party authorities are not intentionally resisting the enforcement of assets disclosure but are not confident in promoting it without damaging the party's legitimacy. The top authority's hesitation may be dissipated if they realized the regulatory regime can strengthen public trust in the government instead of ruin party legitimacy as criminal corruption does.

There are also resistance from the regulators and the regulated officials. For the former, reform on enforcement style and enforcement techniques will require the enforcement agencies to adopt a new enforcement philosophy and new instruments, which means more commitment from the regulators. For the latter, recommendations to cover the unregulated aspects of government ethics, especially conflicts of interest and appearance of corruption will greatly reduce their benefits as a government official. Hence, it is natural to expect resistance from these reforms. However, all this resistance is mainly at the personal, managerial, and technical levels, and thus can be overcome if the party wants these changes to happen.

5.2   Contributions

Contributions of the research are fourfold. First, this research helps explain and understand the fight against corruption in China. Laws (rules) and their enforcement are not new perspectives to understanding anti-corruption in China; it seems superficial to say that both government ethics rules and their enforcement need to be improved in China, as this appears obvious. This research has thrown up fresh ideas with respect to the specific weaknesses of the existing rules in China. It has successfully identified the area which has not been regulated by rules (e.g. representing a third party in dealing with the government), the area where the existing rules are not comprehensive (e.g. the transfer of economic value from a private source to a government official), and the technique problems of rules (e.g. ambiguous language, scattered rules in various documents). Though existing research has pointed out that weak law enforcement is a problem in China both in general and more specifically for fighting corruption, this research, when referring to 'enforcement', largely means investigation, prosecution, or punishment. This current research has shown that it is not only a problem of strictness or toughness (punishment likelihood and punishment magnitude) of punishment, but an issue about a government ethics enforcement regime in China which requires corresponding enforcement agencies, enforcement styles, enforcement powers, and enforcement tools and techniques. Thus, this research can provide a better understanding of the weakness of the rules and the problem of enforcing these rules.

The second contribution that this research makes concerns the development of frameworks that can be used in analyzing government ethics. The four key categories of government ethics (conflicts of interest, appearance of corruption, financial disclosure, and outside employment/ activities) are derived from observing codes of conduct for government officials in the United States, the United Kingdom, and Hong Kong, and allows a systematic analysis of the broad notion of government ethics. The subcategories of conflicts of interest and appearance of corruption, although they are not original, have not been used to examine conflicts of interest and appearance of corruption in China. Extension of these frameworks to China is fruitful. For example, existing research on fighting corruption in China has touched on the notion of conflicts of interest. However, without the subcategories model of conflicts of interest the existing research would not have found that many conflicts of interest forms have not yet been regulated by ethics rules instituted by the Chinese government. Further, in examining enforcement style, this research is the first to systematically extend the nine features of enforcement styles into government ethics enforcement. Previously, these features were developed mainly in the areas of financial regulation, work safety regulation, environmental regulation, and food and drug regulation.

Third, this research offers an original and empirical contribution to the study of government ethics enforcement in China. Corruption is a sensitive topic in China; most existing research mainly relies on easily available official data and other published literature. This research successfully collected rich empirical data from interviewing government ethics officials and reviewing the internal documents of government ethics regulatory agencies. The data collected offers important empirical evidence to the DICs' deterrence-oriented enforcement style. Many interesting and striking findings are based on empirical data, such as the findings in relation to the DICs enforcement of only a small amount of unethical behaviour covered by China's ethics rules, and the DICs' criminal corruption–centred enforcement practice.

Fourth, the research has offered practical implications both for government ethics rule making and the enforcement of rules in China. With respect to government ethics rules, much unethical behaviour (e.g. officials representing a third party in the third party's dealings with the government) has not been covered under existing laws; thus a reform of the rules must fill the gap. Regarding enforcement, reform in a variety of aspects including increasing the number of enforcement agencies, increasing enforcement powers, and adapting enforcement styles and enforcement tools are required. Detailed policy implications of the research have already been discussed in Section 3.6 and Section 4.4.

5.3   Recent anti-corruption developments in China

After party chief Xi Jinping took office in 2013, verification of assets declarations made by officials has been piloted in selected areas of Shanghai and Guangzhou.[4] Now, the CCDI is planning to start random checks on asset declarations made by officials at the national level.[5] The top authorities in China also state that more focus will be given to corruption prevention institution building and everyday graft,[6] and that a regulatory system should be established in the future so that officials' power can be confined within the cage of regulation.[7] It seems that the top authorities in China have realized the current problems that they face in their fight against corruption and are planning to establish a government ethics regulatory system. However, evidence suggests that changes are not likely to happen in the near future.

So far, a regulatory system based on constant and effective monitoring of power is still absent in the war against corruption in China. Though party chief Xi Jinping expressly mentioned about establishing a regula-tory system to curb officials' power, there are signals that changes in anti-corruption legislation will not occur in the near future. Wang Qishan, a Politburo member and the head of party's CCDI, and who is the coun-try's top anti-corruption official, tried to play down public expectations spurred by Xi's speech.[8] Wang said to the media that his agency would pursue the policy of treating the symptoms first by investigating and punishing corrupt officials.[9]

---

[4] Alice Yan, 'Sites unveiled for Guangdong anti-graft pilot', *South China Morning Post*, p. 6, 10 December 2012.

[5] Mei Peng, 'The CCDI is now planning to start random checks on asset declarations made by officials', *Nandu Daily*, p. A17, 30 April 2013.

[6] Nick Macfie, 'China's Xi urges swatting of lowly "flies" in fight on everyday graft', *Reuters*, 22 January 2013, available at www.reuters.com/article/2013/01/22/us-china-corruption-xi-idUSBRE90L0AA20130122 (last visited on 21 April 2013).

[7] Baijie An, 'Power within cage of regulations', *China Daily* (Hong Kong Edition), p. 1, 23 January 2013.

[8] Xiangwei Wang, 'Xi gets off to good start but drastic reforms unlikely', *South China Morning Post*, 25 February 2013.

[9] Ibid.

Wang's words are consistent with recent anti-corruption efforts which still mainly focused on investigation and punishment. The president Xi Jinping has launched an unprecedented anti-corruption campaign since he came into power in 2013. The following three efforts of Xi's anti-corruption drive are especially eye-catching. First, in addition to the Bo Xilai case, a former member of the central Politburo and former party chief of Chongqing city, and the Xu Caihou case, a former member of the central Politburo and former Vice-Chairman of the Central Military Commission, Zhou Yongkang – a former member of the 17th Politburo Standing Committee (PSC), China's highest decision-making body, and the former Secretary of the Central Political and Legal Affairs Commission – was charged with bribery, abuse of power, and disclosure of state secrets in April 2015. Zhou Yongkang is not only the biggest 'tiger' to be caged in president Xi Jinping's anti-corruption drive, but he is also the most senior figure in the Communist party's history to be charged with bribery.

A second effort of the campaign is to catch and punish the corrupt officials who are currently on the run to enhance the deterrence effect. For example, in the 2014 Beijing APEC Summit, China reached consensus with other APEC members in hunting down fugitives at large, recovering their ill-gotten assets, and expanding law enforcement cooperation.[10] In April 2015, China released a detailed list of 100 corruption fugitives and captured the first person, Dai Xuemin, on 25 April 2015.[11]

Another recent effort is to reform the national anti-corruption bureau to better cope with the increasing caseload. In November 2014, the central government approved the reform plan of the anti-corruption bureau. The most important aspect of the reform is the new bureau will be promoted to vice-ministry ranking, which will allow the bureau to break institutional barriers in investigating cases involving higher ranking officials. It is clear that all of the recent anti-corruption efforts are still deterrence oriented.

Further, though verification of financial disclosure has been experimented in several cities and more institutions may be launched, all these new rules or institutions are still enforced by the DICs in a criminal enforcement manner. For example, enforcement campaigns, a regular

---

[10] Wang Hairong, 'Coming together against corruption', available at www.bjreview.com.cn/print/txt/2014-12/08/content_657227.htm (last visited on 24 May 2015).

[11] 'China nets wanted economic fugitive', *Xinhua Net*, available at http://news.xinhuanet.com/english/2015-04/25/c_134184257.htm (last visited on 24 May 2015).

enforcement tool in criminal corruption, have been adopted to enforce the recent crackdown on eating meals paid for with public funds. A political campaign starts from 'a set of political speeches . . . from central level politicians . . . defining a particular, targeted, stricter and swifter, form of law enforcement for a particular period of time'.[12] A local-level law enforcer will take organized enforcement action and then the central-level authority will verify the local enforcement results within the specified period of time.[13] In the crackdown on eating meals paid for with public funds, all these political campaign features apply. Thus, enforcement is still focused on deterrence through apprehension and punishment rather than on constantly monitoring compliance.

5.4   Further research

This research has focused on regulating government ethics in China. Regulation in this research is restricted to official regulation which means that rules are made and enforced by official entities. However, unofficial institutions such as the media, Internet forums, micro-blogs, and especially smartphones, also play a role in monitoring government officials' conduct even if in China there is no free media and the Internet is subject to censorship. Many corrupt officials (such as the 'property uncle' and the 'watch uncle' cases discussed in Chapter 4) in China are first exposed on the Internet by ordinary citizens. Thus, it is interesting to examine to what extent the Internet and other media will play a role in monitoring government ethics in China in the future and what will be the government reaction to this media and Internet exposure of corruption? The role of the Internet in opposing corruption has been noticed recently in China. For example, news articles have been discussing the success of bringing corrupt activities to light by micro-bloggers.[14] The authorities also encourage web users to provide tips to bring the corrupt to justice.[15] However, systematic academic study about this has not yet been undertaken.

---

[12] Benjamin Van Rooij, 'The politics of law in china: enforcement campaigns in the post-mao PRC', *SSRN* (2009), p. 6, available at http://ssrn.com/abstract=1368181 (last visited on 27 December 2011).

[13] Ibid.

[14] Jia Cui, 'Micro blogs make graft fight hot news', *China Daily*, p. 6, 15 May 2013; Richard Fu, 'Claims posted online bring down top planning official', *Shanghai Daily*, p. A02, 15 May 2013; and 'Official falls via Internet', *China Daily*, p. 8, 14 May 2013.

[15] 'Graft tip sites a success', *Global Times*, p. 5, 9 May 2013.

Further, the research mainly focused on the politics related factors in considering the promotion of government ethics regulation in China. It concluded that the regulatory system would not damage the party's ruling legitimacy as it is different from criminal enforcement. Thus, in general, proposed reforms should not face serious resistance from the top authority. Though political aspects are the most fundamental and direct factors that will affect the effectiveness of government ethics regulation in China, other factors may also influence the establishment and enforcement of such a regulatory system against corruption. For example, traditional Confucian culture and Deng's slogan that obtaining wealth is glorious may, to some extent, influence the effectiveness of the implementation of government ethics regulation in China. However, the culture area is a complicated factor to explore. This research did not examine these issues in more detail due to space limitations. Future research can further discuss how and to what extent cultural factors will influence government ethics regulation in China and how to design specific ethics rules and enforcement tools for China.

Appendices

Appendix A: A note on research methods

The research in this book involved both literature and textual searches and fieldwork. The first part of this research mainly included the following materials: academic literature, relevant news articles, government reports, and laws and rules governing government ethics.

The research mainly included two aspects: the rules themselves and the enforcement of these rules. Discussion of the rules is addressed by desktop research. First, the literature on government ethics principles and categories in general was examined to figure out the appropriate frameworks to analyze government ethics rules and their enforcement. Second, government ethics rules in three selected jurisdictions (the United States, the United Kingdom, and Hong Kong) were systematically examined. The features and patterns of the government ethics rules in the three countries provide a standard to examine China's rules. Finally, government ethics rules in China were searched and then analyzed. This part mainly involved rule searching and rule analysis methods.

The second aspect of the research is a discussion of the enforcement of government ethics rules. As enforcement is about how to maintain adherence to the rules in reality, it is not enough to examine this based solely on academic literature, especially for China where existing research on this area is limited. Thus, fieldwork was carried out on government ethics enforcement in China. However, study on theories on enforcement elements and enforcement features in the three jurisdictions was still based on existing research and data available from government regulatory agencies.

More specifically, interviews, internal documents review (archive study), and questionnaires were used in this research. Of the three methods, interviews were the most essential as access to archives was subject to negotiation while the fieldwork was being carried out. Individual interviewees promised access before entry into the field. The questionnaires were designed prior to the fieldwork and the target participants selected; successful collection of a decent number of completed questionnaires could not be guaranteed.

Interviews were conducted in three cities in China: one in central China, one in west China, and one in south China. To protect the identities of the interviewees, the city names will not be disclosed as disclosure of a city's name is tantamount to disclosing the name of the interviewee's government agency. Disclosure may lead to harm or inconvenience for the interviewees.

About ten to fifteen government ethics regulatory officials (specifically speaking, DIC officials) in each city were interviewed to learn about what actions are actually regulated by them, about the scope of their powers, about their enforcement methods, and about any other information which can help us to understand government ethics enforcement in China. About five civil servants under regulation in each city were interviewed to obtain data from the perspective of the regulated (i.e. what behaviours are prohibited and what are not in the eyes of the regulated).

Interviews were not strictly structured by a 'one question after another' format, so that interviewees could tell their stories in the least obtrusive way. However, some key interview questions had been designed in advance to guide the interview. These questions are listed in Appendices D and E. Further, interviews conducted at the beginning sparked other questions, which were not thought of when planning the original interview. These questions were added to the remaining interviews.

Internal documents of regulatory agencies and data from questionnaires were also examined to crosscheck with the information derived from the interviews to increase the reliability of the data.

Appendix B: Key issues addressed in government
ethics rules in the United States, the United Kingdom,
and Hong Kong

Category of Ethics Rules	Framework	The United States	The United Kingdom	Hong Kong
Conflicts of interest	Self-dealing: a public official must disqualify himself from participating in an action related to his public office in case this action may affect his personal interests	• General disqualification • Excise tax and additional tax on self-dealing transactions • Disqualification if officials' former employer/clients involved • Disqualification for ex-lobbyists[1] • Prohibits from holding certain interests which might raise conflict	• General disqualification requirements • Disqualification if ministers retaining conflicted interests	• General disqualification requirements • Diversion of interests which conflict with their official duties
	Transfer of economic value from private source to a public official (not bribery)	• Compensation outside government • Benefits such as gifts and honorary club membership • Reduction in claim for allowed outside payments for travel	• Benefits such as gifts and hospitality • Compensation	• Advantages such as gifts, hospitality, or entertainment

(cont.)

Category of Ethics Rules	Framework	The United States	The United Kingdom	Hong Kong
	Assisting a third party in dealing with the government Profiting from misusing official position; eg, using information obtained in official duties to gain economic value	• Assisting or representing a third party in dealing with government • Accepting a gift from a subordinate official • Using public office for the endorsement of any product, service, or enterprise, or for the private gain of friends, relatives • Using nonpublic information to further one's own private interests • Using government resources for political party purposes	• Act as a paid advocate in any proceeding of the House • Efficient and cost-effective travel arrangements • Avoid official transport for private travel arrangements. • Earned air miles in business travel[2] • Public resource only for official duties • Using government resources for political party purposes	• Representing any person in dealing with government • Misuse official position for personal interests • Use any public resource for private purposes • Flight awards earned in business travel • Using government resources for political party purposes

Appearance	• Proper use of court premises, stationery	• Proper use of judicial office[3]	• Proper use of judicial status[4] • Proper use of judicial stationery[5]
• Behaving in a way creating a perception the official may use his influence	• Appointment impartially and on the basis of merit • Avoid nepotism, favouritism, and unnecessary appointments.	• Appointment on the basis of merit • Other requirements on public appointments[6]	• Civil servants are appointed, managed, and promoted on the basis of merit
• Appearance of favouritism in appointment even if actual favouritism cannot be proved	• Prohibits ex parte communication • Disqualification if a judge has a personal bias or prejudice concerning a party or a party's lawyer	• Prohibited from sponsoring individual nominations for any awards • Personal relations with law practitioners	• Prohibits ex parte communication • Intervention manner in listening to a case • Social contact with the legal profession
• Appearance of favouring one party in dealing with official duties	• Avoid responding to public criticism of a judgment or decision	• Avoid responding to public criticism of a judgment or decision • Disagreements over judicial decisions in the media	• Visiting pubs, bars, karaoke lounges, casinos, or these kinds of places (consider the reputation of the place visited and any concern that the place might not be operated in accordance with law)
• Association with criminals or behaving improperly creating a perception the judge disagrees with the overall justice system			

247

(cont.)

Category of Ethics Rules	Framework	The United States	The United Kingdom	Hong Kong
	Improper statement (or action/behaviour) raising doubt on the basis of an official decision	• Avoid impressions that any person or organization is influencing the judge • Avoid making any public statement that might affect the outcome or impair the fairness of a matter pending	• Avoid public demonstration that associates the judge to a political stance • Expression out of court creating perception of bias or prejudgment in cases that later come before the judge	• Avoid unjustified offensive remarks about litigants • Avoid giving legal advice • Avoid visiting old chambers or law firms. • Avoid using facilities (clubs) operated by or for organizations that appear frequently before courts[7]
	Appearance of bias towards a certain person	• Avoid any display of bias or prejudice on various grounds • Perform duties of judicial office without bias or prejudice. • Require lawyers before the court to refrain from manifesting bias or prejudice	• Avoid any display of bias or prejudice on various grounds • Proper arrangements in cases involves a disabled party so that the disabled face no disadvantage	• Treat all who appear in court without any display of prejudice • Avoid improper intervention, such as interruption of the claimant's or defendant's words

	Who discloses? What to disclose? / Whom to disclose?	Government officers	Ministers and MPs	Civil servants and PAOs
Financial disclosure	Who discloses? What to disclose?	• Assets such as income, properties • Transactions (purchase, sale or exchange) • Gifts • Outside positions such as an officer, director • Liabilities • Agreement or arrangement for future employment	• Land, property, Shareholdings • Controlled transaction • Gifts, hospitality, Sponsorships • Outside positions[8] • Overseas travel • Meetings with external organizations • Clients	• Any interest in land or buildings • Investment transactions[9] • Material benefit, gift, payment, sponsorship • Undertaking such as company directorship • Investment (shareholding, securities, option contracts)
	Whom to disclose (to a commission or the public)	• Senior officials disclose to the public • Other government employees disclose to an agency	• Disclose to the public	• Civil servants disclose to department head • PAOs disclose to the public
Outside work and outside activities		• During office, outside work may divert an official's energy and attention • During office, outside work may arouse, or appear to arouse, conflicts of interest • Restriction on outside income[10] • Outside employment[11] • Permit one's name to be commercially used • Paid teaching, speaking, or writing • Dual pay from more than one position in the govt. prohibited	• Dual public employments • Paid writing and speeches • Making arrangements on the publication of books after leaving office • Acting as paid advocates	• Government's prior call on the abilities, energies, and attention • Outside positions • May advise other government or international organizations after receiving approval[12]

Category of Ethics Rules	Framework	The United States	The United Kingdom	Hong Kong
		• Prior approval before engaging in specific outside activities and employment • Using official influence to further fundraising effort in a personal capacity		• Prohibited from production of any publication in which paid advertisements are reproduced
	After leaving office, it is possible that outside work may still arouse conflicts of interest	• Lobbying in control period • Representing a third party within certain period	• Lobbying in control period • Seeking approval if taking up any employment • Judges prohibited from practicing law as a barrister or as a solicitor	• Lobbying activities • Prior approval before taking up outside work within control period[13] • Bid for government land, property, projects, contracts, or franchises • Representing a third party

[1] For example, ex-lobbyists are barred from participating in any matter that they have lobbied before joining government.

[2] Earned air miles in business travel can only be used for government travel.

[3] For example, a judge shall not allow his residence to be used to, by a member of the legal profession, receive clients or other members of the legal profession.

4 For example, a judge volunteers his judicial status to the police when he is stopped for an alleged traffic offence.

5 For example, writing to complain about an insurance policy.

6 The Ministerial Code 2010 contains many provisions, together with requirements of Civil Service Commissioners' Recruitment Principles.

7 Such as the Police and the ICAC.

8 Including directorships, remunerated employment, office, and profession.

9 Acquisitions and disposals reaching certain value per transaction.

10 Not more than 15 per cent of annual income for government officers with basic pay equal to or greater than $119,553.60.

11 Including receiving compensation for affiliating with or being employed by a firm, partnership, association, corporation, or other entity which provides professional services involving a fiduciary relationship; receive compensation for practicing a profession which involves a fiduciary relationship; or serve for compensation as an officer or member of the board of any association, corporation, or other entity.

12 However, permission will not be given if the officer will retain more than 50 per cent of the fee or honorarium offered for his or her consultancy services.

13 Outside employment will not be approved if that brings unfair advantage/benefit (or such impression) to his or her prospective employer. Outside activities which might negatively affect an officer's official performance or distract his or her attention from his or her official duties must be avoided.

Appendix C: Key issues addressed in government ethics rules in China

Category	Framework	Specific issues addressed
Conflicts of interest	Self-dealing: a public official must disqualify himself from participating in an action related to his or her public office in case this action may affect his or her personal interests	• General disqualification requirements • Disqualified from buying or selling securities for officials who may have inside information • Setting up businesses by party organs and governments prohibited • running businesses by civil servants prohibited
	Transfer of economic value from private source to a public official (not bribery)	• Gifts including cash gifts, coupon, banquets, entertainment (especially connected to his official duties) • Travels paid by private source
	Assisting a third party in dealing with the government	No relevant rules identified
	Profiting from misusing official position: eg, using information obtained in official duties to gain economic value	• Private travel with public funds • Claiming private expenditure in the name of official expenditure • Public car for private use • Using public funds to purchase various club memberships

(cont.)

Category	Framework	Specific issues addressed
		• Unnecessarily or luxuriously use public funds in performing official duties • Misusing office-related information/influence for private gain
Appearance of corruption	Behaving in a way that creates a perception that the official may use his or her influence	No relevant rules identified
	Appearance of favouritism in appointment even if actual favouritism cannot be proved	• Accepts gifts or cash from subordinate government officials • Civil servants with close relationships not allowed to take up posts with immediately subordinate or supervisory relations in the same organ
	Appearance of favouring one party in dealing with official duties	• (For judges) Meeting the party concerned or his or her agent without authorization • Attending dinners or accepting presents given by the party concerned or his or her agent
	Association with criminals or behaving improperly creating a perception the judge is disagreeing with the overall justice system	No relevant rules identified
	Improper statement (or action/behaviour) raising doubt about the basis of an official decision	No relevant rules identified

(cont.)

Category	Framework	Specific issues addressed
	Appearance of bias towards a certain person	No relevant rules identified
Financial disclosure	Who must disclose?	State personnel, senior officials,[1] and core leaders in state-owned enterprises.
	What to disclose?	• Overseas deposits, wealth in foreign countries • Income including outside employment income such as teaching and writing • House property • Investment including investment in partnerships or sole individual enterprises • Outside employment • Employment and foreign residence information of their spouse and children
	Whom to disclose (to a commission or the public)	• Disclose to different departments depending on the ranking status of the reporting official • The information is not available to the public
Outside work and outside activities	During office, outside work may divert an official's energy and attention	• Outside profit-making activity • Paid outside employment
	During office, outside work may arouse, or appears to arouse, conflicts of interest	• Outside leadership positions at NGOs (only applies to senior officials)
	After leaving office, it is possible that outside work may still arouse conflicts of interest	• Take up outside employment or profit-making activity directly related to his or her prior work within control period

(cont.)

Category	Framework	Specific issues addressed
		• (For former judges) Practicing law as a lawyer within control period
		• Invest in companies which has business related to his prior work in control period

[1] Officials at or above the vice county/division (*fu xianchuji*) level.

Appendix D: Key interview questions for DIC officials[1]

Could you briefly introduce your DIC including the structure of your DIC and your specific role at the DIC?

What are the specific areas you and/or your DIC regulate? More specifically, what kinds of behaviour do you and/or your DIC regulate and what kinds of behaviour do you and/or your DIC not regulate?

What is the relationship between your DIC, the Bureau of Supervision, and the Bureau for Corruption Prevention (if you have one) in your province (city or district)?

In addition to regulation at the individual official level, what did you and/or your DIC do (or are doing) in building integrity and fighting corruption at the government department level?

Has your DIC ever sent out inspection work teams (*xunshi gongzuozu*)? How are the teams formed? Have you ever attended an inspection team in your DIC? If yes, what did you and/or your inspection team do in your inspection visits?

Can you think out of all the types of actions you and/or your DIC made in dealing with government officials/government departments under your regulation? (If they do not have any ideas in mind for a minute, then give them some examples such as handling cases, carrying out warning education [*jing shi xing jiaoyu*] . . .).

How do you and/or your DIC interpret relevant rules in handling specific cases? Do you (and/or your DIC) pursue a standard interpretation of rules or are you (and/or your DIC) flexible in interpreting these rules?

How do you and/or your DIC gather compliance information? How do you identify a violation?

It is not uncommon to see corrupt officials being exposed by Internet users. Do you and/or your DIC regularly search the Internet for such

---

[1] The interviews were conducted in Chinese. These questions are semi-structured and serve simply as guides for the researcher.

exposure under your jurisdiction? What is your (or your DIC's) response if you find an online corruption story involving officials in your jurisdiction?

Would you like to talk about the distribution of your, and/or your DIC's, efforts and time spent in different kinds of work activities, especially on the four types of work activities (handling cases, carrying out warning education, meeting with government department officials responsible for discipline inspection, and sending discipline inspection teams [*xunshi gongzuozu*] to prefectures and cities to discover the local leaderships' compliance to discipline rules)?

Could you talk about your, and/or your DIC's, commitments in the fight against travel using public funds? What are the various efforts you have made? Can you comment on the effectiveness of these efforts?

From your internal documents and official website, I learned that supervision of the execution of the party's basic line, principles, policies, and decisions are important parts of the work of your DIC. Can you speak about that? What did you and/or your DIC do (or is doing, or is planning to do) to fulfill that responsibility?

Some party/government rules on anti-corruption and government integrity building [*fanfu changlian*][2] (such as rules prohibiting officials from running businesses, rules on assets/property declaration, rules prohibiting public cars for private use, rules prohibiting luxury office furnishing, and rules prohibiting certain outside employment) have already been issued. But my review of media scandals handled by the DICs and certain DICs' case files shows that officials are seldom disciplined for violating these rules given the background that these kinds of rule violations are very common. Do you agree with my findings? Why, in your opinion, are these officials seldom held responsible for violating these rules?

As a discipline inspection officer (sent out by your DIC [*jijian jiancha paizhu gongzuozu*]) accredited to this bureau/department, what did you do in performing your anti-corruption and integrity-building responsibilities? Can you describe your relationship with your DIC and with the bureau where you are working and which you are supervising?

Is there anything else about fighting corruption and integrity building in your DIC you would like to talk to me about?

---

[2] In the interview dialogue, I used the expression 'party/government rules on anti-corruption and government integrity promotion' instead of 'government ethics rules' because the former is better understood by the DIC officials.

Appendix E: Key interview questions for regulated officials[1]

Which government agencies/entities/departments can make laws/regulation/rules on anti-corruption and integrity building which can restrict your behaviour? Which agencies/entities/departments are actually enforcing these laws/regulation/rules?

In what ways do the above agencies/entities/departments make sure you and your colleagues in this department know these laws/regulation/rules? How do they know whether you and/or your colleagues are complying with these laws/regulation/rules?

Can you summarize, as a government official, what actions are prohibited by the relevant rules on anti-corruption and integrity building? What is the compliance state to these prohibition requirements in your departments? To what extent do the above agencies/entities/departments learn about the state of compliance of your department? What are their reactions to violations in your department?

What are the most common types of violations handled by the above agencies/entities/departments in your department/bureau/agency?

What are the most common types of violations which are seldom handled by the above agencies/entities/departments in your department?

Questions are related to the participants' personal experience of various government ethics violations. Below is an example about 'representing a third party in this party's dealing with the government'.

What is your comment on helping a friend in his dealings with the government? Do you have any experience where you helped your friends in dealing with the government? Do the above agencies/entities/departments know that you have done this (helped your friends)? What is the above agencies/entities/departments' attitude towards and response to what you did? I am not talking about serious offences such as helping your friends bribe other officials or using your position's influence to

---

[1] The interviews were conducted in Chinese.

create competitive advantage for your friends. I am talking about scenarios similar to the following example: Mr Ma is an official of the Legal Affairs Office of the government of Y City. His wife's college classmate, Miss Liu, was running a restaurant in Y city. Miss Liu's restaurant license was revoked recently by Y City Administration for Industry and Commerce on the grounds that she sold expired food. Miss Liu thinks that the punishment is too heavy and asked Mr Ma to assist her in appealing to Y City Bureau for Letters and Calls and to Y City Administration for Industry and Commerce. Mr Ma agreed to help Miss Liu, prepared a letter of complaint, and challenged the basis of the punishment before Y City Bureau for Letters and Calls and Y City Administration for Industry and Commerce on behalf of Miss Liu.

Is there anything else about anti-corruption and integrity building in your department/bureau you would like to talk to me about?

Appendix F: Survey questionnaire[1]

DIC officials (including officials in the Bureau of Supervision at different levels of governments) were invited to complete this questionnaire.

There are twenty-eight statements below describing a government official's behaviour in China.[2] Please judge whether your DIC in practice handles cases concerning the following scenarios. For each statement, please answer the question: have you (or your colleague) ever handled a case concerning the statements below? Handling a case is not limited to opening a case file, investigation, or punishment, but also includes any other action which seeks to monitor the covered officials' compliance state.

Please tick the 'Yes' box *only* when you *indeed* handled such a case or you are 100 Per cent sure that your colleague handled such a case.

1. A government/party official did not disqualify himself when he or she is required to do so by relevant disqualification requirements.	Yes ☐	No ☐
2. A government/party official who may have inside information did not disqualify himself or herself from buying or selling securities.	Yes ☐	No ☐
3. A party organ or government department set up a business.	Yes ☐	No ☐
4. A government/party official is running a business.	Yes ☐	No ☐
5. A government/party official accepted gifts including cash gifts, coupon, banquets, and entertainment (especially connected to his or her official duties).	Yes ☐	No ☐
6. A government/party official was financially supported for his or her travel by a businessman.	Yes ☐	No ☐

---

[1] Questionnaires distributed to participants were written in Chinese. This is a translated copy.

[2] All these statements are violations of existing government ethics rules in China. The researcher intentionally avoids using the word 'violations' as that may induce the participants to tick the 'Yes' box.

7. A government /party official went on private travels with   Yes ☐   No ☐
public funds.

8. A government/party official claimed private expenditure in   Yes ☐   No ☐
the name of official expenditure.

9. A government/party official used a public car for a private   Yes ☐   No ☐
purpose.

10. A government/party official used public funds to purchase   Yes ☐   No ☐
various club memberships.

11. A government/party official unnecessarily or luxuriously   Yes ☐   No ☐
used public funds in performing official duties.

12. A government/party official misused office-related   Yes ☐   No ☐
information/influence for private gain.

13. A government/party official accepted gifts or cash from   Yes ☐   No ☐
subordinate government officials.

14. Civil servants take up posts in organs where they have   Yes ☐   No ☐
close relationships with people who are in immediately
subordinate or supervisory positions.

15. Judges meet one of the parties concerned or this party's   Yes ☐   No ☐
lawyer without authorization.

16. Judges attended dinners or accepted presents given by the   Yes ☐   No ☐
party concerned or his or her lawyer.

17. A government/party official has overseas deposits or wealth   Yes ☐   No ☐
in foreign countries.

18. A covered government/party official does not disclose his or   Yes ☐   No ☐
her income including outside employment such as teaching
and writing.

19. A covered government/party official does not disclose his or   Yes ☐   No ☐
her house properties.

20. A covered government/party official does not disclose his or   Yes ☐   No ☐
her investments including investments in partnerships or
sole individual enterprises.

21. A covered government/party official does not disclose   Yes ☐   No ☐
outside employment.

22. A covered government/party official does not disclose   Yes ☐   No ☐
information about the employment and foreign residence of
his or her spouse and children.

23. A covered government/party official while holding office   Yes ☐   No ☐
engaged in outside profit-making activities.

24. A covered government/party official while holding office   Yes ☐   No ☐
takes up paid outside employment.

25. A covered government/party official while holding office   Yes ☐   No ☐
takes up outside leadership positions at an NGO (this only
applies to senior officials).

26. A covered former government/party official takes up outside   Yes ☐   No ☐
    employment or engages in profit-making activities directly
    related to his or her prior work within the control period.
27. A former judge practices law as a lawyer within the control   Yes ☐   No ☐
    period.
28. A covered former official in a state-owned enterprise invests   Yes ☐   No ☐
    in companies which have business related to his or her prior
    work in the control period.

BIBLIOGRAPHY

Laws, rules, and other forms of binding documents

The United States

18 U.S. Code § 202 – Definitions (18 U.S.C. 202).

18 U.S. Code § 203 – Compensation to Members of Congress, officers, and others in matters affecting the Government (18 U.S.C. 203).

18 U.S. Code § 205 – Activities of officers and employees in claims against and other matters affecting the Government (18 U.S.C. 205).

18 U.S. Code § 208 – Acts affecting a personal financial interest (18 U.S.C. 208).

18 U.S. Code § 209 – Salary of Government officials and employees payable only by United States (18 U.S.C. 209).

41 U.S. Code § 2103 – Actions required of procurement officers when contacted regarding non-Federal employment (41 U.S.C. 2103).

5 C.F.R. Part 2635 – Standards of Ethical Conduct for Employees of the Executive Branch (5 C.F.R. Part 2635).

5 C.F.R. Part 2638 – Office of Government Ethics and Executive Agency Ethics Program Responsibilities (5 C.F.R. Part 2638).

5 U.S. Code § 5533 – Dual pay from more than one position; limitations; exceptions (5 U.S.C. 5533).

5 U.S. Code § 557 – Initial decisions; conclusiveness; review by agency; submissions by parties; contents of decisions; record (5 U.S.C. 557).

5 U.S.C. App. – Ethics in Government Act of 1978.

ABA Model Code of Judicial Conduct 2007.

Executive Order 12674.

Executive Order 12834.

Executive Order 13184.

Executive Order 13490.

The United Kingdom

Civil Service Code, 2010.

Constitutional Reform and Governance Act 2010.

Guide to Judicial Conduct 2011.
Guide to the Rules relating to the Conduct of Members (approved by the House of Commons on 9 February 2009).
Ministerial Code 2010.
Resolution of the House of 15 July 1947, amended on 6 November 1995 and on 14 May 2002.
The Code of Conduct for Members of Parliament (approved by the House of Commons in 2012).

Hong Kong SAR

Acceptance of Advantages (Chief Executive's Permission) Notice 2010.
Civil Service Bureau Circular No. 10/2005 on 'Taking Up Outside Work by Directorate Civil Servants After Ceasing Active Service'.
Civil Service Code.
Civil Service Regulation (CSR) 398.
Civil Service Regulation (CSR) 462.
Civil Service Regulation (CSR) 463.
Civil Service Regulation (CSR) 464.
Civil Service Regulation (CSR) 550.
Code for Officials under the Political Appointment System.
Guide to Judicial Conduct, 2004.
Prevention of Bribery Ordinance.
The Basic Law.

Mainland China

Circular of CCP Central Committee and the State Council on Prohibition of Setting Up Businesses by the Children and Spouses of Leadership Position-Holding Officials (23 May 1985). 中共中央、国务院关于禁止领导干部的子女、配偶经商的决定(1985年5月23日).
Circular of Discipline Inspection Committee of the Central Committee of CCP on Issuing Provisions on Issues Related to Setting Up Businesses by the Children and Spouses of Core Leaders of Party Committees and Governments at Provincial and City Levels (8 February 2001). 中共中央纪委关于印发《关于省、地两级党委、政府主要领导干部配偶、子女个人经商办企业的具体规定(试行)》的通知 中纪发(2001)2号 (2001年02月08日).
Circular of Ministry of Finance on Issuing Provisions on Reception of Foreign Guests by Central Committee of CCP and Central Government (31 December 2013). 财政部关于印发《中央和国家机关外宾接待经费管理办法》的通知 财政部财行(2013)533号 (2013年12月31日).

Circular of the CCP Central Committee and the State Council on Prohibiting Party Organs and Governments and Their Personnel from Setting Up Enterprises (3 December 1984).中共中央、国务院关于严禁党政机关和党政干部经商、办企业的决定 中发[1984]27号(1984年12月03日).

Circular of the Central Committee of CCP and the State Council on Some Recent Issues on Handling the Fight against Corruption (5 October 1993). 中共中央、国务院关于反腐败斗争近期抓好几项工作的决定(1993年10月5日).

Circular of The General Office of CCP Central Committee and the General Office of State Council on Seriously Checking the Enforcement of Relevant Regulations on Prohibitions of Using Public Funds for Private Banquets, Gifts Giving, etc (9 December 1991). 中共中央办公厅、国务院办公厅关于认真检查对严禁用公款吃喝送礼等有关规定执行情况的通知 中办发(1991)17号 (1991年12月09日).

Circular of the General Office of Central Committee of CCP and the General Office of the State Council on Prohibition of Leaders of Party Organs/Government Departments from Taking Up Leadership Positions in Non-Government Organizations (2 July 1998). 中共中央办公厅、国务院办公厅关于党政机关领导干部不兼任社会团体领导职务的通知 中办发(1998)17号 (1998年07月02日).

Circular of the General Office of State Council on Prohibition of Waste and Acceptance of Gifts and Banquets (28 January 1986). 国务院办公厅关于春节期间严禁铺张浪费、请客送礼的通知(1986年1月28日).

Circular of the General Office of the State Council on Prohibition of Pursuing Illegal Interests in Social or Economic Activities (5 June 1986). 国务院办公厅关于严禁在社会经济活动中牟取非法利益的通知 国办发[1986]43号(1986年6月5日).

Circular of the General Office of the CCCPC and General Office of the State Council on Several Issues Concerning the Frugal Spending by the Party and Government Organs (20 February 2009). 中共中央办公厅、国务院办公厅关于党政机关厉行节约若干问题的通知 中办发(2009)11号(2009年02月20日).

Circular of the General Office of the CCCPC and the General Office of the State Council on Firmly Preventing Overseas Travel with Public Funds (20 February 2009). 中共中央办公厅、国务院办公厅关于坚决制止公款出国(境)旅游的通知 中办发(2009)12号2009年02月20日.

Circular of the General Office of the CCP Central Committee and the General Office of the State Council on Tightening Control of Overseas Visit of Party/Government Officials (4 July 1987). 中共中央、国务院关于严格控制党政机关干部出国问题的若干规定(1987年7月4日).

Circular of the General Office of the CCP Central Committee and the General Office of the State Council on Issuing Provisions on Integrity in Conducting

Business for Basic Level Officials in Villages (23 May 2011). 中共中央办公厅、国务院办公厅关于印发《农村基层干部廉洁履行职责若干规定(试行)》的通知 中办发(2011)21号 (2011年05月23日).

Circular of the General Office of the CCP Central Committee and the General Office of the State Council on Issuing Provisions on the Integrity for Officials of State-Owned Enterprises (1 July 2009). 中共中央办公厅、国务院办公厅关于印发《国有企业领导人员廉洁从业若干规定》的通知 中办发[2009]26号 (2009年07月01日).

Circular of the General Office of the CCP Central Committee and the General Office of the State Council for Issuing the Provisions on the Disconnection between Party Organ/Governments and Businesses Run by Them (9 October 1993). 中共中央办公厅 国务院办公厅关于转发国家经贸委《关于党政机关与所办经济实体脱钩的规定》的通知 中办发[1993]17号 (1993年10月09日).

Circular of the General Office of the CCP Central Committee and the General Office of the State Council for Issuing the Provisions on Party/Government Officials' Personal Investment in Securities (3 April 2001). 中共中央办公厅、国务院办公厅关于印发《关于党政机关工作人员个人证券投资行为若干规定》的通知 中办发[2001]10号 (2001年04月03日).

Circular of the General Office of the CCP Central Committee and the General Office of the State Council on the Termination of Business Run by the Army, Armed Police, and Politics-Law Institutions (25 July 1998). 中共中央办公厅、国务院办公厅关于军队武警部队政法机关不再从事经商活动的通知 (1998年7月25日).

Circular of the General Office of the CCP Central Committee and the General Office of the State Council on Settling the Problems of Mixture of Government Functions and Enterprise Management (*zhengqi bufen*) (21 July 1988). 中共中央办公厅、国务院办公厅关于解决公司政企不分问题的通知 中办发[1988]8号(1988年7月21日).

Circular of the General Office of the Central Committee of CCP and the General Office of the State Council on Frugal Spending in Domestic Business Receptions (8 April 2001). 中共中央办公厅、国务院办公厅关于在国内公务接待工作中切实做到勤俭节约的通知 厅字[2001]3号2001年04月08日.

Circular of the General office of the Central Committee of CCP and the General Office of the State Council on That Reception Standards Shall Not Exceed Local Standards (28 April 1994). 中共中央办公厅、国务院办公厅关于党政机关工作人员在国内公务活动中食宿不准超过当地接待标准的通知 厅字[1994]16号1994年04月28日.

Circular of the General Office of the Central Committee of the CCP and the General Office of the State Council on Provisions on Reporting Personal Matters for Officials (26 May 2010). 中共中央办公厅、国务院办公厅印

发《关于领导干部报告个人有关事项的规定》的通知 中办发[2010]16号
2010年05月26日.

Circular of the General Office of the State Council on Prohibition of Giving Money
or Gifts (22 September 1988). 国务院办公厅关于严禁滥发钱物和赠送礼品
的通知(1988年9月22日).

Circular of the State Council on Enforcement Opinions on the Recent Fight against
Corruption (18 September 1993). 国务院关于印发近期开展反腐败斗争实施
意见的通知 国发[1993]64号 (1993年09月18日).

Civil Servant Law of the People's Republic of China (2005). 中华人民共和国公务
员法 (2005).

Criminal law of the People's Republic of China (1997). 中华人民共和国刑
法 (1997).

Government Car Reform Policy for the CCP Central Committee and the Central
Government (16 July 2014). 中央和国家机关公务用车制度改革方案 (2014
年07月16日).

Joint Circular of Ministry of Finance, Ministry of Foreign Affairs, Ministry of
Supervision, National Audit Office, and the National Bureau for Corruption
Prevention on Issuing 'Temporary Rules on Strengthening Management of
Government Spending on Overseas Visits for Business for Party and Government Officials' (5 August 2008). 财政部外交部监察部审计署国家预防腐败
局关于印发《加强党政干部因公出国(境)经费管理暂行办法》的通知 财
行[2008]230号 (2008年08月05日).

Judges Law of the People's Republic of China (2001). 中华人民共和国法官
法 (2001).

Provisions [of Aletai Distric] on Financial Disclosure for Officials at County/
Division Level (Under Trial) (25 May 2008). [阿勒泰地区]县处级领导干部
财产申报的规定(试行)阿地纪发[2008]17号 (2008年5月25日).

Provisions of Central Committee of CCP and the State Council on Saving Expenditure and Prohibiting Waste in Party Organs and Government (29 October 2013).
中共中央、国务院关于党政机关厉行节约反对浪费条例 (2013年10月29日).

Provisions of Shenzhen Party Committee and Shenzhen Government on
Tightening Supervision of Heads in Party Organs/ Government Departments
(25 November 2009). 中共深圳市委 深圳市人民政府关于加强党政正职监
督的暂行规定 深发[2009]14号 (2009年11月25日).

Provisions of the Central Committee of CCP and the State Council on Spending
Frugally and Prohibiting Waste in Party Organs and Government Departments
(29 October 2013). 中共中央、国务院关于党政机关厉行节约反对浪费条
例 (2013年10月29日).

Provisions of the Central Committee of CCP on Integrity in Performing Official
Duties for Party Officials (23 February 2010). 中国共产党党员领导干部廉洁
从政若干准则(2010年2月23日).

Provisions of the General Office of State Council on Sending Officials to Receive Overseas Training (1 March 1990). 国务院办公厅关于派遣团组和人员赴国外培训的规定 国办发[1990]4号 (1990年03月01日).

Provisions of the General Office of the CCP Central Committee and the General Office of the State Council on Allocation and Management of Government Cars (6 September 1989). 中共中央办公厅、国务院办公厅关于中央党政机关汽车配备和使用管理的规定 中办发[1989]11号 (1989年09月06日).

Provisions of the General Office of the CCP Central Committee and the General Office of the State Council on Issues Related to Setting Up Business by Retired Officials in Party Organs or Government Departments above the County Level (3 October 1988). 中共中央办公厅、国务院办公厅关于县以上党和国家机关退(离)休干部经商办企业问题的若干规定 (1988年10月3日).

Provisions of the General Office of the CCP Central Committee and the General Office of the State Council on Domestic Business Reception for Party Organs/Government Departments (8 December 2013).党政机关国内公务接待管理规定(2013年12月8日).

Provisions of the Organization Department of CCP on Supervision of Party/Government Officials Whose Children and Spouse Have Migrated to Foreign Countries or Regions outside Mainland China (21 February 2014). 配偶已移居国(境)外国家工作人员任职办法 中组发[2014]6号 (2014年2月21日).

Provisions on Disciplines for the People's Police of the Public Security Organs (21 April 2010). 公安机关人民警察纪律条令 (2010年04月21日).

Provisions on Financial Disclosure for Officials in Cixi City (Under Trial) (5 December 2008). 慈溪市领导干部廉情公示暂行规定(试行)(2008年12月5日).

Provisions on Punishment for Officials Using Public Funds to Travel Abroad (12 August 2010). 用公款出国(境)旅游及相关违纪行为处分规定 监察部、人力资源社会保障部令第23号 (2010年08月12日).

Regulation of the Communist Party of China on Disciplinary Actions (31 December 2003). 中国共产党纪律处分条例 (2003年12月31日).

Regulation of the State Council of the People's Republic of China on Giving and Receiving Gifts in Foreign-Related Official Activities (5 December 1993). 国务院关于在对外公务活动中赠送和接受礼品的规定 国务院令第133号 (1993年12月5日).

Regulation on the Punishment of Civil Servants of Administrative Organs (22 April 2007). 行政机关公务员处分条例 国务院令[2007]第495号 (2007年04月22日).

Ten Provisions on Establishing and Improving Prevention and Punishment Mechanisms for Corruption [in Liuyang City] (27 March 2009). [浏阳市]建立健全惩治和预防腐败体系的十项廉政制度 (2009年3月27日).

The Constitution of Chinese Communist Party (2007). 中国共产党章程 (2007).

English Sources

'Appointments must avoid appearance of favoritism', *The Southern*, available at http://thesouthern.com/news/opinions/voice_southern/appointments-must-avoid-appearance-of-favoritism/article_2c3bd624-9c82-11e1-ae4c-001a4bcf887a .html (last visited on 15 September 2013).

'Around China', *China Daily*, p. 02, 23 February 2013.

'Beijing's facts, and fictions', *New York Times*, available at www.nytimes.com/2014/ 04/17/opinion/beijings-facts-and-fictions.html?_r=1 (last visited on 20 May 2015).

'China executes former food and drug safety chief', *NewScientist*, 10 July 2007, available at www.newscientist.com/article/dn12230-china-executes-former-food-and-drug-safety-chief.html (last visited on 21 September 2009).

'China jails tainted milk activist Zhao Lianhai', *BBC News*, 10 November 2010, available at www.bbc.co.uk/news/world-asia-pacific-11724323 (last visited on 3 January 2012).

'China nets wanted economic fugitive', *Xinhua Net*, available at http://news .xinhuanet.com/english/2015-04/25/c_134184257.htm (last visited on 24 May 2015).

'Federal 2013 Government revenue', available at www.usgovernmentrevenue.com/ fed_revenue_2013US (last visited on 15 May 2014).

'Graft tip sites a success', *Global Times*, p. 5, 9 May 2013.

'Internet exposes corruption', *China Daily* (Hong Kong Edition), p. 8, 27 November 2012.

'Official falls via internet', *China Daily*, p. 8, 14 May 2013.

'Report of the Independent Review Committee for the prevention and handling of potential conflicts of interests', 2012, available at www.irc.gov.hk/pdf/IRC_ Report_20120531_eng.pdf (last visited on 15 May 2013).

'Salt in their wounds: bereaved parents treated like criminals', *The Economist*, 14 May 2009, available at www.economist.com/node/13650027 (last visited on 17 November 2011).

'To fight corruption, China must push to disclose leaders' wealth', *South China Morning Post*, 19 April 2013.

'Xi gets off to good start but drastic reforms unlikely', *South China Morning Post*, China Briefing, EDT5, 25 February 2013.

An, Baijie, 'Officials whose family owns 31 houses arrested', *China Daily* (Hong Kong Edition), p. 5, 15 January 2013.

'Power within cage of regulations', *China Daily* (Hong Kong Edition), p. 1, 23 January 2013.

'Tougher measures on corruption studied', *China Daily* (Hong Kong Edition), p. 3, 24 January 2013.

Andrews, Claire, *The Enforcement of Regulatory Offences* (London: Sweet & Maxwell, 1998).

Aristotle, *Nicomachean Ethics* (Chicago, IL: University of Chicago Press, 2011).

Ashton, Matthew, 'Comment: fox scandal shows need to reform ministerial code', *Politics.co.uk*, available at www.politics.co.uk/comment-analysis/2011/10/11/comment-fox-scandal-shows-need-to-reform-mini (last visited on 21 April 2013).

Baldwin, Robert, Colin D. Scott, and Christopher Hood (eds.), *A Reader on Regulation* (Oxford: Oxford University Press, 1998).

Bardach, Eugene and Robert A. Kagan, *Going by the Book: The Problem of Regulatory Unreasonableness* (Philadelphia, PA: Temple University Press, 1982).

Barker, Thomas and David L. Carter, *Police Deviance* (Cincinnati, OH: Anderson Publishing, 1986).

Bentham, Jeremy, *An Introduction to the Principles of Morals and Legislation* (Oxford: Clarendon Press; New York: Oxford University Press, 1996).

Better Regulation Task Force, 'Principles of good regulation', 2003, available at www.cabinet-office.gov.uk/regulation/TaskForce/2000/PrinciplesLeaflet.pdf (last visited on 23 October 2012).

Boehm, Rachel E., 'Caught in the revolving door: a state lawyer's guide to post-employment restrictions', *The Review of Litigation*, 15, 3 (1996), pp. 525–550.

Braithwaite, John, John Walker, and Peter Grabosky, 'An enforcement taxonomy of regulatory agencies', *Law & Policy*, 9, 3 (1987), pp. 23–51.

Brown, Jeremy and Paul G. Pickowicz, 'The early years of the People's Republic of China: an introduction', in Jeremy Brown and Paul G. Pickowicz (eds.) *Dilemmas of Victory: The Early Years of the People's Republic of China* (Cambridge, MA and London: Harvard University Press, 2007), pp.1–18.

Bryner, Gary C., 'Trends in social regulation', in David H. Rosenbloom and Richard D. Schwartz (eds.), *Handbook of Regulation and Administrative Law* (New York, Basel, and Hong Kong: Marcel Dekker, 1994), pp. 73–90.

Carson, W. G., 'Some sociological aspects of strict liability and the enforcement of the factory legislation', *The Modern Law Review*, 33, 4 (1970), pp. 396–412.

Chan, Hon S. and Jie Gao, 'Old wine in new bottles: a county level case study of anti-corruption reform in the People's Republic of China', *Crime, Law and Social Change*, 49, 2 (2008), pp. 97–117.

Cheung, Anthony B. L., 'Combating corruption as a political strategy to rebuild trust and legitimacy: can China learn from Hong Kong?', *Research in Public Policy Analysis and Management*, 17 (2008), pp. 55–84.

Cheung, Gary, Fanny W. Y. Fung, and Tanna Chong, 'Former housing chief in fresh controversy', *South China Morning Post*, 14 August 2012, available at www.scmp.com/article/965115/former-housing-chief-fresh-controversy (last visited on 12 June 2013).

Choi, Chi-yuk, 'Xi urges officials' power to be "confined in a cage"', *South China Morning Post*, EDT1, EDT3, 23 January 2013.

Chung, Wayne, 'What the local media says', *South China Morning Post*, CITY2, 9 June 2012.

Civil Service Bureau, 'Disciplinary cases in the civil service', available at www.csb.gov.hk/english/stat/annually/553.html (last visited on 20 January 2013).

'Information note for the LegCo panel on public service: disciplinary mechanism in the civil service – supplementary information', available at www.csb.gov.hk/english/admin/conduct/files/LC_Disciplinary_Mechanism__Eng_.pdf (last visited on 31 January 2013).

'Introduction', available at www.csb.gov.hk/english/aboutus/org/intro/355.html (last visited on 21 May 2013).

'LCQ13: government remains vigilant to fortify the culture of integrity in the civil service', available at www.csb.gov.hk/english/info/269.html (last visited 1 February 2013).

'Legislative council panel on public service: promotion of integrity in the civil service', 2005, available at www.csb.gov.hk/english/admin/conduct/files/paper050412e_2.pdf (last visited on 12 June 2013).

'Legislative council panel on public service: disciplinary mechanism and related procedures for disciplined services and civil grades', 2009, available at www.csb.gov.hk/english/info/files/20090420_panel_discipline_eng.pdf (last visited on 20 June 2013).

'Update on integrity enhancement initiatives for civil servants', available at www.csb.gov.hk/english/info/files/20100222_panel_integrity_eng.pdf (last visited on 15 September 2013).

'Updated overview of civil service conduct and discipline', 2007, available at www.csb.gov.hk/english/info/files/panel070618e.pdf (last visited on 12 June 2013).

Civil Service Commission, 'Annual report 2009/2010', available at http://civilservicecommission.independent.gov.uk/wp,content/uploads/2012/03/Annual%20Report%2009-10.pdf (last visited on 23 June 2013).

'Annual report and accounts 2010–2011', available at http://civilservicecommission.independent.gov.uk/wp-content/uploads/2012/04/Annual-Report-10-11.pdf (last visited on 15 September 2013).

'Annual report and accounts 2011–12', available at http://civilservicecommission.independent.gov.uk/wp-content/uploads/2012/07/CSC-Annual-Report-2011-12.pdf (last visited on 15 September 2013).

'Recruitment principles', available at http://civilservicecommission.independent.gov.uk/civil-service-recruitment/ (last visited on 25 June 2013).

'What we do', available at http://civilservicecommission.independent.gov.uk/about-us/what-we-do/ (last visited on 20 January 2013).

Committee on Standards in Public Life (the UK), 'Annual review and report 2009–10', 2010, available at www.public-standards.gov.uk/wp-content/

uploads/2012/11/2010_ANNUAL_REPORT___Final.pdf (last visited on 17 December 2012).

'The 7 principles of public life', available at www.gov.uk/government/publica tions/the-7-principles-of-public-life/the-7-principles-of-public-life-2/ (last visited on 1 August 2013).

Comstock, Amy, 'Maintaining government integrity: the perspective of the United States Office of Government Ethics', in Cyrille Fijnaut and Leo Huberts (eds.), *Corruption, Integrity and Law Enforcement* (Kluwer Law International, 2002).

Crank, John P. and Michael A. Caldero, *Police Ethics: The Corruption of Noble Causes* (Cincinnati, OH: Anderson Publishing, 2000).

Croall, Hazel, 'Combating financial crime: regulatory versus criminal control approaches', *Journal of Financial Crime*, 11, 1 (2003), pp. 45–55.

Cui, Jia, 'Micro blogs make graft fight hot news', *China Daily*, p. 6, 15 May 2013.

Divjak, Carol, 'Corruption and shoddy construction behind school collapse in China earthquake', *World Socialist Web Site*, 16 October 2008, available at www.wsws.org/articles/2008/oct2008/chin-o16.shtml (last visited on 21 September 2009).

Dobel, J. Patrick, 'The realpolitik of ethics codes: an implementation approach to public ethics', in H. George Frederickson (ed.), *Ethics and Public Administration* (Armonk & London: M. E. Sharpe, 1993), pp. 158–174.

Douglas, Paul H., *Ethics in Government* (Cambridge, MA: Harvard University Press, 1952).

Duan, Mingming, 'The role of formal contracts with weak legal enforcement: a study in the Chinese context', *Strategic Organization*, 10, 2, (2012), pp. 158–186.

Earl A. Molander, 'A paradigm for design, promulgation and enforcement of ethical codes,' *Journal of Business Ethics*, 6, 8 (1987), p. 619.

El-Ayouty, Yassin, Kevin J. Ford, and Mark Davies (eds.), *Government Ethics and Law Enforcement: Toward Global Guidelines* (Westport, CT: Praeger, 2000).

Eliseo Cocciolo, Endrius, 'Checking the integrity of government,' *Droit Administratif Compare, europeen et global seminar paper* (Paris, 2008).

Entorf, Horst, 'Certainty and severity of sanctions in classical and behavioral models of deterrence: a survey', *IZA Discussion Paper No. 6516* (Goethe University, 2012).

Fong, Phyllis K, 'Working together: corruption and integrity investigations in the United States', *Collaborative Governance and Integrity Management Conference* (Hong Kong: ICAC, 2010).

Freiberg, Arie, *The Tools of Regulation* (Leichhardt, NSW: The Federation Press, 2010).

Fu, Richard, 'Claims posted online bring down top planning official', *Shanghai Daily*, p. A2, 15 May, 2013.

Fung, Fanny W. Y. and Tanna Chong, 'Legislators unite to urge justice for milk activist', *South China Morning Post*, 18 November 2010, available at http://topics.scmp.com/news/china-news-watch/article/Legislators-unite-to-urge-justice-for-milk-activist (last visited on 27 December 2011).

Gilman, Stuart C., 'Contemporary institutional arrangements for managing political appointments and the historical process of depoliticization: the experience of the United States at the federal level and in some states', *International Anticorruption Conference*, Seoul, 2003, available at http://unpan1.un.org/intradoc/groups/public/documents/un/unpan010814.pdf (last visited on 28 December 2012).

'Ethics codes and codes of conduct as tools for promoting an ethical and professional public service: comparative successes and lessons', *World Bank Research Reports*, 2005, available at www.oecd.org/mena/governance/35521418.pdf (last visited on 19 April 2013).

'The U.S. Office of Government Ethics', *The Bureaucrat*, 20, 1 (1991), p. 13.

Gong, Ting, 'Dependent judiciary and unaccountable judges: judicial corruption in contemporary China,' *China Review*, 4, 2 (2004), pp. 33–54.

'The party discipline inspection in China: its evolving trajectory and embedded dilemmas', *Crime, Law and Social Change*, 49, 2 (2008), pp. 139–152.

'An "institutional turn" toward rule-based integrity management in China', *Collaborative Governance and Integrity Management Conference* (Hong Kong: Centre of Anti-corruption Studies of the ICAC, 2010).

'The institutional logic of local innovation: an analysis of anticorruption initiatives in Guangdong Provinces', (Shanghai: International Conference on Public Management Research: Seeking Excellence in a Time of Change, 2012).

Gong, Ting and Stephen K. Ma (eds.), *Preventing Corruption in Asia: Institutional Design and Policy Capacity* (London and New York: Routledge, 2009).

Goodwin, Miles and Glenda J. Maconachie, 'Redesigning the inspection blitz in the post Work Choices environment', in Alison Barnes, Nikola Balnave, and George Lafferty (eds.), *Proceedings of the 24th Association of Industrial Relations Academics of Australia and New Zealand Conference – Work in Progress: Crises, Choices and Continuity, Association of Industrial Relations Academics of Australia and New Zealand (AIRAANZ)* (Sydney: Sydney Trades Hall, 2010), available at http://eprints.qut.edu.au/31736/ (last visited on 26 May 2012).

Gordon, Mirta B., J. R. Iglesias, Viktoryia Semeshenko, and J. P. Nadal, 'Crime and punishment: the economic burden of impunity', *The European Physical Journal B* , 68, 2009, pp. 133–144.

Gormley, William T., Jr, 'Regulatory enforcement: accommodation and conflict in four states', *Public Administration Review*, 57, 4 (1997), pp. 285–293.

Gray, Cynthia, 'Avoiding the appearance of impropriety: with great power comes great responsibility,' *University of Arkansas at Little Rock Law Review*, 28, 1 (2006), pp. 63–102.

Guo, Baogang, 'Political legitimacy and China's transition', *Journal of Chinese Political Science*, 8, 1 & 2 (Fall 2003), pp. 1–25.

'Political legitimacy in China's transition: toward a market economy', in Lowell Dittmer and Guoli Liu (eds.), *China's Deep Reform: Domestic Politics in Transition* (Lanham, Boulder, New York, Toronto, and Oxford: Rowman & Littlefield, 2006), pp. 147–175.

Guo, Yong, 'Historical evolvement and future reform of the China Communist Party Discipline Inspection Commission', Opening Ceremony of the Centre of Anti-corruption Studies and Seminar, ICAC, Hong Kong, 2 April 2009.

Hao, Yufan, 'From rule of man to rule of law: an unintended consequence of corruption in China in the 1990s', *Journal of Contemporary China*, 8, 22 (1999), pp. 405–423.

Hardman, Donald J., 'Audit of ethics in government', *International Journal of Government Auditing*, 23, 2 (April 1996), pp. 11–12.

Hawkins, Keith, 'Bargain and bluff: compliance strategy and deterrence in the enforcement of regulation', *Law & Policy Quarterly*, 5, 1 (January 1983), pp. 35–73.

He, Zhengke, 'Corruption and anti-corruption in reform China,' *Communist and Post-Communist Studies*, 33, 2 (2000), pp. 243–270.

Herrmann, Frederick M., 'Empowering governmental ethics agencies', *Spectrum: Journal of State Government*, 77, 3 (2004), p. 33–35.

Heywood, Paul M., 'Integrity management and the public services ethos in the UK: patchwork quilt or threadbare blanket?', Collaborative Governance and Integrity Management Conference, ICAC, Hong Kong, 2010.

Holbig, Heike, 'Ideological reform and Political Legitimacy in China: Challenges in the Post-Jiang Era', in Thomas Heberer and Gunter Schubert (eds.), *Regime Legitimacy in Contemporary China: Institutional Change and Stability* (London and New York: Routledge, 2009).

Holbig, Heike and Bruce Gilley, 'In search of legitimacy in post-revolutionary China: bring ideology and governance back In', GIGA (German Institute of Global and Area Studies) Working Papers No. 127, 2010, available at www.giga-hamburg.de/dl/download.php?d=/content/publikationen/pdf/wp127_holbig-gilley.pdf (last visited on 19 June 2013).

'Reclaiming legitimacy in China', *Politics & Policy*, 38, 3 (2010), pp. 395–422.

Hong Kong Audit Commission, 'Hotel accommodation arrangements for the Chief Executive's duty visits outside Hong Kong', May 2012, available at www.aud.gov.hk/pdf_e/hotele.pdf (last visited on 19 May 2013).

Hood, Christopher, Colin Scott, Oliver James, George Jones, and Tony Travers, *Regulation inside Government: Waste-Watchers, Quality Police, and Sleaze-busters* (New York: Oxford University Press, 1999).

Hu, Jintao, 'Hu Jintao's report at the 17th party congress', available at www .china.org.cn/english/congress/229611.htm#3 (last visited on 16 December 2011).

Hutt, Peter Barton, 'Philosophy of regulation under the Federal Food, Drug and Cosmetic Act', *Food and Drug Law Journal*, 50, 5 (1995), pp. 101–110.

Independent Commission Against Corruption, 'Annual report 2011', available at www.icac.org.hk/filemanager/tc/content_1238/2011.pdf (last visited on 13 February 2012).

Independent Parliamentary Standards Authority, 'Guidance for MPs' business costs and expenses', October 2012, available at http://parliamentarystandards .org.uk/IPSAMPs/Guidance/Documents/Guidance%20for%20MPs%20Business %20Costs%20and%20Expenses%20updated%20(April%202013).pdf (last visited on 15 March 2013).

Jacobs, James, 'Dilemmas of corruption control', in Cyrille Fijnaut and Leo Huberts (eds.), *Corruption, Integrity and Law enforcement* (Kluwer Law international, 2002).

Jiang, Zemin, 'Report at the 16th party congress', available at www.china.org.cn/ english/features/49007.htm#10 (last visited on 16 December 2011).

Kagan, Robert A., 'Editors introduction: understanding regulatory enforcement', *Law and Policy*, 11, 2 (1989), pp. 89–119.

'Regulatory enforcement', in David H. Rosenbloom and Richard D. Schwartz (eds.), *Handbook of Regulation and Administrative Law* (New York, Basel, and Hong Kong: Marcel Dekker, 1994), pp. 383–422.

Kagan, Robert A. and John T. Scholz, 'The "criminology of the corporation" and regulatory enforcement strategies,' in Keith Hawkins and John M. Thomas (eds.), *Enforcing Regulation* (Boston, The Hague, Dordrecht, and Lancaster: Kluwer-Nijhoff, 1984), pp. 67–95.

Kelman, Steven, *Regulating America, Regulating Sweden: A Comparative Study of Occupational Safety and Health Policy* (Cambridge, MA: The MIT Press, 1981).

Krause, Joan H., 'A conceptual model of health care fraud enforcement', *Brooklyn Journal of Law and Policy*, 12, 1 (2003), pp. 55–147.

Lawton, Alan, Michael Macaulay, and Jolanta Palidauskaite, 'Towards a Compara-tive Methodology for Public Service Ethics', *EGPA Conference*, 2009, available at www.law.kuleuven.be/aap-bap/integriteit/egpa/previous-egpa-conferences/ malta-2009/lawton.pdf (last visited on 15 June 2013).

Legislative Council of The Hong Kong Special Administrative Region, 'Report of the select committee to study Mr Leung Chun-ying's involvement as a member of the jury in the West Kowloon reclamation concept plan

competition and related issues', available at www.legco.gov.hk/yr11-12/eng
lish/sc/sc_lcy/report/lcy_rpt-e.pdf (last visited on 27 May 2013).

Legislative Council, 'Annual report 2011-2012', available at www.legco.gov.hk/
general/english/sec/reports/a_1112.pdf (last visited on 15 September 2013).

Levin, Ronald M., 'Fighting the appearance of corruption', *Journal of Law & Policy*,
6 (2001) pp. 171–179.

Lewis, Carol W., 'Ethics codes and ethics agencies: current practices and emerging
trends', in H. George Frederickson (ed.), *Ethics and Public Administration*
(Armonk, NY: M.E. Sharpe, 1993), pp. 136–157.

Li, Cheng, 'The battle for China's top nine leadership posts,' *The Washington
Quarterly*, 35, 1 (Winter 2012), pp. 131–145.

Li, Chengyan, 'Government honesty building up and civil servant honesty management', Collaborative Governance and Integrity Management Conference,
ICAC, Hong Kong, 2010.

Li, Li and Wu Chonghao, 'The application of sentence suspension and exemption
for 'duty offences' in China: special social status and ineffective legal techniques', in Michal Tomasek and Guido Muhlemann (eds.) *Interpretation of
Law in China: Roots and Perspectives* (Prague: Karolinum Press, 2011),
pp. 175–179.

Lievense, Andrew J. and Avern Cohn, 'The federal judiciary and the ABA Model
Code: the parting of the ways', *The Justice System Journal*, 28, 3 (2007),
pp. 272–282.

Little, Joseph W., 'Abolishing financial disclosure to improve government', *Stetson
Law Review*, 16, 3 (1987), pp. 633–680.

Lord Acton, *Essays on Freedom and Power* (Boston, MA: the Beacon Press, 1949).

Macfie, Nick, 'China's Xi urges swatting of lowly 'flies' in fight on everyday graft',
Reuters, 22 January 2013, available at www.reuters.com/article/2013/01/22/
us-china-corruption-xi-idUSBRE90L0AA20130122 (last visited on 21 April
2013).

Mak, Jennifer, 'Opening remarks', *Seminar on Integrity Programme Implementation*, 2001, available at www.csb.gov.hk/hkgcsb/rcim/pdf/english/confer
ence_meterials/speech_d3-2001_11_13_a.pdf (last visited on 24 April
2013).

Manion, Melanie, *Corruption by Design: Building Clean Government in Mainland
China and Hong Kong* (Cambridge, MA and London: Harvard University
Press, 2004).

Mauro, Paolo, 'Why worry about corruption?', *Economic Issues*, 6 (1997), available at www.imf.org/external/pubs/ft/issues6/index.htm (last visited on
23 September 2009).

May, Peter J. and Robert S. Wood, 'At the regulatory front lines: inspectors'
enforcement styles and regulatory compliance', *Journal of Public Administration Research and Theory*, 13, 2 (2003), pp. 117–139.

May, Peter J. and Soren Winter, 'Reconsidering styles of regulatory enforcement: patterns in Danish agro-environmental inspection', *Law & Policy*, 22, 2 (April 2000), pp. 143–173.

Mcallister, Lesley K., 'Dimensions of enforcement style: factoring in regulatory autonomy and capacity', *Law & Policy*, 32, 1 (January 2010), pp. 61–78.

McConville, Mike, *Criminal Justice in China: An Empirical Enquiry* (Cheltenham: Edward Elgar, 2011).

McDonnell, Stephen, 'Chinese outraged at activist's jailing', *ABC News*, 12 November 2010, available at www.abc.net.au/worldtoday/content/2010/s3064557.htm (last visited on 17 November 2011).

Men, Jing, 'The search of an official ideology and its impact on Chinese foreign policy', paper presented on Regional Governance: Great China in the 21st Century, Asia-Link Conference, University of Durham, 24–25 October 2003, available at https://www.dur.ac.uk/resources/china.studies/The%20Search%20of%20An%20Official%20Ideology%20and%20Its%20Impact%20on%20Chinese%20Foreign%20Policy.pdf (last visited on 13 June 2).

Miethe, Terence D. and Hong Lu, *Punishment: A Comparative Historical Perspective* (Cambridge: Cambridge University Press, 2005).

National Bureau of Corruption Prevention, 'Responsibilities of the National Bureau of Corruption Prevention', available at www.nbcp.gov.cn/article/zzjg/ (last visited on 26 April 2012).

Nolan, Beth, 'Public interest, private income: conflicts and control limits on the outside income of government officials', *Northwestern University Law Review*, 87, 1 (1992–1993), pp. 57–147.

Norad, 'Anti-corruption approaches: a literature review', 2008, available at www.norad.no/en/Tools+and+publications/Publications/Publication+Page?key=119213 (last visited on 12 April 2010).

Office of the Ombudsman, 'Powers, Functions and Duties', available at www.ombudsman.gov.ph/index.php?home=1&navId=MQ==&subNavId=ODY (last visited on 11 September 2013).

Oxford Dictionaries (online), 'Ethics', available at www.oxforddictionaries.com/definition/english/ethics (last visited on 15 May 2014).

Parliamentary and Health Services Ombudsman, 'The ombudsman', available at www.ombudsman.org.uk/about-us/who-we-are/the-ombudsman (last visited on 4 January 2013).

Patrick J. Sheeran, *Ethics in Public Administration: A Philosophical Approach* (Westport, CT and London: Praeger, 1993).

Pearson, Margaret M., 'Governing the Chinese economy: regulatory reform in the service of the state', *Public Administration Review*, 67, 4 (2007), pp. 718–730.

Peele, Gillian and Robert Kaye, 'Regulating conflict of interests: securing accountability in the modern state', 2006, available at www.corrupcion.unam.mx/documentos/investigaciones/peelekaye_paper.pdf (last visited 23 June 2013).

Pei, Minxin, 'Corruption threatens China's future', *Policy Brief* 55 (Washington, DC: Carnegie Endowment for International Peace, October 2007), available at http://carnegieendowment.org/files/pb55_pei_china_corruption_final.pdf (last visited on 15 June 2013).

Perkins, Roswell B., 'The new Federal Conflict-of-Interest Law' *Harvard Law Review*, 76, 6 (1963), pp. 1113–1169.

Pistor, Katharina and Cheng Gangxu, 'Governing stock markets in transition economies: lessons from China', *American Law and Economics Review*, 7, 1 (2005), pp. 184–210.

Pope, Jeremy, *Confronting Corruption: The Elements of A National Integrity System* (Berlin: Transparency International, 2000), available at http://info .worldbank.org/etools/docs/library/18416/00.pdf (last visited 17 October 2012).

Public Sector Standards Commissioner (Victoria, Australia), 'Review of Victoria's integrity and anti-corruption system', 2010, available at www.vic.ipaa.org .au/sb_cache/professionaldevelopment/id/193/f/PSSC_Integrity_Review.pdf (last visited on 17 April 2010).

Public Service Commission, 'Aims and function', available at www.psc.gov.hk/ english/aboutus/aim_fun.html (last visited on 31 January 2013).

  'Annual report 2011', available at www.psc.gov.hk/english/ann_rep/files/11rep .pdf (last visited on 13 February 2012).

Reiss, Albert J., Jr, 'Selecting strategies of social control over organizational life', in Keith Hawkins and John M. Thomas (eds.), *Enforcing Regulation* (Boston, The Hague, Dordrecht, and Lancaster: Kluwer-Nijhoff Publishing, 1984), pp. 23–26.

Reiss, Albert J. and Albert D. Biderman, *Data Sources on White-Collar Lawbreaking* (Washington, DC: National Institute of Justice, 1981).

Rhodes, Robert M., 'Enforcement of legislative ethics: conflict within the conflict of interest laws', *Harvard Journal on Legislation*, 10, 3 (1973), pp. 373–406.

Rivkin-Fish, Michele, 'Bribes, gifts and unofficial payments: rethinking corruption in post-Soviet Russian health care,' in Dieter Haller and Cris Shore (eds.) *Corruption: Anthropological Perspectives* (London and Ann Arbor, MI: Pluto Press, 2005). pp. 50–51.

Roberts, Robert N. and Marion T. Doss, *From Watergate to Whitewater: The Public Integrity War* (Westport, CT and London: Praeger, 1997).

Roberts, Robert N., *White House Ethics: The History of the Politics of Conflict of Interest Regulation* (New York: Greenwood Press, 1988).

Rodrik, Dani, 'Growth strategies', *NBER Working Paper Series*, Working Paper 10050, October 2003, available at http://users.nber.org/~rosenbla/econ302/ lecture/rodrick.pdf (last visited on 28 July 2013).

Rose-Ackerman, Susan, 'Corruption and the criminal law', *Forum on Crime and Society*, 2, 1 (2002), pp. 3–21.

Sapio, Flora, 'Shuanggui and extralegal detention in China', *China Information*, 22, 1 (2008), pp. 7–37.

Schoeneman, Brian W., 'The scarlet L: have recent developments in lobbying regulation gone too far?' *The Catholic University Law Review*, 60, 2 (2011), pp. 505–532.

Scholz, John T., 'Cooperative regulatory enforcement and the politics of administrative effectiveness', *American Political Science Review*, 85, 1 (1991), pp. 115–136.

Scott, Ian, 'Promoting integrity in a changing environment: Hong Kong's public sector after 1997', Collaborative Governance and Integrity Management Conference, Centre of Anti-corruption Studies of the ICAC, Hong Kong, 2010.

The Public Sector in Hong Kong (Hong Kong: Hong Kong University Press, 2010).

Shavell, Steven, 'The optimal structure of law enforcement', *Journal of Law and Economics*, 36, 1 (1993), pp. 255–287.

Sherman, Lawrence W., 'Becoming bent: moral careers of corrupt policemen', in Frederick A. Elliston and Michael Feldberg (eds.), *Moral Issues in Police Work* (Totowa, NJ: Rowman & Allanheld, 1985), pp. 253–265.

Shi, Yingying, 'Internet anti-graft effort debated', *China Daily* (Hong Kong Edition), p. 4, 22 December, 2012.

Shipman, Tim, Ian Drury, and Rupert Steiner, 'Secret cash trail that meant Fox had to go: defence secretary resigns after claim he 'personally asked Tory donor to fund his best man', *Daily Mail Online*, 15 October 2011, available at www.dailymail.co.uk/news/article-2049222/Liam-Fox-resigns-Defence-Secretary-finally-quits-Adam-Werritty-scandal.html (Last visited on 27 May 2013).

Shover, Neal, Donald A. Clelland, and John Lynxwiler, *Enforcement or Negotiation: Constructing a Regulatory Bureaucracy* (Albany, NY: State University of New York Press, 1986).

Smart, Alan and Carolyn L. Hsu, 'Corruption or social capital? Tact and the performance of guanxi in market socialist China', in Monique Nuijten and Gerhard Anders (eds.), *Corruption and the Secret of Law: A Legal Anthropological Perspective* (Aldershot: Ashgate, 2007).

Smit, Paul R., Ronald F. Meijer, and Peter-Paul J. Groen, 'Detection rates: an international comparison', *European Journal on Criminal Policy and Research*, 10, 2–3 (2004), pp. 225–253.

Smith, Robert W., 'A comparison of the ethics infrastructure in China and the United States: should public servants be executed for breaches of ethics – or is a $150 fine enough?', *Public Integrity*, 6, 4 (2004), pp. 299–318.

'A conceptual model for benchmarking performance in public sector ethics programs: the missing link in government accountability?' *International Journal of Public Administration*, 30, 12–14 (2007), pp. 1621–1640.

'Enforcement or ethical capacity: considering the role of State Ethics Commissions at the millennium', *Public Administration Review*, 63, 3 (2003), pp. 283–295.

Stark, Andrew, 'Public-sector conflict of interest at the federal level in Canada and the U.S.: differences in understanding and approach,' in H. George Frederickson (ed.), *Ethics and Public Administration* (New York: M.E. Sharpe, 1993).

Stewart, Richard B., 'A new generation of environmental regulation?' *Capital University Law Review*, 29, 1 (2001), pp. 21–182.

Tam, Fiona, 'Exposing loopholes and lax oversight', *South China Morning Post*, EDT/EDT6, 27 October 2012.

Tam, Waikeung and Dali Yang, 'Food safety and the development of regulatory institutions in China', *Asian Perspective*, 29, 4 (2005), pp. 5–36.

The American National Election Studies, '*The ANES Guide to Public Opinion and Electoral Behavior*', Centre for Political Studies, University of Michigan, 2004.

The Civil Service Bureau, 'Civil servants' guide to good practices', 2005, available at www.csb.gov.hk/hkgcsb/rcim/pdf/english/publications/civilservant_e.pdf (last visited 24 April 2013).

'Declaration of investments by civil servants 2000', available at www.csb.gov.hk/english/info/813.html (last visited on 23 April 2013).

'LCQ19: guidelines on avoiding or reporting conflict of interest', available at www.csb.gov.hk/english/info/1610.html (last visited on 23 April 2013).

'Policy and procedures to the civil service code', 2010, available at http://civilservicecommission.independent.gov.uk/wp-content/uploads/2013/03/Policies-and-Procedures-Guide-to-the-Civil-Service-Code-Feb-12.pdf (last visited on13 December 2012).

'A guide for departments subject to a complaint to the Civil Service Commission', 2010, available at http://civilservicecommission.independent.gov.uk/wp-content/uploads/2013/07/CodeGuideforDepartmentsApril2013.pdf (last visited on 13 December 2012).

'Complaints handling procedure', available at http://civilservicecommission .independent.gov.uk/wp-content/uploads/2012/04/Complaints-Handling-Procedure-Jan-2012.pdf (last visited on 13 December 2012).

'The civil service code: a guide to bringing a complaint to the Civil Service Commission', 2010, available at http://civilservicecommission.independent .gov.uk/wp-content/uploads/2013/08/Guide-to-bringing-a-complaint-to-the-Commissioners-Civil-Service-Code-March-2012.pdf (last visited on13 December 2012).

The Hong Kong Judiciary, 'Complaints against a judge's conduct', 3rd edition, 2010, available at www.judiciary.gov.hk/en/crt_services/pphlt/pdf/complaintsjjoleaflet .pdf (last visited on 24 April 2013).

'List of judges and judicial officers (position as at 7 January, 2013)', available at www.judiciary.gov.hk/en/organization/judges.htm#HC (last visited on 24 April 2013).

The New York State Commission on Judicial Conduct, 'Pastrick', available at http://scjc.state.ny.us/Determinations/P/pastrick.htm (last visited on 17 June 2013).

The Official Website of the Independent Parliamentary Standards Authority, available at http://parliamentarystandards.org.uk/TheGuide/Pages/home .aspx (last visited on 3 January 2012).

The Supreme People's Procuratorate Website, available at www.spp.gov.cn/site 2006/region/00027,1.html (last visited on 29 April 2009).

The U.S. Office of Government Ethics, 'Agency supplemental regulations', available at www.oge.gov/Laws-and-Regulations/Agency-Supplemental-Regulations/ Agency-Supplemental-Regulations/ (last visited on 27 August 2013).

'Annual report pursuant to Executive Order 13490', 2011, available at www.oge .gov/displaytemplates/searchresults.aspx?query=annual%20report%20of%20 executive%20order%2013490 (last visited on 15 December 2012).

'All Advisories – 2012', available at www.oge.gov/OGE-Advisories/All-Advi sories/Index/?id=2147488083&LangType=1033&y=2012 (last visited on13 December 2012).

'Budget and appropriations', available at www.oge.gov/About/Legislative-Affairs-and-Budget/Budget-and-Appropriations/ (last visited on 27 July 2012).

'Confidential financial disclosure: OGE job aid – a tool for ethics officials', 2009, available at www.oge.gov/uploadedFiles/Education/Education_Resources_ for_Ethics_Officials/Resources/450_FilersJobAid.pdf (last visited 30 January 2013).

'DO-20-023: 2001 conflict of interest prosecution survey', Case 3, available at www.oge.gov/OGE-Advisories/Legal-Advisories/DO-02-023–2001-Conflict-of-Interest-Prosecution-Survey/ (last visited on 12 May 2012).

'EA-12-03 GPO rider for special edition CFR and compilation books', 2012, available at www.oge.gov/DisplayTemplates/ModelSub.aspx?id=2147488657 (last visited on 13 December 2012).

'Financial disclosure', available at www.oge.gov/Financial-Disclosure/Financial-Disclosure/ (last visited on 23 January 2013).

'Guidance for reviewers of the OGE Form 450, Part I (assets and income)', 2008, available at www.oge.gov/Financial-Disclosure/Docs/Guidance-for-Review ers-of-the-OGE-Form-450,-Part-I/ (last visited on 16 April 2012).

'LA-12-01: post-employment negotiation and recusal requirements under the STOCK Act', 2012, available at www.oge.gov/OGE-Advisories/Legal-Advi sories/LA-12-01–Post-Employment-Negotiation-and-Recusal-Requirements-under-the-STOCK-Act/ (last visited on 15 December 2012).

'Legislative affairs & budget', available at www.oge.gov/About/Legislative-Affairs-and-Budget/Legislative-Affairs–Budget/ (last visited on 27 July 2012).

'OGE advisories', available at www.oge.gov/OGE-Advisories/OGE-Advisories/ (last visited on13 December 2012).

'OGE Conference', available at www.oge.gov/Education/National-Government-Ethics-Conference/OGE-Conference/ (last visited on 24 April 2013).

'OGE Form 1353: semiannual report of payments accepted from a non-federal source', available at www.oge.gov/Forms-Library/OGE-Form-1353–Semi annual-Report-of-Payments-Accepted-from-a-Non-Federal-Source/ (last visited on 29 January 2013).

'PA-12-01: ethics pledge assessment', 2012, available at www.oge.gov/displaytem plates/modelsub.aspx?id=2147485555 (last visited on 13 December 2012).

'Program review reports', available at www.oge.gov/Program-Management/Program-Review/Program-Review-Reports/Program-Review-Reports/ (last visited on 29 January 2013).

'Public financial disclosure: a reviewer's reference', Second Edition, 2004, available at www.oge.gov/Financial-Disclosure/Docs/Financial-Disclosure-Guide/ (last visited on16 April 2012).

'Public financial disclosure', available at www.oge.gov/Financial-Disclosure/Public-Financial-Disclosure-278/Public-Financial-Disclosure/ last visited 30 January 2013).

'Purpose of financial disclosure', available at www.oge.gov/Laws-and-Regulations/Statutes/5-U-S-C–app–4-§§-101-111–Public-financial-disclosure-requirements/ (last visited on 12 May 2013).

'Workshops & seminars', available at www.oge.gov/Education/Education-Resources-for-Ethics-Officials/Workshops-and-Seminars/Workshops–Sem inars/ (last visited 24 April 2013).

The Website of Home for Kidney Stone babies (*Jieshi Baobao Zhi Jia*) www.bullogger.com/blogs/jieshibaobao/ (last visited on 3 January 2012).

The World Bank, 'GDP per capita', available at http://data.worldbank.org/indica tor/NY.GDP.PCAP.CD (last visited on 15 May 2014).

Thompson, Dennis F., 'Paradoxes of government ethics', *Public Administration Review*, 52, 3 (1992), pp. 254–259.

Transparency International, 'Corruption perceptions index 2012', available at http://cpi.transparency.org/cpi2012/results/ (last visited on 21 October 2013).

United States Courts, 'Judicial conference of the United States', available at www.uscourts.gov/FederalCourts/JudicialConference.aspx (last visited on 28 December 2012).

United States Office of Personnel Management, 'Common characteristics of the government', 2013, available at www.opm.gov/policy-data-oversight/data-analysis-documentation/federal-employment-reports/common-characteristics-of-the-government/common-characteristics-of-the-government-2012.pdf (last visited on 15 May 2014).

Van Rooij, Benjamin, 'Implementation of Chinese environmental law: regular enforcement and political campaigns', *Development and Change*, 37, 1 (2006), pp. 57–74.

'The politics of law in China: enforcement campaigns in the post-Mao PRC', *SSRN*, 2009, available at http://ssrn.com/abstract=1368181 (last visited on 23 April 2013).

Von Hirsch, Andrew, 'Penal theories', in Michael Tonry (ed.), *Handbook of Crime and Punishment* (New York and Oxford: Oxford University Press, 1998).

Waller, Spencer Weber, 'Prosecution by regulation: the changing nature of anti-trust enforcement', *Oregon Law Review*, 77, 4 (1998), pp. 1383–1450.

Wang Hairong, 'Coming together against corruption', available at www.bjreview.com.cn/print/txt/2014-12/08/content_657227.htm (last visited on 24 May 2015).

Wang, Gungwu and Zheng Yongnian, 'Introduction: reform, legitimacy, and dilemmas', in Wang Gungwu and Zheng Yongnian (eds.) *Reform, Legitimacy and Dilemmas: China's Politics and Society* (Singapore: Singapore University Press and World Scientific Publishing, 2000).

Wang, Xiangwei, 'Homing in on the corrupt "uncles"', *South China Morning Post*, EDT/EDT5, 17 December 2012.

'Learn from the West on how to curb graft,' *South China Morning Post*, China Briefing, 22 April 2013.

'Xi gets off to good start but drastic reforms unlikely', *South China Morning Post*, EDT5, 25 February 2013.

Warren, Mark E., 'Democracy and deceit: regulating appearances of corruption', *American Journal of Political Science*, 50, 1 (2006), pp.160–174.

Weatherley, Robert, *Politics in China Since 1949: Legitimizing Authoritarian Rule* (London and New York: Routledge, 2006).

Wedeman, Andrew, 'The intensification of corruption in China', *The China Quarterly*, 180 (December 2004), pp. 895–921.

Wei, Shang-jin, 'Corruption in economic development: grease or sand?', *Economic Survey of Europe*, 2 (2001), pp. 101–112.

Winter, Soren and Peter May, 'Reconsidering styles of regulatory enforcement: patterns in Danish agro-environmental inspection', *Law & Policy*, 22, 2 (2000), pp.143–173.

Wrage, Alexandra Addison, *Bribery and Extortion: Undermining Business, Governments, and Security* (Westport, CT and London: Praeger Security International, 2007).

Yan, Alice, 'Sites unveiled for Guangdong anti-graft pilot', *South China Morning Post*, EDT6, 10 December 2012.

Yardley, Jim, 'Infants in Chinese city starve on protein-short formula', *New York Times*, 5 May 2004.

Yeung, Irene Y.M. and Rosalie L. Tung, 'Achieving business success in Confucian societies: the importance of guanxi (connections)', *Organizational Dynamics*, Vol. 25, Issue 2, 1996, pp. 54–65.

Yu, Zhengsheng, 'Speech at the closing meeting of the first session of the 12th CPPCC National Committee', available at www.cppcc.gov.cn/zxww/2013/03/12/ARTI1363071765408886.shtml (last visited on 30 April 2013).

Zhai, Keith, 'Watch that watch: officials' displays of wealth scrutinized', *South China Morning Post*, EDT17, 14 October 2012.

'Watchdog to launch 5-year war on graft', *South China Morning Post*, EDT6, 24 January 2013.

Zhang, James Xiaohe, 'Is the Chinese economic growth sustainable? A macroeconomic approach', *Journal of Business and Policy Research*, 7, 2 (July 2012), pp. 25–40.

Zhao, Lei, 'Hubei official investigated', *China Daily* (Hong Kong edition), p. 3, 19 January 2013.

Zhao, Suisheng, 'China's pragmatic nationalism: is it manageable?', *The Washington Quarterly*, 29, 1, (2005), pp. 131–144.

Zhao, Yinan and Cao Yin, 'Officials voluntarily give Up 771m yuan in questionable gifts', *China Daily* (Hong Kong Edition), p. 3, 23 October 2012.

Zheng, Yongnian, 'The politics of power succession', in Wang Gungwu and Zheng Yongnian (eds.), *Reform, Legitimacy and Dilemmas: China's Politics and Society* (Singapore: Singapore University Press and World Scientific Publishing, 2000).

Zhong, Yang, 'Legitimacy crisis and legitimation in China', *Journal of Contemporary Asia*, 26, 2 (1996), pp. 201–220.

Zhou, Laura, 'Large bed in official's office stirs talk', *South China Morning Post*, EDT/EDT8, 22 February 2013.

Zhu, Andong and David M. Kotz, 'The dependence of China's economic growth on exports and investment', 2010, available at http://people.umass.edu/dmkotz/China_Growth_Model_%2010_09.pdf (last visited on 18 June 2013).

Zhu, Qianwei, 'Reorientation and prospects of China's combat Against corruption,' *Crime, Law and Social Change*, 49, 2 (2008), pp. 81–95.

Zhuang, Pinghui, 'Housing official tied to big assets', *South China Morning Post*, EDT/EDT6, 14 December 2012.

Zou, Keyuan, 'Judicial reform versus judicial corruption: recent developments in China', *Criminal Law Forum*, 11, 3 (2000), pp. 323–351.

Chinese Sources

'A thorough investigation is needed for the luxury office case', *Beijing Times*, p. A02, 22 February, 2013. 豪华办公室须彻查到底[N]. 京华时报, 2013-02-22 (A02).

'An analysis of Wang Guoyan corruption case', *CCP News*, avalilable at http://
    fanfu.people.com.cn/n/2015/0507/c64371-26961961.html (last visited on
    20 May, 2015). 南昌航空大学党委原书记王国炎违纪违法案件剖析[OL].
    人民网, [2015-05-20].
'Annual work report of the supreme people's procuratorate (2000-2008)', available
    at www.spp.gov.cn/site2006/region/00018.html (last visited on 20 April
    2011). 最高人民检察院工作报告[OL]. [2011-04-20].
'Annual work report of the supreme people's procuratorate 2008', available at
    http://www.spp.gov.cn/gzbg/201208/t20120820_2496.shtml (last visited on
    12 June, 2012). 最高人民檢察院工作報告2008[OL]. [2012-06-12].
'Annual work report of the supreme people's procuratorate 2014', available at
    http://www.spp.gov.cn/gzbg/201503/t20150324_93812.shtml (last visited
    on 1 June 2015). 最高人民檢察院工作報告2014[OL]. [2015-06-01].
'Cheng Liangyu was sentenced to 18 years imprisonment for his two offences',
    XinhuaNews, available at http://news.xinhuanet.com/newscenter/2008-04/
    11/content_7959849.htm (last visited on 13 Sep., 2013). 陈良宇一审两项
    罪名获刑18年[OL]. 新华网, [2013-09-13].
'Corrupt officials' confessions will be published as an anti-corruption tool to warn
    other officials', *CCP News*, available at http://theory.people.com.cn/n/2015/
    0325/c49150-26745816.html (last visited on 20 May 2015). 落马官员忏悔
    录被列入反腐'任务清单'透视[OL]. 人民网, [2015-05-20].
'Head of Food Bureau in Luliang City, Shanxi Province, was exposed having a
    luxury queen-sized bed in his office' *Nanguo Zaobao*, p.22, 21 February,
    2013. '糊涂' 官员山西吕梁粮食局长被曝奢华办公室配双人床 [N]. 南国
    早报, 2013-02-21 (22).
'Head of Luliang Bureau of Food was recorded a demerit', *Beijing Daily*, p. 13, 22
    February, 2013. 山西吕梁粮食局局长被记过[N]. 北京日报, 2013-02-22 (13).
'Henry Tang denied concealing his illegal property structures', *am730*, 14 February,
    2012, p. 2, available at www.am730.com.hk/article_print.php?article=92234
    (last visited on 10 June, 2013). 疑似酒窖为挖深车房 唐英年住僭建屋否认
    隐瞒[N/OL]. am730, 2012-02-14(2) [2013-06-10].
'Lei Zhengfu was sentenced to 13 years imprisonment and confiscated of personal
    wealth of 0.3 million RMB', *XinhuaNews*, available at http://news.xinhuanet
    .com/legal/2013-06/28/c_116329205.htm (last visited on 13 Sep., 2013).
    雷政富受贿316万被判13年 没收财产30万[OL]. 新华网, [2013-09-13].
'Luxury Office of a Head of Food Bureau in Shanxi was exposed', *Bao'an Daily*,
    p. A14, 21 February, 2013. 山西一粮食局长奢华办公室曝光[N]. 宝安日
    报, 2013-02-21 (A14).
'Most corrupt officials involved in Fuyang intermediate court corruption cases are
    still in their positions,' 31 March 2008, available at http://www.ah.xinhuanet
    .com/ahws/2008-03/31/content_12836550.htm (last visited on 14 April 2009).
    安徽省阜阳中院腐败窝案大多数涉案官员仍居原位[OL]. [2009-04-14].

'National Bureau of Corruption Prevention's personnel composition is modelled on Hong Kong's ICAC', *Wen Wei Po*, p. A9, 21 March, 2007. 国家防腐局人事构成仿照港廉署[N]. 香港文汇报, 2007-03-21 (A9).

'Net citizens ask "property uncle" in Panyu to "sun himself"', *Southern Metropolis Daily(Guangzhou)*, AII02, 10 October, 2012. 番禺城管 '房哥'网友喊你 '晒太阳'[N]. 南方都市报, 2012-10-10 (AII02).

'Notice of Beijing Statistics Bureau on publishing average salary data for the Beijing City in 2012', available at http://www.bjstats.gov.cn/zwgk/ystg/201306/t20130608_250285.htm (last visited on 15 May, 2014). 北京市统计局关于公布2012年全市有关平均工资数据的通告[OL]. [2013-05-21].

'The 2nd plenary meeting of the 18th Central Commission for Discipline Inspection of the CCP held and four key anti-corruption works decided', available at http://fanfu.people.com.cn/n/2013/0123/c64371-20302846.html (last visited 27 February 2013). 十八届中央纪委二次全会举行部署反腐廉政四重点[OL]. [2013-02-27].

'Wen Jiabao delivers a speech at the fourth meeting of state council on anti-corruption work', available at http://www.gov.cn/ldhd/2011-03/25/content_1831877.htm (last visited on 20 April 2011). 国务院召开第四次廉政工作会议 温家宝发表讲话[OL]. [2011-04-20].

'Why are bribing bosses not sentenced?', *Yanzhao Wanbao*, B5, 19 October, 2007. 为什麼老板行贿没被判刑[N]. 燕赵晚报, 2007-10-19 (B5).

'Xi Jinping revisited Lankao', *Xinhua Net*, available at http://news.xinhuanet.com/politics/2014-03/17/c_119810080.htm (last visited on 10 June 2015). 习近平重访兰考:焦裕禄精神是永恒的[OL]. 新华网, [2015-06-10].

'Xi Jinping's speech at the second meeting of the third plenary session of the 18th Central Committee of the CCP: the work of fighting corruption still faces a complicated and difficult situation', available at http://www.ccdi.gov.cn/special/xilun/zyls/201501/t20150111_49941.html (Last visited on 19 May 2015). 党风廉政建设和反腐败斗争形势依然严峻复杂[OL]. [2015-05-19].

Cheng, Qiao, 'At least 45 officials were involved in the Sinopec corruption scandal', *Beijing Times*, 14 April, 2014, available at http://www.chinanews.com/gn/2014/04-14/6058232.shtml (last visited on 15 May, 2014). 陈荞. 中石油人事地震持续发酵 至少45人因中石油被查[N/OL]. 京华时报, 2014-04-14 [2014-05-15].

Deng, Xiaoping, *Selected Works of Deng Xiaoping*, Vol. 3 (Beijing: People's Publishing House, 1993). 邓小平. 邓小平文选: 第三卷[M]. 北京: 人民出版社, 1993.

Douyun Discipline Inspection Committee, 'Assessment measures for discipline inspection and administrative supervision agencies' cases investigation in Douyun City', available at www.dyjjjc.com/zcfg/ShowArticle.asp?ArticleID=440 (last visited on 12 April, 2013). 都匀市纪检监察机关查办案件工作考评办法[OL]. [2013-04-12].

Feng, Yiqian (ed), *Public Ethics*, (Guangzhou: South China University of Technology Press, 2010). 冯益谦(主编). 公共伦理学[M]. 广州: 华南理工大学出版社, 2010.

Gao, Fusheng, 'Beating both tigers and flies shows progress in anti-corruption', *CCP News Net*, available at http://cpc.people.com.cn/pinglun/BIG5/n/2013/0124/c241220-20314541.html (last visited on 14 April, 2013). 高福生. '老虎' '苍蝇'一起打彰显反腐正能量[OL]. 中国共产党新闻网, [2013-04-14].

Heng, Jie (editor), 'Aletai "eat crabs", breakthrough in financial disclosure for officials', *Honesty Outlook*, February 2009, pp 16–17. 衡洁. 阿勒泰'吃螃蟹' 官员财产申报破冰[J]. 廉政瞭望, 2009, 二月: 16–17.

Hu, Yi, 'Early warning supervision for naked officials', *People's Court Daily*, 27 July, 2007. 胡艺. 管理'裸官' 需前移监管关口[N]. 人民法院报, 2007-07-27.

Jiang, Shuoliang, 'Moral risk for naked officials and its prevention', *Journal of China National School of Administration*, Vol. 6, 2011, pp. 99–102. 蒋硕亮. 裸官的道德风险及其防范[J]. 国家行政学院学报, 2011, 6: 99–102.

Li, Song, 'Problems of promotion of leaders' assistants', *Outlook*, Vol. 45, 2010, pp. 12–14. 李松. 秘书提拔'路径隐患'[J]. 瞭望, 2010, 45: 12–14.

Li, Xiujiang, 'Converging attack "naked officials"', *Insight China*, September 2010, pp.100–101. 李秀江. 夹击裸官[J]. 小康,2010,九月: 100–101.

Li, Yonggang, 'Lin Zhe, professor at central party committee college, proposed that anti-corruption institutions shall be upgraded to anti-corruption statutes', *Huashang Daily*, available at http://sx.sina.com.cn/news/kuai/2012-03-14/18729.html (last visited on 25 May 2013). 李勇钢. 中央党校教授林喆:反腐制度应升级为反腐败法[N/OL]. 华商报, [2013-05-25].

Lin, Zhe, 'What kind of anti-corruption law shall we have', *Honesty Outlook*, 3 (2011), pp. 44–45. 林喆. 我们该有一部怎样的《反腐败法》[J]. 廉政瞭望, 2011, 3: 44–45.

Liu, Renwen, 'Can we create conditions for abolishing the death penalty for corruption?' *Democracy and Legal System*, 22 (2010), pp. 32–34. 刘仁文. 能否创造条件废除贪腐死刑[J]. 民主与法制, 2010, 22: 32–34.

Ma, Sanshan, 'Resisting corruption from six aspects', *Study Times*, p. 11, 5 Aug., 2013. 麻三山. 拒腐防变应从六个方面做起[N]. 学习时报, 2013-08-05 (11).

Mao, Yizhu, 'Will official property disclosure become a sharp anti-corruption sword?', *China Youth Daily*, p. 06, 11 December 2012. 毛一竹. 财产公开能否成为反腐利剑[N]. 中国青年报, 2012-12-11 (6).

Ministry of Finance of the People's Republic of China, 'Government revenue and spending in 2013', 2014, available at http://gks.mof.gov.cn/zhengfuxinxi/tongjishuju/201401/t20140123_1038541.html (last visited on 15 May 2014). 中国财政部. 2013年财政收支情况[OL]. 2014 [2014-05-15].

National Bureau for Corruption Prevention, 'Seminar on "Fighting corruption: theories and practice for preventing conflict of interests" and the fourth Integrity Forum were held in Hangzhou', available at www.nbcp.gov.cn/

article/gzdt/201110/20111000014851.shtml (last visited on 21 May 2013).
国家预防腐败局. '反腐败:防止利益冲突的理论与实践'专题研讨会暨第
四届西湖•廉政论坛在杭举行[OL]. [2013-05-21].

Pan, Duola, 'Do not hurry to be optimistic about anti-corruption Law', *China National Conditions and Strength*, 7 (1999), p. 35. 潘多拉.《反腐败法》且慢乐观[J]. 中国国情国力, 1999, 7: 35.

Peng, Mei, 'The CCDI is now planning to start random checks on asset declarations made by officials', *Nandu Daily*, A17, 30 April 2013. 彭美. 中纪委研究全国抽查干部个人事项申报　三种抽查办法纳入考虑范围,但尚无定论,出台时间未定[N]. 南方都市报(全国版), 2013-04-30 (A17).

Qiao, Yunhua, *Before the Gates of Hell: Conversations with Li Zhen before His Execution* (Beijing: Xinhua publishing, 2004). 乔云华. 地狱门前:与李真刑前对话实录 [M]. 北京: 新华出版社, 2004.

Shao, Dan, 'Feasibility of abolishing the death penalty for corruption crimes: implementing UNCAC', *The Legal System and Society*, 22 (2006), pp. 9–10. 邵丹. 论废除腐败犯罪死刑的可行性——从《联合国反腐败公约》的贯彻与实施谈起[J]. 法制与社会, 2006, 22: 9–10.

Shao, Daosheng, *China: Anti-corruption Campaigns* (Beijing: Social Sciences Academic Press, 2009). 邵道生. 中国:阻击腐败 [M]. 北京:社会科学文献出版社, 2009.

Shen, Lijie, 'How to deal with those who offer huge bribes?' available at www.hndjw .gov.cn/Article/fazhijiaoyu/fazhi/fayan/2009-07-29/5938.html. (last visited on 14 April 14, 2009). 申丽洁. 巨额行贿者应当如何处理[OL]. [2009-04-14].

Tongchuan DIC, 'Tongchuan made new breakthrough in case investigation by adopting six measures', available at http://jjw.tongchuan.gov.cn/structure/ jjxx/jjxxzw_64808_1.htm (last visited on 10 April 2013). 铜川市采取'六抓'取得查办案件工作新突破[OL]. [2013-04-10].

Tsinghua University et al., *An Analysis of Wenchuan Earthquake Disaster Caused by Construction and Countermeasures for Building Design* (Beijing: China Architecture & Building Press, 2009). 清华大学等. 汶川地震建筑震害分析及设计对策[M]. 北京: 中国建筑工业出版社, 2009.

Wang, Qishan, 'Report at the second plenary meeting of the eighteenth central commission for discipline Inspection of the CCP', 21 January 2013, available at http://cpc.people.com.cn/n/2013/0226/c64094-20597121.html (last visited 27 February 2013). 王岐山. 在中国共产党第十八届中央纪律检查委员会第二次全体会议上的工作报告[OL]. [2013-2-27].

Wu, Qiao, 'Legal measures against corruption: confining public power into the cage of regulation', *Beijing Times*, p. A02, 17 December, 2012. 吴乔. 反腐亮剑之法治篇 将公权力赶进法治的笼子[N]. 京华时报, 2012-12-17 (A02).

Xiu, Ling, *The Rise and Fall of Li Zhen – The Li Zhen Case and Li Zhen's Personal Life* (Beijing: Guangming Daily Press, 2004). 秀灵. 河北第一秘: 李真盛衰记 [M]. 北京: 光明日报出版社, 2004.

Yan, Xinwu, 'An government official in Hunan fought with his section chief for the reason that his request of using government car for private purpose was declined', *CCP News Net*, 13 May, 2013, available at http://fanfu.people.com .cn/n/2013/0513/c64371-21457460.html (last visited on 15 Oct., 2013). 颜新武. 湖南衡阳正副科长因公车私用互殴 副科长鼻子被咬掉[OL]. 中国共产党新闻网, [2013-10-15].

Yang, Hongtai, 'Legislative thoughts on the national anti-corruption law', *Law Science*, 9 (1998), pp. 23–25. 杨鸿台. 《国家反腐败法》立法构想[J]. 法学, 1998, 9: 23–25.

Zhang, Guang, 'Estimating government employees' salary based on official data in China', *Financial Times Online (Chinese version)*, available at http://m .ftchinese.com/story/001054761 (last visited on 15 May, 2014). 张光. 从官方数据看中国公务人员工资[OL]. [2014-05-15].

Zhang, Hongge, 'Investigation and analysis of the application of sentence suspension and exemption for duty offences', available at http://hnwgfy.chinacourt .org/public/detail.php?id=33 (last visited on 10 August 2009). 张红鸽. 职务犯罪案件适用缓、免刑情况的调查与分析[OL]. [2009-08-10].

Zhu, Lingjun, *Consensus and Conflict: Rethinking of Relations between the People and the CCP* (Beijing: People's Press, 2006). 祝灵君. 一致与冲突–政党与群众关系的再思考 [M]. 北京: 人民出版社, 2006.

Zhuang, Deshui, 'Discipline Inspection Offices sent out to SOEs must break through the power constraints of the SOEs', *ChinaNet*, 22 April 2014, available at http://opinion.china.com.cn/opinion_94_96894.html (last visited on 15 May, 2014). 庄德水.专职纪检必须突破国企权力羁绊[OL]. 中国网, [2014-05-15].

Zigong DIC, 'Rong County takes four measures to put into practice the spirit of the basic level DICs case investigation promotion conference', available at http://www.zgjw.gov.cn/News/show/play/3488 (last visited on 9 April 2013). 荣县四举措认真贯彻落实全省基层纪检监察机关办案工作推进会议精神[OL]. [2013-04-09].

INDEX

Administration Supervision Law of the People's Republic of China, 91–92

administrative law, corruption under, 4

Anti-Corruption Law, in China, 7–8

anti-corruption laws, 23

anti-corruption strategies
CCP and, 49–61
  through political campaigns, 58–60
in China, 238–240
enforcement strategies and, 192
NIS theory, 2–3
Norad study on, 2
in the Philippines, 17
regulation systems for corruption compared to, 22–49
types of approaches, 2–3

appearance of influence peddling, 75, 77–78

Before the Gates of Hell: Conversations with Li Zhen before his Execution (Qiao Yunhua), 38–46

behaviour changing mechanisms, in regulatory systems, 22

behaviour manipulation tactics, in ethics enforcement, 163–169

bias, by judges, 81–82

Bo Xilai, 239

bribery, in China, 96

Cai Bin, 181–182, 208, 212

CCDI. *See* Central Commission for Discipline Inspection

CCP. *See* Chinese Communist Party

Central Commission for Discipline Inspection (CCDI), 174, 198, 207, 210–211, 214–215, 219, 221, 225, 234, 238

Cheng Xitong, 31

China, corruption in, 1–3. *See also* Chinese Communist Party
Administration Supervision Law of the People's Republic of China, 91–92
Anti-Corruption Law in, 7–8
anti-corruption strategies, 238–240
average salaries in, 227–228
bribery, 96
Civil Servant Law of the People's Republic of China, 91–92, 94
compared to other countries, 14
conflict of interest and, 93–102
  private gain from information, 99–102
  profiting from official position, 99–102, 122–123
  self-dealing as, 93–96, 120–122
  third-party assistance, 98–99
  transfer of economic value as, 96–98
Criminal Law of the People's Republic of China 1977, 91–92
criminalization of, 5–6, 14
death penalty for, 26–27
DICs and, 10–11
  behaviour manipulation tactics of, 213–215
  CCP and, 61
  educational programmes, 214–215

290

CPSIA information can be obtained
at www.ICGtesting.com
Printed in the USA
LVHW081043090119
603029LV00041B/320/P